WEST AFRICA

MALI

BURKINA FASO

• Ouagadougou

Dano •

• Missionary
School

*DAGARA
COUNTRY*

BENIN

**IVORY
COAST**

GHANA

TOGO

Gulf of Guinea

Of Water and the Spirit

Also by Malidoma Patrice Somé

Ritual: Power, Healing and Community

Of Water and the Spirit

Ritual, Magic, and Initiation in the Life of an African Shaman

MALIDOMA PATRICE SOMÉ

A Jeremy P. Tarcher/Putnam Book
published by
G. P. Putnam's Sons
New York

A Jeremy P. Tarcher/Putnam Book
Published by G. P. Putnam's Sons
Publishers Since 1838
200 Madison Avenue
New York, NY 10016

Jeremy P. Tarcher, Inc.
5858 Wilshire Blvd., Suite 200
Los Angeles, CA 90036

Library of Congress Cataloging-in-Publication Data

Somé, Malidoma Patrice, date
    Of water and the spirit: ritual, magic, and initiation in the life of an African
shaman / Malidoma Patrice Somé.
        p.   cm.
    "A Jeremy P. Tarcher/Putnam book."
    ISBN 0-87477-762-3
    1. Somé, Malidoma Patrice, date. 2. Dagari (African people)—Biography.
3. Shamans—Burkina Faso—Biography. 4. Dagari (African people)—Religion.
5. Dagari (African people)—Rites and ceremonies. I. Title.
DT555.45.D35S667   1994
960 ' .049635 ' 0092—dc20   93-39440
                                                                     CIP

Design by Susan Shankin
Illustrations by Tanya Maiboroda
Endpaper map by Lisa Amoroso
Printed in the United States of America
1   2   3   4   5   6   7   8   9   10

This book is printed on acid-free paper.

CONTENTS

INTRODUCTION

My name is Malidoma. It means roughly "Be friends with the stranger/enemy." Because the Dagara believe that every individual comes into this life with a special destiny, some names are programmatic. They describe the task of their bearers and constitute a continual reminder to the child of the responsibilities that are waiting up ahead. A person's life project is therefore inscribed in the name she/he carries. As my name implies, I am here in the West to tell the world about my people in any way I can, and to take back to my people the knowledge I gain about this world. My elders are convinced that the West is as endangered as the indigenous cultures it has decimated in the name of colonialism. There is no doubt that, at this time in history, Western civilization is suffering from a great sickness of the soul. The West's progressive turning away from functioning spiritual values; its total disregard for the environment and the protection of natural resources; the violence of inner cities with their problems of poverty, drugs, and crime; spiraling unemployment and economic disarray; and growing intolerance toward people of color and the values of other cultures—all of these trends, if unchecked, will eventually bring about a terrible self-destruction. In the face of all this global chaos, the only possible hope is self-transformation. Unless we as individuals find new ways of understanding between people, ways that can touch and transform the heart and soul deeply, both indigenous cultures and those in the West will continue to fade away, dismayed that all the wonders of technology, all the many philosophical "isms," and all the planning of the global corporations will be helpless to reverse this trend.

It has taken me ten years of battling with insecurity, uncertainty, hesitation, and God knows what other types of subtle complexes to write this book. The greatest obstacle I encountered was finding a suitable way to tell my story. I could not speak English when I arrived in the United States ten years ago, even though I had taken some English classes at the Jesuit seminary in my teens. Although I have made great strides in orally communicating in that language, it was still very difficult to write this book. One of my greatest problems was that the things I talk about here did not happen in English; they happened in a language that has a very different mindset about reality. There is usually a significant violence done to anything being translated from one culture to another. Modern American English, which seems to me better suited for quick fixes and the thrill of a consumer culture, seems to falter when asked to communicate another person's world view. From the time I began to jot down my first thoughts until the last word, I found myself on the bumpy road of mediumship, trying to ferry meanings from one language to another, and from one reality to another— a process that denaturalizes and confuses them.

I have had to struggle a great deal in order to be able to communicate this story to you. It is basically the story of my initiation into two different and highly contradictory cultures. I was born in the early fifties in Burkina Faso in West Africa, then called Upper Volta by the colonial French government who invaded my country in the early 1900s. Although my parents did not record my birth, and to this day are still in conflict as to the exact date, my papers say that I was born in 1956.

When I was four years old, my childhood and my parents were taken from me when I was literally kidnapped from my home by a French Jesuit missionary who had befriended my father. At that time Jesuits were trying to create a "native" missionary force to convert a people who had wearied of their message along with their colonial oppression. For the next fifteen years I was in a boarding school, far away from my family, and forced to learn about the white man's reality, which included lessons in history, geography, anatomy, mathematics, and literature. All of these topics were presented with a good dose of Christianity and its temperamental god who forced everyone to live in constant fear of his wrath.

At the age of twenty I escaped and went back to my people, but found that I no longer fit into the tribal community. I risked my life to undergo the Dagara initiation and thereby return to my people. During that month-long ritual, I was integrated back into my own reality as well as I could be.

But I never lost my Western education. So I am a man of two worlds, trying to be at home in both of them—a difficult task at best.

When I was twenty-two, my elders came to me and asked me to return to the white man's world, to share with him what I had learned about my own spiritual tradition through my initiation. For me, initiation had eliminated my confusion, helplessness, and pain and opened the door to a powerful understanding of the link between my own life purpose and the will of my ancestors. I had come to understand the sacred relationship between children and old people, between fathers and their adolescent sons, between mothers and daughters. I knew especially why my people have such a deep respect for old age, and why a strong, functioning community is essential for the maintenance of an individual's sense of identity, meaning, and purpose. I used this knowledge as my starting point.

My own elders had experienced French colonialism and the culture of the West as a force that used violence as a means to eradicate traditional lifeways. They had seen their own youth stolen from them as they vainly struggled against the incursions of these intruders. During these years, in which my people were trying to make sense of a people whose every action seemed to go against the natural order of things, creating chaos, death, and destruction, the sense of unified community that sustained their tribal life was profoundly destabilized. These foreigners seemed to have no respect for life, tradition, or the land itself. At first my elders refused to believe that a race of people who could cause such suffering and death could possibly have any respect for itself. It did not take long before they realized that the white man wanted nothing short of the complete destruction of their culture and even their lives.

For some of my people, befriending the white man was the best way they could find to fight back. By doing this, they hoped to get to know how the white man's mind worked and what they thought they were accomplishing by invading another people's ancestral lands. Not all of my people were willing to have this much contact with the whites. Some village people, who chose to see things only from their own tribal perspective, believed that to have become so spiritually sick, the white man must have done something terrible to his own ancestors. Others who knew a little about military culture, imperialism, and colonialism thought that the white man must have destroyed his own land to have to come here and take the land of others. In spite of the best efforts of all my people, the whites kept on coming; kept on doing whatever they pleased; and kept on taking more and more of our land, our beliefs, and our lives.

Many years later, my generation finds itself gripped by a powerful irony. Suddenly it has become popular to defend tribal people, their world view, and their lifeways. But while the West is engaged in a great debate about what it means to preserve culture, the indigenous world is aware that it has already lost the battle. It seems obvious to me that as soon as one culture begins to talk about preservation, it means that it has already turned the other culture into an endangered species. Then you have the purists on either side who want indigenous cultures to remain "exactly the same as they have always been." In many cultures, the Dagara included, it is no longer a question of preservation but of *survival* in some form or another. The culture's own reality has already been superseded by the "fashionable" modernity. I see my position as a two-way passage of information, as both a bridge and a conduit. By agreeing to move between both worlds, I seek to bring about some kind of balance.

I deeply respect the story I have told in this book. I respect it because it embodies everything that is truly me, my ancestors, my tribe, my life. It is a very complicated story whose telling caused me great pain; but I had to tell it. Only in this way could I ultimately fulfill my purpose to "befriend the stranger/enemy." This is not the first task set me by my elders, nor will it be my last.

My first "assignment" after my initiation into the tribe was to seek entrance into the university. I did so equipped with the special knowledge that initiation had provided me with. I had one thing in my pocket—a little talisman. This talisman was an oval-shaped pouch stuffed with a stone from the underworld and some other secret objects collected in the wild. Though it is common to carry talismans in my village, for they are a great source of power and protection, people fear them. Every Dagara knows that powerful objects are dangerous. Depending on the actions of its bearer, such objects have the power to help, but also to hurt. Therefore, talismans are treated with great respect and care. My pouch was sewn tightly shut and then decorated in a way that enhanced its ugliness and scariness. These objects are always made to look ugly and fearsome, perhaps to stress their supernatural quality. Besides, my experience of the other world has led me to understand that anything that crosses from that place into this one is seldom beautiful, as if anything spiritually potent must look ugly and smell bad in order to work. My talisman certainly did. At one end of the oval pouch was a tuft of strange animal hair.

The government of what was then called Upper Volta had a school called the Centre d'Études Supérieures, whose course of studies was the equivalent of a four-year college in the West. It had been built several years earlier by the now-departed French colonials as part of the incentive to the newly independent countries in Africa. The end of territorial colonialism was followed by a period of "neocolonialism" that took the form of bilateral cooperation, economic sponsorship, and professional support in every pertinent department of the new government. And so the college was just one of the many faces of this new colonialism, whose goal is to place the newly independent countries into a state of perpetual indebtedness. It is important to understand that modern Africa does not exist as it is by the will of its leaders, but by the will of the very powers that divided it between them.

Every student in the center was there on scholarship, and every year there was a huge number of candidates who applied for the few scholarships available. Those who obtained them were usually students whose parents were either well-to-do or could pull some strings. The politicians would simply order the scholarship board to grant the awards to their relatives or children. Wealthy people who lacked political power bribed their way to scholarships for their loved ones, but even the wealthy did not always succeed, for after the "political" scholarships were granted, there were few left for the bulk of the candidates.

The year that I applied was no different from any other. I had filled in my application for a scholarship knowing that I had no chance of getting beyond the filing. But I also knew that my tribal elders had given me instructions on how to apply, even though they had no basis upon which to work. How, I wondered, could these people, accustomed to village life, know how to get one's needs met in the city? Yet I felt it was still worth a try. What did I have to lose? To my great surprise, I was scheduled for an interview and was not only informed of my acceptance to the school, but given a full scholarship on the spot. I cannot tell you the details of how my talisman worked, for I prefer not to blunt its effectiveness, but it is still helping me today to speak in big assembly halls. Though invitations come in unorthodox ways, I always seem to be able to get where I need to go and say what I need to say.

I spent four years in that center for higher education, which later became the national university. I walked away from it with a bachelor's degree in sociology, literature, and linguistics, and a master's thesis in world literature. I still did not know why I had been there. The system did not care whether you really learned anything or not. It was based upon the regurgitation of memorized material fed to one by professors who read from their notes in bored, sleepy, and sometimes even drunken voices. Most of what they said was incomprehensible. Our only reason for being there was our need to transcend the alarming social and economic situation in which most of us were caught. We did not need to be told that a proper Western education was the key to good Western jobs and a decent life.

For most people, top performance in that school meant hard work. As an initiated man, I did not have to work hard to get my degrees. I skipped a great deal of the classes, made sure that I was present at the exams, and walked away with my diplomas. The answers to the exam questions were mostly visible in the auras of the teachers who constantly patrolled the aisles of the testing rooms. I just had to write these answers down quickly before any one of them noticed how strangely I was looking at him/her.

During my second year in college, the teachers began to notice me. It was harder and harder for me to cut classes. When I was picked by the professor to reply to a question, I continued to instinctively seek the answer in his aura, as I did during exams. To me it was like being asked to read out of an open book. This method worked so well that one day one of my teachers looked at me suspiciously and asked, "Have you been reading my mind?" Of course, I said no. We were in the modern world, where such things are impossible.

My talisman continued to work for me. I was awarded a scholarship to the Sorbonne, where I received a "D.E.A." (Diplôme d'Études Approfondies) in political science. Later I continued my education at Brandeis University, earning a Ph.D. in literature. I am not writing about all these accomplishments to impress you, but to show you that what I have learned as an initiated man really works (at least for me) in Western reality.

Coming to the United States was a matter of necessity. I could not reconcile myself with what France reminded me of. Every day I was told in a thousand ways that Africa gave its life force for France to look, and its people to live, like this. The temperament of the Parisian was most conducive to irritation, discomfort, and even murderous thoughts. The African had become a pest, reminding the French of their own guilt. My own racial consciousness was heightened as a result, and led me to dangerous behavior such as jumping into the Métro without paying, and eating my way through a supermarket. I came to the United States shortly after my mentor announced it in the course of one of our numerous divination sessions during my first trip to the village. He said I was going to cross the big sea into a land where I will be able to do what I must. A scholarship brought me here. That's the way most Black Africans enter into the heart of the civilized world.

During my time in the West, I have found myself facing an interesting paradox. People approach me not because I am an educated man but because the tribal outfit I wear seems to have an effect on them. It initiates contact. Conversations always seem to begin with someone saying, "Nice outfit. Where do you come from?"

I answer by saying, "Burkina Faso."

The response is invariably, "What?" or "Where is that?"

Sometimes I feel like a walking billboard, but these conversations always give me food for thought. I learn to understand my own culture better by comparing it with others. Ironically, I am more free to be African in the West than I am in Africa. In my country, a man with as many degrees as

I have wears a Western suit and tries to act cosmopolitan. He does not want to be reminded of where he came from or what he has left behind. He has turned his back on "superstition" and embraced "progress."

Here in the West I have a great deal of time for spiritual contemplation and study, and much more time to share things of the spirit with others. If I were still living in my village in Africa, nearly every spare moment would be taken up with scratching a living from the exhausted soil that is all colonialism has left us with. The 600 American dollars I send every year to my family feeds them, and many others, for a year. Although I miss them and would prefer to see them more often, I know I am taking better care of them here than I could by going home and picking up a hoe—even if the elders had left that option open to me.

Living in this culture and being openly African also has its moments of comedy and suspense. For example, when I travel to conferences, I always take my medicine bag with me. I have always been afraid to check it in the baggage for fear that it will somehow be lost—a terrible thought to contemplate since without it and the magical objects it contains, I would not be able to do the many hundreds of divinations I perform for people each year.

The first time I carried my medicine bag through the airport, I realized, when I arrived at the X-ray machine, that I could not have my medicine X-rayed. I did not want my medicine to be seen. I realized that if I did, I would have to explain its strange contents to the guards. This would be awkward, to say the least. Besides, I was not altogether sure what this modern technological contraption would do to my medicine.

The guard asked me if I had films in the bag. I said no, but I had something just as sensitive. That did it. Bristling with suspicion, the security officer poured the contents of the bag out onto the table. I saw his eyes open wide as he asked, "What the hell is this?" Other officers joined him and they all looked in surprise at the content of my medicine bag. One of them, a Black officer, said, "That's voodoo stuff," and ordered them to put it through the X-ray machine while he held a talisman in his hand and looked at it with great suspicion.

I stood there wishing I could have checked my pouch in the baggage to avoid this embarrassment, but I realized I could not part with my medicine. By this time, a small crowd had gathered. My heart was beating rapidly. My medicine had become public. I quickly put it all back into the bag and put the bag on the X-ray conveyor belt. My talismans came on screen. The officer stopped the belt, stared at them intently for an infinite amount of time, then reactivated the belt. I picked my bag up with relief at the other end. From that day on, I began to think about new ways to avoid these embarrassing moments.

Every day we get closer to living in a global community. With distances between countries narrowing, we have much wisdom to gain by learning to understand other people's cultures and permitting ourselves to accept that there is more than one version of "reality." To exist in the first place, each culture has to have its own version of what is real. What I am attempting to share with you in this book is only one of the endless versions of reality.

In the culture of my people, the Dagara, we have no word for the supernatural. The closest we come to this concept is *Yielbongura*, "the thing that knowledge can't eat." This word suggests that the life and power of certain things depend upon their resistance to the kind of categorizing knowledge that human beings apply to everything. In Western reality, there is a clear split between the spiritual and the material, between religious life and secular life. This concept is alien to the Dagara. For us, as for many indigenous cultures, the supernatural is part of our everyday lives. To a Dagara man or woman, the material is just the spiritual taking on form. The secular is religion in a lower key—a rest area from the tension of religious and spiritual practice. Dwelling in the realm of the sacred is both exciting and terrifying. A little time out once in a while is in order.

The world of the Dagara also does not distinguish between reality and imagination. To us, there is a close connection between thought and reality. To imagine something, to closely focus one's thoughts upon it, has the potential to bring that something into being. Thus, people who take a tragic view of life and are always expecting the worst usually manifest that reality. Those who expect that things will work together for the good usually experience just that. In the realm of the sacred, this concept is taken even further, for what is magic but the ability to focus thought and energy to get results on the human plane? The Dagara view of reality is large. If one can imagine something, then it has at least the potential to exist.

I decided to do a little experiment of my own with "reality" versus "imagination" when I was home visiting my village in 1986. I brought with me a little electronic generator, a television monitor, a VCR, and a "Star Trek" tape titled *The Voyage Home*. I wanted to know if the Dagara elders could tell the difference between fiction and reality. The events unfolding in a science fiction film, considered futuristic or fantastic in the West, were perceived by my elders as the current affairs in the day-to-day lives of some other group of people living in the world. The elders did not understand what a starship is. They did not understand what the fussy uniforms of its crew members had to do with making magic. They recognized in Spock a *Kontombié* of the seventh planet, the very one that I describe later in this story, and their only objection to him was that he was too tall. They had never seen a Kontombié that big. They had no problems understanding light speed and teleportation except that they could have done it more discreetly. I could not make them understand that all this was not real. Even though stories abound in my culture, we have no word for fiction. The only way I could get across to them the Western concept of fiction was to associate fiction with telling lies.

My elders were comfortable with "Star Trek," the West's vision of its own future. Because they believe in things like magical beings (Spock), traveling at the speed of light, and teleportation, the wonders that Westerners imagine being part of their future are very much a part of my elders' present. The irony is that the West sees the indigenous world as primitive or archaic. Wouldn't it be wonderful if the West could learn to be as "archaic" as my elders are?

As in the case of "Star Trek," Westerners look to the future as a place of hope, a better world where every person has dignity and value, where wealth is not unequally distributed, where the wonders of technology make miracles possible. If people in the West could embrace some of the more positive values of the indigenous world, perhaps that might even provide them with a "shortcut" to their own future. Many people in the West seem to be trying to find this shortcut through their commitment to learning about indigenous cultures, non-Western forms of spirituality or, most recently, through the Men's Movement. If these seekers fail, and if the modern world lets the indigenous world die, it will probably mean a long, hard trip into the future in search of the values of the "past."

Westerners forget that it is not only indigenous cultures that have a deep commitment to non-Western ideas about reality. Even in a highly industrialized culture like Japan, a connection with the ancestors is taken very seriously. When the new emperor of Japan was installed, many leaders in the West were disturbed by the fact that, as part of his inauguration, he went into the temple and spoke to his ancestors. Why is it that the modern world can't deal with its ancestors and endure its past?

It is my belief that the present state of restlessness that traps the modern individual has its roots in a dysfunctional relationship with the ancestors. In many non-Western cultures, the ancestors have an intimate and absolutely vital connection with the world of the living. They are always available to guide, to teach, and to nurture. They represent one of the pathways between the knowledge of this world and the next. Most importantly—and paradoxically—they embody the guidelines for successful living—all that is most valuable about life. Unless the relationship between the living and the dead is in balance, chaos results. When a person from my culture looks at the descendants of the Westerners who invaded their culture, they see a people who are ashamed of their ancestors because they were killers and marauders masquerading as artisans of progress. The fact that these people have a sick culture comes as no surprise to them. The

Dagara believe that, if such an imbalance exists, it is the duty of the living to heal their ancestors. If these ancestors are not healed, their sick energy will haunt the souls and psyches of those who are responsible for helping them. Not all people in the West have such an unhealthy relationship with their ancestors, but for those who do, the Dagara can offer a model for healing the ancestors, and, by doing so, healing oneself.

Because the world is becoming smaller, people from different realities can benefit from learning about and accepting each other. The challenge of modernity is to bring the world together into a unified whole in the middle of which diversity can exist. The respect for difference works only if connected with this vision.

▲   ▼   ▲

The first time I presented the material contained in this book was at a multicultural men's conference in Virginia. I needed to discover what, in the sequence of initiation experiences, could be put into words, and then see how this information would be received by the audience. I had heard other people tell the story of their initiation, but these stories sounded greatly different from mine. Some of the stories I'd heard seemed to make the process a mild formality, deliberately safe to the point where everyone was guaranteed to come out fine. In the Dagara culture, initiation is a dangerous commitment that can—and sometimes does—result in death, and I did not want to upset people who might be thinking of it differently. Was I not supposed to make friends with the stranger? I did not want to make initiation sound unreachable either. My wish was to strike some kind of balance between the modern person's mind and his heart by communicating to both of them. Within this group of men of opposing color and culture who had gathered together to figure out how to bridge gaps and reach out to each other, the initial atmosphere was one closer to war than to peace.

On the day of my presentation, the room was jam-packed with busy professional men who had cleared a whole week off their schedules to come to this conference. Their expectations were high. As I began telling my story, I could hear the sound of my own voice competing with the pounding of my heart, and the terrible sound of the audience's silence. Images of my initiation rushed into my mind, as if someone stood behind me passing them to me on picture postcards. I merely took them and passed them on. Soon I forgot my heartbeat, then the crowd, then myself. I realized, as I moved through the landscape of initiation, that a great number of episodes were at the periphery of my attention, not because I did not remember them fully, but because they were part of the untellable.

When I finished, something happened that I had never expected, something I was not prepared to handle. One hundred and twenty men gave me a standing ovation—men of European, African, Oriental, Indian, and Native American descent. The intensity of their response filled every corner of my mind, body, and heart and threatened to draw tears out of me. I fought hard to keep from weeping while the clapping seemed to go on for an eternity.

I do not remember how I recovered from this response. The whole time all I could do was to wonder what could be the explanation for this kind of overwhelming response. What was it in those men that understood what I had said about initiation so fully that they responded to it as if it were something familiar to them? They were not simple men. On the contrary, they were sophisticated, highly educated individuals—psychologists, therapists, anthropologists, men versed in myth, medical doctors, sociologists, lawyers, and who knows what else. And they all had the same response.

It took me a week and more to recover from the telling of my story. People came to me afterward to ask if I had written it down so they could have it. I had long had a question as to whether I could tell the untellable. I now had my answer. Some parts at least could be told, and so I knew where to start.

Since then, I have told the story of my initiation many times. The response has invariably been the same, and this response has given me the courage to share more information about elders, youth, medicine, healing, and the indigenous world of the Dagara which my own initiation had allowed me to access.

My grandfather's funeral ritual, described in this book, was one of those realities. I presented it once at a conference, leaving out many of the elaborate magical details. I was hardly surprised to find that it too had the power to touch people in this culture.

I have since then, and with great support, conducted a form of the Dagara funeral ritual with Americans as participants. Watching people of this culture devote themselves to a funeral ritual the Dagara way was as baffling to me as my initiation story must have been to them. I was glad the elders from my village weren't present. They would have thought I had made it up. But something in it, maybe the sincerity of over a hundred men mourning their losses, broke my heart. It is in response to them and to others who desired to know more that I have gathered the energy to write this book. It is also for every old person in this culture who feels abandoned, as if he or she has become useless, and for the young ones in search of a purpose and a blessing from some sacred old hands that I write. These two groups of people need to get their relationship straight. Maybe they will discover each other through this book. Their unspoken support has given me the courage to speak out clearly and explicitly.

It is time for Africans to clear their throats and enter boldly into the concert of spiritual and magical exchange. Books on other indigenous realities, written by native peoples, can be found everywhere. Those that deal with the deep tribal socio-spirituality of Africans are still the exclusive department of specialists: foreign anthropologists or native anthropologists who have been "foreignized," ethnographers, and sociologists. This is the direct result of five hundred years of European looting of the African continent. For those who do not know what colonialism does to the colonized, Frantz Fanon's *Black Skin, White Masks* and *The Wretched of the Earth* are a good starting place. When they are done, I would suggest they go further into reading Chinweizu's *The West and the Rest of Us.* It will suffice to give them a picture of what it means to be on the losing side in the struggle of nations and cultures. The subtle complexes that colonialism has produced in the hearts and psyches of the colonized still linger controllingly in the backyards of our modernity—the third world. It is not fair to think that Africa is only what postmodern specialists have come to tell us it is. Part of the violence in modern Africa is created by leaders who were educated as violently as I have been. I do not know if a person who was raised in terror, then given leadership, can think in gentle terms, for I do not think I would be the kind of person I am today without the powerful experiences that my elders gave me in my village of birth.

Being a man of two worlds is not easy. I have to constantly fight against the depressing energy of exile and homelessness. My degrees did not help resolve the problem of exile, they enforced it. The best degree I hold is the one that my elders have given me. It does not have a paper attached to it—it is ingrained in me, and it too is responsible for my feeling of exile. This feeling has nothing to do with geography, because I don't feel any different when I am in Africa. There I can't wear my African cloak in some quarters without seeming deliberately insulting because everybody else is busy trying to look as Western as possible. In many circles, an African who possesses a Ph.D. is expected to wear a three-piece suit and a matching tie, not an embarrassing village costume. And so, whenever I leave the West, it is not infrequent to see me wearing a cowboy outfit or a tie and speaking "Frenglish" in a Paris airport while I wait for my connecting flight. There an American, Black or otherwise, is treated better than a Black African.

I have to watch where I go and what I do because of this sense of exile. Every year I have to return home to my elders, not to visit them, but to be cleansed. After several years of doing that, I have come to understand that being in the West is like being caught in a highly radioactive environment. Without this periodic checkup, I will lose my ability to function. Speaking with people in this culture, I also have come to understand that a lot of them born and raised in the West share this sense of exile, and that I may be better off than they are because I still have elders that I can go to who will make me feel at home for a while as they cleanse me. Sometimes I find myself wondering, however, how long can this last.

Alienation is one of the many faces of modernity. The cure is communication and community—a new sense of togetherness. By opening to each other, we diminish the pressure of being alone and exiled. I have told my story here with the wish that it will be of help to those who pick it up with a sense of hope, searching for answers of their own.

CHAPTER I

SLOWLY BECOMING

 The story I am going to tell comes from a place deep inside of myself, a place that perceives all that I have irremediably lost and, perhaps, what gain there is behind the loss. If some people forget their past as a way to survive, other people remember it for the same reason. When cultures with contradictory versions of reality collide, children are often the casualties of that contact. So, like many dark children of the African continent, my childhood was short, far too short to be called a childhood. This is perhaps why it has stuck so vividly in my memory. Exile creates the ideal conditions for an inventory of the warehouse of one's past.

When I was little, two people in my family fascinated me: my mother and my grandfather. I loved my mother because she loved me. Although she would sometimes storm at me for my insatiable greed, she provided me with anything I asked for. Every now and then, when she went to the village market to sell her grains, I knew she would come back home with some treats such as cakes, European bread, or even a worn-out garment.

Every market day then was a new day for me, a day of excitement and expectation. Until I was three years old, my mother would carry me tied onto her back whenever she went in search of wood or grain or simply to farm. I loved to be knitted so closely to her, to watch her collect wood and carry it home on her head singing. She loved music and perceived nature as a song. While walking any great distance, she always sang to me. The story was always chosen to match the length of the journey, and was usually about some unfortunate girl or woman, usually an orphan.

One I remember in particular was about a girl named Kula, whose mother died and left her with a little sister, Naab, to take to their aunt. Kula asked Woor, her slave, to do the packing while she dressed herself as a queen, putting on gold necklaces, rings, and beads for the journey. Woor, who was more practical than her unmindful mistress, packed a lot of water along with her personal things.

On the road Naab, the little sister that Kula carried on her back, felt thirsty and asked for water. The only person who had brought any water was Woor, but she wasn't about to give it away for free. In payment, she asked for a gold ring.

The day was terribly hot and dusty, and a little while later, Naab cried again for water. Kula again begged Woor, this time trading her gold earrings for the water. This went on and on until the slave girl was dressed up like a queen, and Kula, stripped of her finery, looked like a slave. The next time Naab cried out for water, her sister had nothing left to trade. Woor suggested that she herself carry the child.

Thus, the three girls arrived at the house of the aunt, who welcomed them, mistaking the slave girl for her niece and the niece for the slave girl, and thus their identities were reversed. The slave girl was treated well and kept in the warm comfort of home, while the niece was treated as a slave and sent out to the farm to guard the crops against wild creatures.

As the days went on, the queen-become-slave sang the story of her life to scare the birds and animals away from the crops. A singing human voice in the middle of a farm always keeps the intruder away. As Kula cried out her plight, her tremulous melody touched the hearts of the winged and the four-legged creatures alike. One day the *Kontombili,* the spirits who live in the underworld, were passing by and heard Kula's song. They stopped and listened carefully as her mournful voice rose and fell amid the tall, end-of-rainy-season grass. When she stopped to catch her breath, the Kontombili approached her and asked her to sing her song again.

After she had finished, they asked, "Is this story true?"

And she said, "I only sing what I know."

The Kontombili said, "Go home, little lady. Your troubles are over. Your aunt's eyes will be opened and she will know who you are."

Kula went home and, as the Kontombili had promised, the aunt recognized her at once as her true niece. She was given her beautiful clothes and jewels back and placed in the bedroom where Woor the usurper had been sleeping. But Kula had learned true humility during her time as a slave, and she did not wish to switch from such hardship to such immense luxury and comfort. She asked if she could continue to stay in the slave girl's room and be given the leftovers from the rich folks' meals. Dumbfounded, sorry, and confused, her aunt could only keep apologizing for having treated her so badly.

Meanwhile the real slave girl was sent out to the farm to guard it against the creatures of the wild. She could not sing, so she sat and made raucous noises when birds landed on the crops. Along came a different group of Kontombili who had been told of the farm girl and her beautiful singing.

They begged her for some music, saying, "We heard that your voice brings tears to the heart. Please let us hear that song you sing every day."

Unaware who she was speaking to, Woor replied rudely, "What are you talking about? I ain't got no song to sing to nobody." Then she barked harshly, thinking that would scare these beings away. To the sensitive ears of Kontombili this sound was like the smell of vomit.

Disgusted and puzzled, the Kontombili asked Woor once more for a real song. Answering their courtesy with rudeness, the girl rebuked them in the same way. Believing they had been deceived by the girl, the Kontombili grew so angry that they turned her to stone.

I never liked the ending to my mother's stories. Someone always became something or someone else. When a story threatened to end before our journey did, she expertly extended it. I heard the story of Woor and Kula many times, but each time something different happened. Sometimes my mother would depict Kula's life with greater misery, as if she guessed that I did not like the fact that the usurper was turned to stone and, therefore, wanted to make a better case for her punishment. One time she had the little queen eat not just the crumbs from the table, but had her share her meals with the dog.

"But, Mom," I protested, "she didn't do that the other day. She ate only the leftovers."

"Yes," answered my mother, "but if she eats what the dog eats, then she can all the more enjoy returning to her queenhood, and you can enjoy watching the wicked slave die."

For those who think that dogs eat dog food in Dagara land, let them know that dog food is human excrement.

Although her songs were sweet, my mother's tremulous voice made me wonder sometimes if she was not mourning something or someone. I was too young then to suspect that her life and her marriage were not as happy as I thought, and that her heart held hidden sadness.

▲   ▼   ▲

It felt good to be suspended behind her, but I did not like being unable to see where we were going. Being so small, I could not see over her shoulders, and mostly she would cover up my head with an extra piece of cloth, hoping I would go to sleep. Consequently, the journeys to the savanna were less enjoyable than the journeys home. Once at the wood-gathering spot, however, she would set me free. I would then go wild, running all over the place as if to recuperate from the immobility of the trip. Sometimes, however, she would yell at me to come back to her, or to show me certain things. This is one of the tricks mothers use to keep children within reach.

Children learn by watching adults work and by doing the same things on a smaller scale. With the help of grown-ups, they obtain the range of skills they need to confront their own adult duties. Collecting wood is essentially the work of women, but it is also the work of boys. Bringing dry wood to your mother is a sign of love.

I loved to pursue rats, snakes, rabbits, virtually anything that moved. Though most of the time she let me indulge my wild nature, my mother always seemed to call me when I was in the midst of a feverish chase—and at precisely the moment when my victim seemed most vulnerable.

One day something very odd happened. As I was running around madly, I stepped on a rabbit. It dashed out of its hiding place and a wild race ensued. Looking for a place to hide, the rabbit ran straight toward a small forested area in the bush. I rejoiced when I saw the rabbit run in that direction because I often picked the fruits there and knew every corner of that little bush. I ran faster and we almost arrived there at the same moment. I had to slow down to avoid crashing into a tree, but the little rabbit, having no such fear, disappeared into the bush like an arrow shot into a pot of butter.

I followed with caution, trying to guess where the rabbit might be hiding. The tall grass put me at a disadvantage. I had to beat my way through while the little rabbit slipped along easily. When I turned over the first clump of grass, the rabbit was not there. I checked another part of the bush where I knew there was an animal nest. This nest was an earthen hole dug in a little hill, its opening covered with grass and its inside filled with soft straw. I removed the grass and was ready to leap headlong onto the miserable rabbit, but I never completed the action. All my movements were suspended as if by an electric shock.

Where I had thought there would be a rabbit there was instead a tiny old man as small as the rabbit itself. He sat on an almost invisible chair and held a minuscule can in his right hand. His head was covered with hair so white and so shiny that it seemed unnatural. His beard was long and white too, reaching almost to his chest, and he wore a traditional Dagara mantle, also white.

All around him there was a glow, a shiny rainbow ring, like a round window or portal into another reality. Although his body filled most of that portal, I could still see that there was an immense world inside it.

But what surprised me most was that the laws of nature in that world did not seem to operate like anything I had seen before. The little man's chair was sitting on a steep slope, yet he did not fall over backwards. I noticed that something like a thin wall sustained him. He was not leaning against the chair he was sitting on, but against that thin wall even though he still appeared upright in the window.

As my eyes moved from that wall and the world behind it back to the man, I saw that his thin legs were bare. His toes were so tiny I could barely see them. Petrified by something that was neither fear nor mirth, but felt like a tickling all over my body, I forgot to scream as the man said, "I have been watching you for a long time, ever since your mother started bringing you here. Why do you want to hurt the rabbit, your little brother? What did he do to you, little one?" His tiny mouth was barely moving as he spoke, and his voice was very thin.

Confused, I tried to reply. "I . . . I . . . don't know."

"Then be friendly to him from now on. He too likes the freshness of this place, he too has a mother who cares for him. What would his mother say if you hurt him? Now go because your own mother is worried."

While the little man was speaking, I spotted the rabbit, which had been hidden behind him in the magic circle all that time. It moved farther into that steep marvelous place, and then disappeared behind a tree. Meanwhile, I heard a cracking sound, as if the earth itself were splitting open. No sooner had I heard this than the old man stood up, slung his chair over his shoulder, and walked into the opening as if he had commanded it. The earth closed up on him, leaving a gust of fresh breeze in his place. At the same moment, I heard my mother's faint voice calling me, "Malidoma, please answer me, where are you?"

Still caught in the intensity of the experience, I opened my mouth to answer, but no sound came out. She called again and again and finally I was able to scream back at her. I could not see her, but I heard her give a yell and run toward me.

When she reached me, she lifted me up in the air and ran out of the bush with me as quickly as she could. "I have been looking for you since noon," she said, gasping for breath. "It's almost dark. What have you been doing all this time?"

"I saw a man in the bush and he said I should be friends with rabbits."

"What man, what rabbit?" my mother said in a panicked voice. "What are you talking about?" Not waiting for an answer, she provided one herself. "Oh, my poor child. Some witch must have taken his soul away. Please, spirits of nature, help me get him home alive." She went on and on, making sounds that seemed like gibberish to me, but were the primal language with which she conjured the protecting spirits.

When I was able to get her attention again, I said, "The man is very small and very old, Mama. He lives there, in the bush, but he just left."

"Oh, dear ancestors, my child has seen a Kontomblé. What else can it be? Don't talk anymore. Let's get out of here. I'll never take you out again."

Saying this, she loaded me onto her back, tied me to her with a piece of cloth, and walked breathlessly to her basket, now filled with heavy pieces of wood. She then lifted the whole thing onto her head and proceeded toward home. There was no singing or talking on that whole six-mile journey. As we neared the house, she finally spoke. "You will not tell anyone about this or I will never take you with me again. Do you hear me?"

"Yes," I replied. And that was all she ever said about the matter.

There was a reason for my mother's unwillingness to discuss this experience with me or to have me discuss it with others. The Dagara believe that contact with the otherworld is always deeply transformational. To successfully deal with it, one should be fully mature. Unfortunately, the otherworld does not discriminate between children and adults, seeing us all as fully grown souls. Mothers fear their children opening up to the otherworld too soon, because when this happens, they lose them. A child who is continually exposed to the otherworld will begin to remember his or her life mission too early. In such cases, a child must be initiated prematurely. Once initiated, the child is considered an adult and must change his/her relationship with the parents.

▲   ▼   ▲

My grandfather had been my confident interlocutor for as long as I can remember. There is a close relationship between grandfathers and grandchildren. The first few years of a boy's life are usually spent, not with his father, but with his grandfather. What the grandfather and grandson share together—that the father cannot—is their close proximity to the cosmos. The grandfather will soon return to where the grandson came from, so therefore the grandson is bearer of news the grandfather wants. The grandfather will do anything to make the grandson communicate the news of the ancestors before the child forgets, as inevitably happens. My grandfather obtained this news through hypnosis, putting me to sleep in order to question me.

It is not only to benefit the grandfather that this relationship with his grandson must exist. The grandfather must also transmit the "news" to the grandson using the protocol secret to grandfathers and grandsons. He must communicate to this new member of the community the hard tasks ahead on the bumpy road of existence.

For the Dagara, every person is an incarnation, that is, a spirit who has taken on a body. So our true nature is spiritual. This world is where one comes to carry out specific projects. A birth is therefore the arrival of someone, usually an ancestor that somebody already knows, who has important tasks to do here. The ancestors are the real school of the living. They are the keepers of the very wisdom the people need to live by. The life energy of ancestors who have not yet been reborn is expressed in the life of nature, in trees, mountains, rivers and still water. Grandfathers and grandmothers, therefore, are as close to an expression of ancestral energy and wisdom as the tribe can get. Consequently their interest in grandsons and granddaughters is natural. An individual who embodies a certain value would certainly be interested in anyone who came from the place where that value existed most purely. Elders become involved with a new life practically from the moment of conception because that unborn child has just come from the place they are going to.

A few months before birth, when the grandchild is still a fetus, a ritual called a "hearing" is held. The pregnant mother, her brothers, the grandfather, and the officiating priest are the participants. The child's father is not present for the ritual, but merely prepares the space. Afterward, he is informed about what happened. During the ritual, the incoming soul takes the voice of the mother (some say the soul takes the whole body of the mother, which is why the mother falls into trance and does not remember anything afterward) and answers every question the priest asks.

The living must know who is being reborn, where the soul is from, why it chose to come here, and what gender it has chosen. Sometime, based on the life mission of the incoming soul, the living object to the choice of gender and suggest that the opposite choice will better accommodate the role the unborn child has chosen for him- or herself. Some souls ask that specific things be made ready before their arrival—talismanic power objects, medicine bags, metal objects in the form of rings for the ankle or the wrist. They do not want to forget who they are and what they have come here to do. It is hard not to forget, because life in this world is filled with many alluring distractions. The name of the newborn is based upon the results of these communications. A name is the life program of its bearer.

A child's first few years are crucial. The grandfather must tell the grandson what the child said while still a fetus in his mother's womb. Then, he must gradually help him build a connection with his father, who will help him with the hard challenges up ahead. My father used to complain that his life was calamitous because he never knew his grandfather, who disappeared before he was born. Had he known him, my father said, he would never have lost his first family, never spent his youth working in a gold mine or later embraced the Catholic religion with a fervor grander than the one that linked him to his ancestors. His stepbrothers, who knew their grandfather, did not have the kind of restlessness that plagued my father. The frustration of a grandfatherless male child has no cure.

In the beginning, the intense intimacy between the grandson and the grandfather might create feelings of jealousy in the father. While a grandfather is alive, the grandchildren do not have much of anything to learn from their father—until they reach their preadolescent age. And the father knows that. He knows that a conversation between a grandson and a grandfather is a conversation between brothers of the same knowledge group. To know is to be old. In that, the grandson is as old as the grandfather. Consequently, the father is too young to have a part in this relationship between wise men.

I used to spend much of my days in the company of my grandfather. He was a man worn out by hard work, who at the age of sixty was virtually a child—weak and sick, yet with a mind still as alert as that of a man in the prime of youth. He also possessed incomparable wisdom stored over the course of half a century of sustained healing and medicine works.

Grandfather was thin and tall. Since I had first known him, he always wore the same traditional *boubou*. It had been white when he first got it, but in order to avoid the cost of maintenance, he had changed the white color of the cloth into red, using the juice of some roots that he alone knew the secret of. In use twenty-four hours a day, the boubou was simultaneously his daily outfit, his pajamas, and his blanket. After more than a decade, it had turned into a remnant of himself, blackened by sweat and dirt. Though most of the boubou had fallen off under the weight of filth, it still hung firmly on his shoulders, its general architecture intact. Unlike modern Christianity, which links cleanliness to godliness, Dagara culture holds the opposite to be true. The more intense the involvement with the life of the spirit, the more holy and wise an individual is, the less attention is paid to outward beauty. Grandfather owned a walking stick carved with artistic dexterity, its wood also darkened from long usage. His movements were slow, and I found it easier to be around him than around the other kids, who were older, stronger and more agile than I was. So every day, while everybody was at the farm, I was with Grandfather.

Grandfather knew every story ever told or even heard of in the tribe. And at his age he looked as if storytelling were the only thing he could still do with success. He utilized this talent very well since that was the only way he could gain attention. Each time I sat in his lap, he took it as a request for a story, and he would always begin by asking a question.

"Brother Malidoma, do you know why the bat sits upside down?"

"No. Why?"

"Long, long time ago, and I mean long when I say long because that was when animals used to speak to men and men to animals and both to God."

"Then why don't animals speak to men anymore?"

"They still do, only we have forgotten how to comprehend them!"

"What happened?"

"Never mind. We're talking about bats, and why they all sit upside down."

"Yes. I want to know why they do that."

"Well, see, there was a time when Brother Bat died and no one knew who he was. The town crier took his body to the crocodile, saying, 'The jaws of this damn thing look like they were borrowed from a crocodile. I thought he might be your relative or something.'

"The crocodile said, 'It's true that this guy's got a mouth like mine, but I ain't got no brother with fur, let alone with wings.'

"So, next the town crier took the dead bat to the head of the birds tribe."

"And who's that?"

"It's Mother Sila, you know, the bird that flies high and shoots herself down like an arrow when she goes to catch her dinner. Mother Sila said, 'This animal looks like it's got good wings and reasonable claws, but I never saw anyone in my family with so few feathers.'

"And so, finally the town crier gave up and threw the bat into a ditch. But when Papa Bat found out about this, he was very angry. He rebelled against God and ordered the whole tribe never to look up to God again. Since then bats never turn their faces upward."

"Grandfather, this is too sad. Tell me another one."

Grandfather never had to be begged. He would tell you a story even without your asking. And the times you asked, he would keep on talking until you "unasked" him.

He also knew how to hypnotize you—to speak you to sleep—when he needed to be left alone to do some important work. He never chased a child away from him; in fact, he always thought children were the most cooperative people on earth. One just needed to know how to use their generous services. A sleeping child is even more obedient than a child awake, and so he would often hypnotize one of us, then awaken us into a state where we would be dispatched to run errands for him. Any child seen silently looking for something, who would not respond when you asked,

"What are you looking for?" was a sleeping child on an errand for Grandfather. He did not like to request the services of grown-ups because they would grumble and swear the whole time. He always said that the good in a service has little to do with the service itself, but with the kind of heart one brings to the task. For him, an unwilling heart spoiled a service by infecting it with feelings of resentment and anger.

Grandfather knew how to talk to the void, or rather to some unseen audience of spirits. Among the Dagara, the older you get the more you begin to notice spirits and ancestors everywhere. When you hear a person speaking out loud, alone, you don't talk to them because he or she may be discussing an important issue with a spirit or an ancestor. This rule applies more to holy elders than to adults in general. When I was with Grandfather, I felt as if there were more people around than could be accounted for. When he knew I was not following his stories, he used to redirect his speech to these invisible beings. He never seemed bothered by my not listening.

▲　　　▼　　　▲

Grandfather's respect and love for children was universal in the tribe. To the Dagara, children are the most important members of society, the community's most precious treasures. We have a saying that it takes the whole tribe to raise a child. Homes have doorless entrances to allow children to go in and out wherever they want, and it is common for a mother to not see her child for days and nights because he or she is enjoying the care and love of other people. When the mother really needs to be with her child, she will go from home to home searching for it.

When a child grows into an adolescent, he or she must be initiated into adulthood. A person who doesn't get initiated will remain an adolescent for the rest of their life, and this is a frightening, dangerous, and unnatural situation. After initiation, the elders will pick a partner for the young person, someone who is selected for their ability to team up with you in the fulfillment of your life purpose. If one obediently walks their life path, they will become an elder somewhere in their late forties or early fifties. Graduating to this new status, however, depends on one's good track record.

A male elder is the head of his family. He has the power to bless, and the power to withhold blessing. This ability comes to him from his ancestors, to whom he is very close, and he follows their wisdom in counseling his large family.

Wealth among the Dagara is determined not by how many things you have, but by how many people you have around you. A person's happiness is directly linked to the amount of attention and love coming to him or her from other people. In this, the elder is the most blessed because he is in the most visible position to receive a lot of attention. The child is too, because it "belongs" to the whole community.

Some elders are chosen to sit on the village council. There they participate in decision making that affects the entire village. Women have their council separate from men because of their unique roles and responsibilities. Dagara culture is matrilineal—everybody in the village carries the name of their mother. The family is feminine, the house where the family live is kept by a male. The male is in charge of the family security. The female is in charge of the continuity of life. She rules the kitchen, the granaries where food is stored, and the space where meals are taken. The male is in charge of the medicine shrine and of the family's connection with the ancestors. He brings the things that nourish the family, like food.

For a full fifty years, my grandfather had been the priest, the leader, and the counselor of a family of over fifty souls. Faced with domestic problems of all kinds, he had had to be tough. Judging from his physical appearance—muscles still protruding from tired biceps, square shoulders that looked as if they could still carry weight, big chest that seemed to hide massive lungs—one could see that he had been a robust young man capable of sustaining long hours of demanding physical labor. Grandfather's greatest fame, however, came from his spiritual accomplishments. In the village, everyone knew him as the "upside-down arrow shooter." He was one of the people in the tribe whose name made people shudder, for if he wished to destroy an enemy, he would retire to the quiet of his chambers, place an arrow upside down on his bow, and magically hit his target. The arrow would kill whomever or whatever he named, then rematerialize in his chamber ready for more. The slightest scratch from such a weapon is mortal.

Other tribes did not dare go into conflict with ours because they did not possess the secret of such deadly magic. Consequently, Grandfather rarely had a chance to demonstrate to the tribe his power in battle. The arrow did have peacetime uses, however. Grandfather used it to protect our family farm from the nocturnal raids of wild beasts. Although he could no longer work the fields, Grandfather could still in this manner contribute to our food supply. He also displayed the upside-down arrow as a persuasive weapon to warn evildoers away from our family, the Birifor.

Grandfather was no longer strong enough to walk the six miles between the house and the farm every day, and as far as I can recall, I never saw him go there. Because the people of my tribe practice slash-and-burn agriculture, their fields are often very far away as people keep moving them around year after year to avoid exhausting the soil. I was born too late to know Grandfather as a more vigorous man. When I was a child, he spent his days sitting in the same place in the central yard of the labyrinthine compound that housed our family group. Sometimes he was pensive, calmly and wisely dispatching legal matters without so much as raising his head or the tone of his voice. He had great knowledge of healing matters as well. Without so much as glancing up from the pots that held the food and medicinal items he dispensed, he could tell young people who had physical problems which roots they should dig up and bring back to him in the evening for their cures.

At night, when everyone else was asleep, Grandfather would watch over the farm and the compound from his room. Through the use of complex and magical security devices, his thoughts were constantly tuned in to the vibration of the farm, and he could always determine whether the fields were being raided by wild animals. The device he used to keep vigil consisted of a clay pot filled with "virgin water," rainfall that had never touched the earth in its fall from the sky. He saw everything that happened throughout the farm by looking into this water. The precision of vision it afforded superseded the simplicity of this device.

Grandfather's magical guardianship had enabled our family to always have enough food to eat. Two thirds of the tribe did not share our surplus and could never put aside enough extra food to avoid the hardship of the hunger season, which ran every year from July to September, when stored food ran out. During this time, a mild famine visited many compounds. Children would stop singing and laughter would vanish from the houses at night. Every morning during that time, a long line of people stood at the door of the Birifor house, waiting for a calabash of grain. Distributing food to all these needy people was another of grandfather's tasks. So, every morning of those misty days of July and August, after he had given orders to the men and women of the family regarding their daily assignments, Grandfather would drag himself to the door of his room. There, he would take all the time he needed to be seated comfortably. I would wait calmly until he was settled, then I would sit on his bony lap. Aided by a woman whose charge it was to measure up the proper amount of millet to be distributed to each of the needy, Grandfather would dispatch his task until shortly after noontime when the heat became unbearable.

Usually, at that particular time of the day, I would fall asleep on his lap. He would wake me up later with a song that rang more like a cry— Grandfather's voice was terrible. Then he would say, "Brother Malidoma, my legs can't hold you any longer. Please allow them to breathe too." And still half asleep, I would stand up and wait, wondering what had happened.

After the rite of charity, one of the women brought food to Grandfather and me, and we ate together. Grandfather was very frugal. I remember him once explaining to my father that the weight of undigested food closed the body and the mind off from the ability to perceive the surrounding good and bad vibrations. He who ate too much increased his vulnerability. The good taste of food hid the danger it put the body into. Grandfather's philosophy was that food is a necessary evil.

For this reason, the attitude toward food in our family was strange. One ate only when absolutely necessary. Grandfather could tell who was eating too much. For children under six, he encouraged food. For adults, he encouraged frugality. He used to rage at certain adolescents who, in his eyes, had no control of their appetite, saying, "Initiation will be a bitter experience when you come of age. Now is the time you must learn to control the drives of your body. Be alert and firm. Do not let the desire for physical satisfactions temper your warriorship. Remember, our ancestors are spirits, they feed only their minds and that is why they can do things beyond our comprehension."

When Grandfather started speaking, he did not particularly care whether someone was listening or not. Speaking was a liberating exercise for him, an act of mental juggling. He would sometimes speak for hours, as if he had a big spirit audience around him. He would laugh, get angry and storm at invisible opponents, and then become quiet once more. When he had a real audience, as he did every evening at storytelling time, he would teach us all through his tales. He would speak until everyone fell asleep, then would rail at us, saying that sleep was a dangerous practice no different from that of eating too much food. For Grandfather, sleep was tribute we pay to the body far too often. He would often say that the body is merely the clothing of the soul and that it is not good to pay too much attention to it, as if it were really us. "Leave your body alone, and it will align itself to the needs of the spirit you are."

I loved Grandfather's company, and he loved having me next to him. He used to call me Brother when he had something serious to tell me. Otherwise, he would call me by my tribal name, Malidoma. I asked him once why he called me Brother and he said, "I call you Brother because you are the reincarnation of Birifor, the elder son of my parents, and someone I used to love very much. Birifor's name is now carried by the entire family, and I will tell you why.

"Our father, Sabare, was a priest and a hunter. Before he went hunting, he used to give directions to Birifor about running the family, for Sabare would often disappear for months at a time. One day he left and never returned. We waited for a year, then another year, then we decided we should perform the funeral ritual, believing that our father must have been devoured by a wild beast. We planned to celebrate the rite for six days instead of three. The day before the funeral, Birifor and I were sitting on the roof of the house planning the final details when we saw our father coming toward us on a white horse. He was riding so fast the feet of his mount barely touched the ground.

"Mesmerized by the sudden vision, we waited in silence. The closer Sabare got, the slower he rode until he stopped just under the big baobab tree in the yard. He dismounted, walked to the ladder, and climbed up to join us. He still wore the same clothes he had the day he left long ago. His bow still hung solid and real on his back, and his quiver and aimer were still there by his left elbow. He was clearly not dead.

"The only strange thing was his horse. We knew what a horse looked like, but we didn't have horses here in our region. We couldn't imagine where he had found one. While we were busy wondering about all these things, he arrived on the roof, produced a little bench out of nowhere, and sat down. Instantly, we all sat. We greeted each other and I asked if he needed anything to wet his throat before we talked.

"'No,' he said. 'I have come to tell you to abandon your funeral plans. Even though you will not see me again, know that I am not dead, nor will I be for a long time, I have shifted to the other side of existence without going through the door of death, and I have done this for the benefit of the family. Do not, I repeat, do not perform any funeral rite, for my soul does not need rest. Whenever you need me, say these words' (Grandfather never told me what the words were) 'and I will be there. As long as I can come to you, the family will never be in danger, there will always be prosperity, and you will have a world of medicine to share among you. Do not mourn my absence, for I am present among you without a body.'

"Saying this, he stood up and the bench he was sitting on vanished. Ignoring this magical occurrence, he walked straight toward the ladder without saying goodbye. We were so surprised, we couldn't think of anything to do or say. Finally, I gathered all my strength and begged, 'But at least stay with us a day or two. You must tell us where you are and talk to the family about what happened. You know we are all anxious to hear about you.'

"His reply came quickly: 'Nonsense! I have already told you what I came to tell you. No more should be said or the thread will be cut between you and me. Know only that where I exist is not on the earth, but in a universe of its own. I see you better from there than I ever could from here. Not a word, not a thought, not a single movement of my family escapes my attention. Now be content and go about your duties, I have spoken.'

"Saying this, he climbed down the ladder. We watched him get on his horse and start to ride away. After he had gone a very short distance, he and the horse began mounting up into the sky. Stunned, we watched them rise higher, then vanish.

"After that we canceled the funeral. My brother Birifor was installed as priest and family leader, and an era of extreme material and magical prosperity began for us. We discovered the secret of the upside-down arrow, the surveillance of remote areas, and many, many other medicine secrets you will learn later. You see all these people who come to ask us for food. Because of what Sabare has taught us, we have food and they don't. When you grow up, you'll learn about the secrets of the Birifor Magic. Do you want to know them?"

"Yes," I said. "I want to know all about the upside-down arrow, I want to be a hunter like Sabare and fly in the sky. But Grandfather, you have not told me why you call me Brother yet."

"Yes, that's right," he replied. "So, like I was saying, your other grandfather became the *Baomale,* the healer of the family. But he died in the war against the white man."

"What? They killed him?" I inquired anxiously.

"No, Brother," Grandfather said mournfully. "The upside-down arrow killed him."

"But it was not supposed to," I said, confused.

"Yes, Brother, it was not supposed to do that. But someone made a serious mistake. I'll explain all that to you when you grow bigger. Now it's my turn to remind you that I have not answered your question yet. So let me do it now."

Grandfather never tackled a question directly. He had the habit of introducing an answer by way of a whole bunch of stories that often placed the question being asked into a wider context. Your answer would arrive when you were least expecting it, nestled into the middle of a litany of fascinating narrations. Thus one would go away with more than they came for, enriched with fantastic tales.

With me it was different. I would keep reminding Grandfather of my question and, at length, he would announce the answer before giving it to me so that I would know when my thirst was being quenched.

"After the death of my brother Birifor and the ceremony of investiture that gave me the leadership of this family," Grandfather continued, "my father, Sabare, came to me in spirit and told me that he was ordering Birifor to return to the family. Your sister had already been born then. A year later, your mother became pregnant again, and the baby inside her, whenever he would speak to me, would call me Brother. I knew it was Birifor about to be born again, and that you would be a boy. So I waited for your birth. And since that night when you came to life at dawn near the river, between here and the house of that white devil on the hill, it has been my turn to call you Brother. Now do you understand?"

"No," I said. This was a lot to take into my young mind. "If I am Birifor, why do you call me Malidoma? And if I am Malidoma after all,

why do my father and other people like the Jesuit priest at the mission on
the hill call me Patrice? Between Malidoma, Brother, and Patrice, what is
my true name?"

"None of them tells the whole story of who you are. However, there is
one that almost does, the one your ancestors call you by: Malidoma. Do
you know why this is so?"

"No, Grandfather, tell me everything." I moved closer to him and
hugged him. His clothes exhaled an unbearable smell and I pulled back
sharply to avoid suffocation. Noticing this, Grandfather smiled briefly and
regarded me gently. He laid his left hand on my forehead, took my right
hand in his, and looked up at the sky for a long while before speaking.

"You do not like smell of a dirty old man's clothing? You love fra-
grance, the kind flowers have. Do you know that these sweet fragrances are
born from horrible ones? Before it can liberate the sweet part of itself, the
flower must rot. You see I have to rot too so that the Birifor family can
smell good. This is the order of things."

"But Grandfather, you were talking about names and my birth. Now
the flower story . . ."

"Yes, the flower story is a little bit of a detour. I do not want to scram-
ble your little growing mind. Now! What was I saying? Oh, yes. Your true
name is Malidoma. This is what your ancestors call you. The other names
are things like tools that will get you out of trouble later. 'Patrice' was
given to you by the Jesuits shortly after your birth. Your parents, as you
know, are friends with that white-bearded priest up there on the hill. They
seem to like his medicine and the God he serves, and that is why he comes
here to visit so often. But let me tell you that a God who would send people away from their land must be drinking a very strong wine all the time.
Long ago that priest changed the names of your parents so they would
come to his church more often. I do not know what your parents and the
priest do up there, and I don't think I want to know either.

" 'Patrice' was the name given to you by that priest up there on the hill.
Use it whenever you are out of the tribal boundaries. 'Brother' is the name
I call you by. Nobody else has claim to it. 'Birifor'—well, nobody will ever
again call you that. 'Malidoma' is the name you will start hearing a lot
when you become big. So be alert and prompt to answer. You never know
what name another person will address you by. This is something you'll
have to live with. That's enough for today."

It was dark already, and the farmers were returning from their day's
work. My mother was the first to arrive, loaded down with a pack of dry
wood that she balanced high on her head. To pass through the gate into our
courtyard, she had almost to kneel double to avoid hitting the top and sides
of the narrow doorway.

My mother walked to the middle of the compound yard, tilted her head, and dropped the wood next to the central cooking pot. Relieved of her burden, she breathed deeply, wiped the blinding sweat from her eyes, and unfastened the wide flat carrying basket from her head. My sister entered with her own small load of dry wood—nothing heavy, since she was so small. She had no trouble passing the gate. She was only six years old, but her education had already begun. Every morning she had to follow my mother to the farm and perform the duties of her sex, on a smaller scale.

She dropped her load carelessly and went into the kitchen in search of food. Shortly after, my father arrived, always the last to come home. He rode a bicycle that he had brought back from the Gold Coast, where he had spent three and a half years working in the gold mines of Takouradi and Sakoundé. It was a huge English bicycle. He used to call it *gawule,* after the lengthy branches of the ga-tree, which grows in the savanna.

This bicycle was a blessing to my father. Thanks to it, he was always the first to arrive at the farm and the last to leave it. I used to watch him ride in, amazed at his dexterity. Balancing his slim form on the narrow iron seat, he rode so elegantly, it seemed there was a conspiracy between him and the bicycle.

The machine had lost its brakes shortly after he arrived home from the Gold Coast. To stop it, he always had to jump off as it neared the gateway and run along with it for a while. Then he would park it against the wall of the compound.

Father never left the farm until he knew everybody else had gone. Once he was home, one of his responsibilities was to check the seventeen living areas of the compound, where the seventeen families of the Birifor family group live, to make sure that everyone had returned safely. These family groups comprise our clan. The Dagara tribe consists of roughly ten clans encompassing over half a million people, covering a surface perhaps the size of Massachusetts.*

Our living area was the first one he checked. In it lived my parents, Grandfather, my sister, and myself. It was the leading unit, bigger than the other spaces yet containing less than 10 percent of the people a living area that size ordinarily does. That was because half of the rooms in our area were spirit rooms, the sacred shrines of ancestors, and therefore accessible only to Grandfather, my father, and other family heads.

Typical family living units consist of two main areas—the men's quarter and the women's quarter—which face each other across the courtyard. In my village, the husband and wife do not share the same bed, and the

---

*Today, colonialism, new and old, has displaced them in three different sovereign nations: Ghana, Ivory Coast, and Burkina Faso. In the fifties there were fewer than two hundred and fifty people in my village. There are fewer than two hundred today. The reasons for this are the migration of the youth due to clashes between the old and the new ways of living, starvation because of destructive "modern" farming techniques, and the melancholy of indigenous life.

children take turns sleeping in the lodgings of both parents. The building that housed my mother was called a *zangala*. It was a large oval structure built with mud and wood, with extensions on the side that looked like extra-large closets. This windowless, wigwamlike lodging was always dark. My mother, and every other woman in the village, preferred it that way. Built against the side of the zangala were two little houses, one for the poultry, the other for the goats and sheep. Across from the zangala was my father's quarter, which was more modern in construction and about the size of a three-bedroom apartment. The floors and walls of all of these buildings were sealed with a kind of polish made from mud and liquefied cow dung to avoid the cracking common to mud houses.

Between these two quarters was an enclosed courtyard—a large open space for evening and community gatherings. The only entrance to the compound was built into the wall of this courtyard, and next to it was a little hole that served as a door for the dogs and cats. On one side of the courtyard was a kitchen where people made fire and cooked food. The ceiling of this kitchen was black with soot and God knows what else. On the other side, to the left of my father's quarter, was a toilet and a shower room.

Lastly, a set of small buildings joined together by a common back wall constituted the quarter of Grandfather and his spirits. Nobody in the compound entered these small buildings without Grandfather's presence, but at night one could hear him conversing with unknown beings. It was from these rooms that he surveyed the farm in the bush six miles away from home.

Grandfather's space housed the pharmacy of the entire Birifor clan—an array of roots, daily collected, nightly prepared, to face emergencies of all sorts. These little dwellings contained the prosperity—spiritual, material, and magical—of the Birifor. Some of these roots were good for physical illness, but most of them were good for illness of the soul. These little buildings held the spiritual destiny of every member of the family. There, each one of us existed in the form of a stone, silent, docile, available. The stones represented the birth certificate of every person in the clan. This is where Grandfather went to examine the physical and spiritual energy fields of the people under his care. Through this magical means, Grandfather could check on each of us at his leisure.

He took care of people outside the family too. Strangers used to come now and then to seek medical help, and Grandfather would begin long ceremonial rites that took most of the day. Sometimes the strangers would bring chickens and, speaking breathlessly in an unintelligible magical language, he would cut their throats and direct the spurting blood onto some statues, representing different spirits, carved out of wood or built against the wall. He never tired of rituals. It took me many years to understand the reasons behind these visits and how Grandfather was able to help these strangers.

After my father had finished his tour of the family units, he had to make sure that all the domestic animals were where they ought to be. Then he would close them in for the night. Finally, he would close the main gate and secure it from the inside by tying it to an old bicycle pedal fastened to the wall. This "lock" was one of my father's inventions since his return from the Gold Coast.

Because my father was such a quiet and rather gloomy man, it was hard to be around him. Grandfather explained to me that this inner conflict had intensified since my father had become a follower of the priest on the hill. His unfocused and taciturn air was the result of the many trips he had made outside the limits of the Dagara tribe early in his youth. "A youth who leaves the village shortly after initiation is vulnerable. He runs the risk of never dying properly," Grandfather always said. My father started traveling when he was fifteen, and never stopped until he was thirty.

These conversations between me and my grandfather may sound very "adult," but it is not uncommon for grandchildren to learn about their fathers—and about everybody else—from their grandfathers. Grandfather was always very open toward me. So open that in retrospect it sometimes seems that he even forgot that the life of the person he was constantly analyzing in my presence was that of my own father. Most of what he said about my father did not make sense until I was much older, but I remembered it because he repeated it so often. Grandfather always spoke to me as an equal, perhaps because his belief that I was his brother implied, in some sense, that I already was an adult. Again, this is not an uncommon attitude among the Dagara: it is not unusual to hear someone exclaim in front of a newly born child, "Oh, he looks so old!"

So, when I became older, I came to understand more about the nature of the emotional problems that contributed to my father's gloominess and absentmindedness. His first marriage had occurred at the age of twenty after he returned from the Ivory Coast. There he had served as a soldier in the colonial army. From this first marriage twin daughters were born. My father was supposed to perform the ritual that every person who becomes a father of twins must perform. It consists of filling up two clay pots with root juice and burying them at the entrance of the compound. These pots symbolize the link beween this pair of humans and the spirits that invited them to come into the family. The original reason for this ritual, as with many others that the Dagara practice, has been lost in oblivion, but people always perform them because their fathers did before them. It is also a very real incentive, borne out by long experience, that those who do not perform these rituals most often meet with disaster. The purpose of ritual is to create harmony between the human world and the world of the gods, ancestors, and nature.

My father's adherence to the new Christian faith made him doubt the validity of such rites. Grandfather had warned him whenever he could about the urgency and importance of the ceremony, but because Grandfather was my father's father, he couldn't do the ceremony himself. Each time he would remind his son of his duty, my father would play deaf, neither refusing nor accepting the responsibility. The truth was that he did not want to offend the white priest, appearing like a pagan devil worshiper in his eyes.

My father genuinely feared going to hell. As he confided to me much later on, the white priest had told him that the Almighty God would take good care of his newborn twins and that He could do it better than the ancestors. According to the priest, our ancestors had been condemned to eternal hell and were busy burning. They had no time to enjoy sacrifices. I wondered what kind of expression Grandfather wore when he discovered that his own son actually believed this nonsense.

As the years passed and the twin girls, Elizabeth and Marguerite, grew without a problem, Father was convinced that the priest had been right. Even though Grandfather continued to remind him of his duties toward his firstborn, nothing could shake his obstinacy. His faith in the Christian religion grew stronger every day. Finally, Grandfather switched from simple warnings to threats. Father began to see himself as a martyr, like those of Uganda who, in the mid-1800s, preferred to die at the hands of their own "pagan" elders rather than deny their faith in God. The Catholic church later canonized these black men as saints. Convinced that his own suffering at the hands of my grandfather meant free passage to heaven, my father endured it gladly.

In the meantime, two other children were born to him. The Catholic priest poured water on them immediately and named them Daniel and Pascal. By this time Grandfather had become a lone observer. Because they were boys, and it was his duty, he secretly gave them Dagara names. Meanwhile, the twin girls grew to the age of initiation. The missionary warned my father against such practices, and Father refused to allow the girls to become initiated, a terrible decision because it doomed them both to being stuck in adolescence for the rest of their lives, bereft of the secret, adult knowledge that initiation would have given them. At this point, Grandfather was tired of struggling with his stubborn son. His grandchildren had grown beyond his protection, and he could only watch helplessly as disaster struck, faster than was possible to take action against.

One morning Elizabeth caught a mysterious illness that no one could diagnose. She died at noon before the missionary could give her extreme unction. During her funeral Marguerite died while running wild with grief. The funeral intensified.

The sudden death of Marguerite had affected Father beyond repair. Her funeral, however, was brief. People knew what was going on. Twins don't die on the same day. The people in our family asked my father to perform a reconciliation rite, thinking it would delay further disaster until the twin ritual for the girls could be done posthumously. It must have been my father's fate to not listen. Instead, he prayed to the foreign god harder than ever, offering him his pain as a gift. In his confusion, he saw his tragedy as a test sent by the Lord to try his faith. He kept repeating the famous sentence from the Lord's prayer, "Thy will be done."

And the Lord's will was done, beyond his expectations. Pascal, the eldest son, expired two weeks after the funeral of Elizabeth and Marguerite. Nobody knew what killed him. He had been playing with his friends and suddenly cried out loudly that he was dying. Julia, the unfortunate mother, died of sorrow during the funeral of her son. She was already too worn out by the shock of the death of her two daughters to endure any more pain. There remained only Daniel and my father. In my imagination I picture my grandfather emitting sounds of immense sorrow and helplessness. The first time he told me this story, my father himself groaned with grief.

My father was a stubborn man to have stood his ground through so much destruction. The missionaries could do nothing but counsel him to pray, and then to pray harder, attributing these calamities to the weakness of his faith in God. All during this time, my father told me, the ghosts of his wife and children haunted his dreams with the question, "Why did you do this to us?"

After a few days of living in terror of these ghostly visitations, Father went up to the hill to seek the interventions of the priest. He returned home with a terrible empty look, as if his soul had already gone out of his body. The Jesuits had given him the same worn-out counsel: "Keep praying." Ruined by pain, eroded by continuous hopeless effort, he discontinued all social activities and voluntarily ostracized himself for months. The only time he would leave his quarter was to check that the only survivor of the holocaust was still alive. Daniel did not care. Who would? His soul was gone. No one could save him from the danger his father had exposed him to, and he was old enough to understand this. He awaited helplessly for death, his anger against his own father for the boundless losses he had endured barely hidden. Daniel died many years later while I was away at the mission school.

Perhaps my father could not stand all of this, for after a few months he disappeared. Consumed by restlessness, he suddenly fell in love with adventure once again. He went to the Gold Coast, first in the town Takouradi, then to Sakoundé, where he hoped a change of scene could help him rid himself of the pain that had taken hold of his body and soul since the death of his children.

He went to work, mining gold for the white man he had sacrificed his children to. Three years later, he returned from the Gold Coast, somewhat healed emotionally, but seriously ill physically. His face was emaciated like an old man's, and his swollen chest grew larger with every breath. His eyes were bloodshot and he looked ghastly, as if he had seen a ghost. He moved like a drunken man, zigzagging randomly. His legs looked more like sticks than limbs, and they struck against each other when he tried to walk.

Grandfather tried to tell my father why he was sick, reminding him yet again of his duty toward his children, living and dead. But, as if accursed, my father always answered in the same way, saying he would think about it.

My father was proud of the English bicycle he had successfully smuggled into the tribe. He paid more attention to it than to his health, which was deteriorating more every day. He even decided to get married again. I have always wondered on what grounds my mother married someone so ill. Was it because of the English bicycle, or because the presence of Grandfather as head of our family represented hope to her that everything could be put right again? Meanwhile, Father had returned to his religious activities with the white priests as if nothing had happened. But everyone knew that the ancestors never forget.

Things continued to go downhill for him until he was incapable of even moving around. He spent his days sleeping and his nights groaning with the pain in his chest, his belly, and his back.

Finally, Grandfather had to warn him that he had only a few days left to live unless he performed his duties. Panic-stricken at the idea of dying at a time when he had just married, my father ordered the ceremony of the twins to be performed.

Two clay pots were brought and filled with water from the underworld. This water was kept on a special shrine at the entrance of my mother's room. Then my father ceremonially sprinkled ash on the ground around the compound to keep malintentioned spirits away from the house. Then the ritual proper began. It lasted a whole day. What was normally a simple gesture toward the spirit had now become painfully elaborate because of my father's constant postponements.

It was not long after this event that my father began to feel better. His health was improving almost visibly. At the end of the first week he had recovered his ability to move around, and by the end of the following week he decided he was strong enough to return to the farm. His pain had almost entirely disappeared.

He developed a better attitude, perhaps because he realized how much death is contained in the way of the white man and his spirituality. He began to hear the ancestors once again. My father still attended Sunday masses, and still maintained friendship with the white-bearded priest on the hill who misled him, but he also listened more carefully to Grandfather now. My sister was born after all this tragedy, and my father performed the proper ceremonies. The happy event revived him and my sister benefited from the joy he took in her. Yet she too was brought to the hill to be baptized.

I was born three years after my sister, shortly after the harvest festival. It was dawn and very cold. My birth took place in the open air, halfway between the family house and the white man's hospital. I still wonder what would have happened if I had been born in that modern, sterilized place. My fate surely would have been different. I like to think that perhaps I knew this in the womb and decided to take matters into my own hands by insisting on being born in nature. Was this the reason why, twenty years later, I was able to find my way back home? And I often wonder if coming into this world between the village and the white man's compound has something to do with the feeling I have of being sandwiched between worlds.

Like my sister, I was baptized at the mission hill and given the name Patrice. But Grandfather registered me in the family ledger as Malidoma, he who would "be friends with the stranger/enemy." He knew that the bulk of my life was going to be lived outside of the tribe, and that meant countless challenges, all aimed at securing friends. His duty toward me consisted of delivering this bad news to me before he died.

Grandfather had also named me Malidoma for reasons pertaining to ancestral law. Because he was the guardian of the house, the link between the dead and the living, he expected his grandson to be recognized by the ancestors. As the first male of my family, my responsibilities had already been predetermined. The first male must be prepared to take charge of the family shrine when his father, the current priest, dies. I found out later that my education had somewhat broken that tradition because, after all, my fate would be to respond to the challenge of being swallowed up by the white man's world.

CHAPTER 2
A GRANDFATHER'S FAREWELL

 Grandfather died while I was still completing the fourth rainy season of my life. I had been so used to being around him while the grown-up men and women were laboring at the farm that it took me a while to admit the stark truth that I was never going to find him again. Since my strange experience in the bush, my mother had kept her word and never taken me along with her when she went in search of dry wood. So on those days my only companion was Grandfather.

One morning when I went in search of him, I saw that the dew was still lingering on his door. I was puzzled because he was usually awake and about long before the penetrating heat of the rising sun. Earlier I had seen my father go into Grandfather's room and stay there a long time. When he came back out, he had looked sad. Staring straight in front of him, he walked into my mother's zangala, taking no notice of me at all. When he emerged, his hand was full of ash. Some he poured in front of Grandfather's door and some in front of his own door, making a straight line in front of each. He went outside the compound and dropped more ash in front of the main gate, making another straight line. I had been staring at him the whole time he was conducting this strange ritual, but when I went outside to try to talk to him, he jumped nervously onto his English bicycle

37

and left without saying anything. I lost sight of him as he rounded the corner of the house. Disappointed, I went back into the compound, wondering where to go. Nobody else was at home except me and Grandfather.

First I thought I'd call him out, then I thought I would go into his room. But I thought better of both those actions. Grandfather's sleeping room was also a spirit room, and I had been told never to disturb him when he was cloistered there. Deciding to wait for a while, I went outside the compound.

Our millet fields formed a green carpet as far as I could see. In the middle of this carpet was the dark circle of the well that served as our water supply during the rainy season. Birds and chickens were busy around it. I could not see them because the millet hid them, but the cackling sounds that came from the general area suggested that there were a lot of them. Far to the left, two majestic green baobab trees made me think of all the stories Grandfather had told me about them. He said that witches of all sizes illuminated their branches at night, burning the leaves with a milky fire that did not consume them. He also told me how these very same witches possessed the secret of separating their souls from their bodies at night, and of turning their souls into light expanding to infinity. I had managed to get Grandfather to promise that he would take me to see their fireworks from the roof of the house one night, but he never did. While thinking about all of this, I had unconsciously wandered over to the baobab trees and now stood in their deep shade. Standing beside their gigantic trunks, beneath their enormous branches, heavy with gray fruits in the prime of their growth, I suddenly felt small. I walked around their great trunks, searching carefully to see if I could find some remnants of the orgiastic rituals the witches had indulged in the night before.

I decided to run back home, for I knew Grandfather would surely be up by this time. But I was disappointed to find that his door was still tightly closed. I looked into the room shared by myself, my mother, and my siblings. There was nobody there either. I went over to my father's door and tried to open it, but it was locked. Returning to my grandfather's door, I contemplated it for a while, then took a deep breath, knocked hesitantly, and called, "Grandfather."

"Come in," a faint voice replied. "I can't come out."

Panting, I opened the door and walked up two little stairs, then down another two stairs, and stood in Grandfather's room. I could see nothing. It was like entering a cave, or walking into night. The room was so dark that I was sure one could sleep forever in it. Apart from a tiny hole on the ceiling that framed a tiny fragment of the immense firmament outside, everything else, including Grandfather, was buried in the darkness.

"Come over here, Brother. And be careful not to step on my medicine," Grandfather said in a faint, tremulous voice. "What have you been doing?"

I hesitated a little before speaking. "Where are you, Grandfather?"

"Right here in front of you. Can't you see me?"

Reassured, I crept toward the voice and sat down when my toes touched the mud elevation that served as Grandfather's bed. He was still stretched out upon it, millet straws serving as his mattress and a burlap sack filled with sand as his pillow. He was dressed the same as I had always seen him, in his ancient boubou.

It took a while for my eyes to adjust to seeing in the dark. Grandfather had never taken me into his room before, and I was anxious to inspect his secret dwelling. Grandfather's room was, in truth, a magic workplace so unfamiliar it did not even seem that I was still in our family compound. Each wall held a row of containers of various sorts. Most were clay pots, but others were just battered old cans and bottles. Each one seemed to contain something. From the ceiling hung dozens of gourds. Some, almost all the same size, were lined up perfectly against each wall. Bigger gourds formed a circle around the center of the ceiling. Another circle of gourds formed a smaller ring around the tiny opening in the roof. The arrangement of these clay pots, tin cans, and gourds seemed to fit together somehow in an intricate and interrelated pattern. They were the work of someone who knew perfectly well what he was up to. A rope coming through the opening in the ceiling was tied to each gourd, and all the gourds were tied together in a complex design that finally terminated at Grandfather's bed. The artistry of this was amazing.

"Have you been into this room before?" Grandfather asked, drawing my attention back to him. He had been watching me without saying anything all the while I looked around.

Surprised, I protested, "But you've never let me in!"

"That's right. As long as my departure was not yet decreed, I could not allow you in here until you reached the age of initiation." In the dim light I could see him looking at me with eyes full of tenderness. I could think of nothing to say.

He continued. "Soon I will go. But before I go I must tell you the message of your ancestors." Grandfather put on a grave face and gazed up at the ceiling as if his eyes were fastened on the beyond.

"Malidoma, you're not yet prepared to hear what I am about to tell you. But perhaps it is better that you're not prepared. Don't stop me while I talk. I will not speak out of my own thoughts, nor is what I am telling you just a story. It is a set of things about you that you must keep in mind as you grow up. The spirit behind the things you see in this room is using me to talk to you now. It has no mouth. But I have one, and we are friends. You understand? If you do not understand, do not worry. It does not matter right now. Later, when you're older, somebody will remind you of what I said today."

Grandfather was right. When I became older and was ready to hear, Guisso, one of the elders of my tribe, helped me to remember. So what I tell you now flows from that remembering brought about by Guisso, who understood the painful uniqueness of my destiny and hoped to help me to fulfill it after I became an initiated man.

Every word my grandfather said that day was said slowly, every sentence was given an interminable time for utterance, every sentence was followed by a long silence, grave and filled with meaning. It seemed as if Grandfather had suddenly ceased to be human. He was disconnected from his voice, as if somebody else next to him were speaking through him. I could feel the presence of that spirit being, below the sand pillow upon which rested Grandfather's head.

"Malidoma, the sweat of one person has significance only when it serves everybody. You have been designated to follow the white man so that you may serve as the eye of the compound, the ear of your many brothers, and the mouth of your tribe. Remember my words. You came from the water, which in our tradition is the symbol of peace and reconciliation. This water has a direction in our mythology, the north, the direction you face each time you stand in the place where the sun rises on your right. This is the place where those who have something to say to the souls of others come from. Now you must go west to learn the wisdom of the people there and represent to them the truth we profess. You are going to be initiated into the white man's witchcraft. Your people ask you to do it. I grieve for you. Many ambushes await you. But my spirit will stand by your side.

"Very soon you will leave your family—it is happening already—and very soon I will not be here with you anymore. In times of turmoil, however, Tingan, the god of the land, will be your shelter, shielding you from the storms of antagonism and blunt hatred. Your journey will never be a lonely one, but from it you'll never come back whole. The ways of the whites consume. When you come back, what you have learned outside the tribe will look suspicious to all of us. You will be only partly a Dagara. You will suffer great frustration, for you will call for a father who will not be here to console you. You will call for a mother who will want you to act as you used to before she will listen to you.

"Later, when you must go away once more from the warmth of your family compound, you will be forced to make up a new world for yourself. It will be a world where Patrice will be very present, and Malidoma very absent. Do not be confused when this happens. The Dagara rite of initiation must be completed before you come to full understanding of who you are. In your labyrinthine journey in the white world, the world of iron, learn to catch the thought behind the machine or it will swallow you."

▲   ▼   ▲

Grandfather seemed to have completely disappeared from my sight. Although I was seated right next to him, I could no longer see him. The voice I was hearing had ceased to have a location, but seemed to be coming out of the numberless containers lining the room. It was as if the walls themselves were speaking, the sound of it echoing everywhere as if in a bell jar. Grandfather had taken me into a world of wonder, for I myself was transformed. Thousands of images of a civilization I had never seen rushed at me, all alive and real: immense metal birds gliding high above the sky, their bellies loaded with humans; dwellings and roads covering the earth as far as the eye could see; houses that challenged the vault of heaven and dwarfed men, trees, and anything else around them. . . .

I began to feel a kind of vertigo that made me want to lie down. In lying down, however, I never reached the cold floor of Grandfather's room. I was suddenly transported into a high region of my consciousness where I stopped being a child. I was simply a knower without age. I had never seen nor dreamed of such a place before. From there I understood perfectly what my grandfather was saying. Stunned, suspended in my thoughts, I kept listening to the voice coming through Grandfather.

"A long, long time ago, the whites came into the land of our people and waged war against us. They were equipped with enormous machines that roared like an approaching storm as they took the life away from our tribesmen. But in the end, we won the battle thanks to the magic of the *Pintul,* the upside-down arrow. It sowed in them the seeds of death. I shot it myself countless times from this room. It saved the Birifor and the Dagara, for a while. The white men died without ever knowing what killed them.

"After that we had peace. But not for long. Very soon more white men appeared. The French came from the west and the English from the east, and we were caught in the middle. We sent our children and women into the thick of the forest, and all initiated males were requisitioned to die for the tribe. Your great-grandfather trained more people in the secret of the Pintul. Animated by the fever of their last victory, our men were confident. The war raged for an entire season. For as more of these white pigs were sent to their deaths by our supreme warrior, Pintul, even more appeared, as if by enchantment. During the day our men were in a pretty bad state, for that was when those pigs fought best. Then their machines would roar iron into our men by the hundreds. But at night the whites would disappear into the forest, a place not at all hidden to the Pintul. The dreadful arrow would send death to their sleeping places and come back to be recharged. Thus, they won by day, and we won by night.

"Then one day, one of the men who guarded the women's secret hiding place came and told us a strange story. He said some white men were in the women's quarters giving them food, medicine, and clothing. The messenger himself was clothed like a white man. We were confused about what to do, for our law says that you do not hurt someone unless they hurt you. A war council was ordered and we agreed to make peace with the enemy. Oh, woeful decision, fools as we all were! No demands were made, no compromises decided, we simply ended the war by refusing to fight.

"So the whites came in and settled. They built hard houses and large roads all over the area, and forced our men to do the work. They even asked us to pay them taxes. They had infiltrated our territory and we could do nothing. They told us that our fetishes were disempowered and that we must cleanse our houses of them. Many heads of family did so in fear for their lives. My father was among the few who refused to obey their orders. That's why today our family is one of the largest left. Those who threw away their fetishes died shortly after. The Tingan made sure of that. The families who obeyed the white man were dispersed. Dozens of families were thus wiped out in no time.

"So you see, some say that the white man became smarter, stronger than us through the help of the avenging spirits of the ancestors. He conquered us through confusion. Your father is one of their victims, but fortunately he is a victim who is still alive. And do you know why? Because we did not destroy our fetish. One day he too will come to understand why one should never, under any circumstance, forsake one's own ways. If you do not abide by the ancestral law, you tacitly ask for your own punishment. In your father's case, it was prophesied that his heart would melt in the face of the white man's fetish, that he would follow him. But it was not part of the plan that he go too far into this maze, just far enough so that our people would have something to work on, a sample of the white man's ways. Your father's illness was a warning from the ancestors that he should stop. See! His troubles have made him wiser. I don't think he wants to travel anymore. . . ."

Grandfather paused. The strange vibration in the room stopped. My consciousness shifted. I was back in the everyday world and could now see him as a normal man. His face was shining with sweat as if it had been anointed with sacred oil. His cheeks were smooth and round and had almost no wrinkles, as if he had reclaimed his youth. He looked twenty years younger. His eyes, wet with tears, were shining with intensity and I wondered why he had been crying. He looked like somebody who had just come back from the emotional intensity of a funeral rite and was still in the process of adjusting to the ordinary world. He was soaked with sweat. His double voyage into the future and back to the past had taken a great deal of energy. Later, when I was older, I would recall this moment with Grandfather as the most intense learning experience of my life.

Outside, the burning disk of the sun was slipping toward its resting place. I thought of my parents on the farm, far away, and how they were getting ready to return home and take their hard-won rest. Suddenly the sound of a breaking clay pot shattered the silent air—probably the one we had used for dinner the night before. Nobody ever had time to clean them before going to sleep. People worn out by an entire day of heavy labor, who must be up at dawn to repeat the same monotonous work, have no time for housework. The noise was immediately followed by the sound of hooves. The main gate had been left open, and the goats and sheep had crept in, searching for scraps of food to supplement their diet of grass.

"Go kick these animal's asses out of the yard," Grandfather ordered. I jumped to my feet, ready to run out and chase them out of the compound. ". . . And close the gate before you come back," he added. I was already at the door. The animals knew somebody was coming because they all turned and ran out quickly before I could kick the ass of even one of them. They had broken the clay pot and licked out anything that tasted like food. I knew that when my mother got home she would storm at me for my negligence in forgetting to close the door behind me when I returned from my trip to the baobab tree. But there was nothing I could do about that now except shut it quickly and rush back to Grandfather's room.

"It took you long enough to return. Didn't those goats want to leave? Come, let me finish with you, then you can go wait for your parents. I would like to take a rest."

Grandfather was sitting up now and leaning back against the sand pillow. I approached and settled at the bottom of his sleeping mat, which was warm and soaked with sweat, as if he had just sat up. Presently he resumed his unearthly aspect, and the voice began speaking, shrilly, through his body again.

"Very soon you will leave this house to investigate the land of the *nipula,* the white man," he began. "It will not be an easy experience. In fact it will be the hardest thing you will ever do. I am in pain for you, but there is nothing I can do about it. What is decreed is decreed. Our ancestors have told us that the best way to know who the nipula is, is to get closer to him. Iron cuts iron. But iron can only cut iron if it rubs itself against iron. The desire for such knowledge is good, but actually getting that knowledge is another story. Let the ancestors' will be done. Remember, however, that in the process of fulfilling your life's mission, you must not forget that your roots are here with us. I say this because I know the hardships that await you. You will soon be shot into the void like an arrow, flying like a bird, diving the way an alligator dives to the bottom of the river. But remember, the arrow shot into the air always returns to earth. The bird, however high it may fly, never fails to return to the ground. The alligator can dive deep into the water, but it must always return to the surface to breathe. Remember where you come from. The day you pluck the nipula's secret, run. Even if you are at the other side of the world, run back and tell us. You are Birifor, my brother, former priest of the tribe, you hold the destinies of thousands of souls, the souls of your people. Remember, to suffer for them is a credit to your name. Be prepared, Birifor, you have come back for that. I salute you. Now I must go."

Saying this, Grandfather stretched and lay back down on the mat with his eyes fixed upon the ceiling. I could think of nothing to say. I did not really comprehend what he had told me anyway. Understanding would come later, when I was older and was helped to remember. Grandfather closed his eyes and remained still, as if sleeping. My thought slumbered in response to his stillness, and I could not decide whether to leave or to stay in this darkening room. My indecision embarrassed me, but at the same time I felt a deep peace flowing into my body through my back. It seemed as if a spirit was breathing fresh air onto me. This freshness invaded my body and I became so cool and so relaxed I thought I was going to fall asleep too.

I do not know how long I remained in that state. What I do remember is the return of the field workers from the farm, and the great explosion produced by my mother as she dropped her load of dry wood in the middle of the yard. These sounds dragged me back to reality and I wondered at how quickly the day had passed. Slowly, I crept toward the doorway, avoiding the row of gourds in the middle of the room.

Outside it was dark. The sky, as usual, was peopled with countless bright spots, all dancing to the rhythm of an unheard drum. Far in the west I could still see the place where the sun went down. Everything else was shrouded in a veil of mysterious darkness.

Soon my father arrived. He pushed his English bicycle into the yard and rushed into Grandfather's room. I walked around searching for my mother, for I hadn't eaten the whole day and was mournfully hungry. I found her catching her breath in the huge hall. As if knowing what I was coming to her for, she pointed to her left breast and assumed a quiet position. Even though I had been weaned a long time ago and was used to eating solid food, my mother still breast-fed me from time to time as a snack when no food was readily available—or when she sensed that I needed ten-

derness and reassurance. The day with my grandfather had been bewilder-
ing and had stretched my young limits to the utmost.

I do not know how long I hugged on my mother's breast. Suddenly, I
was startled by the noise of an engine outside the house. My mother pushed
me away and rushed out. Disoriented, I remained in the dark for a while,
then followed her. Father Maillot, the Jesuit priest who always visited the
family, was standing there in the yard, speaking very loudly and in very
bad Dagara. Several people surrounded him, most of them from the other
compounds. Father Maillot barked out a command and my father and one
other person went into Grandfather's room and came out carrying him.
The little crowd joined in the carrying, and together they moved him out
of the yard. I followed them. They put Grandfather and a few of his personal belongings into the car. Shortly after, the car groaned and illuminated the whole yard, turned around, and headed toward the mission hill.

My father grabbed his bicycle. I ran to him and asked, "Where are they
taking Grandfather?"

"To the dispensary."

"I'm going with you," I said.

"The night will be very cold, and you are not well protected. Just go
inside and wait here. I will return."

I screamed and yelled and fell down on the ground, pedaling my feet
in the air with frenzy. My father sighed deeply, as if he didn't know whether
to get angry at me or not. The next thing I knew, I was behind him on the
baggage rack.

The dispensary was built a few years after the missionaries settled in
Dano. It was the same dispensary that I had avoided being born at. The
first Jesuit to arrive in our territory looked like an explorer. He spent his
first six months living in a hut down the hill. An administration building—
connected to the white colonial government and the church—now sits on
the site where he used to live. He paved the way for the other Jesuits by
maintaining a steadily growing Christian community. When the others
came, they built a huge house for themselves and a church for everybody,
all on top of the hill. From the valley eastward, everyone could see the
steeple of that church. I knew none of the people up there except Father
Maillot, who was a frequent visitor to our village.

Next to the church were a couple of houses where sick people were
treated with modern medicine. It was there that Grandfather was taken. A
pudgy man examined him as we waited in silence. Next, Grandfather was
taken to the dispensary room, where he lay unconscious. Calling his name,
I rushed over to him and grabbed his hand.

"Don't touch him!" my father roared. But Grandfather opened his
eyes, and seeing me, smiled faintly and closed them again. I sat next to

him, my left hand in his right hand. Nobody said anything more. All the faces around me were shrouded with sadness. I didn't know why, but I did not care as long as Grandfather was there.

When I woke up in the morning, I was not beside Grandfather, but in one of the corners of the tiny cement room. I stretched my legs, rubbed my eyes, and looked around me. The sun had already risen. Its penetrating rays were already biting my skin through the corrugated iron roof of the building. Grandfather was still lying where I had seen him last night and he seemed to be in a deep sleep. I got up and walked to him. Picking up one of his hands, I called him aloud. He did not answer. When I called again, he remained quiet. My father was not around, and I didn't know any of the many villagers in the room. I sensed however that they must be the leaders of other compounds. I looked at them for help to find out why Grandfather was still sleeping.

"You will never hear him speak again," one of the strangers said.

"He has become a spirit," another one said.

I still didn't understand, but I hesitated to ask for further explanation. Confused, I sat quietly. It was a long time before my father returned with the doctor who had examined Grandfather the night before. The doctor did the same ritual and left. Then my father stood in front of Grandfather's bed and put on a grave air. He held up something that looked like a tail mounted with two handles decorated with cowrie shells, stretched it out, and put it in Grandfather's hand.

As soon as the tail touched his hand, Grandfather opened his eyes and sat up, all in slow motion. His behavior seemed strange. Because he wouldn't let go of the tail my father had given him, he could not use his other hand to support himself while maneuvering to sit up. This seemed very odd to me. Ordinarily, Grandfather took an endless time to get up from his couch. He would begin by grinning and groaning while he turned himself over. Then he would grip the mat with his hands, and one by one bend his legs. From then on, every movement upward would force a yell out of his mouth, until he was on his feet. But this time nothing of this sort happened.

Grandfather's torso sat up as if moved by an invisible hand, then became immobile. Following the same impulse, his legs bent over the side of the bed, although they were cracking like dry leaves. Fascinated and speechless, I watched. Everybody seemed captivated. Then he began to rise, as if under a slow and steady impulse, his body resembling one of the village spirit statues. I was not only fascinated, but also afraid that he might lose control and break his back. No one could possibly get up this way without using one or both of their hands to balance their weight. But Grandfather's only contact with the ground was with his bare feet, and one could see the muscles of the lower part of his legs compressed and straining under the thin dark skin. Presently, he was standing straight up.

This miracle completed, I rushed to him and grabbed his right hand, the one that was free. My father made a movement to stop me, but decided against it.

Keeping his authoritative tone, my father spoke to my grandfather in secret primal language. Grandfather said nothing in response, he just walked out of the room preceded by my father and followed by the delegation. I walked at his right side, still holding his hand. He moved strangely—too straight, too rigid, unnatural, yet very conscious of any obstacle. Once outside, the crowd joined to make a circle around us. Although I was too young to understand the significance of this ritual, or why all these people were not speaking with one another, I was glad to return home with Grandfather—even if he did not seem to want to speak to me.

The four-mile walk took an equal amount of hours. Dead people don't walk very fast. They are not in a hurry. We must have reached home around noontime, for upon our arrival we were each walking on his own shadow. People we encountered along our way stopped, left the road, and assumed a somber mood. At home men and women were everywhere, having come from all directions to wait for Grandfather. Those who had arrived earliest were sitting under the shadows of the trees surrounding the compound, others stood under the biting sun. Many more were still arriving. When we reached the yard outside the main gate, our delegation stopped. Five old men came out of the compound and saluted us in mystical terms, each one kneeling down with a grave air. I felt proud to be at the center of so much attention. They murmured something to Grandfather. He continued to be unresponsive, but they did not seem to mind his silence at all.

I'm going to stop here for a moment to make a point. Different cultures have different relationships with their dead, and I know very well that in a culture of skyscrapers and high technology, dead people don't walk. Instead, they are placed in nice expensive caskets and driven to the cemetery in elegant black cars. They are put quickly out of sight so that life can go on.

Why do the dead walk where I come from? They walk because they are still as important to the living as they were before. They are even more meaningful, as the breadth and depth of our funeral ritual shows. We do not hide their bodies away—because we want to see those bodies to help us remember the person's life and all the good they did for us. We need to remember that they are well on their way to becoming an ancestor. We must see our dead so that we can truly mourn them, all the way through, without restraint, to release the grief from our hearts once and for all. True, every dead person is not asked to walk. My grandfather died on the mission hill, thus in a foreign land. He was an elder and a leader of great power, and should have died at home. The only way to correct a death of such an important person when it occurs in the wrong place is to walk the dead home. Once the funeral ritual is at an end, his body would be carried to the burial ground.

Grandfather's eyes were peering at something beyond them, his face and body expressionless. Of all of us, he was the least concerned about what was going on. Presently, the people were cleared away from the gate and he walked into the compound. Looking behind me, I noticed that the crowd under the trees had stood up and were reverently taking part in everything that was going on. Beyond them the whole millet field was colored with men and women in blue, white, yellow, red, and black clothing, still arriving.

As I marveled at this colorful panorama, I was dragged into the present by a pull from Grandfather, who had begun walking again. We walked into his room. There a kerosene lamp cast a faint yellow light, disturbed now and then by the wind penetrating from the skylight in the roof. As Grandfather moved toward his mud bed, he looked both comic and dramatic. His stiff movements and his almost ghastly air gave him a look that was both authoritative and indifferent. He leaned forward, just as he was about to reach the low elevation of his bed. He lifted his left foot and put it hesitantly upon the platform, as if doubting the propriety of his actions. Then he stepped straight up until he was standing on the bed. Once his equilibrium was established, he turned around and faced the entrance door as if to contemplate the small crowd that had followed him into the room. There was no real eye contact, however, because Grandfather was now existing in a space that was beyond the living. Although he was physically present with us, he was only really alive in the world of the spirits.

My father came to Grandfather and took the hyena tail out of his hand while two robust men supported Grandfather from the back. Grandfather let himself fall into their hands and, with due ceremony, he was laid out on his couch. Once again he looked as if he were deeply asleep. Disoriented by his sudden immobility, I looked around me in search of an explanation.

The crowd outside was growing rapidly and I could tell something was very wrong. A little more than twenty-four hours ago I had been transported into the future by Grandfather's speech. Now he was sleeping, peaceably, as if indifferent to what was going on around him.

The five or six men who had accompanied us into Grandfather's room were now busy. Some were rearranging the order of the gourds and cans in the room, others were preparing medicine or lighting aromatic plants.

My father had once again disappeared, but I could hear him speaking to a group of old women who were standing at the entrance of Grandfather's room. "Get the material ready for the meal, and warm up the water. Make haste. Everything must be finished before the sun cools down."

He came back to Grandfather and proceeded to strip him of the remnant of clothing he wore. Then he massaged his body slowly and carefully. One of the men brought a clay pot containing some foaming liquid, inside of which was a double-edged knife. My father lifted Grandfather's head while another man proceeded to shave his white hair. He wetted a portion of the snowy skull, then cleaned away whatever hair was there. Then he collected the fallen hair and handed it up to another man near him, who passed it to another, and so on until I lost track of it. The shaving went very slowly. When there was nothing left, the hairdresser put the knife back into the pot, then pronounced some lugubrious words. The gourds and cans in the room responded by knocking against one another.

At that moment the women entered the room. They put down an enormous clay jar full of warm water and three other medium-sized pots. One contained more water, another some seasoning ingredients, and the third one some millet flour. The women left without a word. The men rushed to the potful of warm water and carried it to Grandfather's death-bed. They mixed the water with three different roots and two liquid substances that they picked out of some of the surrounding gourds and washed his body carefully. Grandfather's last toilet took an interminable time. Those who labored on him were singing solemnly in harmony, a sort of genealogical recital. I can still recall some of the names, and later I understood that they referred to my very ancient ancestors.

After that the men recited the prayer of the dead. Other men who had not entered into the earlier singing now sang the canticle to the spirits, who know no death. These spirits live in the underworld, in the air, in the water, and in the fire. The awesome voices of the men, tremulously mounting in the air like a mournful complaint, were seconded by other voices outside, at the entrance. The women's song was the most thrilling. Men who heard it groaned a brief *sanwéi,* which means in our language, "Oh, Father." The women's shrill voices rose sharply like daggers and penetrated every heart, blocking our throats, sending chills all through our bodies, and causing tears to well up from our eyes. I was crying not because Grandfather was dead—for up till now I had but a faint idea of what death meant—but because these female singers made such a miserable lament that I was beginning to suspect some sort of tragedy had occurred.

The room was suddenly overtaken by a blanket of darkness, thick and heavy, punctuated here and there by something that resembled a yellow glitter, a mild lightning. Behind the singing voices, there was a continuous murmur, an unfailingly monotonous buzzing sound that was coming out of the surrounding gourds and cans. They were hitting against one another as if moved by the ropes that held them in place. Next, I heard the sound of marching feet, pounding the ground everywhere in the tiny room. The darkness became deeper and more terrifying. Footsteps also sounded on the roof of the house, and little bits of dirt falling from the ceiling seemed to indicate that the roof was groaning under their weight. Inside, the invisible marching people shouted at each other cacophonously and stomped loudly in every direction, bumping into invisible objects that fell catastrophically on the ground. The noise was getting to be unbearable.

Then everything began to revolve in a circle around me. I had the feeling that I was on a raft that kept turning and turning and not going anywhere. On the raft were half a dozen elderly people, each one my grandfather, and each one making fun of me. They were laughing loudly, mindless of whatever I wanted to ask them. I kept trying to speak to them, but my mouth wouldn't form the questions that my eyes kept asking over and over. The raft finally took off into the air. In an ultimate movement, it dived into the void like a spaceship. Overtaken by fear, I yelled. Everything ceased instantaneously, and I saw my father bending over me with an anxious face asking, "Are you all right?" I realized I was lying next to Grandfather, on his bed. They had dressed him up the way they dress everyone who dies. I wondered what had happened to me.

Singers, washers, and hairdressers had finished their cabalistic activities and were now all interested in another no less mysterious one. They had transformed Grandfather's room into a kitchen where everything was happening upside down. A clay pot full of water was boiling quietly on the ceiling, its bottom sitting against the roof. Beneath it was a fire dancing inside a triangular fireplace, its boundaries marked off by medium-sized stones, each of which could easily have weighed ten kilos. The whole—fireplace, fire, stones, clay pot, and water—were suspended as if by enchantment on the wooden ceiling. Beneath this vertiginous fireplace, men were busy readying the many condiments necessary for the preparation of a meal outside the force of gravity.

I was fascinated by this upside-down boiling pot of water. The whole thing appeared to me like a joke. I had never seen anything like this before, and Grandfather had surely never mentioned it.

One of the men poured some flour into a basket of water yellowed by a mixture of herbs, stirred it carefully, and tossed its contents toward the boiling pot. Instead of falling down onto the floor, the contents obeyed another law. They landed in the boiling water, which splashed upward onto the wood of the ceiling. Everybody went about their tasks as if unmindful of how strange their activities appeared. It was as if they were operating in a circle that defied natural laws, involved in a strange conspiracy to challenge the Great Master of the Universe.

Soon, the clay pot was filled with a gelatinous mass which roared like a volcano in action. Cooking vapors filled the entire room. The man who had poured the flour into the boiling water grabbed a flat wooden stick called a *vuul* and plunged it into the roaring, sticky porridge in the upside-down pot. He began stirring clockwise, then counterclockwise. Meanwhile, another man standing next to him poured dry flour from a basket he was holding into the pot at regular intervals. The millet cake in the clay pot was slowly increasing in size, thickening, hardening, and making the stirring movements harder and harder. The first man was perspiring, his muscles contracting with each movement; he and the cakes were now growling in unison.

When the first man was finished, he put his vuul down on the floor next to the second man, grabbed two pieces of cloth to protect himself from the heat, took hold of the clay pot and its contents, and pulled very strongly, holding his breath. The clay pot resisted for a while, then gave up and rushed toward the ground. The man quickly executed a rolling gesture, turning the clay pot upright, to avoid pouring any of its contents onto the ground. That way, container and contents were deposited safely on the floor of the room, unspoiled. Almost immediately another man performed the same rolling movement backward with another clay pot half filled with water. The new pot rose in the air, made a U-turn in the middle between the ground and the ceiling, and backed up onto the fireplace. Before the water began to boil, the man had already put some okra flour in it, along with some condiments.

He added some dry monkey meat and a huge number of other medicinal products. In the meantime other people were serving out the millet cake. One portion of the cake was put near Grandfather's deathbed. The other portions were placed in smaller pots and distributed to the women who were waiting outside at the entrance. When the sauce in the second pot was cooked, the men took it down just as they had taken down the previous pot. The sauce was also served into clay pots and distributed, and a portion placed near Grandfather's deathbed.

At that time the cooks and my father approached Grandfather and sat around the still-smoking meal. My father pulled out the terrible hyena tail once again and put it into Grandfather's left hand. Grandfather had been sleeping all this time, indifferent to what was going on in his own room. Now he jerked as if bitten or shaken by an electrical shock. He opened his eyes and fixed them on the ceiling.

My father said, "Father, get up. The last meal has arrived. Eat with us this food that strengthens the body and keeps the mind in a state of wakefulness. You cannot begin the trip to the ancestors on an empty belly. It is a long trip, a difficult journey. Eat with us that which, while living, you never wanted to miss."

Grandfather did not answer. He stretched slowly upward until he was sitting. He gazed inquiringly from left to right, and from right to left, as if to inspect his own room, then brought his lifeless eyes down to the dish in front of him. Everybody was silent and fascinated. There was a calabash full of warm water near Grandfather, and he plunged his right hand into it and washed, while his left hand continued to hold the hyena tail. Then he picked up a piece of the millet cake, plunged it into the sauce, and carried the whole toward his mouth.

Five pairs of eyes vigilantly watched his every gesture. I noticed that the food disappeared before reaching the interior of his mouth. An invisible force simply absorbed it before it reached his lips. Nobody said anything or seemed surprised by any of this, so I stopped watching. Following the example of the other guests, I began eating. I was hungry enough to swallow an entire roasted monkey and a few gallons of its gravy. We ate without a word as Dagara customs command: "The mouth that eats cannot be the mouth that talks."

Grandfather was the first to stop eating. He let his hand fall onto his upper leg for a short time, then lifted it toward the calabash and again washed his fingers. That activity took a comparatively long time. He did not seem to be in a hurry at all. When he finished, the other men followed his lead; all washed their hands, and I was left alone to eat the leftovers. I pulled the two clay pots and their contents nearer to me. Everybody was looking at me, and without a word I understood that I better eat fast.

Years later, when I was older, I would come to understand what I had seen that day. The out-of-gravity culinary art was a secret practice performed only when a leader of exceptional standing died. The day of my grandfather's death was the first and last time I ever saw it. For, as things changed in our tribe, the practice passed away, perhaps along with the secret. Today it has become a tale. But for those who had direct contact with the reality of *satulmo*, as it is called, it is a sad thing to realize how much my people have lost and how much yet of our reality is to be buried in the pit of oblivion.

The food preparation within the precinct of reverse gravity was a symbolic enactment of the realm that the great ones enter through death. By leaving his body, Grandfather had escaped the laws of physicality; therefore, only food cooked according to the laws of the new realm he now inhabited could be eaten and digested effectively. There are secret plants in nature that are very powerful. By using some of these plants, known only by healers and men and women in touch with the great medicine of Mother Earth, our cooks were able to produce, for a short time, an area free of gravity.

▲ ▼ ▲

The sun was about to set. The compound was black with men and women, girls and boys, who had arrived from the four corners of the tribal territory to pay homage to Bakhye, my grandfather. I ate faster. The dishes were soon clean and one of the guests took them away. My belly full, I looked up toward the wooden stove that had yielded such a great meal, but there were now no traces of stove, fireplace, or fire on the ceiling above.

By now the sun had sunk behind the mountain and a crepuscular dew had freshened the air. The wind had stopped blowing and time was still, as if waiting. My father, who had vanished for a while, now reappeared dressed in a ceremonial outfit. His huge cotton blouse had been woven by expert craftspeople. It was decorated at the neck with a circular arrangement of alligators, each one holding the tail of the one in front of it in its jaws. On the front of the blouse was an immense embroidered zodiac, a symbol of our tribal cosmogony, and the medicine wheels embroidered on the garment gave my father a powerful and occult air. At the bottom of the blouse, a series of stars of different colors made him look very wide and muscular. Beneath the blouse, which ended midcalf, could be seen an immense pair of trousers whose ankles were decorated with a series of smartly rendered arabesques. The bottom of these trousers was so narrow that I wondered how he had managed to stick his legs through. Beneath the pants I saw a pair of modern shoes, so highly polished they shone even at twilight. This entire outfit was topped by a tightly fitting traditional hat, shaped something like a Western beret. Slung over his back was his medicine bag made of antelope skin and filled with cowrie shells.

When my father entered Grandfather's room, everybody stood solemnly. I wanted to get up like everybody else, but I was paralyzed by the heavy meal I had eaten. Fortunately, I didn't have to, for in the next moment everyone departed, leaving my father and me alone with Grandfather. My father knelt down in front of Grandfather's still-seated figure, took out some white, powdered substance, and dispersed it into the air. Like most magical things, it smelled terrible. I was suffocating, but my father seemed perfectly at ease with this smell.

"Here I am," he said humbly.

At these words Grandfather opened his eyes, which had been closed since the end of the meal, tightened his grip upon the hyena tail, and said mechanically, "Everything is ready; I relinquish the destiny of the family into your hands. Though I must go, yet I will always remain here. From the realm of the dead, I will be more useful to you. I will be there and here at the same time, because I have no flesh anymore. Son, the time has come for you to become an authority, a well of wisdom. Behind this tribe of men and women you must stand vigilant. Sleep only when it is necessary, eat only when it is necessary. Guard the wellness of the Birifor; the prosperity of this family is in your hands."

As he spoke, Grandfather's voice had changed timbre, progressing from deep and rich to thin, shrill, and extremely distant. He spoke without moving his lips, without gestures and without intonation; but the power of his speech was incontestable. As he continued to speak, a glow, first yellow then green, came out of the crown of his head and spread through-out the tiny room. The medicine boxes started bumping against one an-other as if moved by an invisible force. Distant spirit voices could be heard behind Grandfather, emitting sounds of approval at what he was saying. My father had a dramatic air. Frowning, he bent his head in humility and abandoned himself to the will of the voice that spoke to him.

After a brief silence, Grandfather continued. "Son, I have preserved within myself a sense of honor, truth, and faith to our traditions. I grew up in the shadow of the sacred rites of the tribe and the family, and as a youth I labored to use what I had learned from the school of our fathers. As I accepted more and more responsibilities, I pushed myself further than I thought I could go so that the family would prosper. Our prosperity is at its height now. Our name, the Birifor, is known everywhere, even in other lands across the big river. Remember then, the higher the rise, the more painful the fall. Keep the family's prosperity and honor up there where I have kept it. This is the least you can do: to not allow our family to sink. Let me stand next to you to continue working with you. When you are confused, I will come into your dreams and tell you what to do next.

"There is yet another thing that you must know about and accept for what it is. Your own experience with the new knowledge that the whites brought here must serve you well. There are dangers in being with them, in studying what they know. One of these dangers is forgetfulness. If your knowledge of their ways must mean forgetting yours, I ask you to aban-don this relationship with them now. But I do not believe that will happen. On the contrary, I believe that your dealings with them will prove benefi-cial. You will, by your priviledged connection with them, prove to other families within the tribe that the dog and the cat can live peacefully to-gether.

"That is why we must open the family to the new era that has envel-oped the entire Black race. We must, with care, expose our children to this new wind that comes from the West. Who knows, maybe tomorrow our medicine bag will be enlarged.

"This is the hour of experimentation. We cannot sit with our hands folded and surrender passively to this alien threat. By sending our children to mix with these people, let us begin our quest for a resolution to our dif-ficulties. The time has come for a new definition, new visions, new war-riorship. Remember, it is the ignorance of submission that cost you a wife and three children. You do not want to remain passive anymore, your ex-perience must become useful to you now. The war against our enemy must now begin with a peace treaty. I am offering you an intelligent way to con-front a problem we do not yet understand the exact nature of. My word stops here. Farewell."

Grandfather had finished his speech. A heavy silence fell upon the room. In ceasing to speak, he had ceased to be the life force of the family. Outside, the crowd had grown larger than ever and a thick blanket of darkness was gradually overcoming the twilight. For a brief moment, my father knelt silently in front of Grandfather. Then he stood up, took the magical tail out of Grandfather's hand, helped him to lie down, and left the room, walking backward.

No sooner had he stepped outside than an uproar filled the quiet air. An immense cry that began in the compound spread like fire, reaching every single person within hearing distance. At the same time the sound of the funeral xylophone could be heard from the roof of our house. Two sharp notes, swiftly rendered, followed by a development at the octave, then a central note continually sustained completed the musical message: "A great chief, Bakhye is his name, left this morning for the great journey . . . the living are mournful." Almost at once the same sound was heard further off, transmitted by another xylophone.

I ran into the compound, attracted by the violent and sudden uproar. Women were lamenting as if caught by a boundless calamity, my mother the most pitiful of them all. Assisted by half a dozen elderly women, she was running here and there like a cow painfully stung inside her ear by a bee. The elderly women followed her everywhere she went, running or walking in symphony with the risings and fallings of her grief. Her cries had a devastating effect upon the women around her. I too cried, moved by the pain Mother was expressing. But nobody aided me in my grief. Crying without help, I walked alone outside the compound. There the scene was even more turbulent. A couple of hundred people were offering, each in their own way, their condolences to the Birifor.

Some men were literally barking their grief, some women were whispering words made unintelligible by the general howling. The women were the best vessels of pain. Their laments rose out of their throats and went up like a witch's fire, vanishing in midair as if by enchantment. Then the same laments would begin again, sharpened, as if they had attained the roof of the sky and were now traversing the atmosphere in their descent toward earth. As if they had bodies of their own, their cries seemed to fall upon the ground, becoming grave and slow, as if chiding the ungrateful Earth for having deprived them of someone they cherished. All Dagara funerals are accompanied by great mourning, but this level of grief was even greater than what was usually experienced. I think that all of these women remembered Grandfather's generosity. A great many of them were still alive because of him, and they knew it. They mourned for his loss and for what a tomorrow without him might bring.

Under the two-hundred-year-old baobab tree in the middle of the millet field, men and women were regrouping slowly around a pair of xylophones and a drum. Grandfather's funeral had begun.

CHAPTER 3

GRANDFATHER'S FUNERAL

 Father, whom I had lost sight of because of the immense crowd and the ever-thickening darkness, suddenly appeared, with half a dozen men behind him. He was moaning with despair and calling Grandfather's name repeatedly, expressing his feelings so intensely it was as if someone had told him this would be his last public opportunity to release his grief. He was weeping not only for Grandfather, but for all the unfinished griefs accumulated during his life. His tear-streaked face was distorted and the faces of those accompanying him, sharing in the full force of his grief, were no less ghastly. He walked slowly from east to west and back again, stopping now and then as if to try and digest the pain of this death that had befallen the Birifor. Then he would make a sudden violent turn, as though his efforts to understand were frustrated by the powers of darkness themselves. He constantly called, "Bakhye, Bakhye"—each summoning would end with a hoarse clearing of his throat, as if he hoped for a response.

The six males whose duty it was to assist him participated discreetly in his sorrow while keeping an eye on him. At Dagara funerals, it is always necessary that the members of the immediate family be accompanied by a group of friends in order that they not injure themselves in the paroxysms of their grief. And it is these very paroxysms that are necessary if one's grief is to be purged. Unlike people in the West, the Dagara believe it is terrible to suppress one's grief. Only by passionate expression can loss be tamed and assimilated into a form one can live with. The Dagara also believe that the dead have a right to collect their share of tears. A spirit who is not passionately grieved feels anger and disappointment, as if their right to be completely dead has been stolen from them. So it would be improper for a villager to display the kind of restraint and solemnity seen at Western funerals.

Although there are certain ritual forms of mourning, it is no less sincere for all that. Public grief is cleansing—of vital importance to the whole community—and people look forward to shedding tears the same way they look forward to their next meal.

It was getting dark. As the pair of xylophones under the big baobab tree began their funeral dialogue, the drum responded with dry syncopated sounds. The chanters, standing behind the musicians, began their mournful songs, piercing the hearts of the crowd with sorrow. It was their job to provide a structure for the crowd to release their pent-up feelings. Each doleful phrase was followed by a huge howling, begun by the men and concluded by the women. It takes millions of tears to produce a flood capable of washing the dead to the realm of the ancestors, so refraining from weeping wrongs the dead. Rhythm and chanting crack open that part of the self that holds grief under control. But grief unleashed without the help of ritual drummers, musicians, and chanters runs the risk of producing another death. It is a force without a container. To the dead, it is useless energy, like food that is wasted while people go hungry.

A constant, rhythmic call and response flowed between the chanters, the crowd, the male and female xylophones, and the drum. One chanter sang that an immense fire had been extinguished in the Birifor compound, and that the living must reawaken it; the male xylophone acquiesced in a woeful tone. The second chanter began another lament. It fell from his lips like a grenade into the thousands of hearts in the crowd, provoking an emotional explosion, pitiful and pathetic. The one experience that all humans share is grief, and it takes the right kind of poetry to set grief ablaze. This is why the griot chanter, the guardian of the mythopoetic doors of the tribe, is an invaluable engineer of emotion.

Meanwhile the xylophones and the drum began a frenetic race of rhythm and sound. In eerie harmony, the men in the crowd released their lamentations in a tearful song. Their voices made me shiver. The wailing of a grown-up male makes a child's world grow dim, but it also teaches the child about the adult world he will someday inhabit. An adult who cannot weep is a dangerous person who has forgotten the place emotion holds in a person's life.

The general atmosphere was calamitous. Together, the voices of the mourners seemed to cast a malediction upon the dark cloud that had fallen over the Birifor family. Though funerals are a group activity, there is also space within them for individual initiative: the container created by ritual is big enough to satisfy everyone's needs. Occasionally the men and women touched by sorrow would move out of the singing crowd, their faces wet with tears, their arms outstretched as if to beg one last time for the return of the departed. Promptly but gently, these individuals were escorted back into the thick of the crowd by friends and relatives. They would comply, crying helplessly and submissively to the Great Master of the Universe who holds life and death in his hands.

Within the immediate family of the Birifor clan, some of the more inconsolable would suddenly leap out of the crowd and run quickly as if pursued by a herd of ghosts. Drunk with pain, they were running to quicken the slow process of catharsis. When activated, emotion has a ceiling it must reach. At its apex, grief turns the body into a vessel of chaos. But it is just such a climactic chaos that can cleanse both the person and his or her spirit.

The assistants of these wild runners would immediately launch a rescue behind them. The ensuing race looked like a mad escape from pathos. Soon the mourner would stop and allow his pursuers to take hold of him or her. Together they would conclude that bout of weeping and execute a mournful dance before rejoining the crowd.

During a Dagara funeral ritual, all kinds of grief are released—not just regret for the departed, but all the pain of everyday life. The chanters, accompanied by the male xylophone, might sing that only an unmarried man has the right to cry for a meal, for there is nobody to serve him. The female xylophone would respond with her double note of agreement. Or a man who lost his crop to bad weather could use the funeral space to release his complaint, chanting his loss in unison with the melody of the funeral. Meanwhile the drum would broadcast its deafening rhythm, penetrating every heart in search of hidden miseries.

The chanters were ecstatic, drunk with words. When the xylophones speak, everyone experiences the meaning of poetry. Slowly, by groups, the men began to move out of the crowd and walk rhythmically in a line toward an open area. There they stopped and began to perform a kind of jiggling, carefully synchronized dance consisting of rhythmical movements of the torso and hands. It was as if something deep inside each person was being pulled out of its secret hiding place. The women followed the men, either in a column or in compact groups. Meanwhile people tossed cowrie shells to the musicians—cowries are the currency used for sacred occasions such as divinations, rituals, and marriage ceremonies.

At the start of the dancing, the climactic first day of Grandfather's funeral began to come to an end. Although some would dance far into the night, many of those who had been present since the middle of the day started leaving. One or two more songs and the bulk of the crowd of several hundred people would dissipate. Certain persons would take turns staying awake during the night. They were needed to assist the musicians, who would not rest as long as the funeral rites continued. It was important that the music be kept going. Without music and chanting there is no funeral, no grief, and no death. Everybody else camped in the funeral space or, if they lived nearby, went to their homes. Even grievers must rest. Worn out, I walked to the house and went to sleep next to my snoring sister.

The sun was high when I awoke. At the funeral circle, the crowd was already as thick as the day before. In the compound kitchen women were busy, gossiping and laughing amid a thick cloud of aromatic smoke.

The general atmosphere appeared festive. It was hot and everybody was sweating. Outside the compound I could hear the music of the xylophones, the songs of the chanters, and the crowd's monotonous, persistent murmur. Everywhere cries and laughter mixed to create an atmosphere of festive tragedy. The apex of grief had been reached by most the day before. The reality of death had been absorbed and people were more relaxed. A brightly colored mass of humans waited in the yard in front of the house. Some were talking, others were bartering, buying, or selling grains, meat, fresh fruit, and vegetables. This always happens at funerals, otherwise how would so many people get fed? Others simply sat in the burning sun, baking slowly, carelessly.

Under the baobab tree I saw a cozy little tent covered with colorful fabric. It had not been there the day before. Inside, Grandfather sat enthroned, facing east, his eyes closed. He had a grave air and wore an immense gala costume of immaculate white, crowned by a hat decorated with the symbol of the Birifors: two crocodiles and a chameleon. In this medicine garb, the ancestral scepter grasped in his left hand, he looked majestic.

Near him was a bow and an immense quiver loaded with arrows to remind the people of his glorious warrior past. One of the arrows had been taken out and planted upside down in the ground. Those who knew about the magic of the Pintul understood. Facing Grandfather were numberless skulls—lions, panthers, buffalos, and humans. These relics were there to remind those who had come to render ultimate homage to their great chief of Grandfather's heroism. On either side of him stood two women elders with sticks made of fresh leaves to protect him against flies.

At a brief distance from this palatial tent, the crowd was crying, laughing, and dancing in harmony with the liquid sound of the xylophones, male and female. In compliance with the theme of the funeral's second day, the chanters tirelessly spoke of the deeds of the departed one. They sang the genealogy of the Birifor from top to bottom, exulting in their oratorical art. As the crowd enthusiastically tossed cowrie shells in their direction, their narration of the deeds of the Birifor family became more and more elaborate.

Some of the more emotionally sensitive mourners still responded to the energy of the chanters with weeping and wailing. People would run wild when they could no longer contain themselves, then they would stop and enact the funeral dance until they were freed from their crisis and could return to the group.

These activities lasted the entire day. People took turns standing near the musicians. They went to nearby villages to sing, to cry, and to dance their condolences, or to dilute their own personal pain with that of the assembled crowd. Certain tribal situations obligate one by law to shed tears. Funerals are one of them. Anyone who doesn't cry on these occasions is subjected to a tornado of unpleasant gossip. Shedding tears in public is not difficult for women, for they can weep anytime. Adult men, however, have a more difficult time expressing public grief, for they are forbidden to except on special occasions. In fact, it is generally believed that if a man weeps outside of ritual context, the day will end in disaster.

So, to shed tears, the man must call upon his dead for help by saying "*sanwéi*," "my father," half a dozen times while looking upward. These words will unfailingly help one to shed tears, especially when one is assisted by many other people.

Many had come to Grandfather's funeral in order to pay him a debt. Few were present who had not directly benefited from his generosity, which most often took the form of medical help or donations of food during times of shortages. For these indebted ones, the funeral was the perfect occasion to liberate themselves from their moral or material debts. Some were so fanatic in their grief that they had not returned to their homes since the first day. They wanted it to be absolutely clear to everybody that their attachment to the late chief was limitless, and they made sure they did everything they could in order to draw other people's attention. They planned to be there through the final moment when Grandfather's *Zanu*, his material, spiritual, and moral legacy, would be shown.

The second day of the funeral of an adult is usually awesome, not because of an increase in the level of common sorrow, but because of the demonstrations of esoteric art that so many among the tribe practice or aspire to practice. To be literate in an esoteric practice one must belong to the school that teaches it and have the ability to keep silent about the school's secret practices. A promise is not enough, because the very existence of the technology practiced by secret societies depends upon its members' silence. To the Dagara, the esoteric is a technology that is surrounded by secrecy. Those who know about it can own it only if they don't disclose it, for disclosure takes the power away. For example, some people are supposed to know how to heal elephantiasis, the disease that makes your legs swell. If one person in the clan explains to anyone outside the clan how they manage to heal the disease, the potency of the medicine is immediately lost. If you cannot keep secrets, everyone in the tribe will soon know about it, because in a self-contained community there is no anonymity. Everyone's track record is a matter of public record. The number of secret societies is proportional to the number of technologies that must be kept alive to make the tribe what it is.

The second day of funerals is therefore the day when magical practices are performed, either in memory of the deceased or against any undesirable elements within the tribe. Those who have "gone private," who have failed to obey the laws of nature in some way by withdrawing from proper social interaction or by practicing an esoteric art outside the moderating influence of a secret society and have not done penance, are very vulnerable because their personal energies no longer flow in harmony with the general community energy. To go private is to break the laws of nature by which the community sustains itself. When a member of a secret society must practice his art publicly, those who have gone private must vacate the area or the force field of the art will be deadly to them.

This sudden release of energy is like a purge—it will harm only those who are no longer in alignment with the community. So funerals are a time when hidden wrongdoings come to light. Justice is not effected by humans but by nature. Unfortunately, not only the evildoers are punished. When persons who have gone private come to funerals to try their art, more often than not they end up hurting innocent bystanders or one another.

No one can practice tribal magical arts without a stable and supportive community. A stable community reflects the laws of nature and dances with them. Within this framework, art, because it celebrates the powers of the underworld, where the true nature of the natural order is administered by the gods, becomes the greatest healing tool that a community can have. When this support system is broken, art no longer functions the way it is supposed to. It becomes dangerous and in turn endangers the person practicing it.

The magical arts are Dagara technology, a technology characterized by practicality—what is needed, what is useful. When one of our elders carves a double-headed serpent or an amphibious mammal, he is not just creating an image out of his imagination, but cooperating with the spirits of those beings for the maintenance of the natural order. Through this carving, spirits from the underworld manifest themselves to heal us in the world above and to repair our world. To the Dagara, art is the form in which spirits choose to exist with us here in this world.

The most common technique utilized by people who have gone private is the *lobir* (plural *lobie*), an invisible projectile known to warriors of the secret societies. A lobir can take any form. The most primitive is an object that is thrown into a person's body. The most advanced is a living thing, ranging from a lobir the size of a worm to one as big as the practitioner can guide.

Funerals provide the ideal context for all sorts of wizard wars. After each funeral celebration a certain number of unfortunate men and women become gravely ill because they have been shot unaware by an enemy or have been hit by a lobir intended for somebody else. Those who attack people with lobie hide themselves and their doings. They may come to the funeral with strange feline-skin bags on their backs containing a secret arsenal invisible to the uninformed eye, or they may mix with the singers unnoticed.

The contents of these bags are kept secret because no one checks the contents of another person's bag. Most males, especially those who are directly related to the deceased, carry animal-skin bags on their backs when they attend funerals. These bags are a kind of Dagara first-aid kit, and contain cowrie shells and medicine objects used for healing. Because funerals are not a closed circle, and since everybody is morally obligated to participate at one time or another, many different kinds of people show up.

Most of the time those who have gone private can harm their chosen victims without being noticed. With a simple movement of their hand, they can fire the invisible projectiles intended for their enemy. Once hit, this unfortunate person feels little pain. In fact, they experience nothing more than the need to scratch. Later, however, the itching will become worse and worse until the person is finally debilitated and forced to leave the funeral circle in search of a healer.

Why would someone who lives within a tribal community want to harm others in this way? Because such actions give pleasure to an evil person. As they say, this person is possessed by bad spirits. For those of you who have begun to construct a romantic picture of indigenous life, let this be a warning. For the indigenous world is not a place where everything flows in harmony, but one in which people must be constantly on the alert to detect and to correct imbalances and illnesses in both communal and individual life.

Like bullets fired from the barrel of a gun, lobie can work against anyone. Just as one must wear a bulletproof vest to ward off bullets, one can have a "lobirproof" vest magically placed over one's body. Unlike the bulletproof vest, which has its limitations, the lobirproof vest is perfect. Once built into your body's energy system, it will be part of you for the rest of your life. Moreover, anyone who shoots at a person thus protected could very well find himself being hit by his own lobir because this "vest" has the power to deflect the hostile projectile back to its sender. This is very dangerous for the evildoer, for as they say in my tribe, you can't defend yourself against your own bullet once it is returned to you.

I remember a story my father once told me about a lobir. He was attending a friend's funeral. In the middle of one of the cathartic communal dances, he was stung on the left hand by something that looked like a bee. This bee, however, tore straight through his skin and disappeared into his arm. My father could feel it moving around under his skin, its wings still whirring.

The pain was so excruciating that he fell onto the dusty ground and passed out. People carried him into the emergency room of the local healer, who looked at the moving lobir and recognized its maker by the speed with which Father's hand was swelling. After stilling the moving lobir, the healer made a tiny incision and chased the "bee" out by plunging an arrow into Father's body. When the bee-lobir flew out, he squashed it before it could escape.

Father was given medicine to restore his strength. Before he was able to return to the funeral, he had to wash himself with a special potion designed to form a shield against such invisible projectiles. Since that day, Father has been extremely cautious about lobie, even with his immunization. I have heard numerous similar reports. And, when I was four years old, I saw my grandfather extract lobie that looked like bones, needles, feathers, and fur from the bodies of victims. A person in my tribe who ignores these warnings because he or she feels invulnerable is exhibiting a dangerous vanity.

During the second day of Grandfather's funeral the *nimwie-dem*, "those who have eyes"—medicine society members, initiated people, and some people who had an exceptional eye for observation—kept tabs on what was happening around them so that they could take appropriate actions. An ordinary person cannot see lobie. To have that ability you either have to know how to use them or be immunized against them. To the average person, lobie might look like something as harmless as the sun's rays, but to trained seers they might, for example, appear as a multitude of tiny shooting stars, traversing space at varying speeds. Some of the "stars" disappear when they hit a human body.

If a person is struck by a lobir, he or she will inevitably scratch where the thing has vanished, alerting the shooter that the lobir has found its mark. But sometimes these minute "stars" land on the ground, endangering anyone who happens to walk on them. The unfortunate victim might leap into the air like a cat who has accidentally stepped on a hot coal, but there will be no further complications beyond a simple skin burn. A lobir cannot hurt you if it is not specifically designed to hurt you. My father once explained that the reasons some projectiles fail to hit their target is because the shooter has an incomplete knowledge of the victim's energy field. The missile becomes confused shortly after being fired. It falls on the ground and sometimes dies quickly thereafter. Those who are able to see them urinate on them when they fall onto the ground (assuming they can do so without infringing on the laws of decency). To urinate on a lobir is to kill it instantly. The thing catches fire and burns to ash.

On the second day of Grandfather's funeral, as I stood at the periphery of the circle of mourners, a brilliant object on the ground caught my attention. It looked like a conic crystal, so incandescent that to look at it directly made my eyes water. Intrigued and curious, I stared at it, trying to figure out what it was. Then I picked it up. It was not hot, but the palm of my right hand became white with light. I thought somebody had lost something valuable because the dances at funerals sometimes become so wild that objects fall out of people's pockets. I decided to show it to my father or my mother—whoever I saw first—so that it could be returned to its owner. But I could see neither of them in the seething crowd.

I went to look for my mother in the compound. Outside the door to her room, I met my aunt and asked her if she knew my mother's whereabouts. I didn't understand her mumbled response, so I decided I would forward the object to Mother through her. When I showed the shiny object to my aunt, she let out a yell so loud that everyone in the compound was alerted. She zigzagged outside, too fat to be agile and too short to take long steps. Seized by sudden terror, I let the object fall. Hearing my aunt's cry, a crowd of people, including one of the elders, arrived at Mother's door. All around me people were asking, "What is it?" Those who were close enough to see the shiny thing were too petrified to answer. The elder ordered everyone to step back. Then he picked up the shiny thing with his left hand, grabbed me with the other, and led me into Grandfather's room.

There I found my father, seated in the middle of a group of elders who were gesturing and speaking. They stopped when we entered the room. I ran and sat next to Father and started telling him what had happened. In the meantime the old man who had taken the shiny object dropped it into one of the many pots of magical concoctions sitting around the room. As soon as the object hit the liquid in the pot, the liquid began to boil frenetically, as though there were a fire under the pot. Everybody was staring at me; I was fascinated by what the shiny thing was doing to the liquid.

My father broke the heavy silence. "Never again pick up these things when you find them."

"Do not interfere with him," ordered a tiny old man with a beard like a goat's. "You cannot tell what this boy can do with these fearful things. He already has a natural immunity against them, and he can see them. Why not tell him what he should do with them instead of pretending that there is some mystery here?"

Another old man who had been chewing tobacco since I entered spat and answered, "With children you are never quite sure what to teach them and what not to. Tomorrow he might forget what he knows today. Then what will happen?"

The little old man did not seem to like this fellow's observation. He too spat, and growled in response, "Keep your tongue where it is. How do you know what this boy does not know? His *siura** has shielded him and everyone around him from harm. He'll grow into knowledge without your help. Weren't you here yesterday? Don't you remember? Then let me tell you. This boy is the reincarnation of Birifor himself. Nothing is going to happen, or Birifor is not the man we have all known him to be. This kid is the original possessor of the secret we are using so badly today. It's he who gave it to Bakhye, the dead man we are honoring."

"Good talk," said another man. He was younger than the others. His eyes were red and extremely mobile, and his teeth had turned black and red through years of addiction to tobacco. They clacked softly against one another like kola nuts as he spoke. Nobody answered. Nobody dared to confront him. This man's name was Guisso and his power was regarded with the same deep respect as Grandfather's had been when he was alive. Even then Guisso was on my side, and years later he would be the person who would help me reconstruct most of the events of Grandfather's funeral. Now he stood up, stretched noisily, and went to the pot where the object had been placed. The liquid had stopped boiling. Plunging in his hand, he brought the object out. It was not shiny anymore, but had turned to charcoal.

He inspected it for a long while, then declared, "This is the work of Dadiè. He makes these kinds of things. But what was it doing on the ground? Perhaps he sold it to a client who does not know how to shoot. I have warned him time and again about this evil practice. He has ruined himself by allowing this to fall into my hands."

He then blew on the object. As if by enchantment, it became air. Then he resumed his seat and said to the man who had brought me into Grandfather's room, "Thank you, Kpire, for what you just did. You can leave now." In a gesture of acknowledgment, Kpire stood up, bowed to the old man, and left the room. Exhausted by my adventure, I went over to Grandfather's bed, stretched out, and soon fell into a deep sleep.

On the third day of the funeral, the crowd was thicker than ever. It had rained the night before, but now the sun was bright in a cloudless sky.

*A human representative in the world of the spirits. The guardian angel.

Early in the morning, the elders of the village had a meeting in Grandfather's room. I could sense the excitement of the people all around me, as if something were about to happen.

The tension of the last two days had receded. People were singing and dancing, visibly relaxed, enjoying the last day of the funeral by celebrating rather than mourning. The catharsis they had been seeking over the last couple of days had been found, and groups were dancing joyfully, as if Grandfather had never died. The musicians, tireless, were now playing merrier tunes. The male xylophone sang, "We made it through the night. He made it through to the shore of the spirits. Now let the departed one be the nourisher of the power we carry."

To this, the female xylophone echoed, "Death is life and life is death. The dead live while the living die. Living or dying, we have joy."

The chanters too had stopped aiming their pointed words at people's hearts. In a merrier mood now, they were singing comic songs.

Toward midmorning, musicians, dancers, and singers all stopped. The crowd around the *paala** where Grandfather was still sitting was cleared. One could now see Grandfather, seated calmly as though unconcerned about the goings-on, but at the same time looking attentive and slightly defiant about the ceremony on his behalf.

After three days most corpses begin to exhale embarrassing smells and to degenerate rapidly. Grandfather, on the contrary, appeared freshly dead. Except for his forward-bent head, one might think that he was merely playing a trick on us.

The crowd was obviously waiting for something to happen. They faced the entrance of the gate to the compound two hundred feet to the north. I found my way through the middle of this crush of people and went in search of my aunt, who was selling freshly fried bean cakes. She served me a few in a calabash.

I sat next to her and ate. Before long we heard a noise like a thunderstorm. This sound was followed by a long procession of elders. They came out of the main gate, dressed in colorful ceremonial outfits of different styles, each one describing the specialties of its wearer. Each elder wore a tall, regal hat with seven points, like a king's crown. On one side of these hats a chameleon was brightly embroidered, the emblem of transformation and service; on the other side was a bird, which signaled a messenger. On the front of these hats was a big star, which symbolized that we were one people.

The most outstanding part of their costumes were their large impressive cloaks, which were intricately embroidered around the chest area with

---

*A funeral tent or a makeshift or temporary house for the dead.

dozens of images. On the back of each cloak was the tribal emblem, a cross in the middle of a square. On either side were images expressing the function of each medicine man. Most of the healers held a scepter in one hand, signifying the special nature of their powers. Others had this symbol painted on their outfits. The scepters resembled strangely sculpted amphibious forms, Kontombili, and the tails of mysterious animals. Each scepter was smartly decorated with cowrie shells or arabesque beads patterned to symbolize the nature of each healer's secret. The medicine men and healers were solemn, and their appearance imposed silence upon the crowd.

The people stood transfixed, contemplating these men of power of the Dagara tribe as if they were seeing them for the first time. The healers walked in a line to the paala, silently circled it three times, then returned to the compound. A hush fell over the crowd. The Zanu ceremony, the enactment of Grandfather's spiritual and moral legacy, was about to begin. The intensity of this ceremony was all the more exceptional because the dead man had been a sacred healer and a leader. The crowd anticipated that something unprecedented would happen—something magical.

Suddenly, slowly and methodically, someone blew a *wélé*, a hunting whistle. Its sharp notes penetrated every ear. In the special language of hunters, it proclaimed that a herd of *walpiel* (deer) was heading southwest, straight toward the compound. The whistle attempted to count their number, gave up after the first dozen, then talked of their speed, making the sound that meant, "They are running chest down," which is the position the walpiel run in when they are coming fast. The whistle went on to describe their sizes, but nobody was paying attention anymore, for behind the crowd, a little distance away, a cloud of dust darkened the sky and everyone could feel the rhythmical cadence of hooves pounding the ground.

Then the yell of a woman, echoed by many others in the outer part of the crowd, announced the nearness of the herd. Finally, we could see them clearly. Heads bent, growling like exhausted war horses in the midst of a battle, the walpiels rushed toward us, tossing their branchlike horns in the air in front of them. Unmindful of their proximity to such a huge mass of humans, they charged the crowd.

A general alarm ensued. People ran for their lives, screaming unintelligibly, in search of hiding places. Some men hid behind trees. Others, realizing the uselessness of any attempt to confront these ferocious animals, hid just behind the huge baobab tree trunk outside the compound.

The most courageous among the crowd never moved. These few individuals knew that the herd was created and being controlled from Grandfather's room, where only a few minutes ago the council of elders and healers had gone. The materialization of this herd was a perfect illusion—these animals were as harmless as the air. Yet the sound of their stampeding hoofs pounding on the ground was growing deafening as the distance between the crowd and the herd narrowed. Under such conditions, there was an exceptional demand upon the will of those who had chosen not to move one inch from where they were. I was watching this scene from the sidelines, next to my Aunt Pony. The herd finally ran directly into the crowd and, with a cavernous noise, melted away into the air. Everything became quiet. Before anyone had a chance to figure out what had happened, the elders and healers appeared in the thick of the crowd as if by enchantment and rallied around the paala of Grandfather. They stood and gave a moment of piety to the dead, then walked back into the compound in a line.

The medicine men created the illusion of this herd of wild beasts because of Grandfather's close relationship, as hunter and healer, to the animal world. They wished to bring this world into the funeral ritual. Even though the villagers knew that what they were seeing was an illusion, it took a great deal of self-control to remember that.

The last *boburo*—medicine man—had barely disappeared into the compound when all of a sudden there was a piercing noise right above our heads. All eyes looked up at the sky, searching for its source. There was light circling Grandfather's paala, about three hundred meters above him. The arrow's speed was so dazzling that, had it not been for its luminosity and the dark trail of steam it left behind, nobody would have seen it. The arrow of light circled three times around the paala, then shot straight into the midst of the crowd, which instinctively tried to make space. The arrow sank into the wet ground and reappeared twenty meters away, shooting up from between the legs of a woman who was seated with her back toward the compound.

The woman leaped to her feet and executed a bizarre dance. Petrified by terror, she raced toward the crowd with her arms upraised, yelling. No one seemed to be concerned for her, nor did anyone laugh at her. They had seen these kinds of scenes countless times, and besides, women in intense grief act like that. After this first surprise, the arrow of light shot once more into the sky, then arched toward the northern horizon, where it was quickly swallowed out of sight. Soon its whistling was heard again, this time from the south, as if in that short time it had circled the Earth. As it neared the crowd, it began to slow down and lose altitude. Finally it flew straight toward the house where the elders and healers were, entered through the wall, and disappeared. The crowd greeted the end of this demonstration with a thunder of *kuyis,* a shrieking sound that women often emit in lieu of applause.

The funeral participants had barely recovered from the display of the magical arrow when the next wonder appeared. Because my grandfather had been a very great medicine man and the leader of our family, it was fitting that the supernaturals who had befriended him and aided him in his work would come to pay their last respects. Within the world of the Dagara, so closely aligned with the worlds of nature and the worlds of the spirit, these beings are commonly seen—just as angels and other heavenly apparitions were once commonly experienced by devout Christians in the West.

Approaching Grandfather's paala from the north came a strange group of beings, short red creatures who looked like humans. They had pointed ears and were two feet tall at most, with genitals so long they had to roll them around their necks, and hair so long it touched the ground. As they neared the crowd, Aunt Pony brought her hands to her mouth and mumbled fearfully, "Oh! The Kontombili!" Women hid behind their husbands. Men lowered their heads, too frightened to run. The boburo and healers stayed out of sight in Grandfather's room.

Ignoring the crowd, these bizarre beings moved toward Grandfather's paala and gathered around it in a semicircle with an air of solemn homage. My grandfather had told me many stories about these beings, but this was the first time I had actually seen any of them. Though they looked tiny and helpless, the Kontombili are the strongest, most intelligent beings God ever created. Grandfather told me they are part of what he called "the universal consciousness," but even though they are immeasurably intelligent, like us they too do not know where God is. They come from a world called Kontonteg, a fine place, far bigger than our Earth, yet very difficult to locate in time and space. They make their homes in illusionary caves that serve as the portals between our world and theirs. When the boburo and healers in our tribe need their counsel, they perform rituals in caves to access the world of the Kontombili.

"The Kontombili live very long," Grandfather once told me. "They can live as long as they want, but they can die when they are ready. We owe them most of the magic we know—and much of our joy. For example, before we met them, we did not know how to brew millet beer. One day one of our women met a Kontombilé when she was out in the bush hunting for dry wood. He gave her a calabash full of a foamy liquid, and when she drank it, she was delighted. She felt merry and wanted to sing. When she asked the Kontombilé what she was drinking, he said it was *dan*, made from millet grains. 'I am saying it, but I am not saying anything,' the Kontombilé chanted:

For three days and two nights
let the grain soak in water
under firm ground.
I'm saying it
But I'm not saying anything.
On the third day bring the wet grain
into air below the sky
and let it rest

below a blanket of green leaves
for another three days.
I'm saying it
but I'm not saying anything.

Then separate the grains
one from the other, slowly
and let the sun dry them, slowly.
I'm saying it
But I'm not saying anything.
Pound the dry grains
cook the meal for two days
and drain,
take the juice and add
some ferment.
Let it mix and foam.
I'm saying it
But I'm not saying anything.
When the juice is under a white foaming blanket
enjoy the whole of it.
I said it
But I didn't say anything.

The woman went home and did as she was told, and since then we have
dan. Many other secrets were thus divulged to selected villagers in the
same way. Kontombili soon became the village consultants. Day and night,
they would wait in the bush, crossing the frontiers between the worlds under various disguises, waiting for humans to come to them.

Their sudden appearance at the funeral was an indication that they
knew Grandfather very well, and were coming to pay their respects to a
great leader. Ignoring the people around them, they marched back and
forth between the paala and the room where the boburo and healers were
housed, as if participating in a ritual of mystic communication with the
dead. After a quarter of an hour, apparently satisfied, they marched off
into the bush without addressing a word to anybody and disappeared behind the first tree they came to.

▲　　　▼　　　▲

Before the burial, the grave must be *muul*, literally "looked into," a ceremony that allows a viewing of the final residence of the dead. This ritual is
for children only. They get the opportunity to see what a grave is like, and
to remember the last resting place of a person of status. For years after-

ward they will always be able to recall the name of the person whose grave they looked into, and this helps determine how much time has passed since then. For the Dagara, the child's memory works better than the adult's. If you trust something important to a child, he or she will keep it as long as he or she draws breath. There are also rituals that stimulate the child's power to store and recall things. One of the reasons why our elders are important to us is because the child within the elder is able to constantly retrieve things from the past that the community needs. The elder also knows how to transfer what he or she knows to the youth so that there is a continuity of special knowledge.

Dozens of children had been gathered for the occasion. Guided by adults, they went in groups of five or ten to spend a few minutes at Grandfather's grave. I was part of the last group. I walked to the opening along with six other children from the house. The grave was noticeable only by the huge amount of dirt surrounding it. The hole itself was a tiny incision cut into the ground that, as it went deeper, became wider and wider. Its entrance was circular and no more than ten inches in diameter. I wondered how they could fit a human body through such a narrow path. But apparently no corpse is too big for this tiny entrance. In the meantime the musicians had carried their instruments closer to the paala and were busy tuning them. In small groups of ten to fifteen, women began singing the celebration songs of harvest ordinarily heard only at the new year's festival. Most grief ceremonies end in celebration—after such strenuous mourning, the human psyche needs to play.

The women sang in a circle, clapping their hands. In the center one or two of them would execute complicated dance steps, then let themselves fall into the hands of two or three other women. Each woman would then be lifted up, then, at the exact moment the song ended, they would be released and land gracefully in the middle of the circle. Then everything would begin over again with new women in the center.

The women soon broke off their dance to join the musicians, who had finished tuning up and agreed on a song. This time the music had a more festive rhythm, contrasting with the tense and mournful music they had been playing for the past two and a half days. They began with a *siaw* tune, a song with a heavily cadenced rhythm that had the effect of being both physically demanding yet relaxing at the same time as the musicians became more and more involved with the beat. The female xylophone began singing playfully:

> *My dog caught an antelope—*
> *But who ever saw a headless dog*
> *catch an antelope?*

Led by the head dancer, men and women joined in the festivities around the funeral paala, singing and dancing. The head dancer held a cow tail in his hand, which he swung comically while he himself looked very serious. The drummer who led the rhythm was sweating under his dusty *balbir* (village shirt) and soon the whole paala was surrounded by a cloud of dust while the air smelled of sweat.

It was then that the boburo and healers, who had not appeared since their last display of magic, marched out of the compound. With a solemn air they moved toward the dancing circle. Everybody stopped at once: singers, drummer, musicians, and dancers. There was complete silence. The women moved east and the men rallied west, leaving the musicians in the middle ground, next to the paala. The boburo and healers arrived and stood in front of Grandfather.

The time had come for the ultimate homage. The musicians began a tuning ritual, testing their instruments nervously. Then the boburo and healers began the closing ritual as one of them intoned:

> *We may never hear*
> *The thunder come out*
> *Of the lion's mouth.*
> *We may never see his claws.*
> *The claws that once served*
> *The peace of our village.*
> *How much longer can we survive?*
> *Yé Yé Yé.*

Another medicine man, a dwarf too small to have been seen before, leaped out of the group and lifted his scepter. In a loud voice he responded:

> *Lightning brings the tone*
> *Of coming thunder,*
> *But thunder came alone*
> *Without his messenger.*
> *Oh, the wrath of nature*
> *Yé yé yé yé.*

First the men began to sing, and soon the song was transmitted throughout the entire crowd. Once again, people began to weep, tears streaming from their eyes. A man let out a long lamenting cry that was drowned out by many others and carried over into the women's thrilling voices. The male xylophone chose that crucial time to begin a mournful song known by the crowd:

Pélé pélé, pélé pélé
Bo mweri kyi
(Empty, empty, empty. The granary broke with the millet.)

The leaves of the branches
The branches of the tree
All fed on the roots.

Now leaves without branches
Branches without roots
How do you stay alive?

The lead medicine man's voice rose above the xylophone, and his words filled the air with doom. The dwarf jumped out of the circle once more and intoned:

The circle has lost its guide
His breath flew out
Now Birifor is waiting to be a ghost.
Ah! this compound is lost. Yééééé.

Once again this utterance was followed by a mournful wail begun by the group of men and sustained by the women. It died away into oblivion as the crowd's attention was directed toward the refrain of the xylophone mourning the tension of this last moment. The gravediggers broke into the circle around the paala and gently carried Grandfather's body away from the weeping circle to the grave. For a while the ritual of farewell continued in front of the empty paala.

It was hot, though the sun was declining toward evening. The funeral ground emptied slowly until there were only a few people left to attend to the last business. The gravediggers returned; the routines of everyday life resumed. A few women still wept as if incapable of consolation. Their high-pitched wailing rose into the dusty air. Without resistance I followed Aunt Pony and her bean-cake equipment into the yard empty of people, where the quiet spoke as eloquently as speech itself. Grandfather had really died. A new era had begun.

CHAPTER 4

A SUDDEN FAREWELL

 The sun had already risen. A few scattered clouds were speeding across the empty zenith as if running away from the threat of the burning disc. The air was heavy, saturated by humidity as the wet soil yielded up its moisture under the boiling work of the sun. It was a few weeks after Grandfather's funeral. The rainy season had arrived: it had rained the night before.

I knew it had rained in the middle of the night because my mother had wakened us suddenly, yelling to my sister Zanta and me to get up so that she could move our sleeping mat a little closer to the fireplace. Water was dripping onto us through a hole in the roof, and our mat was wet.

Mother was always impatient and sometimes brutal when it came to waking my sister and me. She thought that we lived more in the spirit world than in the village world. She often used the word witch to refer to us—me because of my meeting with the little man in the bush, and my sister because of the deepness of her sleep. My mother thought my sister's spirit went flying off at night, as is customary with witches, leaving her body behind, sound asleep, and that is why mother was so violent when she tried to waken her.

My sister had more or less confirmed her suspicions. One night, when my sister had fallen asleep outside, my mother tried everything to waken her, with no results. Then she decided to abandon my sister in the rain, thinking this would teach her to sleep more lightly. Nothing, however, woke my sister up. Toward dawn, when the storm had diminished, she came in, soaked and stiff as death. Since that night, nothing could convince Mother that her daughter was not a witch.

Among the Dagara it is not a bad thing to be a witch. Those who aren't witches aren't afraid of them, but they do find the idea of becoming a witch frightening. No one wants to embrace talents and abilities that would take so much energy out of them.

After mother had awakened me and moved me out from under the leak, I heard Father's footsteps on the roof. He was trying to locate the hole through which the water was dripping into the house. The frequent flashes of lightning must have helped him, for soon I heard him pound heavily on the roof and then climb down the ladder. A few seconds later he came into the huge zangala to ask Mother if the dripping had stopped. She said it had and, without another word, Father disappeared back to his quarters.

Grandfather used to call the rain "the erotic ritual between heaven and Earth." The rain represented the seeds sown in the Earth's womb by heaven, her roaring husband, to further life. Rainy encounters between heaven and Earth were sexual love on a cosmic scale. All of nature became involved. Clouds, heaven's body, were titillated by the storm. In turn, heaven caressed the Earth with heavy winds, which rushed toward their erotic climax, the tornado. The grasses that pop out of the Earth's womb shortly after the rain are called the numberless children of Earth who will serve humankind's need for nourishment. The rainy season is the season of life. Yes, it had rained the night before.

The sun appeared, drying everything and increasing in heat the higher it climbed. In the compound, two elders were sitting on the wet wooden bench next to the kitchen. I remembered having seen them a month and a half before among the group of healers and medicine men who were leading Grandfather's zanu—especially the dwarf. I wondered if I should go and greet them, but I had to pee so badly, I decided I would think about that while I was in the toilet. Just as I was about to enter it, the dwarf called out to me, "My friend, pee and then come here." I hurried into the toilet, wondering what he wanted me for.

"There is plenty of blood in this kid," the white-bearded dwarf said to the man sitting next to him. He held me between his knees as he spoke, a great honor, for in the village it is a sign of tenderness for an elder to have a child sit on or between his legs while he talks to that child. The dwarf smelled like tobacco.

"Yes, *Bie Ku*,"* the other man answered and spat. A dark stream of tobacco shot through the air with a nicotine smell.

"Where is your father?" the dwarf asked, addressing me now.

"I don't know," I said.

It was getting harder and harder to bear his smell. His boubou, dyed with pink root juice, had not been washed for years. The accumulation of sweat, tobacco, and decay had combined to form a halo of suffocating perfume around him strikingly similar to Grandfather's. He coughed, cleared his throat, and spat out a mixture of kola nut and tobacco. He wiped his mouth with his left hand, then cleaned his hand with his boubou, all the while pounding his foot on the mess he had spat onto the floor, attempting to make it disappear. It eventually vanished, leaving a wet spot.

In the Dagara culture, elders don't care about cleanliness or the affectations that young people think they have to put on. The nature of the other world is pink, so the elders dye their boubous that color. The aura of disgust that elders love to create around themselves is the result of their having let go of certain social pretenses, and especially of their unyielding concentration upon the spirits. They don't have any spare energy to invest in being polite. Among the Dagara, the more you dwell in the other world, the more you shock those who don't.

Just then my father came out into the compound from his room.

"*Sê*," the two men said together, greeting my father solemnly. *Sê* means to dance. In its imperative form, it refers to a synchronized dance called *sew*. Elders use this word as a greeting when they require someone's cooperation.

"*Sê ni lè*," my father responded—the dance is on. He inquired about their health and the situation of their households, then added as an extra measure of politeness, "Is anyone not in good health? I mean the children, their mothers, and everybody else."

"There is nothing wrong with anyone," said the dwarf. "Is everyone in your family in good health?"

"I feel so," my father replied, "but I've been counting the pieces of wood on the ceiling night after night." By this he meant that he had been finding it hard to sleep because of anxiety.

"That's all we're good at these days. It's like a plague. You have to be constantly on the alert to earn a few more days of life. You never know when calamity will hit. And the most disciplined is the one who will live the longest." While the dwarf spoke, he had his hand in his pocket, searching for something.

He brought out a kola nut, which he split into two. He gave one half to

*A statement of acquiescence.

my father, bit into the other half, and gave the rest to the other man. The three men were quiet while they chewed thoughtfully on the nuts, stopping now and then to swallow the juice.

It was not long, however, before the dwarf broke the silence again. "Our health is linked to our capacities to manage our responsibilities. A weary mind in a restless body is likely to forget what he must do and with whom. That is why our fathers say one man needs the eyes of another man to see what the shadow of the tree hides. I suppose you know why we are here."

My father cleared his throat and said, "It is indeed a matter that requires no explanation. The sick do not expect the medicine person to explain why they are being visited." Then he added, "Let's proceed. Past experiences have taught me that procrastination in my duties has been the enemy of me and my family's health. Since my father decided to become a ghost, he has visited me quite often in my dreams, urging me to be faithful to my duties when the time comes. I have already been reminded of my responsibilities and you need not do it again. Let's proceed."

"Good talk," the little man said.

"The beer preparation for the ceremony will begin a market from today," my father replied. "We will make everything ready."

"That's good," the tiny shaman replied. "Then we will get this out of the way before the dead become angry at us."

In light of my father's past, it was not surprising that these elders had felt it necessary to come and speak with him. Everyone in the tribe knew of the disastrous consequences of his dealings with the white Jesuit priest. Now that my father was head of the entire Birifor clan, the two elders had come to make sure that he intended to perform his duties.

Since Grandfather's funeral, my father had been under an intense transformation of the type that had burdened him when his first wife's children had died, one after the other, under his helpless eyes. A few days after the last person had left Grandfather's funeral circle, Father, as if trapped in endless troubling thoughts over what to do in order to escape the responsibilities that so suddenly faced him—responsibilities that he feared because they entailed a conscious giving up of the new religion that had won his heart—decided to take some time to meditate upon this recent turn of events.

First he locked himself into his room for a few weeks and would not speak to anyone. During this time of seclusion, he would come out of his quarter and walk to Grandfather's door, which had been quarantined since the funeral.

I wasn't really sure that Grandfather's room was off limits, but I had heard whispering to the effect that it was. People intimated that Grandfather's ghost was at work in that dark room and wouldn't let anyone disturb it. Father frequently stood at Grandfather's door and stared at it as though he could see something no one else could. Then he would go back to his quarter after a quick stop at the bathroom.

It was obvious that Father was not enthusiastic about being in charge of the elaborate collection of medicines, the magic tools that had made Grandfather unequaled in our tribe. In a traditional culture, power and regard are based upon medicine and upon its related spiritual training and growth. But the more you know, the more obligated you are to serve the community; the more you own, the more you must give. Consequently, it is easy to understand why people are reluctant to embrace spiritual secrets and their attendant responsibilities. By departing this life, Grandfather had passed his medicine on to Father, and if Father chose to assume that burden, he would have to change the entire pattern of his life.

One does not jump enthusiastically into being big: status can swallow every bit of your life energy. Those who serve are not equal to those who are being served. They are higher than those they serve because they are in the spirit world. Those that are served are lower because they are in the material world. The irony is that each wants to sit where the other sits. The healer dreams about being human, that is, "normal," while the normal person wishes to become as knowledgeable as the medicine man. My father was in a dilemma because he understood this.

As if in perfect synchronization with Father's mood, the entire Birifor compound was living in a suspended life. All day, and late into the evening, men and women walked about in silence. Heads of families would come into our quarter in the morning and enter Father's room. They would linger there for a while and then leave without a word.

I noticed that each of them, before leaving, would stand for a few minutes in front of Grandfather's door. As the weeks passed, the silence became unbearable. The coming of the two *Baomale,* or medicine men, one morning was a major turn of events. For the first time, people in our compound began to talk out loud again. Something was about to happen.

Before the arrival of the medicine men, Father Maillot had come to see us. It was as if he sensed the spiritual battle that was going on and was determined to sway my father from his duties. He arrived in midmorning. Everybody was out except my father who, following his habit, was sequestered in his quarter. In contrast to Grandfather, who was eager to talk to me whenever the two of us were left alone, Father liked his solitude. He did not care what I was doing in the meantime. So when the priest appeared that morning, I was the first person he saw.

I had never had a close look at this white Jesuit missionary before. His sudden appearance in the compound scared my soul out of my body. Father Maillot looked like a ghost. Dressed from his neck down to his feet in an immaculately white robe, he looked almost as if he were floating. As he strode in my direction, his arms outstretched toward me, I somehow had the impression that he wanted to suck my life force out of the crown of my head and my eyes. As is well known among the Dagara, never let a ghost look into your eyes. You will never live to find out why.

I tried not to look at him, but his presence was so overwhelming that I could not help it. His face was mostly hidden behind a thick carpet of dark floating hair. Unless he was laughing out loud, as he did when he first saw me, one would think he had no mouth. Protruding from beneath his forehead was an immense nose the size of an anthill, which looked down on his thick beard like a giraffe upon a small tree. His eyes were petrifying: two round blue mirrors, so transparent one would swear they were made out of the stuff of the world below. They exerted an irresistible magnetism.

Like his mouth, his skull was generously hidden under a thick layer of undulating hair that formed a ring on his back below his neck. Father Maillot looked like a woolly sheep from the neck up and like a ghost everywhere else. So when this apparition came into the compound and walked straight toward me, I almost fainted. I opened my mouth to scream, but nothing came out. Father Maillot did not seem to notice my bedeviled appearance. He grabbed me with both hands and lifted me into the air, all the while speaking in a foreign language. Then he brought me down against his chest and hugged me. He smelled funny, a real ghost smell. But his body, I was sure, was not a spirit body.

Grandfather had once told me that ghosts look like they have flesh but don't. So I figured that people who looked like ghosts but did have flesh were those he used to call the "shaved pigs," the name he gladly gave to French people because their skin was so unnaturally pink. I could see Father Maillot's pink skin shining even beneath his hairy covering.

He asked, "Where is your dad?"

His Dagara was execrable. One had to rebuild the entire sentence to extract any meaning. I could make out only the word "dad." I pointed to Father's door. I was too numb to speak, and too close to the vicinity of the priest's jungle face. Father Maillot put me down, spoke his gibberish again, and walked to my father's door. He opened it without knocking and walked in. As he was closing the door behind him, I saw my father move toward him.

My body was still shivering from the panic fit Father Maillot had caused in me. I sat for a while in the compound under the sun to calm down. But the door leading to the outside was not closed. This priest had left it wide open when he entered. Chickens and goats began pouring into the compound. I knew I was supposed to do something, but I couldn't get my wits together. The chickens overturned a clay pot that contained some leftover millet cakes and began pecking at them frenetically and fighting with each other. The large crumbs were rapidly swallowed by the grown-up hens. The smaller chickens, which could not get their share because of the infernal rhythm of eating and squabbling around the clay pot, stood around waiting for an opportunity to steal some crumbs from the mouths of those who couldn't swallow fast enough.

I became fascinated by the scene and wondered, "Do chickens really enjoy their meal? They don't seem to taste anything they eat."

I remembered Grandfather's attitude toward chickens. He believed that they spoke. He said that if you wished to comprehend this language, you should stop eating chicken. Next you should bathe at dawn, at the third crow of the rooster, in some water mixed with chickenshit. After that, you should rub your body with the fat of a three-year-old hen.

I don't know if Grandfather had been through this disgusting process. But I know he used to amuse himself by listening to chickens. One day he translated their language to me while a flock of them stood around a one-eyed woman who was pounding millet for the evening meal. The woman first had to separate the grain from the chaff. To do this, she had to pound the millet in a mortar, then use a calabash and a big basket to perform the actual separation. After filling up the calabash with the pounded millet, she would hold a basket in her other hand and gradually pour the pounded millet into it. Before the millet reached the basket, the wind would blow the chaff away from the grains. Only grain would fall into the basket.

Grandfather told me he had heard a rooster say to a hen, "Go over to her blind side and jump into the basket on the ground. When she notices you, beat your wings and kick hard. Do not leave until you're sure the basket is overturned and the millet is on the ground. Don't worry, she won't kill you. Women are harmless."

No sooner had Grandfather translated this than I heard the woman get into a fight with one of the hens. The hen had jumped into the basket that contained the sorted millet. The woman was yelling and beating the hen. The hen was kicking everywhere in the basket as if she could not jump out. The fight ended when the basket was upside down and its contents on the ground, uncollectible.

The entire flock moved a few meters back and became silent. The woman swore and muttered while the poultry waited. Then she picked up her equipment and disappeared into her compound. Grandfather repressed a laugh as the chickens moved in for a feast.

After his death I missed my grandfather immensely: his life had been so much a part of mine. I remembered his story as I watched the chickens near the clay pot eat the millet cake. Soon they were making so much havoc that I knew Father would come out if I didn't do something. I stood up, grabbed a stick, and went to war against them, knocking them at random. Yelling and cackling, they ran away from the pot and out into the open air. Then I went in search of the goats. I knew they were in Mother's zangala, looking for her condiments. But because the zangala was dark, it would take a while for my eyes to adjust.

As I stood there in the compound wondering what to do next, Father's door opened and he and the human ghost came out. Father Maillot stretched out his hands once more and walked toward me. But this time he did not scare me. I avoided him by running over to my father and sticking close to him. Father Maillot stared at me with a pair of eyes that looked like fire in the night, and I felt a chill on my back. Then he spoke to my father in such bad Dagara that I failed to understand anything.

My father, however, seemed to have understood. He said, "I don't know. But if that is the will of God, I hope this time his will doesn't mean death."

Father Maillot barked out a laugh that stopped so suddenly that I wondered if he really meant to laugh. He shook hands with Father and walked out of the compound without looking back.

Father stared at me for a while, then mumbled something and said, "Go play outside, and keep the gate closed."

I walked outside the compound. It was hot. I sat under the tiny nim-tree on a piece of wood facing the Puré River. My mind was smoking with thought. What was my father's relationship with this man? Why was Father Maillot so happy? Because of him so many people had died in this family. Could he have killed Grandfather too? I was too young to know how to answer these questions, but my instincts told me that something serious had been decided.

▲　　▼　　▲

After Father Maillot and the two medicine men came to call, life gradually began to return to the compound. People began to speak about a forthcoming ceremony. I was too young to really understand the details, but I knew it was somehow related to Grandfather, Father, and the entire Biri-for clan. All around me preparations were in progress. Dry germinated millet was brought to the grinding stations that were built in every one of the women's compounds. And every afternoon women were busy at their grinding mills, pounding the red millet grain necessary for the preparation of beer. Millet beer has always been a part of major rituals. Our rituals are long, and one gets thirsty.

The job was demanding in time and energy. A basketful of millet required all afternoon to grind into flour. Although my mother was among the grinders, I could never figure out whether she liked the job or not. If a job needed to be done, Mother always did it, whether she enjoyed it or not. She confronted every duty as if determined to get rid of it in the most efficient way possible.

The grinding was a case in point, for her efficiency was beautiful to watch. Moving rhythmically, her arms drove the smaller piece of granite back and forth over the surface of the grinding mill. At every third stroke, her right hand would release the stone and push a small quantity of unmilled grain forward. Then, with increased energy, she would push the small piece of granite over the larger surface all the way to the ditch and back. Her flat breasts pounded against her chest with each forward and backward movement of her slightly arched body.

Each afternoon, during the preparation for the ceremony, the compound was full of songs. In order to combat the monotony of the labor, the women would sing genealogy songs, which were long enough to last the six hours it took to grind a bucket of millet.

Mother's grinding songs were now sad, for every woman in the village knows that if her husband becomes a leader, she must dedicate her life to helping him fulfill his obligations to the community. To be a leader, or the helpmate of a leader, you have to first die as a person, and Mother was mourning for her approaching death as just a simple village woman.

Unlike the other women, Mother did not sing genealogy songs. Instead, her trembling voice spoke the litany of the orphan sisters:

> *Heartless ghosts of the ancestors,*
> *They cut the breath of almost*
> *Every flesh in that house.*
> *A mother, a father, and two daughters*
> *Were left altogether.*
> *And the ghosts thirsted for more blood,*
> *And the ghosts came and cut the breath*
> *Of the mother and the father.*
> *Only the two lonely daughters remained.*
> *Oh, the wrath of Tingan!*
> *Hunger liked to play with them.*
> *Fear of death lingered in them.*
> *To the tribe they were accursed.*
> *And the sun set, and the sun rose;*
> *Dry and rainy seasons on the row.*
> *No clay pot warm with food*
> *Ever went their way.*
> *And the daughters cried*
> *And marched to their parents' single grave;*

"Father, Mother," they sang. "Wake up!
Our bellies hurt."

As Mother sang the first few stanzas, sweat popped out on her face and her bare back. Each stanza was punctuated by heavy breathing. She seemed to commune with the intensity of work with her litanies, her arms pounding harder and harder on the grains. Each movement shook her body as it leapt forward and backward.

After a few hours she ran out of verses. Without transition, she improvised additional ones. I wondered how she could combine such heavy work with such creativity. But it seemed as if she drew her power from the strenuous labor. Without her improvisational singing, she might not have been able to sustain this monotonous work from noontime till dusk.

When the last few grains were squashed and turned into white flour, she stopped singing and remained in her position for a while as if suspended. Then, slowly she straightened up, breathing heavily, and with a calabash began collecting the flour into a basket.

▲   ▼   ▲

Father's consecration ceremony took place about two months after Grandfather's funeral. It was harvesttime and the rain had ceased. The dry season had begun. Every morning the sun, unperturbed by the vanished clouds, rose triumphantly as if convinced that it would reign for the next six months.

Early that morning people started coming to the Birifor compound by groups. The crowd thickened rapidly as the sun rose higher. Something unusual was going to happen.

Apparently the two Baomale who had visited Father the previous week had been busy with him in the medicine room since before dawn. I had heard their voices in the wee hours of the morning when I had woken up to go to the bathroom. When I went back to bed I could not get to sleep. I knew this was a big day for the compound. I heard noises in the poultry room. Somebody was trying to catch a sleeping chicken and had provoked an uproar. The rooster that was caught yelled his head off.

That got me out of bed. I did not want to miss anything. I looked out my doorway and saw Father standing in the middle of the compound with the rooster. When I walked over to Father, I could see that he was examining the rooster in the fading light of the moon, lifting its wings and feathers. When he was finished, he walked into Grandfather's room and I followed him.

Inside, darkness prevailed and my father melted into it. I was convinced there was more than one person in the room, and these unseen presences made me all the more uncertain about what to do. Scared, I crept toward the mud elevation of Grandfather's bed by thinking its shape into place.

No sooner had I walked a few steps than I bumped hard against a clay pot and fell headlong onto someone who was not my father. The man's boubou smelled unfamiliar. He cleared his throat and grabbed me. As I wrestled to get free, he tightened his grip. I thought about biting him, but gave up and remained still. "Where do you think you're going?" he asked.

I recognized the dwarf's voice. His sticky hands released me and I relaxed.

"Be careful when you walk around in the dark," he said in a friendly manner.

Another person noisily cleared his throat and said, "How many adults know how to travel without light?"

The voice was very close, yet I could not see its owner. The dwarf still held me loosely, not replying.

Then my father spoke. "Come this way, Mado." He grabbed my arm and pulled me toward him. I sat down next to him on Grandfather's bed.

The dwarf began a prayer that lasted forever. He spoke very fast. The speech was punctuated here and there by spitting, coughing, and growling. Grandfather's name kept coming up over and over. I could also hear the regular occurrence of the refrain *k'a suo mwan kur, k'a kur mwan suo,* meaning, "so that iron can cut iron." The man was obviously conjuring up the world of the ancestors for protection against evil forces. Every time higher forces are invoked to intervene against other higher forces, elders use these terms. Meanwhile the other medicine man was repeatedly shaking a *kontonbgele,* the bell that calls the spirits, and a *kuor,* a ritual drum. The cacophony was hallucinatory.

Images crept into my mind. I saw Grandfather on his deathbed, speaking to me. But this time he was very young, almost a teenager. He looked radiant and he floated in a ring of green, red, and yellow light. His lips were moving as if he were saying something, but I could not hear anything. When he vanished, I realized that the infernal cacophony had ceased.

Just then the rooster crowed. The dwarf asked for him and my father handed him over. Some timid light began to filter into the room with the sunrise. I could now see the white rooster and part of the dwarf. He was seated on the floor, his legs crossed, facing the statue of *Bèru,* the god of the compound. In one hand the dwarf held a sacrificial knife and in the other he held the rooster by the wings. He lifted the rooster's head and bent his neck back. While his big thumb held the rooster's head tightly against the wing, he slashed the rooster's throat.

A stream of blood dashed out and hit the wall behind the statue of Bèru. The dwarf lowered the bird's neck and directed the stream onto the statue. "Drink," he murmured. Many Dagara rituals are private, attended only by medicine men, but ceremonies involving sacrifices are open to anyone, including children. Children get used to sacrifices very quickly and even look forward to them because they get to eat meat, a rather rare food in the village.

The dwarf put the knife away, pulled out a few feathers from the rooster's tail, and threw them against the statue of Bèru. Then he dropped the rooster near the entrance to the room. The rooster stood up and tried to walk away as if he had been through a mere inspection, but he soon realized that something was wrong. He staggered forward and backward, then sat, facing the door. Each one of his movements was accompanied by an "*ooon*"—the Dagara sound of acquiescence—from the dwarf.

Watching a rooster sitting on its backside is funny. He seemed to be thinking about something, but he quickly gave it up and tried one more time to walk away. This second attempt was as unsuccessful as the first. So he lay down, then suddenly got up and dashed out toward the yard with a shriek of surprise—a rooster can shriek even with his throat slashed. He landed heavily on the ground and took off one more time. The dwarf acknowledged each effort with an "*a baa*" of satisfaction.

The rooster landed on his back and spread his wings, legs frantically pedaling in the air. If it died belly up, it would mean the ritual was good. Finally, the rooster died on its back. Its ghost was accepted—its relatively lengthy death had constituted the proper response to the elders' invocational prayer.

The sun had risen and the compound was filling up with joyous people, each one holding a calabash full of foaming millet beer.

Father gave the rooster away to a man I did not recognize. Then, without a word, unmindful of the greetings that poured from every direction, Father walked back into Grandfather's room.

A man called out to me, "*M'bara,** come take a drink!" He was so tall I had to bend my neck back to see his face, most of which was hidden by the smoky air. All I could really see of it were his two shiny and mobile eyes. The man knelt down to my height and directed a calabash of beer toward my mouth. The more I drank of the sweet, biting, red liquid, the more I wanted to drink. Unable to breathe and drink at the same time, I didn't know whether I should stop to catch my breath or continue till I had enough of this sweet stuff. Noticing my predicament, he said, "This calabash isn't going anywhere. You can pause and breathe if you intend to drink more."

On the verge of passing out from lack of oxygen, I stopped drinking. The man stood up and waited while I caught my breath.

*An affection term meaning "my dog."

"Ready for another round?" he asked.

I bent back my neck and saw a row of bright teeth smiling down at me. Their hilarity was frightening. I said, "No," and went to the fireplace, where I stretched out on the floor and blacked out.

When I woke it was dusk and I was lying on Father's bed. I ran out into the yard. The crowd was gone. Only a few people remained, still drinking, Father seated in the middle of them. When he saw me he said, "Do you feel hungry, drunkard? Go to your mother. You missed it all."

"Why? Where was he all day long?" asked a young man from the compound next door.

"A member of the Dabiré clan managed to get him drunk," Father said, smiling.

"So he saw nothing. To choose a day like this to sleep . . . you must be sleeping your last," the young man commented.

There were a few women in Mother's zangala, some singing quietly, others speaking about the day, and a few sitting silently. Each one held a calabash of beer in her hands.

Mother brought me some food, a cold millet cake with some chicken and spinach sauce. I ate without paying much attention to how the food tasted. I was starving.

The next morning, early, Father disappeared into the bush with Mother. This was unusual, since neither of them ever went into the bush together. Because Father did not take his bicycle with him, I knew that they were going to conduct some business with the spirits and the ancestors before going to the farm. As she left, Mother asked my sister to meet her later at the farm for the collection of dry wood. Left alone to guard the compound, I went outside where the other children were playing and joined in their game.

From far off came the sound of an engine. Although the millet was too tall for anybody to see what kind of vehicle it was or where it was heading, it drew everyone's attention. As the sound approached, we waited breathless and speechless. We knew it was a white man coming to the house. The idea of having to face a white man caused panic. Who among all of us kids would dare to stand his or her ground in the presence of one of those frightening ghosts? Kids began to disappear rapidly into the safety of the millet field.

I waited, thinking it might be Father Maillot coming to see my father, but as the roaring became deafening I too took to my heels. The thought of being lifted up into the air toward that bushy face again was unbearable. I ran toward the house as fast as I could, trying to think of a good hiding place. Father's quarter was closed, so I could not get in there. Mother's zangala was open, but it was large and there was too much light in there. I would surely be found. The vehicle stopped right outside the compound and roared like a mad dog. Out of time, I ran into Mother's zangala and hid behind one of the huge clay pots.

The engine stopped and I could hear footsteps in the yard. I held my breath as the intruder walked toward Father's quarter, shook the door violently, and shouted, "Elie, Elie—where are you?" As if disappointed, he walked into the zangala. I was frozen with terror. As if all the dogs of misfortune had chosen me that day, an irresistible need to cough took hold of me. Though I vainly tried to repress it, I coughed. Father Maillot heard me. Without a word he grabbed me from behind the huge clay jar and lifted me into the air. I opened my mouth to yell, but nothing came out. But when my head bumped against the wood of the ceiling, the pain helped, and I cried out.

Father Maillot did not seem to notice anything. Still holding me, he walked out into the compound yard and stared at me for a while before speaking. "Where is your dad?" he asked. His Dagara had not improved, but I understood him, probably because I heard the word "dad." He talked some more, but this time I understood nothing.

After he finished speaking he put me down on the ground and dragged me by the arm out of the compound and over to his enormous motorcycle. Mounting it, he placed me on the fuel tank in front of him, then started the engine, which roared like a lion caught in a trap. Paralyzed by terror, I remained still. The BMW groaned and coughed, then shot like an arrow in the direction it had come from.

CHAPTER 5

IN THE WHITE MAN'S WORLD

 The presbytery where Father Maillot took me was one of the few modern buildings in the whole county. Small but stout, it seemed built to challenge the environment, especially the periodic hurricanes that destroyed many other structures. The walls stood high and straight, their red bricks smartly arranged and held together by concrete. The interior was attractive. Unlike our compound, whose floor was made with cow dung and was soft to the foot, the house of the priest was hard inside and out.

Father Maillot's room was like nothing I had ever seen before. Instead of a mud elevation for a bed and a burlap sack for a pillow, he had a four-legged platform about two feet tall, four feet wide, and nearly six feet long, so soft-looking it seemed as if its very purpose was to generate sleep. All of it was white, so white it was intimidating to look at. Surrounding the bed on all sides was a misty, transparent veil. I was to learn very soon that it was a protective device against mosquitos.

I began to think that my rough journey to the hill was not so bad, since I was learning so many new things. It would even be great fun to tell Mother about them when Father Maillot took me home. Poor Mother! If I had only known that I was not going to see her again for a long, long time, I would have taken the opportunity right then to run away.

My introduction to a Western house and a Western bed was the beginning of an end. Grandfather's prophecy had begun, and with it my childhood was coming to an end. Never again would I hear the melancholy songs of Mother at work, the fairy tales of Father at dusk, and the songs and dances of the Birifor compound.

▲ ▼ ▲

The mission hill was only five or six miles away from my parents' house, yet it was forbidden to go home. Father Maillot's orders were enforced by the catechists and the workers who lived on the mission hill. No contact was supposed to take place between us and anybody who was not part of Father Maillot's crew. There were about ten other boys at the mission, most of whom had preceded me to Father Maillot's establishment, and most of whom had been kidnapped as I had. Slatin was from my village. He was taller and stronger than me, and he became my good friend. Father Maillot had driven him up the hill a week earlier. Daniel was also from our village, but he was so quiet no one could get anything out of him. The rest of the boys came from six different villages. Uruber and Kritor came from a village called Maber. They arrived one night after dinner, looking like they had been wakened in their sleep. Gartien and Proper said they were from the faraway village of Pontié. Marcellin was born in Dasara, a village east of Dano. Betin came from Sori, a village whose people are renowned for their hunting prowess. Matin was from Guibal. He said his father left him at the mission hill and never came back. The last boy I met was Cloter from Bolem, who arrived a few days after me.

As the days passed, I began to be afraid. I longed to go home. I longed to speak to my mother. I longed to be away, far away from the home of this man. Mantié told us about some other kids, adolescents, who had been at the mission school for a long time, but now were gone. They had been sent, not back to their respective villages, but to a so-called seminary far away somewhere in the jungle.

My life at the mission was much different from the relaxed, freewheeling life I had enjoyed as a child in our compound. Here, every moment of the day was planned, with little time off for fun. Our day began at around seven, when we were taken by the catechist to a well, where we washed our faces in a bucket of water. Then he took us to the church, where Father Maillot recited the mass. It was all most of us could do to stay awake during the thirty or forty minutes this mass took. Then we finally got to eat our breakfast. The food was served in a large container, which we ate from with our fingers in enforced silence. The next two or three hours were spent in class. Then we had to go work on the mission farm, pulling out weeds until lunchtime. After lunch we had singing, followed by two hours of religious instruction, followed by a one-hour French class. Late in the afternoon, we were brought to the sacristy of the church for a little prayer. Dinner was taken the same way as lunch and breakfast. Our nightly entertainment consisted of more songs and review of the things we had been taught during the day. By 8 p.m. we were in bed. The only variations in our schedule were the occasional replacement of farming and gardening with physical education, which consisted of running around. I liked none of this.

The first time I got the chance to ask Father Maillot why he had taken me away from my family, he locked me in a room with concrete walls and a metal door and walked away, speaking in a foreign language. His mood had become arrogant and intimidating, but I did not care. I wanted to go home. I banged on the door so hard and so long that in the end someone opened it. It was a catechist and behind him was Father Maillot. The catechist had a whip in his hand. He spoke fluent Dagara, and when he ordered me to bend over, he called me Patrice. This was the first time someone had directly referred to me by my Catholic name. I had heard that name spoken each time Father Maillot came to the compound to see my father, but I did not know they had been talking about me. Since that was not my name, I refused to respond to it or to bend over. The catechist began to lash out at me. I could see Father Maillot smiling broadly and I screamed insults at him, but they were diluted by pain. This was the first time anyone had ever hit me so hard. The pain of the first blow was so bad that I didn't even notice the many other times the whip struck my body. Very soon I doubled over, then lay flat on the floor. My nerves were so tightly strung I could not produce a sound. I realized I was suffocating and I felt as if I were going to die. All I could hear was the rhythmic sound of the whip landing on my back, and then I felt an irresistible desire to sleep. In my dream I saw an old familiar man whose name I could not remember. When he poured water on me, it soothed me.

When I woke up it was pitch dark. I knew the man I had dreamed about was Grandfather. I tried to move, but my body was on fire and I was very thirsty. Beginning to cry again, I kept calling for my mother to bring me some water. Although my misery and the reason for my beating were incomprehensible to me, what was happening was all too real. The door opened and the catechist came in and ordered me to shut up. To this day I remember him telling me that he was my mother now, and that I should never call for her again. In my confusion the gentleness in his voice even sounded like my mother. It would be years before I understood that tenderness is the weapon used by the torturer to win over his victim. For me, the world ended that night.

When I woke up in the morning, I was lying in the dispensary on my belly, covered with bandages. I didn't dare turn over. The simple thought of doing so brought me tremendous pain. A stranger held some water to my lips and I drank profusely. As my mind returned to me, I wanted to talk, but I was too weak to say anything. How many days I was kept there and treated for the wounds I sustained, I never knew. But it taught me my first lesson: to stop being innocent. There were quite a few kids like me in this ill-fated place, so I felt I was not alone.

When I met Father Maillot after my recovery, I was trembling with fear. He, however, had not changed. He smiled as usual and even handed me a piece of sugar. But I saw him as such a monster that I felt I was better off just doing what he told me to do rather than asking him any more questions about my fate. My barely healed wounds were powerful evidence that this man would have things his way no matter what, nor was I the only boy who had been beaten. There was not one of us who did not bear the scars of Father Maillot's rage. My life had become so absurd anyway that I felt as if I were in a bad dream that I would wake up from some day if only I could stay with it. Whether some unknown force had put the thought of hope into my mind, I never knew. Meanwhile, I became submissive, though that meant losing all my enthusiasm and spontaneity. In my dream world an impossible drama was unfolding. Reflecting on this event twenty years later with Mantié, who had long ago retired, I realized that my instincts had been correct.

On the mission hill, time stopped being my friend and became instead an overwhelming force. I could no longer tell how fast or how slow it moved. Something in me had stopped working. A year could have gone by, and I would not have known unless someone had told me. Our days were lived in fear, fear of being beaten for the things we did or the things we neglected to do. None of us knew what was really going on or what was expected of us. We were sheep, going whichever direction the shepherd ordered us to go. Over and over we asked ourselves the same questions. Why were we here? Why couldn't we go home? Why were we being taught French and ordered to go to mass every morning—except on Sundays, when we were hidden from the Christianized villagers who came to worship. Our own Sunday service began very early in the presbytery. It was a quick mass and we did not participate in the communion.

One of the classes that has stayed most clearly in my mind was the French class taught by a teacher named Mantié—the local name for Matthew. Every morning Mantié would flog us to inject a few letters of the alphabet into our recalcitrant brains. Ruthless, he held us under his tyrannic supervision from breakfast till noontime, using every trick he knew to make us learn. His task was not only to turn us into men of letters, but also to familiarize us with French civilization. On the mission hill, my Dagara language eroded gradually as French painfully took its place.

I still remember my first class. Mantié came to class with a textbook that he held like a sacred artifact. He also brought a huge stick and a broken engine belt. He started out by drawing some strange signs on a large dark surface on the wall. I counted twenty-six of them.

Then he began sullenly, "To know the ways of the white man, you must be an artist. Just as our carvers do with wood, you must be able to carve speech, just as I did, for this is speech made flesh. These signs won't talk until I make them talk. Today, I will disclose to you the secret of the first six carvings. Tomorrow I will tell you more. By the end of the week, you will have to know all of them. Then I will show you what they do when they get mixed up together.

"Now, let us begin. I obtain the first sign by moving my hand upward with this white thing called chalk, then downward. Finally I link the two pieces of wood together . . ." While speaking, Mantié was writing the letter A slowly in its majestic capital form.

"See, it looks like the roof of a hut. You call this Aaaa. Repeat."

And we all went "Aaaaaaa."

"The next one is like a village child with a swollen belly. You carve a piece of wood straight up and give it a belly, then you call it Beee. Repeat."

And we went "Beeeeeeeeeee."

Mantié seemed satisfied. He looked like the head dancer who led the village dances, except that only his hands were dancing. He went on. "Good. The third sign is even simpler. It's like a ring with half of it missing. But the missing part must be to the right. The white man calls it Ceeee. Say it together."

We all said "Ceeeeeeeeeeee."

"You remember what we called the kid with a big belly?" Mantié was already reviewing. He pointed to the letter B. "What did we say it is?" Mantié pointed to me. I had forgotten what B was called. Being fingered all of a sudden like that did not help either. Petrified, my mind went blank. Mantié waited, but fear had blocked my memory. Then he put down his book and picked up a stick. "Maybe this will remind you."

As the stick landed on my head, my skull exploded with pain. I remember something about a belly. I said, "It's a belly."

"Like your big fat belly," retorted Mantié. The stick landed on my head once more as he spoke. Tears streamed out of my eyes. I could not stop them. Mantié pretended not to notice and turned to another student. "Slatin, what did we say this thing was?"

Slatin stood up, folded his arms and screamed, "Beeeeeeeeeeeee-eeeeee."

"Good brain. Good brain. Did you hear this, Patrice? What did Slatin say?"

I said between two sobs, "Slatin said, 'Beeeeeeee.'"

"Good. I'm sure your stupid brain has caught up with us now. Sit down."

"Now," continued Mantié, "if you look carefully, the belly of 'Beee' is looking toward the right side. When the same belly starts looking toward the left side, the white man calls it Deeeeee. Your turn."

We sang "Deeeeeeeeeeeeee" in unison.

"One more time."

And we repeated the same thing. Cloter asked, "What do all these carvings mean?"

Mantié seemed to have been taken by surprise. He looked up at the ceiling, then said, "This is not the time to learn meaning yet. When you know how to remember all of them, I will tell you what they do."

Another student stood up and said, "I know what they mean."

"Oh, really! Marcellin, you should be here teaching, then. But please, tell us what they mean."

"I don't know about Aaaaaaaaa. But it seems that Beeeee, Ceeeee, and and Deeeee are Dagara. Beeeeee means cooked; Ceeeee means to skin, and Deeeeee means to eat."

It all suddenly became clear in our minds that this is what these letters should mean. It was obvious. It was as if their very visibility had hidden their meaning. Now that Marcellin had thought of them in Dagara, they all made sense. They were alive. But the teacher did not like this translation. He grabbed his stick and called Marcellin to the platform next to the blackboard.

"I will teach you that this is not a Dagara class but a French class. Bend over with your butt toward your fellows."

Marcellin was shaking while he did so. The teacher pounded on his behind, then said, "You may go sit on it, though I know it burns."

It seemed as if Marcellin was making a monumental effort not to scream. His face tight with pain, he zigzagged back to his bench and sat. The teacher went on with the identification of the alphabet without paying any further notice to what had just happened.

My first day of foreign language class filled me with terror and curiosity. It happened two or three weeks after I arrived at the school. None of us knew exactly what Mantié was up to, but his stern face warned us of the seriousness of the work ahead. And then there was the stick and the strap. These learning aids forced an atmosphere of fervor and inevitability into us. The first session was so emotionally intense that we were not even able to comment on what we had learned. The ghosts of A's, B's, and C's kept flowing in our child minds. We did not want to forget, especially those of us who had experienced the teacher's stick.

In a few days we could all identify the alphabet easily. Memory works well when threatened with punishment, and the teacher's stick was its trigger. In a few weeks we were able to write all the letters of the alphabet. We were not in any hurry to know their meaning or to even attempt to speculate about it. But, somehow, knowing how to carve words or the components of words was captivating. I was able to think, for the moment, that young as I was, I knew something secret. Although holding the pencil was not easy, the capacity to carve visible speech was like an initiation into a secret practice. I cherished my performance because somehow I had the impression that these mysterious letters possessed the ability to say miraculous things if combined properly. I was like my grandfather, who knew how to communicate with the dead by using the hieroglyphics of gourds and water. For me, the silent reproduction of letters was enough. There was no need to assign meaning to them because then they would lose their power. Wasn't this the reason Father Maillot spoke the mass in Latin?

Pride and passion were associated with this manner of discovery of a language. Mantié, however, was still the terror of the class. He looked like an envoy with terrible news, both wanted and dreaded, and he could not tolerate mistakes. The atmosphere of terror created around every session was for him a sure way to avoid failure as an instructor. On the one hand, he enjoyed our progress, but on the other hand he seemed to be disappointed in the results we were producing. It seemed to me that he would rather see us forget, to provide him with a golden opportunity to utilize his stick on us. Beating and learning went together in his mind. And Father Maillot had officially granted him this dreadful right.

In less than half a year we had reached the point where we could manage basic reading. It appeared that as we moved more and more into French, the language was getting all the more complicated. Mantié liked it this complicated. During each session he could whip us at will. Sometimes when nobody could figure out a grammatical riddle, he would put us together by pairs and order us to slap each other's faces while he watched.

One day Slatin and I were assigned together. He and I had become quite close and it was hard to hit a friend. When Mantié noticed that we were not slapping each other hard enough, he came over to help. He held Slatin's head with his left hand and smacked him with the other. Disoriented by the shock, Slatin stumbled around in a circle.

When my turn came, I also laid my head against the palm of Mantié's hand. Then I closed my eyes and waited. All I remember was a loud noise like an explosion and then silence. When I awoke, I was in the dormitory with Mantié. He glared at me with his red eyes, said something I couldn't understand, and walked out of the dorm. I went back to sleep.

The first year on the mission hill was thus dominated by an apprenticeship to the language of Father Maillot. He was jubilant the first time I was able to say, *"Bonjour mon Père,"* to him and ordered everyone else in the class to greet him in French thereafter. I didn't consider Father Maillot my father, and had said this only because the teacher had told us to greet him that way. Actually, it was a total mystery to me why the priest was called "Father." He had no wife, nor did he seem to worry about having one. I decided that perhaps he needed us around so that *some* children would call him Father.

Religious colonialism tortures the soul. It creates an atmosphere of fear, uncertainty, and general suspicion. The worst thing is that it uses the local people to enforce itself. Our teachers were Black, from the tribe, yet they were our worst enemies. The question I often asked myself in later years, when I thought about how Black nationals are leading our country, is whether a person schooled in an atmosphere of such abuse can actually lead with compassion, justice, and wisdom. My experience was not uncommon. Today, Africa's leaders are mostly people who were educated in this manner. Is it surprising that there is so much instability in so many African countries?

▲　　　▼　　　▲

The one exception to the harsh rule on the mission hill was Zan, our religious instructor. His afternoon lessons were in striking contrast to Mantié's morning terrorism. Zan's task was to prepare us for communion. Though he could not read, he taught us out of his prodigious memory. We learned morning prayers in Dagara and evening prayers in Latin. Though Zan did not know what the prayers in Latin meant, it did not seem to matter much, for he would always make up a story to explain them.

Zan laughed when relating stories from the Bible. He used to tell us that when Mary became pregnant with Jesus, his father, Joseph, was surprised. Somebody had figured out a way to get Mary pregnant without his knowing. When Mary's belly started to protrude, this same person told her to tell her husband that God had done it in the only way he knew how, by an immaculate conception. Zan found everything funny. I wondered why he even stayed in the mission if everything was a joke to him. I never figured it out, but I was convinced that Zan was there with us for a very good reason.

This man was our last contact with our roots. He did not know how to be serious in the face of anything. He saw the whole world as a story, a funny story, and he thought that what you couldn't understand was not meant to be understood. Although Zan had translations for the prayers in Latin, he did not believe in them, so he would make some up. In this manner, he might have believed that he was preserving the arcane mystery and power of Latin. After all, when he was a boy, his Dagara elders had not provided translations when they conducted their rituals in "primal language."

There was one prayer he spent a long time teaching us. The prayer ran like this:

In mali touas domine comment do sipiri tu meo. *

Zan translated it as, "I want to follow Domine** once again to see if he will give me something to drink." Zan thought he could adapt this phrase to Dagara since the words sounded strangely like that language. He did not think that Father Maillot knew the meaning of the words anyway. But Zan often wondered who Domine might be. He told us it was probably one of Father Maillot's close friends. He himself knew somebody in his own village by that name, but he was sure that person could not possibly be a close friend of Father Maillot. So Zan concluded that Domine must be living somewhere across the sea.

Zan's teachings were a process of discovery both for him and his students. Catechism was a series of questions and answers. Zan would ask the question, then provide the answer along with a funny comment before asking us to repeat after him. One of the catechism questions was "Who created man?" The answer Zan gave was "God created man along with everything else." But Zan always added that God created drinks too, not for Father Maillot only, but for everybody, and that meant for him too. Zan was always complaining that Father Maillot drank all the holy wine on the grounds so there was not enough for everybody.

Although I enjoyed Zan's teaching much better than Mantié's, I learned very little from him about the Bible till I was able to read it myself. Once I learned to read, it became a wonderful escape. Books were a world into which we were authorized to escape—though we always had to come back to reality. In the meantime I had become accustomed to a life without my real parents, especially because I was able to speak a little French after the first year in the mission hill. I was now finding it difficult to remember how to speak Dagara.

It took a man like Mantié to make me fluent in French. His imagination for finding insidious ways to make us learn had no bounds. After Father Maillot heard us greet him in French, he declared that speaking Dagara at school was now a sin, so Mantié declared Dagara illegal within the precinct of the mission. To enforce this new law he found a goat skull and tied a rope to it so that it could be hung around the neck of a trans-

---

*In manus tuas, domine, commendo spiritum meum.

**Dagara way of calling somebody whose name is Dominique.

gressor. He called it the Symbol. Whoever was found guilty of uttering a word in Dagara was to wear this ugly skull around his neck until the next pupil was caught sinning.

To liberate himself, the sinner had to listen for a misused word—speaking poor French also counted as a sin—or for a Dagara's word that had slipped into a French sentence. When someone erred, the symbol wearer would declare him a sinner, and with the help of his comrades would transfer the skull.

One night in the dormitory we were talking about the way our lives had changed since we came to the mission hill. Slatin said he did not even remember his real traditional name anymore, though he wished he would be called by this name once in a while because it would help him recall his home. I found his forgetfulness outrageous and I said, "I can't imagine that I would ever forget that my Dagara name is Malidoma."

The current unfortunate bearer of the Symbol, Cloter, promptly declared me a sinner because I had spoken Dagara by uttering my traditional name. Everybody agreed with him because "Malidoma" is primarily a Dagara word before being somebody's name. So, in the middle of the night, they hung the hideous object around my neck. That was the first time I experienced the horror of living with the Symbol. The rope was itchy and too short and the skull itself had a terrible odor because it was still in the final stages of decomposition. It was very hard for me to get to sleep.

The skull had other applications beyond the simple fear it produced. It was a memory enhancer. The wearer of the Symbol became a spy, a listener and observer. The Symbol functioned like an extension of Mantié, who had invented it to make sure that we didn't limit our apprenticeship to our few daily sessions with him. So we learned and studied hard because we did not want to wear the Symbol. Yet it was always with us—a terrible presence. Somebody always had to wear it, and it could not switch necks until one of us spoke Dagara by mistake.

So our intellectual life was ruled by the Symbol and by Mantié. And we learned fast; understanding did not matter: the Symbol did not give us time for that.

Years later, when I was a student in the seminary, I would think back on the Symbol and realize that human ingenuity is boundless in times of threat. There is no limit to productivity in those times. He who wore the Symbol was asked to be more creative than the rest. He had to play the devil's advocate and also the trickster. He had to engage all of us in conversation, waiting for one of us to slip.

Life presents us with an infinite number of choices. Discipline is perhaps a way of narrowing them down. But to learn to limit one's choices, one must first have a specific goal. When I was at the mission, I never knew what my goal was supposed to be. My life had been taken away from me because during the years I was there, this institution assumed that its goal was my goal. The result was, of course, the slow death of my identity and the understanding that I was in exile from everything I had held dear.

I would like to tell you more details of my years at the mission hill, but for the most part, it was a child's dream journey. Most of its episodes have been buried deep within my unconscious mind and cannot be remembered. As an adult, I have learned that this state of mind is not uncommon for children raised without parents by caretakers who really do not love them. The memories of these children become undependable, flat and one-dimensional, like paper.

I began to wake up from the dream around the age of twelve, when Father Maillot decided that we were old enough to be sent to the seminary at Nansi. I remember the night I arrived there by truck with the dozen other graduates of the mission school. My first impression was of a harsh brightness caused by the rows of floodlights that lined the road that led to the seminary. The driver of the truck stopped at the main building, a tall, brightly illuminated brick house. A priest came out and spoke with the driver, then we were taken into the guest quarters—an immense dormitory lined with metal beds that seemed to go on indefinitely. Some were occupied by sleeping bodies, others were empty. The priest assigned beds and ordered us to go to sleep immediately.

My bed faced the entrance door. There was a straw mat on it and a blanket. I had never seen anything like it before nor have I since. It was made of four steel bars, about three inches in width and five feet in length. I put my bag underneath the bed and stretched out on it. The straw mat was not firm enough to keep me from falling between the bars, and, with a loud cracking noise, I found myself wedged between two of them. Overcome by exhaustion, I went to sleep without trying to dislodge myself.

Before we left the mission hill, Father Maillot told us that our years there had provided us with an adequate preparation for the next step in the journey toward encountering Christ. How strange it sounded to be meeting Christ through the agency of literacy! The day the truck came to pick us up, the Father was so happy and so proud of us all that he couldn't stop smiling. A crowd had gathered, some out of curiosity because they had never seen a truck, others because this was a distraction from their heavy work.

My longing for my family never stopped while I lived at the mission hill, even though I could not remember when I had seen my parents for the last time. For some strange reason the memory of Grandfather was even more vivid than that of my parents. I could feel him around me in ways I cannot explain. This feeling was not there when I thought about my mother and my father. As I took the 120-mile journey to the seminary, every mile seemed to deepen my separation from them.

CHAPTER 6

LIFE BEGINS AT NANSI

 The boarding school was a fortress—a state within a state, bursting out of nowhere, a garden of order within the chaos of the African jungle. Rows of houses more beautiful even than Father Maillot's mission house were spread out among trees, gardens, and flowered pathways. Their stone and concrete walls painted bright glittering white shocked the eye and intimidated the newcomer. They were all covered with tin roofs and most of them had wooden ceilings. Next to the teachers' residence, the church was the tallest. The chapel was built of cement bricks and steel. Its high ceiling was a complex arabesque of steel on top of which was laid a metallic cover that resonated loudly when it rained. Then came the classrooms and the dormitories, each of which contained over a hundred of the Spartan metal beds. Each classroom was big enough for eighty students, although a good hundred were sometimes stuck in there during morning classes. In all, the institution contained well over five hundred children, aged twelve to twenty-one.

This titanic religious establishment was the dream-come-true of the missionary crusade that had followed imperialism into the continent of Africa. The kids came from everywhere in French West Africa: Mali, Niger, Togo, the Ivory Coast, and Benin. Some were brought there fresh from baptism after a few years of parochial brainwashing. Others, schooled privately as the protégés of white missionaries, arrived there still longing for their white father.

There were two sections to this religious campus. We called them divisions. The First Division, nicknamed Roman Campus, was occupied by about three hundred kids from twelve to sixteen. It consisted of an immense classroom building, two dormitories, and a spiritual lecture hall. The lecture hall was where we met every evening at 7 to hear a priest lecture on a religious subject, usually the life of some European saint whose anniversary fell on that day. Some student usually bore the same name as the saint, in which case it was that person's birthday too. We did not have formal birthdays. Since being baptized meant being reborn a lot cleaner— which is why our traditional name was replaced by a new and better Christian name—the anniversary of that saint was also the birthday of the student who had borrowed his name.

Evening lectures were tedious: to listen to God on an empty stomach is like refraining from laughter at the grimaces of a monkey. Thanks to the one freedom we had—to daydream—it was possible to endure the lecture. If for the most part we looked attentive, the priest did not care very much what we did as long as there was silence.

There were three classrooms in the school building. The first, the *septième*, was for the newly arrived seminarians who had to be taught everything from composition and geography to mathematics and science. French was the language that carried all this baggage. The second classroom, the *sixième*, was reserved for those who had survived their first year in this institution. The third classroom housed the *cinquième*, those preparing to enter the upper division, which the students called the Greek Campus. The same subjects were taught to everybody, but according to their appropriate levels.

The upper division had five classrooms instead of three and was housed in two dormitory buildings similar in size to those of the lower division. Their classroom building was adjacent to ours. The refectory stood alone, away from the dorm and the school. Divided into two sections, it belonged to both divisions.

The upper-division boys, the Greeks, did not like to mix with the Romans, nor were the two groups authorized to mix outside of school hours. The Greeks had their own spiritual lecture hall situated next to their classroom building, and an extra structure called the Mechanics Building where all kinds of skilled activities—sewing and weaving, woodworking, metalworking, and indoor athletics—took place every Thursday and Sunday afternoon. The higher division ranged from one to two hundred teenagers and students in their early twenties. In front of the classroom building was the basketball court, the athletic field, and the soccer field. There was no library. Each teacher had a sizable collection of books, sufficient for the specific intellectual and spiritual needs of the subject he taught. Each teacher taught one subject. All books were in French. Second-language training included English even though there was no book about it. Latin was a requirement, but it too had no book. There was no German or any other European language taught. The students were encouraged to borrow books from the teacher.

One thing was certain: this coming together of all of us—not just strangers from the same tribe but strangers from many different tribal communities—demonstrated the possibility of unity amid tribal diversity. Suddenly French became useful far beyond its power to introduce us to literacy. It became a means of linking us to each other. It was our only bond within the heterogeneous community assembled by the Jesuits. There was no need to enforce the speaking of French here or to ban the use of local languages. Most of us had none we could remember, and besides, who would understand them? Because my Dagara friends from the mission school were scattered throughout the mass of kids in the seminary, it was not easy for us to stick together.

The seminary at Nansi had appropriated the name and the land of a nearby village occupied by a tribe whose members watched the whole maneuver astonished and speechless, horrified at being politely asked to quit their own land. But in the eyes of the Jesuits, how could such a theft be considered a crime? Who would dare to question the divine need for land? The students had no contact with the villagers. Only the priests who ran the seminary did, and that took the form of a church in the village.

Within the institution, the smell of France and its impressive order prevailed menacingly yet majestically amid the stubborn surviving perfume of the wild. No one could survive in an institution like this unless he developed the habit of removing his mind from the "vocation" that had been imposed upon him. The steel structure of its very architecture spoke resolutely to each student about the might of the God the white man served. The seminary had ripped nature from its order and reordered it into concrete houses, into paths, lawns, flower gardens, canals, and roads— into a new beauty that man served assiduously because it was divine.

Outside of the institution's boundaries we could smell the unmediated perfume of the wild and glimpse the cold silent beauty of its mysterious order. We often went out on botanical field trips, identifying and studying an endless variety of plants. Way off in the distance, carefully separated from the boys, was the novitiate, a similar but smaller institution for girls, but it would be years before we enjoyed any contact with that place.

▲   ▼   ▲

"This is a day of miracle and wonder. A day when our Lord Jesus Christ has proven once again that his heroic death on the cross was not in vain.

"Dead because he wanted to save his children from perdition, he is now resurrected to prove that he meant what he did—that his suffering was a commitment: the Lord died with you in mind.

"Thus, you are Christ's chosen disciples, endowed with the vocation of the priesthood to rescue, in the manner of the apostles, the erring souls of your brothers and sisters, and to return them to the divine path."

It was a hot Easter day in the seminary of Nansi. The mass was more solemn than usual because Easter marks a peak time in the calendar—sometimes on the same level as Christmas, but sometimes considered higher because birth is common and resurrection is not. Above all, it was the end of Lent, which for most of us was a period of gastronomic deprivation. During Lent, the school was vegetarian, and for a lot of us, this was dreadful. Why eat grass because God was in pain and needed us to support him by some form of deprivation?

Father Superior was presiding over the mass, which was concelebrated by the entire professional corps, all Jesuits. Dressed in a majestic chasuble with crosses at front and back, Father Superior displayed a dramatic flair in all his movements, as if he himself were the center of the event and the attendant crowd. His concelebrants looked dedicated too. Each one knew his role so well that he performed it almost mechanically.

For the past ten years or so, Father Superior had been the sole leader of the Nansi resurrection mass. As the director of this impressive institution, he always presided over the masses and often delivered the homily after the gospel was read by another colleague.

Ordinarily, Father Superior spoke about the meaning of the Christian holiday that was being celebrated. He often compared Christ's resurrection to Africa's awakening into Christ, and never missed an opportunity to glorify the Jesuit order for its splendid achievements in Black Africa. To him, every man and woman who was brought to the baptismal font was a resurrected being following the example of Christ and an example of the appropriateness of religious colonialism in Black Africa. But this day, for some reason, breaking his own rules, he decided to speak about our vocation.

"You are candidates within a very special discipleship in Christ's community. Not only have you been baptized in his name, but you will dedicate your lives to the service of his cause. This is important because our world is crumbling, torn apart by the work of Satan and his many followers throughout this land of God.

"Born sinners, your people grew in sin. They cultivated a fellowship that glorified in the practice of those very acts that every day kill our Lord Jesus Christ, who died precisely for these macabre sins.

"But do you know why these sinners still live? They still live because they are still given a chance—the chance to repent and to be saved. I suppose there is no need to say that every simple action you perform here in this holy place increases the chances of their salvation as well as bringing it closer to hand.

"The bulk of your task resides there among these disciples of evil who are every day blackened by the blood of satanism, stone worship, false beliefs, and attachments to a world structure devoid of sanctity. While these conditions still exist, you must not sleep until the light of resurrection is brought forth to them.

"This is the calling to which you must respond. This is the light you must intensify and keep alive every day. This is the good news you must bring out and disseminate to your people. As they suffocate in the steel grip of the devil's hand, only *you* can come to their rescue—because Christ was resurrected for you. This is your calling."

Father Superior had a way of making you feel sorry, anxious, and guilty. I wondered how I could possibly go tell my people to drop their age-old traditional habits of belief and be prepared to be saved because somebody had died for them without even telling them. It had been so long since I had left these people that I could barely remember how wicked their spiritual life supposedly was—what it was that they were doing wrong in the first place. And in any case, would they recognize me, wearing a white robe and a rosary, when and if I returned to them?

Though Nansi was sealed away from the outside world, many stories about the deeds of the colonials had slipped in. For example, in a nearby village missionaries had attempted to convert the people by using the symbol of Christ on the cross. One unfortunate man had taken the risk of objecting. "This man is not Black," he said. "He never came to any Black village. No one among his disciples was Black. So how could he have died for us, too? Are you trying to transfer the guilt of your ancestors upon us? Look—your ancestors killed somebody they should not have killed, then they found out that this man was a divine man. So they decided to share their regret with the rest of the world. Our ancestors never told us that you had committed such a crime against humanity. And if this man was a god, Mother Earth would have told us about it before you arrived here. Be clear about what you are saying."

It may or may not have been a coincidence that this man fell into the hands of the territorial army and nothing was ever heard of him again.

Was it a calling to have been grabbed by Father Maillot out of my parents' compound while they were away working, to have been driven to the mission on a BMW and to this seminary light-years away from home just so that I could go tell them later that they should believe in Christ?

These were the thoughts that were always with me after I came to Nansi Seminary.

▲   ▼   ▲

Between the higher division and the lower division buildings were the faculty buildings or, as we called them, the pantheon. Each of the two dozen Jesuit missionaries in charge of the school had a divine nickname. They all knew they had nicknames, but they pretended they did not. Father Superior was called Zeus, for his quick temper and love of punishment were legendary. Slim and tall in his white turtle-necked robe, he never smiled. Though some students claim that he did on rare occasions, I don't think he knew how. Zeus did not teach anything profane. He was a great, ofttimes bombastic and convoluted deliverer of homilies. His assistant, a white-haired World War II veteran, was called Scylla because his voice was so thin one could barely hear him. He sang well, although his voice was nasal. He was so emotional that he cried each time he spoke to us about the holy war waged against Nazi Germany—this was a favorite subject. He worked closely with the bursar, whom we nicknamed Hermes because he was gone all the time to run errands for the seminary. He was in charge of feeding us and did his job with dedication.

He was a close friend of another priest we named Bacchus. Bacchus was in a good mood only when under the influence. When it was his turn to say mass, he consecrated more wine than he should and drank it all. So each time he presided over the mass, he came out of it drunk and cheerful. Bacchus never got angry at anyone. He was dull and even-tempered, therefore not dangerous. This was not the case with Cerberus. Tall and heavily bearded, with terrifying eyes that rolled in their orbits, this priest from Holland was a friend of no one, including his colleagues. He barked instead of talking, yelled instead of singing, and changed color at the slightest shift of events. We called him Cerberus because he once caught a villager stealing flowers from a garden. He grabbed the poor sinner by the neck and almost shook him to death, like a dog with a rat. When he let him fall, you could not tell on which side of existence the poor lad was situated.

On the north-central side of the campus was the double-storied building where the professorial corps resided. At the heart of the campus, its steeple overlooking the entire institution, was the church. The tallest and newest building in the seminary, it was the place we went first after waking up and last before going to bed. The church was beautiful. Inside there was space for nearly a thousand people. It had a balcony too, but we never knew who sat there. The front pews were reserved for the people of the lower division, who sang alto and soprano. The back rows were for the higher division: the tenors and basses. Singing was a major part of life at Nansi, and we rehearsed in this building as well as prayed. Singing was good for the psyche. It established an independent relationship between us and God, and song carried our emotions more readily than the rote recitation of canonic prayers.

Meetings between the higher division and the lower division took place at the church every morning, and at the refectory, where we took our meals, every morning, noon, and evening. Our daily schedule ran like this:

5:30 a.m.	Wakeup
6:00 a.m.	Morning prayers
6:30 a.m.	Mass
7:30 a.m.	Gymnastics/athletics
8:00 a.m.	Breakfast
9:00 a.m.	First class
10:00 a.m.	Second class
11:00 a.m.	Third class
12:00 p.m.	Lunch hour
1:00 p.m.	Siesta/rest period
3:00 p.m.	Fourth class
4:00 p.m.	Manual work
5:00 p.m.	Study hour
6:00 p.m.	Spiritual lecture
6:30 p.m.	Evening prayers
7:00 p.m.	Dinner/recreation
8:30 p.m.	Study hour/higher division
	Vespers/lower division
8:45 p.m.	Bedtime/lower division
9:30 p.m.	Vespers/higher division
10:00 p.m.	Bedtime/higher division
10:30 p.m.	Lights out everywhere

At 5:30 a.m. one of the priests would come into the dorm, clap his hands, turn the lights on, and scream *"Benedicamus Domino!"* We were supposed to scream back: *Deo Gratias.* But most of the time we couldn't waken fast enough to respond immediately, so the priest would have to repeat his morning greeting until satisfied with the general response. Then he would walk down the aisle and pinch those whose sleep had survived the screaming ceremony. In the meantime those who were up grabbed their towels and went for a quick morning ablution. This was taken in a cement trough about sixty feet long. Two feet above the trough was a pipe. When the faucet was turned on, cold water poured out of holes punched into the

pipe. Our washing was done in silence, for silence was one of the most important rules in that divine realm. From wakeup till sports, free talking was forbidden. In the beginning it felt like the worst kind of rudeness to walk next to another person without saying a word. In the village such behavior would mean that a funeral had just ended. It was hard to keep your mouth shut for so long. But you got used to it fast. Anybody who talked would have his butt put to fire.

Speech does not have to be uttered out loud. I discovered that I could comply with the rule of silence by simply creating speech within myself in the form of a dialogue with an imaginary person. Topics were not lacking, for I could never stop thinking about what was going on back home. Trying to tap into the activities of my family opened up a vast field of mental speculation. These thoughts sometimes led to tremendous anger as I discovered that I was, after all, an abandoned person longing for a culture I no longer had.

But if my thoughts often led to sad and angry feelings, they also offered a cozy resting place to a mind that could not deal with the same bland diet every day. I learned the art of retreating within my thoughts quickly and well. By doing this, it was easy to eliminate the uncomfortable feeling of the presence of my walking partner, without impinging upon his space. Another aspect of silence is the opportunity it provides us to discipline our mouths, and to learn to attend to the still small voice from within. Consequently, if the seminary was quiet most of the time, for me at least this quiet was only external.

I learned to swim at Nansi. It was not an amusing experience. Though it was the appointed job of the higher division kids to teach the lower division the art of swimming, we were better off knowing how to ahead of time than being submitted to their ministrations. The lower division experienced the higher division as tough, even brutal. Ultimately, you had to be the protégé of one of them before you could ever find peace. So it was vital to become friends with somebody.

I was taught to swim by a student from the higher division who called himself Carib. As I stood on the shore of the river, watching him approach, my heart was pounding with fear and apprehension. He walked up to me and said, "Hi! Ready for the water baptism? . . . Better be. Ah! Ah!" He grabbed me in his arms and lifted me up into the air. I tried to resist his grip, but I was like a mouse between the paws of a cat. He did not even notice that I was fighting back. Carib walked to the edge of the water and jumped high into the air, still holding me in his arms like a pet. We shot into the middle of the water. All of a sudden I could not breathe. I opened my mouth and inhaled water. But Carib did not look like he intended to swim up to the surface. We stayed there at the bottom of the river, and I could see his globular eyes glaring at me while his grip tight-ened. Feeling like I was being crushed in a narrow cage, I tried every signal I knew in a supreme effort to communicate to Carib that I was drowning. Every breath was so liquid that I could feel the water rush into my belly. Carib only squeezed me tighter.

Finally, he swam up to the surface and left me on the shore, saying, "Enough for today. You were pretty good. I'll see you on Sunday."

Carib did not seem to notice that I was vomiting water. The experi-ence was so horrible I could not help crying. A sudden sense of insecurity and vulnerability produced the specter of death in me. My sufferings at Father Maillot's mission school seemed nothing in comparison to the swimming lessons. I finally stopped leaking water, but I continued to cry, sitting at the edge of the river with my feet in the water. My memory searched backward in time for a season of comfort that had not been avail-able anywhere since my separation from my native compound. The only emotions I could feel were anger and sadness, mixed with an inexpressible feeling of betrayal. My past contained nothing to feel joyful about except perhaps those faint memories of the sweetness that I felt beside my grand-father and my mother. They appeared briefly in the panorama of my mem-ory. I was struggling hard to produce a clean, lucid image of home from the dark negative of a four-year-old brain.

I tried to pray to God, but it was like praying to the very person who had caused my misfortune. When that failed to bring me a sense of relief, I tried hard to recall Grandfather's face and wished hard that his spirit would do the job if God would not. I kept thinking that God had too many peo-ple to take care of—too many who were more important in his eyes than I was. So I prayed instead to the spirit of Bakhye, thinking that at least he would hear me since he did not have so many people to worry about.

"Stop making a fool of yourself," someone said in the midst of my mourning and praying. I rubbed my eyes rapidly and took a look. The face was somewhat familiar. It was another kid, thirteen years old like me, and a little smaller in size. He had just come out of the water—as if he had gone in intentionally! Embarrassed, I stopped crying, but I could not help com-plaining, "But he almost killed me."

"Who? Carib? He didn't know. Everybody here will pretend they didn't know. I've been at the bottom of the river too. If you think your mom will come and take you away, you can keep on crying. But if you don't, you'd better keep an eye open and think for yourself."

"Who are you, anyway?" I asked.

"Antoine. My name is O. Antoine. And you?"

"Patrice, Patrice Somé. I come from—"

"Doesn't matter anymore. We're all here. Come on! Let's go back into the water, Patrice, and I'll teach you a couple of things. Otherwise next time you'll be a peeled banana by the time that Carib releases you."

I figured that if the two of us could not prevail against Carib, we could at least do him some damage. Although it was unlikely we would ever have the courage to attack him, the thought made me feel better. I had found a friend, and that evening we sat at the same table together. We did not say very much to each other, but friendship does not need words. It often speaks louder in silence.

As I grew older, I discovered that life in a boarding school, where discipline is at its most rigorous, triggered a psychological reaction that forced students under this kind of dispensation to invent new ways of existing as a community. Older students looked at young newcomers as girls and possible sexual partners. Their friendliness was stimulated by an attraction that could not find real girls to satisfy itself. So it settled on a substitute.

There were as many boys in their twenties as there were in their early teens. My first two years in the seminary were ones of intense nightmares and deep psychological trauma for one important reason. I was shaped like a girl. At age thirteen, my breasts were the size of apples. This condition was attributed to the starchy food we ate, and the doctor said it would melt away as I grew older. Our diet was essentially vegetarian of the worst kind. We ate leaves from trees we didn't know, for usually there was no name to what was on for lunch or dinner except when we recognized yams or sweet potato on the menu. Breakfast was always rice or millet porridge. It was so slimy, you had to add a lot of water and lemon to swallow it. On Sunday we had bread at lunch and dried fish for dinner. On Christmas and Easter lemonade was added to the meal. But, while waiting for that, I discovered that I had become an object of desire. . . . Everything about me was referred to as feminine. My voice was so thin and soft that I was nick-named Eros. I fell into a deep psychological chasm in which I saw my manhood denied. I looked at other boys with envy. They at least did not look like girls.

One of the priests, Father Lamartin, had taken a special liking to me, but I never understood its nature until far later. He was the tall, fat priest from Holland, the one we called Cerberus. His eyes were so blue and distant they seemed as if they did not belong to him, and he had the look of someone who is permanently bedazzled and about to be upset. One evening while everybody was gathered for a spiritual lecture, Father Lamartin, my Latin teacher, called me into his office. He was holding a stick, and his face was scarlet. As soon as I came into the room, he closed the door and said, "You are a lazy boy, and I must teach you to obey. Take your clothes off."

I looked at the stick in his hands and my blood went hot. I was ashamed of taking my clothes off in front of a person so heavily dressed. But more seriously, I did not want to show him the two apples growing on my chest. He roared at me again and I understood that there was nothing I could do but obey. So I took my shirt off first, unzipped my shorts and let them fall to my feet, and looked at him imploringly. His eyes protruded so hard that, in a snap, my underwear was down. I was so ashamed that I had to lower my eyes. I felt like I would rather die a hundred deaths than stand like this is front of someone.

After a moment that seemed like an eternity, Father Lamartin came to me and touched my breasts. They were so sensitive and so painful that I emitted a light sound.

"Do they hurt?"

"Yes, Father."

He caressed them.

"Do they still hurt?"

"Yes, Father."

"How did you get them?"

"I don't know, Father. It just happened."

He sat, and then made me lie down on his lap while he slashed me on the back with his stick, speaking words that I did not understand. The beating did not hurt, and I wondered why he was going through all this trouble to tell me that I should work harder in his Latin class. When he was done, he had me sit on his legs, facing him, and he put his arms around me. At that time he was a different person, soft, tender, and protective. I closed my eyes. I did not want to see his face.

Meanwhile the students had finished their spiritual lecture and were going to the refectory for dinner. Those who knew me and Father Lamartin came walking by the office, looking like they were searching for something. Father Lamartin ordered me to dress and leave.

"Did he hurt you?" Antoine asked outside the office.

"No."

"Yes, he did. You're trying to hide it."

"No. He hit me but it didn't hurt."

"He hit you where?"

"On the back."

"Did you take your clothes off?"

"He ordered me to."

"The bastard. He's done that to others before. Be careful."

The other students began joking with me. They said I was Father Lamartin's girlfriend and asked when he was going to marry me and take me to France. That didn't bother me nearly so much as the experience itself. The shame for me was to have stood naked in front of a priest.

Similar things happened, not just with Father Lamartin, but with older students who broke into the dorm in the middle of the night and would threaten to kill you if you made a noise or told anyone what happened. Everybody in the dorm knew what went on at night, but no one dared say a thing about it except in jokes about so-and-so being the girl-friend of such-and-such. It was a nightmare to be young and good-looking in that divine institution. I longed to grow up and prayed that my breasts would go down as the doctor had said they would. These experiences made me stupid in class and absentminded in church. I did not know who to pray to, as I felt God had betrayed me in some deep and unforgivable way. I only wished I could find an opportunity to show him my contempt. I became gloomy, dreaming of a better world in which no one could rape anyone and where no boy would look like a girl or be misnamed as a girl. The god who made this possible was a dreadful god.

One night Father Lamartin called me once again into his office, right before lights-out. After the now familiar ritual beating on the butt and the squeezing and heavy breathing, I asked, as he dismissed me, if I should confess my sin on Friday. Every student was supposed to confess on Friday afternoon and be absolved from the sins committed during the week. Most sins, or confessable sins, were venial. They ranged from eating in excess to having negative intentions against a neighbor to personal failings like laziness, carelessness, or forgetfulness. These sins were mechanically absolved by the priest while we recited our act of contrition by rote.

Father Lamartin jumped to his feet and became red. He mumbled a few words that sounded like curses to me and said, "No!" Then, as if realizing that he might have gone too far, he composed his voice and asked, "Why do you think this is a sin?"

"I don't know. Am I fine then?"

"Of course you are fine. Have you ever talked about this at confession?"

"No. I wanted to ask you first."

"You did a good job. You don't confess sins that are not sins. Who is your confessor?"

"Father Rémy."

"Don't talk to him about this. I'll take care of it myself."

As I walked to my dorm, my mind was working hard, trying to understand why Father Lamartin did not want me to confess that I had stood naked in front of him several times in his own office. The nakedness for me was a sin. The rest I didn't know about. Why didn't Father Lamartin think I should confess what he ordered me to do when he considered such simple things as being awake in bed when one should be asleep as a sin? I was not afraid, I was only beginning to understand something dreadful about life in a Catholic boarding school.

CHAPTER 7

THE REBELLION BEGINS

 The first three years in the seminary were lived almost outside my body. There are certain wires in the psyche that one must cut under certain abusive circumstances in order to survive. Unlike the school at the mission hill, where most of the brutality came from the staff, here it could come from any direction, students included. Among the boys secret anarchy reigned, and the fear of being tormented, sexually or physically, kept me in a state of strained vigilance and emotional numbness. In the boarding school at Nansi, one had to grow up fast.

It was not until I was transferred to the higher division that my plight began to be bearable. The main cause for my improved situation was the shift in my physical appearance. By now, my breasts had receded. Even though they were still lumpy, they did not protrude from inside my clothes, and I was less ashamed of myself. I had also developed a certain amount of physical strength and size. I was more manly than before, more aggressive. But I did not know that my former condition had taught me deceit, conceit, anger, pretense, boldness, and aggressiveness as expressions of my frustrations.

I channeled most of my rage into my studies, which all of a sudden took off. Studying hard was a way to feel vindicated and at the same time keep myself busy. Every new subject came with a book that opened up a strange new world into which I could escape. It was easier to stay there in that imaginary freedom than to go out and face the boring reality of the sanctified realm. But though fascinating, the world of the book was an alien place altogether. History focused on the white man's deeds, and was a tale of violence and death. It was about war, and the strife that arose from man's greed for power. It was about the instability and insecurity of an existence where one's life was constantly at risk, either to serve the ego of another life, or to be plainly wasted. From the pages of our history books sprang figures of violence and terror who were presented as symbols of strength and models of civilized humanity. Occasionally a bright spot shone through: I saw the French Revolution as an example of humanity's reaction against oppression. But most of the time history seemed one long tale of irrational violence. We learned that war was peace and peace was war. *"Qui para pacem, para bellum"*—if you want peace, get ready for war.

Our history teacher always insisted that we understand the meaning of power, and of peace and freedom, but these values were presented to us only in Western terms. Utilizing the white man's violent philosophy, even the terrible commerce of slavery became comprehensible—justifiable even. In our history books there were illustrations of ships full of slaves heading west. All of this sounded unreal to me until some of the students who came from the coast confirmed having heard stories from their grandfathers about people who were deported and never returned. One subject we never studied was African history. In our classroom, the African continent was mentioned only in the context of the white man's involvement with it. Otherwise the world was clearly run by whites.

From the testimonies in our textbooks, the whites were the great thinkers, the great inventors. Our teachers stressed scientific discoveries. Johannes Gutenberg discovered printing. Galileo unlocked the workings of the heavens. Newton solved the mysteries of gravity and physics. Everything they did eventually enabled God to come to Africa—and we began to understand why our people were considered primitives. I came to realize that wherever the white man went, he brought trouble because he had no scruples. He brought a kind of meanness that no one could face because it made no sense to anyone, and eventually he took over because no one loved blood and killing more than he did. Sadly, our young minds were being formed by the vivid images of death and suffering in these books. One day in our history class Father Joe, speaking about the beauty of colonialism, likened it to a mother trying to protect her son. Out of kindness, France had taken a large portion of Africa under her wing, and that was a heavy burden. "We must remember," he added, "that resistance always brings havoc, chaos, confusion, and ultimately destruction. Europeans came into Africa for the purpose of bringing to fruition the immense wealth that had been kept dormant by the ignorance of the African people. When the soldiers arrived, there was resistance everywhere. When you resist a peaceful mission, you invite force. When force renders you inoffensive, it reminds you at the same time of the sweet taste of peace. If force was utilized from time to time in Africa, it was not out of any pleasure in bloodshed. A truly civilized person hates shedding blood, but at the same time knows how to defend himself."

I raised my hand to speak. I felt stabbed in my spirit and thought that, after all, this was a class, a time for the exchange of thoughts.

Father Joe motioned to me with his head. "What is your question?"

"I don't know if it is a question, but it goes like this: if I come to your father's house and I want to get in—even though your father does not want me as a guest—do I force the door anyway?"

Father Joe turned dark red, and the class was as silent as if no one were there. Then, as if trying to control himself, he asked quietly, "What are you suggesting?"

"I am suggesting that perhaps colonialism cannot be justified on the grounds that some people decided it was their right to disturb the quiet lives of others. Obviously this book was written by someone who thinks it is right to put whole villages into forced labor or to summarily liquidate them. Somebody who does not care about other people! This history may make sense to his mind, it does not make sense to me or to anyone else here."

"Speak for yourself, Patrice." It was the voice of one of the students. I did not have time to notice who he was, because Father Joe was talking to me.

"Patrice, sit down," Father Joe ordered. He was trembling with anger and had lost sight of me. I was not standing, yet he had ordered me to sit. I felt the urge to tell him that I had been sitting down all the time, but I realized that if I said this, I would make things worse. Then he ordered me to follow him into his office. We left the class in turmoil.

When he closed the door of his office and sat down behind his desk, I moved to sit down as well. He jumped up from his desk and roared, "You will sit when I order you to sit. Who do you think you are? Do you think the Christian mission would invest so much money in you just to train you to become an ideological delinquent? This institution does not tolerate this kind of freethinking. You are here to learn to become a soldier of Christ—and that's it." He pulled a rubber truncheon out of his drawer and came after me. But now I was sixteen and would not let myself be beaten. I had already been chastised for looking like a girl and for being lazy, and now I was not going to allow anyone to flog me for participating in class.

Father Joe made his move and I avoided him. That irritated him. He walked from his chair to the other side of the desk where I was standing and ordered, "Stay still." I stood still, but when he tried to hit me on the head, I moved away just in time. Instead he hit a pile of books delicately balanced on a narrow shelf and they came tumbling down. His temper became red-hot. "Bend your back." This time I obeyed him. But I made my thoughts go away from my body so that when the first blow fell, I was not even aware of it.

"What's going on here?" It was the voice of another priest, Father Michael, standing outside.

"It's none of your business. This boy's been interrupting class with subversive questions." While saying this, Father Joe kept lacerating my back.

"Curiosity is not a crime."

When Father Joe kept beating me, Father Michael rushed into the room and grabbed the truncheon from Father Joe's hand. "That's enough!"

I was absent from all of this, having retreated far into myself. I did not care what happened, but I was glad the thing had ripped open a difference of opinion between these priests.

Father Superior, who must have heard all the noise, now came running. "What's going on here?"

"I'm disciplining Patrice," Father Joe told him sullenly.

"Oh . . . Patrice . . ." Father Superior said patronizingly.

"He is beating Patrice without a cause," Father Michael said, still trying to defend me.

"You have no authority here. You've been ordered back to Europe." Father Superior's voice was vindictive.

"*What?*" Father Michael demanded.

"I made the recommendation to Paris a long time ago. The order came through yesterday. I was waiting for an appropriate time to tell you, and now seems very right."

It took a while before Father Michael regained his wits, then he said, "All right, but while I'm still here, I'm going to do what I can." He snatched the truncheon from Father Joe's hand. The two priests glared at each other like two roosters about to fight. Father Joe was the first to give in.

"*Assez*"—enough. He turned to me. "Patrice, you will write two hundred times, 'I will not disobey.' Now get out of here. Remember to mention this at confession. And be a good lad from now on. . . ."

I was filled with deadly hatred toward Father Joe and Father Superior, but I said nothing.

"You shouldn't have done that," I heard Father Superior say to Father Michael as I stood outside the door, listening. "I've warned you many times about interfering."

After Father Superior had left, I heard Father Joe's voice rise. "You—

it's no wonder you're being shipped back to Europe. Your weakness has cost you your calling."

Do your people a favor and get free of this madness, a voice said inside of my head. I never knew where that thought came from, but something was happening to me.

▲　　▼　　▲

Geography opened up worlds far different from the one we learned about in history class. It was amazing for those of us who were born inland to realize that there was so much water on the Earth. Soon the tiny forms of the five continents came into view. As our horizons became wider, it was both wonderful and disturbing. During the break we would regroup to comment on what we had heard in class. What came to me as good news from the beginning was to learn that the Earth is round and that it is hanging in the middle of nowhere and moving very fast. I never knew why I was happy about that, but sometimes I found myself wishing the whole planet would just quit its trajectory and go somewhere else.

The world outside of Africa came into even sharper focus with French literature, which crystallized history by resituating it in a larger social and ethical context. I was astounded by the ease with which Racine and Corneille put words together. How could they make their characters go mad, seek death, and die so poetically? I was stunned by La Fontaine, who told stories strangely similar to those Grandfather used to tell me, stories in which animals spoke and acted just like humans. I was astonished by Molière and his eccentric, egocentric, avaricious characters. I loved Baudelaire. He was blasé toward morality, and for a good reason. He had discovered that the whole French world was a monumental lie—and I believed him. I was endlessly amazed that all of these people could come alive on the thin pages of a book, always there for anyone who was interested.

Because mastery of French was fundamental to good apostolic output, we were more concerned with it than with anything else. The study of vocabulary and the memorization of texts, especially excerpts from the great French poets, was very important. Composition was crucial. Every Monday we had dictation, something that required the ability to hear and spell words correctly. The *dictée* was about two hundred and fifty words. To misspell five words meant failure. Grammatical errors were considered the worst, and punctuation errors minor, costing only a quarter of a point. We came to call them capital sins or venial sins. Zero misspellings made you a hero.

In composition, we always aimed at using the rarest words possible in order to prove to the teacher how far we had gone into memorizing vocabulary. Rhetoric was conceived of as a technique by which to prove through argument that a fact, obviously wrong, was right. This skill was important because it meant that we were equipped to defend Christianity in the face of every contradiction.

Once we were asked to prove, in the middle of the day, that it was night. Dismayed, we looked at each other hopelessly. I wrote that everything came with its opposite, and so behind the shining noontime sun were the dark shadows of midnight. I argued that light could not occur without its opposite, and that the presence of the one was a message about the coming of the other. Then I became crafty. I added that the same principles applied to the present domination of the world by Europe because this condition foretold the coming of its own end. To substantiate my argument, I spoke about the rise and decline of the Roman Empire, the rise and fall of feudalism, and the danger incurred by any person in a position of power, no matter what denomination. I was one inch from denigrating the institution.

Father Joe was also a French teacher. He was nicknamed Joe the Spartan. He was the only Black priest in a white world of educators. As an African priest he was dead to Africa, a fine specimen of European brainwashing and indoctrination. No wonder I always annoyed him. For a while I was stupid enough to think that because he looked like me, he would agree with and support me. Little did I know that he had been brainwashed to brainwash us. We called him Spartan because of his athletic looks. Father Joe played basketball with us every Thursday and was very agile. Ever since the incident in the history class, he and I had each other under surveillance. He knew I did not like him and so he was going to use his authority to torture me whenever he could.

The next day I was called to his office. I understood immediately that he was going to talk to me about my paper.

"What do you mean by this essay?"

"I was just trying to write a good essay. It was a tough topic. I knew I didn't have much chance."

"I said, what do you mean by this essay?"

"Nothing."

"What's in your mind?"

"Nothing." I was growing tense. My blood was heating up in my veins and I sensed trouble ahead.

"Listen, this is not the kind of mind that the Catholic community is spending money to train. The things you are insinuating here are very grave and your punishment could be great if Father Superior were told about this."

"But I did nothing."

"You were not asked to do nothing."

"But what did I do, then?"

"You insulted God's work. You insulted the effort of thousands of people working to make this place a good place for everyone."

"But I was asked to write a paper."

"You can't feel free to say anything you want here. You know that. It has already brought you trouble. I wonder what's in your damn brain that you can't get this one lesson into it."

I understood immediately what my own words had done to me. There was no denying that I had said something incriminating. All of a sudden I understood the power of the written word. Its stark naked visibility could not be denied. I apologized to Father Joe, employing the argument I had used before to get myself out of trouble. It consisted in pleading guilty and in asking for forgiveness in the most demeaning way possible, acknowledging my ignorance of the sanctity of missionary work and the feebleness of my character. This, because it created an atmosphere of mini-confession, always produced a result favorable to me. Father Joe promised not to bring the paper to the attention of Father Superior, but on one condition: that I never do this again.

I had no luck with Father Joe. He was just too present in my life, and his presence weighed on me intolerably. In French classes he would pick on me every time, asking me to go to the blackboard and write sample outlines for essays in order to show the others what the anatomy of an argument should look like. He knew I was good at arguing things, but he would never say it. I was getting to dread rhetoric classes.

As time passed, so we too learned to change our lives in accordance with the rules of the place. We constructed support groups to help each other, since we had learned very quickly that God was not going to give us the aid we so desperately needed. Belonging to a group provided the opportunity to obtain a personal identity far more in tune with our inner impulses. Because we were teenagers, those impulses presented great risk. For most, being part of a group meant being able to break the rules, being able to prove that we could outwit the eyes of God.

In the course of three years, my friend Martial and I had developed a very solid relationship based on intellectual speculation on the pros and cons of being an apostle of the divine. We were joined by others who, like us, wandered lost in the midst of the crowd, trying to make our impossible dreams come true. We named our group the Garibaldis, after the Italian nationalist Giuseppe Garibaldi, who was described in our history book as a master of guerrilla warfare and a powerful revolutionary leader. What struck us most about his tempestuous life was his love for insurrection and his ability to escape when captured or condemned to death. I was particularly struck by his attempt in 1862 to capture Rome from Pope Pius IX and save Italy from the tyranny of Catholicism. For having attempted this, Garibaldi seemed to us like a good example of defiance toward priestly authority. Everyone in our group pledged to be bold on all levels—intellectual, spiritual, and psychological—and to always challenge conformity. We craved to prove to ourselves and to each other that we could face the danger of breaking the rules without being caught.

Most of our activities consisted in being awake somewhere when we were supposed to be sleeping. After lights-out, the priest on duty would join his colleagues at the forum. We would then, one by one, crawl out of the beds where we had been snoring. After arranging our belongings so that it looked like someone was still beneath the blankets, we would rally somewhere at the periphery of the institution, just to be together in a freer way. Most of the time that's all we did. The good in the adventure was the feeling we got of being bold. Soon, however, it became obvious that just getting together was no real deed—all it did was to deprive us of much-needed sleep, especially after long hours of soccer or basketball. So we decided to find ways to be more creative.

One night a Garibaldi named Robert brought a cigarette to our meeting. He always had to be doing something or else he would go crazy. But no one would have ever believed he would go so far into risk taking. Everyone was shocked. How could he have managed to find a cigarette? There were a few among the teachers who smoked the famous Gauloise, but to get a cigarette from any one of them was unthinkable. Cigarette smoking was not just prohibited, there was a ban on even bringing cigarettes into the precincts.

"I can't believe this," François said.

"Where did you get it?" Antoine demanded.

"Father Superior." There was an air of victory in Robert's words.

"You mean he gave these to you?" Antoine asked skeptically.

"No, I took them from his study."

"Are you the burglar they reported stole Father Superior's tape recorder a few days ago?" Antoine asked.

I hadn't heard about this, so I voiced my surprise. "Wow! Somebody did that?"

Robert wanted to clarify his deed. He asked for the group's attention and explained, "I'm not a thief. I merely liberated a few cigarettes from Father Superior's desk when I met him in his study this morning. The guy who took the tape recorder was from the city. They say he had a gun and everything. You see, thieves come all the way from the city to steal things here because they know there are things to steal."

"But where did you get the matches?" I asked.

"The cook gave them to me."

"Do you think we should be doing this?" It was François speaking. He was uneasy.

Robert answered him sarcastically. "So you wanted me to go to Father Superior and ask permission? 'Would you please give me a couple of your cigarettes? I would like to share them with the Garibaldi group tonight.' No! You see, true revolutionaries, true patriots, don't ask or beg, François. They already have permission because they carry it in their blood."

We could not smoke the cigarette because the only match Robert had brought with him was wet. We decided we had to find a fire somewhere so we could share this precious Gauloise. Robert came up with a bright idea: The cooks came from the nearby village. We could not go to the village to get fire, but we could, if we had the guts, ask one of the cooks to give us some dry matches. But in order to do that we needed someone who would act as an emissary.

I had liked being part of the Garibaldis as long as our activities consisted in not being asleep when we were supposed to be, for there are times when disobedience heals a very ailing part of the self. It relieves the human spirit's distress at being forced into narrow boundaries. For the nearly powerless, defying authority is often the only power available. But as much as I admired Robert for bringing this cigarette and looked forward to finding out what smoking was like, the idea of being picked for a solo mission scared me. Fortunately, I was not the one selected to retrieve matches. Nevertheless, I was worried. What if the chosen boy was followed? What if a cook decided to report this strange request to a priest? I had been in trouble before, and I did not feel like jumping into more.

I tried to intervene. "Wait a minute, what do you think you're doing?"

"We need fire. Someone has to go get it."

"But do we need to put ourselves at risk over a cigarette?"

"What are you afraid of?"

"Nothing. I just don't want to throw myself into the hands of those cooks. How do I know which side they are on?"

"This is a good way to find out."

"We may not be able to make use of our finding, though."

"But I know the cooks are on our side. Where do you think I got the match in the first place?"

"You mean you didn't steal the useless match from Father Superior's office too?"

"Well, at least I was able to convince the cook to give me a match."

"Then you already know one of the cooks. Why don't you yourself go ask him for more instead of risking one of us?"

"All right, I'll do it this time. But next time someone else has to prove he's a Garibaldi—I've proven that *I'm* one!"

So Robert left to get the matches. He soon returned with them and a couple more local cigarettes called Camelia Sport that the cook had given him. We lit the cigarettes and passed them around. We did not know how to inhale, so we just took the smoke into our mouths and let it out again, feeling good anyway because we were defying authority. What we were really enjoying was the risk.

While we were smoking, Antoine observed, "This must be why the Fathers are so very, very pleasant. See, they have a good education, a roof over their heads, and the promise of visiting the divine realm anytime via cigarettes, wine, and beer." He took a puff of the cigarette he held between his fingers and offered it to me, inquiring, "And how have you been, Patrice?"

I knew he wanted to talk to me about my growing reputation as a troublemaker, but I did not feel like letting anyone spoil my evening. I just wanted to go on enjoying the bliss of the present moment. Antoine didn't press the matter and we remained quiet, savoring our first cigarette.

CHAPTER 8

NEW AWAKENINGS

 When I first came to the seminary, I sincerely tried to believe and pray, but any spiritual grace I found gradually dissolved in the face of continued and re-peated brutality. There came a time when I rebelled against God. In spite of all my prayers for him to come and help me, nothing happened. As I grew older, I found it more and more difficult to rely on prayers and hope for my redemption.

That period in my life coincided with the creation of the Garibaldi group. Not only did we spend our time figuring out ways to attain enlightenment through breaking the rules, but we were also determined to prove ourselves in class as exceptional students. Consequently, my last three years in the seminary were devoted to the cultivation of dissidence, ego, and intellectual pursuits.

I managed to do well in most of my subjects, but I was only so-so in science and poor in math. Actually, math was decipherable until the letters of the alphabet got involved. I had reserved them for literary pleasure and found them out of place in this region that belonged only to numbers. So when confronted by a mixture of letters and numbers, my mind went blank. Science was basically all right, especially the natural sciences and anatomy, but the learning process became nauseating when a frog, then a rabbit were involved. Supposedly, these poor animals were being ripped open for our scientific education, but I could only feel their pain. My psyche shut down, and with it every interest I ever had for anatomy.

I enjoyed all my other subjects, especially reading and writing. Writing was cathartic. Through it I escaped from the reality of institutionalized life into a world in which I seemed to have the power to regulate things. One day we were asked to write a story, any story in which someone would occupy a position of authority and be a symbol for others to follow. The paper was due in a week.

That night something strange happened to me. It was after lights-out and I was walking around in the dark, near the dormitory, like a good Garibaldi, waiting for my fellows and enjoying my solitude. Suddenly, a few yards from me, I saw an old Black man dragging a white priest by the hair. As he came closer, I thought I recognized Grandfather. *Am I dreaming?* I felt a chill of apprehension and my whole body broke out in a sweat. Grandfather dropped the white priest and walked closer, beckoning me to come to him. He was talking to me, even though I could not hear him. My petrified body could not move. Grandfather beckoned more urgently. I desperately wanted to go to him, but couldn't. Seeming disappointed in me, he began walking toward me, and when he was a few feet away I realized it was not Grandfather but Robert.

"What's the matter with you, Patrice? I asked you to come here and you stand there like a dummy." I did not know what to say. I was confused. Why did I think that Robert was my Grandfather?

"What was that you were dragging?" I inquired, eager to know what I had seen.

"A bench from the forum for us to sit on. It's still there where I left it. Would you tell me what's the matter with you? You look like you've seen a ghost."

"You bet I have. I didn't expect to see you coming from that direction. Why did you go to the forum to steal a bench? We don't need a bench to sit on."

"Why not? We always stand up for hours. I thought tonight we could sit down for a change. And what's this about stealing a bench? I didn't steal it. I was planning to take it back when we're done with it. Is there something wrong with you?"

"Never mind," I said, letting the subject drop. I was afraid to tell Robert that I thought I had seen Bakhye. That night I couldn't stop thinking about him, nor could I dismiss what I had seen. It had seemed so real—yet how could I prove that I had seen Grandfather while wide awake? For days to come, Grandfather crowded my conscious life.

So, when given the assignment to write a piece about a figure of authority, I wrote a play about him. In it I depicted him as a person who possessed supernatural powers that he used to protect his community. I resurrected him into a story in which he led the whole tribe to victory against the colonial oppressor. I invented graphic details about how he personally fought the leader of the colonial army in a duel and spared his life in the end on the condition that he go away and never return to the area. I even had the French general kneel down and pray to my grandfather to spare his life and declare that the French ideology he lived by was wrong. Finally, I had the general ask Grandfather's permission to study with him and learn the wisdom of the tribe. As the play ended, Grandfather and the French general were initiating a new era in which tribal wisdom was taught to white people, and nothing else.

I had been in trouble with Father Joe in the past with this kind of subject, and I was smart enough to know that writing the play was an explicit invitation to more trouble. But some evil was working in me and I could not help it. I never knew why, but I took my chances. The war I was depicting was not against any religious authority, and I thought that would help, just in case I had to defend myself ideologically. The fascination that drew me into writing this play was deeper than I can explain. Everything in my logical mind said I was begging for a serious beating. My deep self refused to admit it and won.

Father Joe, our Black African priest, read the play and at first did not have anything to say. I believe he experienced a mélange of fear and amazement at what I was able to do. Something told me that his deeply buried roots were shaken and his identity temporarily confused. Miraculously, Father Superior selected the play for performance at Nansi's anniversary celebration. I chose to play Grandfather. The rest of the cast consisted of members of the Garibaldi group. The rehearsals promised that the play would be great. The night of the performance I dressed the way I remembered the elders being dressed. There was no way to re-create their formal outfits with the materials on hand and the limits of my childhood memories, but, with a high level of motivation, much that was missing was reconstructed.

That night the whole novitiate was invited. Visitors even came from outside of the institution, and there were more priests present than I had ever seen together in one place. There were also high local and national authorities. The play began. From the stage it was impossible to see the audience with clarity. As I played Grandfather, I felt an inexpressible sensation surge through me. I was not acting but being. I was not Patrice, conscious of a role being played, trying to make an audience believe in a clever illusion. Instead I felt a true merger between my person and a spirit, and it felt as though I had come home. This force moved my whole being into a timeless place in which I sensed the possibility of being captured by the soul of another. I was coming into life through my own creative work. God did not exist. I was restoring the old wisdom of the ancestors.

The play ended. A roar came from the audience, mostly from the students who, for a little while, had been reconnected with their roots. They were responding freely to how they felt. But the response of the priests was quiet, reserved, even confused. It seemed as if they clapped their hands because none of them could guess quite clearly what the others were thinking. They stole quick glances at one another while they applauded.

In the dressing room, Robert observed, "Expect to meet Zeus before sunset tomorrow. I don't know, but I have a feeling that they got something a little more controversial than they bargained on."

"What do you mean?"

"Didn't you watch them at the end of the play?"

"Sure, I did. But why should I believe the worst just because someone's face didn't light up or someone doesn't know how to clap his hands?"

"Because that face has the power to frame your fate."

"And I have the obligation to do what I am asked to do to the best of my ability."

"Your best may be too good to be seen as best. But look, I didn't mind your play at all. I think it was very Garibaldi for you to do what you did. At certain moments I had the clear feeling that you were explicitly attacking the pigs in the audience, and not any vague, remote, and insubstantial colonial ghosts. I appreciated that because that is the real war we went out there to wage on stage."

"But now I've started another war that I can't win. Is that what you mean?"

"I'm afraid so. I fear that you may have tipped off these people too explicitly. Now they will know where to look for us. But hell, the worst that can happen is that we will all be expelled from this place, never to return."

The next morning I was called into Father Superior's office. Having a private visit with Zeus was like having a visit with thunder and lightning. When I entered he was browsing through a row of books on a shelf. I sat down and took a look at the man beside the bookshelf. Inside his ample robe he was slim and tall. His almost lipless face was as stiff as if it had been carved out of a rock and was waiting to be given some kind of life. His eyes were too deeply recessed to be seen.

I decided I was not going to let myself be pulverized without some resistance. Father Superior finally stopped pretending to look at his books and turned toward me.

"What were you thinking about last night while up on that stage?"

"I was asked to do a job, and I was busy trying to do it well."

"That's not what I asked you."

"What did you say?"

"In this office I ask the questions and you answer."

"Yes, Father."

"Now, what were you thinking about last night?"

"Nothing, Father."

"What is this ancestral crap about?"

"I don't know, Father."

"Why did you write it?"

"I was asked to write, Father."

"And you chose to write about paganism."

". . ."

"Listen, we can't tolerate any suggestion that we are here to encourage anyone to remain in ignorance and disease. You came close to creating a scandal last night, do you realize that?" He remained thoughtful for a while, his face so puckered with frowning that he looked older than his half a century. Then, for a moment, his face lightened a little.

"Did you have a grandfather?"

"I think so, Father. He died shortly before I was taken away."

"You mean your vocation began after his death. Were you close to your grandfather?"

"Very close, Father."

"Was it him you were trying to play?"

"I don't know, Father," I lied.

Zeus was obviously uncertain as to how to approach me. He was neither angry nor appreciative, but I knew he was suspicious and uncertain and that he wished he could catch me at something. When he let me go, I was unsure of why he had not accused me of being heretical or profane. But deep down I knew what was going on. I knew that Father Superior had been responsible for creating the situation that led to my play being selected for production. So, ultimately, he couldn't blame me.

He was, I learned later, an anthropologist who had spent his first years as a missionary in Africa, studying the relationship of the indigenous cultures to the divine. In an article he wrote about one tribe, he argued that the indigenous man or woman's instinctual worship of the inanimate is an indication of his or her innate longing for God. He emphasized the good being done for indigenous peoples by finally revealing the true God to them. One of the central postulates of his article was that a deep craving for God can call up a warlike spirit in an indigenous man, and he attributed the surprising victories that some tribes had won over better-armed colonials to that. He stressed that the coming of Christ has reversed that savage fierceness and turned entire African tribes into humble servants of God.

Perhaps Father Superior believed that I, in all my untamed rebelliousness, would make all the greater disciple when he finally conquered me.

But I suspected that the spirit of my Grandfather was trying to precipitate me into another stage of my tumultuous life. I felt invulnerable, like a man beyond error. My heart was calm and I felt no alarm. If the Father was giving me a rope to hang myself with because he suspected me of something, I had just the opposite feeling—as if he were the one getting ready to do himself in. Whatever forces were at work in me, at that moment I experienced invincibility.

Regardless of the neutral outcome of my meeting with Father Superior, I had now fallen under constant surveillance, like the rest of the Garibaldis. We were praised for our intellectual performance and dreaded for our undisciplined attitudes.

One night I was sitting in the forum with Robert, Antoine, and François. It was toward the end of Lent, in the middle of holy week. The atmosphere of the whole seminary was desolate and silent because of the imminent death of Christ. Every evening we said the *"Christus factus est obediens usque ad mortem"* with mournful voices, as if to convince ourselves that it could have happened differently. All this singing and wailing was a nuisance to the Garibaldi society. The seminary was awake almost all night, every night, because the priests kept a vigil. We could not gather for any length of time or get up in the middle of the night to go adventuring. We could only take advantage of the short recreational period following dinner to have our meetings.

That night we were discussing the really serious issues of life. François had overheard something that he said was going to have tremendous importance in our lives. We had met so he could tell us about it.

"I heard Father Pascal talking with Father Michael about loosening the rules here because of the end of the colonial era. You know what that means."

"Sorry, but no."

"It means that we're free."

"Free from what?"

"From this religious colonialism. Isn't that great?"

"It isn't that easy," I said. "Don't you see that the conditions under which we've been living for so many years aim at imprisoning everybody? The freedom you are talking about is impossible. You can't get rid of your own shadow. You, me, Father Joe, we can never be free again. For one thing, the church has obliterated our past. Now we may as well all be Europeans, only we're the wrong color."

"What about this free will you've been talking about?" François asked, challenging me.

"Free will—not freedom from the past."

"And who wants freedom from the future? Our destiny is the destiny of the civilized. In an independent country we will get the biggest slice of the pie because we know how to play the game."

"Independent—meaning what?" I asked.

"Meaning no more references to the ancestors. It means that the literate get all the recognition. This kind of independence has tremendous implications for us."

"François, aren't you going to become a priest?" I asked him.

"You know damn well that we're not supposed to speak about priesthood and colonialism openly. Just whose side are you on?"

"My question is very clear."

"Aw, Patrice, don't be a pain."

Suddenly, from out of the blue, Robert jumped into the conversation, taking it far away from anything like what we were speaking about.

"And as for the necessity of bringing light into the darkness, in fact, the life of the Father . . ."

We all understood. Was it too late for us to change the subject? There, a few feet away and coming toward us, was Father Superior.

"Sharing spiritual matters, boys?"

"No, Father," I said.

"Yes, Father," Robert said.

"No—that is . . ." I wanted to correct the impression I had made, but I wasn't doing a very good job.

François took over. "Yes, Father Superior, that is, we were all appalled and deeply overwhelmed by the idea of death associated with Christ. This high moment is always suggestive of that awesome event that obliterated history. I mean, just think about it—a God killed by men! I was expressing my thoughts about the matter when you arrived."

"Leave that mystery for tomorrow. Now it's bedtime."

"Thank you, Father," François responded with sincerity.

▲   ▼   ▲

That year, on high holy days like this, the nuns and female students at the novitiate were going to join us for the resurrection mass. The novitiate was a mile or so from the seminary, in a world of its own—a zone we were forbidden to even think about. We knew that in that place there were girls, whose fate was exactly like our own, but we hadn't seen them until now. The rules were really loosening! When the news broke, it stirred sentiments of wonder and awe within us—we were going to see real women! We wondered where they were going to sit in the chapel. Everyone wanted to be able to gaze at them. Going to mass suddenly became something that we had to prepare for seriously. We got ready to go to the church the way you do for a date. Weren't we going to meet *girls*? And the Garibaldis made it a rule to look impeccable. We were warned not to speak to the girls or to shake hands with them, but in our imaginations, all of that was going to happen, and much, much more. . . .

The girls were our age, pretty-looking, but lamentably shy. They walked into the chapel, herded together bewildered and encircled by uniformed nuns. We waited outside as they entered and took their seats upstairs.

"They are going to see us from the back and we aren't going to get a look at any of them," Robert said, disappointed.

"Don't worry, they'll have to come down from there to go to the communion rail," I said. "Then we'll get a good look." Nonetheless we felt cheated.

The resurrection mass was intense. We sang with our best voices. Each of us assumed that his princess was watching him from behind, taking note of every subtle movement. Even though we did not know anything specific about the princesses, we trusted that they were all beautiful beyond our wildest dreams. At communion time, as anticipated they came down from the balcony and walked, one close behind the other, to the rail. We watched them. The priests at the altar watched us. Mentally, we took our pick, deciding which girl had taken notice of us during the mass. At the end of the service, the girls exited first, packed together as before. By the time it was our turn to go, they had disappeared forever.

▲　　▼　　▲

The Garibaldis were having another one of their nightly meetings. Robert was not there, and we didn't know where he had gone. He wasn't in his bed. Antoine had brought a small map of the world that he had stolen from some priest's room, probably his confessor, and we decided that we were going to locate exactly where we were on it. All I was interested in seeing was my own village. I was bitterly disappointed. There was no Upper Volta, let alone my village.

Paul noticed that I was downcast and asked, "What's eating you, man?"

"It's all about Europe," I said, pointing to the map. "Don't you realize— all we study is Europe. Where are we, anyway? I thought we were in Africa. All we get about Africa is a lot of whitewashed propaganda that tells us nothing. What if—"

Paul was not listening—he was lost in some world in a far corner of his own psyche.

"Paul," I asked him, "do you want to be a priest?"

The question woke him up. He looked around as if the trees were listening. "No."

"What the hell is the matter with everyone?" I asked. "What the hell are you doing here, then?"

"I'm going to be a writer," Paul said. "Or at least a professor. I'm going to go to Europe and study the theater—Molière, Racine, Shakespeare . . ."

Paul brought out a book that I had not noticed at first because he had placed it in the dark somewhere. I did not want to ask him where he had gotten it. By now I knew that the Garibaldis were good at removing other people's property. He showed it to me. It was a book of photographs of artists, Black and white, sitting together in cafés in Paris, in the late forties. I was still shocked at the idea that Paul did not want to be a priest.

"That's nauseating. Antoine, François, and now you. Doesn't anyone want to be a priest?"

"No. So?"

"You're all hypocrites."

"I don't have a choice," Paul said angrily. "I can go mad and become a priest or I can stay sane and nourish my own dream. You're the one who is off the deep end, buddy. You're the one still willing to become a priest after all that's happened to you."

"Wanting to be a priest doesn't mean wanting to be a European," I said. "I want to be a priest as much as I want to be an African. We have people we need to help. To fight a system effectively you have to be on the inside. What's the harm in that?"

I knew I wanted to be a priest, but not the kind I was being asked to be. I knew I could be one who would place dynamite in the middle of the whole system and explode it. That was what I wanted to do. I thought that, after all, our group activities were preparing us to do this kind of job together, to send the Catholic establishment to the very hell it pretended to save people from. So I was shocked when I learned that my fellow Garibaldis had different plans.

"How you've made it so far, I don't know," Paul said in disgust.

"What about you?" I asked. "How are you going to get out of here? Do you think that someday they'll come up to you and say, 'OK, now you're free to choose. You can either be a priest or we'll send you to Europe to sit in cafés in Paris, eat little cakes, and scribble little notes'?"

Paul looked at me in a very odd way. Perhaps he was trying to measure the amount of eccentricity I carried in me. "So, very good. You've proven the age-old truth, then. There's madness in every action. Grow up, man!"

About this time Robert showed up. He was sweating. François rushed up to him and grabbed him. "Where have you been, man? You look like you've seen a ghost."

"Yeah. I probably did. You look pretty shitty yourself."

"What happened?" I asked, knowing that Robert had done something he wasn't supposed to.

"I went to see my girlfriend, and I ran into the priest in charge of the novitiate."

"A girlfriend? You went to the novitiate? *Jesus Christ in hell.* What's going to happen now?" Paul was panicked.

"Calm down and listen. See, ever since I saw this girl on Easter day, I couldn't sleep. My dreams were filled with her. I had to see her, even if it was only going to be for a second. All I needed was her name. But who the hell was going to help me? That's why I decided tonight to drop by and see her for a minute."

"But how did you imagine you would see her?" I interjected. "There are almost two hundred girls in that place."

"Trust, trust. I knew she would come. I knew that the first window I was going to knock on would be hers. I needed to see her so bad. And I would have, only I got there at the wrong moment, when the priest in charge of the novitiate was getting ready to come back here for the night."

"He does that every night around eleven. You knew that," said François. He was beginning to get the picture, and it was irritating him.

Robert continued. "As I walked past the fence and into the novitiate, it was so dark that I didn't notice anything at first. I located the girls' dorm and was just about to do the impossible when I heard the sound of urine falling onto the ground. That damn priest was pissing next to a tree. No wonder I didn't see him. Where he was it was a lot darker.

" 'Who is it?' he roared. I took two steps backward. I knew I had been caught and I was thinking very fast. The priest repeated his question. I was so scared I decided I was going to run, and so I did. Suspending his relief, the man ran after me. He moved so swiftly that there were no way I could outrun him. So I stopped and turned around. 'Father Simon—is that you?'

" 'Who are you?' he said. He was now convinced that he had me in his hands.

" 'It's me—Robert.'

" 'What are you doing out here at night?'

" 'Father, oh, Father! I'm so glad it's you! I was going to the latrine to relieve myself. I have diarrhea, and I haven't been able to sleep since lights-out. On my third round to the latrine, I heard a noise down there—see that light in the forum area? There have been so many thefts in the past couple of months that I thought it was a bunch of thieves sharing what they had stolen. I decided to go do something about it, but I couldn't go straight there. They would have heard me long before I got there. So I decided I'd take a detour through the woods. When I got there, I heard the noise you were making, and I thought the whole area was infested by thieves. When you asked me who I was, I wasn't sure it was you until you spoke the second time.'

"Father Simon looked at the light where I had pointed, and said, 'Gee, Robert, I think you're right! Let's go find out who's down there. Just stay behind me.' We crawled together through the tall grass and the trees. When we were near the light, he told me to hide behind a tree while he went to take a look. He came back and said, 'Oh, *mon pauvre* Robert—it's only your teachers playing chess in the forum. Go back to sleep. And next time don't take that kind of risk. You could be killed.'

"'Thank you, Father,' I said. I went to the dorm and lay down for a while because I still couldn't believe I'd escaped."

"You're the craziest Garibaldi," I said, feeling my heart pounding inside my chest as if trying to warn me of an impending danger. "Why would anyone put himself at such risk?"

Robert sighed. "The world is calling me," he said. "It says, 'Robert, Robert, you've suffered long enough.' Besides, Patrice, I don't think I can live any longer without a woman."

Excited by Robert's confession, Antoine jumped in. "The only reason I look forward to Christmas and Easter is because I know I'll see the girls. I feel guilty, but at least I look forward to the mass."

From his pocket he pulled out a crumpled picture of a naked woman. He had gotten it from the cooks and been hiding it until now. To my dismay, I was discovering that all of the Garibaldis had the same intention: to leave the seminary at the first opportunity. I began to wonder why I had been hanging on to the need to become a priest. *I must be crazy,* I thought, but I had wanted to be a priest all along, as far back as I could remember.

Antoine looked at me intently and I felt as if he had read my thoughts. "Aren't you curious about what it's like to be inside a woman?"

"I have no desire to inflict the pain of sex on anyone," I said.

It stunned me to suddenly realize the extent to which my religious experience had molded my psyche on the issue of male/female relations. Without knowing it, I had come to see women as both attractive and repulsive. This attitude had begun with the endless homilies on hell, Satan, and, most vividly, on mortal sins fed to me by the Jesuits. From the minute I entered my teens, I began to hear that women had the doors to hell built into their bodies. Even thinking about them could endanger our souls. I could concede that thinking about them was dangerous, in light of the events that transpired in the Garden of Eden so long ago. After all, wasn't it Woman who had first tempted Man to sin? I also understood that

Woman was born punished since her body poured blood every month and she gave birth amid incredible pain. But why women were so cursed was as difficult for me to comprehend as their total absence from our lives.

To even think sexual thoughts was to invite damnation, since we were taught that there was no difference between thoughts and deeds. In such an unbalanced context, sex was presented as a sin as wicked as suicide or murder. The specter of sexuality became a nightmare in the quiet of my spiritual life. As I traversed puberty, the topic became laden with terror. My normal hormonal disturbances seemed like the very devil invading every part of my being, and I felt like a frail leaf adrift on the shores of hell.

Thus, over the last fifteen years the association of sex with death and hell had surreptitiously taken a grip on me, and to me, what Robert had done was beyond the daring of even the most insane mind. He was the most active of the Garibaldis and the most unpredictable. How he had managed to survive so many years of brainwashing on sexuality to respond to the imperative of seeing a princess in the forbidden land, I could never fathom.

After Robert's adventure, sex became a regular topic among the Garibaldis. Once, while we were arguing in the forum during siesta, Father Michael approached us. After his skirmish several years ago with Father Superior, we had expected him to leave. Instead, his influence continued to be felt in the most flagrant way. He was known among his colleagues as the one who spied for the students and helped them break the rules. Father Michael knew what the other priests thought of him. He had discussed it with us several times, and our general impression was that he did not care what people said about him.

When he arrived our talk died. He greeted us. "Hello, there. What's on today?"

Our response to these friendly overtures was invariably deferential and cautious, even though we knew that Father Michael was more trustworthy than anyone else. Our caution today stemmed from the subject matter of our conversation—the wrinkled nude female image that Antoine had gotten from the cooks. To carry around a picture like that in a seminary was the worst crime one could possibly think of committing, and we all found the battered photograph attractive and frightening. I was drawn to it because I wanted to take a good look at the anatomy of the Keeper of the Gateway to Hell; I had a strong yet vague sense of the relationship of beauty to evil. If hell were to recruit likely candidates, it had to construct a presentation of itself that contradicted its nature; and so, it seemed to me, it was logical that a naked woman should look so beautiful.

Father Michael had a keen flair for uncovering the hidden. He could detect the presence of something important behind our heavy silence, and this instinct invited him to investigate. "Politics, literature, art?" he queried.

No one answered. We were busy trying to act normal while our minds were still locked onto the very subject his shrewdness was going to guide him toward.

"Sex?"

This time he hit it. Antoine, who had introduced the subject in the first place with his nude photograph, jumped right in, obviously feeling responsible. "Uh, we've just learned that countries in Africa are being freed."

"Yes, that's true, but this isn't what you've been talking about. I'll bet it's sex. Right?"

"Women," capitulated Antoine.

"Love," François corrected.

I felt that I too should say something along that line to provide a general impression of unity and credibility. "Father, do people really like sex?"

"It's not always that bad, is it?" Antoine asked, relieved. We were all relieved from the anxiety of being caught with our hands in the cookie jar.

Father Michael undertook to give us a little sex education. "It can be an act of choice," he said. "It's like a supplement to the fire of love that two people maintain for each other. Without sex, there is a certain sense of incompleteness and unfulfillment. One consummates love by making love. I don't mean 'make' in the sense of manufacturing something, but in the sense of—"

"But why is there is so much danger associated with sex?" I asked this because I hoped for a refutation of what Father Rémy had told us for so long—that women are the doors to hell.

"The dangers are more symbolic than real. See, when God commanded humans to reproduce, he did not warn them that the particulars of reproduction could be undermined by the danger of going to hell. We, for example, are an institution that does not encourage reproductive thinking. Chastity is one of the promises we must make as part of our vocation. This has nothing to do with believing that we must hate women or think of them as evil. There is no hell in the body of a woman. Beauty is not hell."

The truth of what he said had a demystifying power over the teaching we had all received. But his views of celibacy implied a profound contradiction: here was an ideal that said a priest could go to heaven only if he first placed an anathema on sexual relations. No one knew what to say. After a while François changed the subject. "Father, are they going to let you remain a priest?"

"I don't know. Once a priest, always a priest. So the business isn't about letting me remain a priest, but what to do with the kind of priest they've got in me."

"Are you leaving, Father?"
"Yes, someday—like everyone else."

▲　　　▼　　　▲

One of the high points in the life of the seminary was the festival of pro-
cessions called Fête Dieu, which coincided with the coming of spring.
This festival was preceded by a day of drawing and painting on the surface
of the processional path. About a kilometer long, the path was divided
into as many parts as there were classes, and each class had to demonstrate
its dexterity at making its part of the processional route look the most
beautiful. We drew stars and angels and geometric patterns—taken mostly
from history books and our imaginations—and we brought flowers from
all over the seminary to cover the ground. At the end of the day, the processional pathway looked as celestial as if God himself were going to descend the next morning and walk on its beauty with us. Sometimes at
night it would rain and most of the paintings would be washed away, but
when the whole pathway survived the night, it was great to be able to walk
on it hand in hand singing *gloria tibi domine*. Saying the mass outdoors in
good weather provided greater distractions and more signs of the divine
presence than saying it indoors.

The year the Garibaldis were born, we had a confrontation with Father
Superior over the content of our contribution to the processional path. Toward the end of the day we had spent decorating, Zeus decided to inspect
the masterpieces of the different classes, something he seldom did.

Unfortunately for us, our group had decided to work a few innova-
tions into the traditional patterns by providing some discreet nonreligious
representations. I in particular was bitten by this bug. Drawing from my
previous experience at encoding African tradition into drama, I had painted
a village medicine man at work, commanding the natural order to interact
with him. Old and bearded, he stood in the midst of trees and birds. In one
hand he held a staff, and his other was stretched out like Moses commanding the waters of the Red Sea to split. Excited by this, I drew another medicine man performing a healing ceremony on a person more wretched than
the paralytic that Jesus healed in the Bible. Then I wrote in golden letters,
GOD IS IN EVERY MAN.

There were a lot of other drawings in our section of the procession
itinerary, and it was not easy to determine whether any one of them was
inspired by paganism or Christianity. None of them was meant to do
anything other than sincerely beautify the processional path, and mine intended to include thematic diversity. When Zeus passed by on his inspection tour and saw what we had done, he went into a frenzy of anger. At the

spiritual lecture that night, he announced that there would be no general recreational time for us, and that we would not get to see the Charlie Chaplin movie *Charlot*. He also declared that there couldn't be a procession this year because God would be very insulted. Some of us had taken their own creative freedom out of bounds and desacralized the entire processional path.

At this, Robert raised his hand.

"What do you want?" Zeus roared.

"I just want to know how desacralized the entire processional space is because I want to see if there isn't a way to save it by performing a little editing."

"It's very bad, and you contributed to it. The worst spot was that assigned to you older students. You really botched it up."

"I just don't think we deserve to be punished like this. The truth is—"

"There's nothing more to be said! The punishment stands."

That night we ate in silence, even though we were permitted to speak to each other. After dinner we decided that since we were in charge of the mass, at least as far as the music went, we were not going to sing songs of grace and joy, but the kind of dismal songs we sang during Lent and holy week.

Our silence drew everybody's attention. Zeus, who thought he could get away with this punishment, found out he was dealing with individuals who felt deeply wronged. But he sustained his verdict, and we maintained our silent resentment. The next day the mass was a ritual mourning addressed to the divine. We sang:

> *Christ, son of the Father,*
> *Who came to Earth to save*
> *Those who were lost,*
> *See the depth of our misery,*
> *Grant us your pity*

In place of a celebratory Kyrie, we sang the Kyrie memorial for the dead. And our voices rose with unmistakable sincerity toward a God whom we took as our witness to the misery we suffered. Father Michael was in a good mood all through the service. Father Joe looked confused, as if he did not know which day it was or which gospel text to preach from. The worst face was that of Father Superior. Fried into crust, it expressed immense pain and subdued will. He had tried to punish us, and we were appealing to God, his God. He could not interfere with that—if he did we would say he did not want us to pray or to speak to the divine. The whole purpose of a seminarian is to express his feelings sincerely and honestly to God anytime. Father Superior was the first to insist on that. What we sang, we felt, and Father Superior knew very well why we were singing mournful songs. God was in the middle of our conflict with leadership. This was good for us.

During communion we sang:

> *The people who dwelt in the dark*
> *Shall arise;*
> *The people who slept in death*
> *Shall awake;*
> *For here cometh Jesus*

Everything else went on as if it were a celebration day. After the mass we spent the day in quiet, whispering to each other when we had to communicate. In the evening, at the spiritual lecture, Zeus, departing from the norm, actually apologized to us. "I know you all feel resentful about what happened in the last twenty-four hours. I am only a human being with the responsibility of a large family, and I must try to do my best to ensure that everything is in order. If you are directing your protest toward me as a person, here I am. But if your protest is against the higher authority for which I work, I am unable to meet your needs. The bishop will have to decide on that."

It was so touching to hear Zeus appear defeated for the first time that we lost the wit to speak. Something in the rigidity of the rhythm of our lives had cracked. I didn't quite know what it was, and I didn't know how long it would be before it took effect or how it would express itself. But something had changed. From then on students were bolder, more daring in their defiance of regulations. It was this new climate of change that brought about my downfall.

One morning Father Joe was giving us our weekly French dictation—the *dictée*. There was nothing very special about this, yet for the Garibaldis, competitive in every area, nothing regarding the French language was to be taken lightly. I had proven myself in textual analysis, but I was never able to spell correctly, so I never did well in dictation, and Robert and François were always ahead of me.

That week I decided to even the score by intensifying my studies. I had had four different practice dictations read to me by Antoine. That Monday I was ready for battle. Everything went well until the last fifteen minutes, when we were supposed to proofread our work for misspellings and grammatical errors. Father Joe was walking up and down the aisle of the classroom, glancing here and there at the texts. He stood next to me, reading my dictation for a time that seemed infinite. It irked me to have someone peering over my shoulder. I could not concentrate, nor could I tell him to get away from me because I was unable to work while he stood there. I tried to ignore him, but my blood was too hot for that. I could only pretend to read my *dictée*.

As if to confirm my suspicion that he was spying on my work, he pointed at a word two lines before the end of the text. I looked at the word and, yes, it was misspelled. Instinctively, I started to correct it. Father Joe knocked my hand off the paper and my pen went flying. Bewildered at the violence of his gesture, I thought he had been accidentally pushed by someone. But when I looked up and our eyes met, his were red with anger and resentment. This made me even angrier. I bent down and picked up my pen to correct the misspelled word. As I was about to do so, he pushed my hand away again. I felt deeply wronged—helpless and alone.

"Why?" I asked out loud.

"I found it, you did not."

"But this is correction time."

"It doesn't make any difference. You did not find the word. I did. You can't correct it."

Suddenly my mind went blank. I felt weak all over. Tears began to stream out of my eyes. "But why?" I implored. "Why shouldn't I verify my text like everybody else?"

"Nobody said you could not."

I felt I could not argue. Torn by a mixture of anger, weakness, shame, injustice, and God knows what else, I went numb. A big lump surged up in my throat, blocking my every word. At that point nothing that happened could atone for the injustice I felt. I grabbed the notebook and flung it on the floor, saying, "Take it then, since it has become yours."

Father Joe picked up the notebook and brought it back to my desk. I pushed it away. He pushed it back. I pushed it harder. He slapped me and said, "You undisciplined brat—you fail at this exercise."

I stopped breathing. I had been struck—insulted in front of the whole class, I, a twenty-year-old grown-up, member of the Garibaldi group. No one in the higher division was ever hit. That punishment ceased after we reached the higher division. It meant that I was going to be the laughing-stock of the class, and probably of the entire division, until someone else took my place as victim.

Something in me switched into a war mode. I shoved Father Joe, saying, "You could never dream of having a son like me. You have no right to hit me."

Speaking gave me more strength and boldness. The priest stared at me, dumbfounded. I shoved him again. He slapped me hard across the face and I saw stars twinkling in the middle of the day. Crying, I bent my head and rammed it into his belly. He emitted an "uh" sound at the impact. I moved back and stood on the defensive.

"I will allow no one to hit me without reason," I said, feeling stronger and stronger, as if I were avenging years and years of silent submission. Father Joe swung at me again, but I ducked. He got carried away by his own momentum and lost his balance. I took that opportunity to run to the front of the classroom. He came after me. I was able to fend off another blow, but this time he grabbed me. I resisted and we fought. We were close to the window, and his every movement seemed to edge us closer to it.

I managed to land a couple of blows on his ribs while he pounded my back. I grabbed his leg. While he struggled for balance, I pushed him hard. He crashed against the window, which shattered as he yelled, and went through it backwards.

I felt for a few seconds like jumping through the window to continue the battle outside, but I slowly became aware that the entire class had leaped to its feet in horror over what had happened. It was then I realized I had made a terrible mistake.

CHAPTER 9

THE LONG JOURNEY BEGINS

 The cup was full; it had to be drunk, bitter as it was. The impulse to raise my hand against my superior had triggered an unstoppable flow of events pushing me like an avalanche toward the chasm of the unknown. In retrospect, my actions seem inevitable. Inside me was a void of rage so deep, so carefully nurtured over the past fifteen years, that I could have done nothing else, finally, but respond to violence with violence.

Father Joe had trapped me in my pride. I read my fate in the sepulchral faces of my classmates. In an instant I had lost one identity and acquired another. And I felt as alone as I ever had before. Nothing could change the course of things as they stood. In a moment of excess I had inadvertently ceased to belong to the seminary. This realization echoed in me endlessly, forecasting immense tribulations ahead.

Father Joe was sitting in the dirt, trying to get up. He was grimacing like a monkey, and his white robe was pierced all over by thorns and stalks of wiregrass. A crowd was slowly gathering around him—students from the lower division next door who had heard the noise of the argument followed by the sound of breaking glass and Father Joe's cry as he fell. They were more fascinated by the spectacle of a priest wearing a formerly immaculate soutane, sitting on the dusty ground, than curious about how he had got there.

Inside the classroom, the students were still standing. Their consternation seemed to have worked a paralysis on their nervous systems. I, on the other hand, felt an urgent need to end the suspense I had created by my impetuous actions. I stood there sweating, facing my dumbfounded schoolmates, my confusion rising in proportion to their apprehension.

I began to speak, partly to myself to keep my blood flowing and partly to make a show of composure. "Friends, I have committed a sin of the most terrible nature, vastly worse than those we have been allowed to take to the confessional every other Friday. I do not think any priest will mediate for me in any attempt I make to seek divine forgiveness. I have attacked God by attacking his closest ally. I didn't mean to do this. I still can't believe it has happened to me. Can no one help me? I feel so alone."

I wanted help from my closest friends, but I knew they couldn't offer it because there are certain limits beyond which help is impossible. I was too numb to even feel pity for myself. For a while, I stood there looking stupid.

Antoine was crying, but in a rather manly fashion. He made no sounds, but I knew that the two lines of tears running down his cheeks were for me.

I bowed my head. As if I were a bottle just emptied of its contents and made useless as a result, words died out of me.

"Where are you going?" inquired Robert in a tone that suggested that he was desperately seeking some sort of compromise. He was the first to regain his wits and was now trying to play the role of mediator. "This was just an accident. We all saw it. We'll back you up in front of Father Superior. At the worst, you'll get away with a series of minor punishments. Don't be so dramatic."

Though I wanted to believe what he said, I realized there could be no mercy for anyone who attacked a priest in a seminary. Nothing like this had ever happened before at Nansi. I would be seen as a godless savage who had willfully resisted the purifying powers of this Christian institution and returned to the uncouth primitivism of his original state.

"I don't know what to do," I said vaguely. My mind was racing. "I suppose I should put as much distance as possible between me and this place."

"Stay," cried François. "Hell, we're all sinners here, right?" He was looking at everybody in the classroom as if seeking agreement from them. There were murmurs of approval—or were they of disapproval? By this time I did not care. I had run out of answers. With death in my heart, I crossed the threshold of the classroom, knowing that I would never be able to return. Meanwhile the crowd had thickened around Father Joe. A few were helping him clean up his soutane, while others watched the procedure piously, arms folded. Was the presence of all these witnesses the reason he didn't leap back in through the window to kill me?

No one seemed to notice my departure. The classroom was less than fifty meters from the latrines, which were built a few meters from the outer rim of the seminary. Beyond the latrines was a semi-jungle of trees and tall grass: easy to disappear into it.

Every step toward the wild outer rim of the seminary seemed like a step toward doom, dragging me backward in time. In front of me was the infinite green mystery of the jungle, speaking a language I could not decipher; behind was the sealed door of a haven of security and protection that had suddenly been transformed into an inimical alien world.

My first taste of freedom made me wish that I had never wanted to be free. I was frightened by the immensity of the jungle—its silent and cold invitation. Now that I had the opportunity to respond to the longing to go home, had I lost faith all of a sudden? Was I fearful because, for the first time in sixteen years, I was expected to make my own decisions about what to do and where to go for the rest of my life? If I had gambled on the odds and stayed in the seminary, I asked myself, wouldn't that have been better than my present mess? Surely my classmates and Father Michael would have supported me? I felt stupid for having acted in haste. I felt angry at myself for attacking a priest and leaving without being asked to. But even if I could return, what would I say?

To have nothing to do and no one to answer to is a frightening thing. Here I was, facing the world and yet incapable of assuming my own freedom. When I finally moved on, it was only because I heard voices behind me. Without thinking, I walked into the jungle to avoid being seen. Thus I began my voyage home.

All I knew was that home was east. How far east? I could not tell. The jungle was not too dense and I could see reasonably far ahead of me. The late-morning sun was ablaze in the savanna-blue sky, promising great heat. I walked steadily eastward, as if trying to complete one of those assignments we were given in the seminary every morning before eight o'clock, which we had to do without any thought. Here and there unrecognizable natural sounds reminded me of the precariousness of my situation. Images of the comforts left behind me rushed through my mind: the quiet orange groves and banana plantations of the seminary, the arrays of flowers on either side of its meditation trails, the comforting thought of a meal always at hand whenever one was hungry and the security of a bed to rest on when one was tired. Why had I ever left? What could possibly replace the life I had grown accustomed to over the last sixteen years? I felt like a domesticated beast abruptly released into the jungle. I had lost my vital instincts. But, I decided, as long as the sun was up there bright and hot and I could still see where I was going, I would keep moving.

My white seminarian's shirt was soon soaked with sweat. The forest was still, as if petrified by the heat of the flaming sun. This deep silence created something like a vacuum inside me, filling me with images of a new world about to be created the split second I became aware of it. I was thirsty. Maybe I was seeing things. The sound of an insect broke the trance of suspense I was walking in and brought me back to the stark reality of my desertion.

As the sun traveled down the vast blue sky toward the horizon, I came to a wide-open dirt road. Judging by the position of the sun and the direction of my own shadow, it ran east/west. I walked along the edge of it until the sound of an engine caught my attention. Far behind me I could see a huge cloud of red dust, indicating that the vehicle was a truck. If it was one of the huge trucks used to bring supplies to the seminary, it would probably be piloted by one of the priests. The thought of being seen sent a chill through me that ran like lightning down my spine. I instinctively hid myself behind a tree and waited for the truck to pass.

Soon I could see the driver busy at the wheel, trying to keep the huge machine straight and avoid the holes and heaps of sand that crowded the highway. Though I did not know his name, I saw that he was a priest. Seated next to him was Blaise the cook. They were probably on their way to the nearest supply center. *How far could that be?* I wondered. Were there a lot of people there? Could I get there before sunset? The truck roared past me, covering my white uniform with red dust. For a while I could see nothing. Up ahead I heard the engine wail and groan and emit a series of frightening explosions. Then its noise receded rapidly. The heavy silence of the bush was restored. I resumed my journey hoping that at least this road would take me to an inhabited place where I could get some information about my whereabouts.

To avoid the thick dust, I moved to a trail that ran parallel to the highway and that kept it carefully in sight. I walked, aware of nothing but the unspecifiable distance I was covering, till the sun disappeared behind a far mountain. The narrow trail I was following became faint, then almost invisible in the twilight. Countless sounds came from everywhere, welcoming the fall of the dew, and my shoes became progressively more wet as I walked. The cool that evening brought seemed to have an invigorating effect on the jungle. Its moisture awoke thousands of insects that became noisier, the darker it got.

I realized that I had walked a whole day without eating. My mind was so crowded by thoughts, my body so stiff and soaked with sweat, that I could not even think about what I was going to do when complete darkness fell and I had to sleep.

Very soon it became impossible to go any farther. The night was dark as charcoal. I felt as if I were walking with my eyes tightly closed. The crisis that had provided the impetus to keep moving all day was far behind me now. My motivation to keep going was being undermined by hunger, fear, loneliness, and a desolate sense of homelessness. I had to gain a sense of direction and control. Two things were becoming more important than anything else: food and rest. But for a person accustomed since birth to having these needs met by other people, it was not natural to think creatively about how to obtain them for oneself. In the seminary, when one felt hunger, there was always the guarantee of a meal within the next hour or so. After all these years my system was like a clock that would register hunger shortly after morning mass, then later after the Angelus at noontime, and in the evening prior to Vespers. But these were sweet triggers, because the food was always there.

Imagining the good meals I had enjoyed at the refectory only worsened the experience and enhanced the fear I was beginning to feel.

What was I supposed to do with this fear? What was I supposed to do with my hunger and thirst? While I walked, I thought about food. It was getting harder and harder to move my body. Each step was beginning to require all my attention, and my progress had slowed dramatically since dark.

I finally decided that the need for rest was more urgent than the desire for food, and more easily available. I quickly filled my arms with some fresh leaves from the dwarf trees I walked past and soon had enough of them to make a bed. Big trees were everywhere. I picked the closest, dropped my leaves beneath it, and sat on them with my back against the trunk and my legs outstretched. At that moment I felt all the weight of stress and fear and exhaustion register in my body in a way that nailed me stiff where I was. I tried to stay awake a while longer to sort out some of my most urgent thoughts, but sleep was coming upon me fast. Fleetingly, I wondered how safe I was at night in the middle of the bush. . . .

An immense bird was flying toward me from the south. Its wings were spread very wide on either side of its slender, muscular body, and it prepared to land on me. The movement of its wings produced a fanlike wind that quickly chilled my body.

My first thought was to somehow hide on the other side of the tree to avoid being hurt by this huge and frightening creature that had erupted out of nowhere, but I could not move. I had lost control of my senses. My mind was still operating, but my body had ceased to be connected to it. The bird grasped me by the shoulders and emitted a shrieking noise as it took off with me hanging underneath. It was so dark I could not tell where

I was being taken to, but I knew we were covering a great distance. Then, as if by enchantment, all of this vanished, and I found myself sitting on a soft, hairy body that somehow felt very familiar. To make sure it was a body, I ran my hand up and down it and pulled out some hair. I also felt as if a wet sponge were being applied to my face and that my body was producing a cool sensation.

I could feel myself sleeping, yet I had no power to open my eyes to see what was going on. I felt no fear and no sense of hurry. The sensation of being taken care of canceled out every instinct to try and find out what was really happening to me. I heard voices—or was it just a voice? I did not understand what it was saying, but it spoke for a very long time as if reciting some discourse in an obscure language. The strangeness of the language did not frighten me. Nothing in the tone of the voice did. Asleep or awake, I could feel myself profoundly participating in the restoration of my fatigued body, as if I were a hungry person imbibing a good meal. I was enjoying the experience and I liked the homey sensations it generated. I had buried the hardships of the day in an experience that, though strange, was comforting.

When I woke up, it was almost dawn and the sun's rays were trekking across the skies. I did not know where I was until I tried to move and found out I was sore all over. It was then that the memory of the dream rushed back into me with great clarity. I looked about as if remembering something I just finished doing. Scattered all around and over me were soft feathers mixed with hair. The tree under which I had slept had been freshly scratched by something large, as if someone had battered the trunk with a powerful tool. In some places the bark had been peeled off, leaving fresh gaping wounds on the trunk. I stood up and stretched, feeling my muscles ache with the pain of my long march away from the seminary.

It had been an agitated night. I could scarcely believe I had had such incoherent and hallucinatory dreams. They were the kinds of images that come to one as an expression of excessive fatigue. But had something real also happened? I could not explain the presence of the feathers and the hair on the ground all around me. What about the bird that had flown away with me? And the hairy thing that had touched me as if it knew me? In spite of my initial fear, I remembered comfort, the kind of comfort that puts the mind to rest from its torments. In a very real way I was still drawing support from the dream, as if a powerful, nurturing presence lingered nearby. I convinced myself that something good was following me, looking out for me—that an ungraspable force was expressing itself around me. Maybe it had always been there, but I had not been able to perceive it because too much had been distracting me in my old life. The incident presented me with a great puzzle, but the puzzle did not feel like a challenge.

To resolve it, I felt I had only to stick with my commitment to keep going amid the silence of the tropical flora, in the deep mystery of its bosom.

Thoughts of my home reminded me of the horrendous reality of my situation. I was lost, sandwiched between a past that had utterly forgotten me and a future that was undecided.

I arose and began to walk toward the rising run. The fresh air of the morning was powerful, but it reminded me of my hunger. *If only I could eat something,* I thought over and over. My mouth felt as if it were plastered with a layer of a sticky substance I could not get rid of. I kept thinking of a good toothbrush and some sweet Colgate toothpaste. But where in the jungle could I find the running water that is so important for brushing your teeth?

Then I remembered that my father used to have a fresh twig stuck in his mouth when he was not eating. His constant chewing of it obliged him to spit frequently. What tree was it whose branch he used as a toothbrush? I decided to try out some fresh twigs just to see how they would work.

By this time the sun had risen behind the tall trees. Its rays sporadically stole through their foliage, coloring the forest with enigmatic patterns of light and dark. The trees around me were getting thicker and thicker. Their leafy branches gave me a canopy of cool darkness. The grass was getting rarer and rarer. I found a small tree and broke off one of its branches, revealing a whitish interior. I sliced the upper part away and kept a short piece. At first chewing was hard and the wood tasted bitter. But the bitterness was better than my sticky mouth. The more I chewed, the more watery my mouth turned, and I swallowed every bit of it.

I was uncertain about whether I was going the right way, yet I didn't have any better ideas. In front of me I noticed a tree loaded with fruits that looked like oranges. Their bright color exerted a powerful attraction, but I found out that they were either inedible or not yet ripe. They were very sour and resisted every bite. The sight of a fruit tree alleviated my panic somewhat, however, reminded me that I was, after all, in the bush, where natural food was plentiful. I began to look harder and harder as I walked. Almost one tree out of ten carried some fruits, but most hung high above my head, defying my curiosity and my hunger that, seeing the possibility of fulfillment, raged more and more inside of me.

Fully occupied with my hunger, I had discontinued dwelling on my fate. I began to feel like it was perfectly natural to be out there in the middle of nowhere trying to go somewhere. *Is this the first sweet taste of freedom?* I thought back to the seminary, now lost in the jungle far behind me. Looking at my wristwatch, I saw that it was 7:45. I imagined the mechanical operation of hundreds of lives as they listened to the end of the morning mass. They were all thinking about the warm rice porridge waiting for them at breakfast. But before they could eat, they would have to go through physical training, a time most of us despised.

My progress slowed as I moved into the mountains. As I reached the top of the first one, I realized I was close to a town. The setting sun was shedding its light on countless roofs, which reflected back into my eyes, making it too bright for me to see anything distinctly. But the town was definitely there, a few kilometers down in front of me. The reddish thread of another dirt highway, bisecting the one I was following, glowed to the north. It too was going toward the rows of shining tin roofs in the middle of the valley.

When I reached the edge of town, it was almost dark. The houses looked miserable and small. It was a suburban shantytown. I was exhausted, dusty, and desperate to know my whereabouts. This town was very different from anything I had seen before. First of all, there were no nearby farms. The town was full of streets, and each street was lined with houses, one next to the other. In every direction people were walking or driving or riding bicycles or mopeds. People walked in groups most of the time, groups that paid little attention to one another. I was anonymous. Nobody cared who I was. In a sense it was comforting not to be asked questions, not to be exposed as a deserter from the divine. I was invisible as long as I looked like everybody else. The road that had taken me into town had become a dirt street, then a paved street that ended in a square where several streets met. On the far side of the square was a street that went east. There was no sidewalk alongside it, just dirt covered with scattered city debris, some of it hidden in the grass. The stench of human excrement and other rotting things filled the evening air.

Soon I was walking under tall trees that lined a paved street, straight and dark. As I walked, my path was lighted by the clair-obscure diffused by courtyard lamps from the rows of dwellings. Everywhere around me there was life. Now and then I heard sounds coming from the houses. The cry of a baby followed by the appeasing voice of its mother, the cries of children playing in a courtyard, and the voices of men assured me that there were other human presences around me even though they spoke in a tribal language I didn't know. In another house a radio blasted local music so loudly that I wondered how anyone could hear anyone else.

I did not realize I was the only person walking in that area until I reached another part of the street illuminated by neon lights and encountered other pedestrians. They were young people, tough-looking and too preoccupied with their business to notice me. They spoke French. Taking a deep breath, I hurled a swift *"Bonsoir"* at four men walking in a group as I was about to pass them. They looked up briefly and returned the greeting. I asked what town it was. They stopped and looked at me with interest. I cleared my throat and asked again, "What's the name of this town?"

One of them answered, "You mean this part of Bobo? It's Ouezzin-ville, man. Where are you going?"

"I'm going to Dano."

"That's far away. The station is up the street."

"What station?"

"Where people take the transport to go to that part of the world."

"You mean there is a bus to Dano tonight?"

"I don't know, but somebody at the east station will tell you if there are any departures tonight."

"How far is the station?"

"Just another half a dozen blocks, past the Lycée Ouezzin."

I thanked the man and walked away. *This town is Bobo,* I thought. On the map it is nearly a hundred kilometers from the seminary. I had walked all that distance in about two days. There was a bus station too. I was delighted by the possibility of having a ride home.

The bus station was an open dirt space where buses, cars, vans, pickups, and trucks were parked. Even though there was a streetlight, the moonlight dominated the area, giving indistinguishable shapes to the people. At one of the corners of the station there was an open-air restaurant, something like a grill. A woman was selling rice and fried fish while a man was busy grilling meat. Scattered around the area were men and women in transit.

I asked the man at the grill, "Where is the bus to Dano?"

The man replied in a tribal language I did not understand, but he seemed to have understood my question, which was posed in French. He pointed to a nearby truck. A tough-looking man was loading fat burlap sacks, probably full of millet. The cargo area of the truck was of wood and steel. It did not have a roof, but a metal structure arched over it that looked like it could be covered with canvas. One man was standing in the truck while the other stood on the ground, hurling merchandise up to him with split-second timing. I waited till they stopped to ask if he was going to Dano.

The man on the ground nodded and added, "We will leave as soon as the truck's full. It's five hundred francs for the trip."

"I don't have the money, but I want to go home."

"Then go borrow it quick before we leave."

"I'm new here, I don't know anybody."

"That's none of my business. If you have five hundred francs you get in and you go. If you don't, go find it first."

I found a place where they cooked meat over an open fire. People sat on stones with their feet in the mud while they ate. They came and left in groups, speaking loudly in a mixture of poor French and local dialects that kept changing as the groups changed. They laughed abundantly. The food was so blackened by the fire that I wondered how they knew what they were eating. No one paid any attention to me. I liked that: In an odd way the proximity of people felt reassuring. They were present, yet absent, and they probably experienced me in the same way.

CHAPTER 10

THE VOYAGE HOME

 Since I had no way to get five hundred francs, I had no choice but to keep going on foot. But that did not seem so unpleasant, for in these circumstances one does not think distance or speed when facing a journey: the focus is on the process.

There are stories in my village about people walking all the way to the Ivory Coast or to Ghana during the first half of the century, when the French decided to use unpaid indigenous labor to construct railroads. As a young man my father had participated in the construction of the railroad—the one that was designed to link the jungle to the desert but never made it to the yellow sands of the Sahara. He had stories of interminable walks through the savanna and the jungle, going toward the ocean. By order of the colonial commandant, people were requisitioned by the village chief and packed into the administration warehouse before being sent northward on foot. The journey, which lasted about a month, was to remain in the memories of those who made it as the most physically demanding and mentally demoralizing experience of their lives. Almost all who were requisitioned were used as bearers. Those who were not loaded with goods were in charge of providing the impetus for this human locomotive so that it could proceed at an acceptable speed. Overseers had whips to lash the travelers and keep them walking fast and steady. Those who did not know how to put their thoughts elsewhere and endure succumbed on the road, where their carcasses were abandoned to the vultures, hyenas, boars, and lions. Stories like this were common. They testified to the challenges of the new time, the white man's time in the African realm.

Mine was a much different experience from that of the people who had preceded me. I did not have any baggage and was therefore lighter than the lightest. When I took to the bush, walking along the dirt highway going east, I had all the time in the world to waste.

The landscape around me was beautiful because of its diversity. The succession of mountains and valleys added to the panoramic aspect of the place. There was a creek or a river in every valley I crossed. The unpolluted water was refreshing to drink. The abundance of fruit trees saved me from my fear of starvation. I had gotten used to living in the bush as a good deserter of God, but my spirit did not want to forget. It acted as a counterforce to my motion forward and produced in me the feeling of someone running away because he was too guilty to be forgiven. I could see with my mind's eyes what would have happened had I decided to stay: the total character thrashing, the gossip, the whip, the isolation, and the unhealable wound to my soul. Things would never have been the same again. Were they the same presently? No one could live so many years in such a strict institution and leave it unhaunted. I felt the seminary following me, judging me, slowing me down—wanting me back and accusing me of violating the physical integrity of one of its sacred members. Images rushed into my crowded consciousness with insistent clarity. The bearded face of Father Maillot appeared and looked down on me as he wondered how to save a soul as messed up as this. Then Father Superior's stentorian voice invaded my ears within: he wanted me to take the punishment as a man totally committed to the divine. He wanted me to submit as an example and be corrected in a way that would also set an example. I heard myself singing requiem songs in a weeping tone. It was a cacophony of arguments launched in every direction within my consciousness. How I was able to keep going forward, I could not tell.

My first night in the mountains I slept well because I did not dream. But when I woke up, I regretted being awake because what visited my conscious mind was the unending problem with guilt. I felt sandwiched between worlds, going toward the one (my village) that had abandoned me, to the other, now haunting me as if a good confession would have set things straight. As I walked with the heaviest baggage of thoughts ever, I could hear the agonizing sounds of trucks trying to conquer the unforgiving dirt highway.

My anxious ruminations ended when I arrived at a village at a crossroad. The new road went north-south and I wondered if it was the same road that I had seen from the top of the mountain. There were people everywhere. I noticed a man at a gas station. "Which road is this?" I asked in French.

The man stared at me, then said, "We first greet people in this corner of the country before asking questions. The new era has not changed the rule yet." This was spoken patronizingly, in passable French.

The man was filthy. He seemed to be an extension of the oil and grease he sold. He was perspiring profusely, even though the weather wasn't that hot, probably because he was so fat. The shirt he wore had once been white. I apologized for being so informal and greeted him again politely in French.

He pointed south, saying, "This road goes very far. If you stay on it, it will take you into Ghana. The other direction [west] goes into Bobo, and if you stay on it, it will take you into Mali. The road that goes into Ghana ends down there into the real Bobo road, the road that goes also to Ouagadougou."

He pointed his finger northward. Then he asked sarcastically, "Now— what do you want?"

"I want to go to Dano," I said, assuming that his knowledge of roads included cities and towns.

The man looked astonished or embarrassed, I couldn't tell which. "You see this road?" he said, pointing south. "Take it and go very far, then ask someone. I think that this Dano place must be a savage region hidden from the light of history. I don't remember seeing it in any book."

He returned to his work as if he wanted nothing else to do with me. I knew that my village was close to Ghana, so I resumed my voyage even though my mind could not stop asking how far is "very far."

The highway was heavily traveled. Every time a truck, a car, or a horse cart passed, it was followed by a thick cloud of red dust that stuck greedily to the body whether there was moisture on it or not. To avoid choking, I tried to stay as far away as possible from the highway, but I could never seem to get far enough. That, I soon learned, was because I was on the wrong side of it. The dust never blew to the other side.

For three days and four nights I encountered no village, only my thoughts and feelings mixed together in a fierce competition. I encountered birds, rabbits, monkeys, and antelope. Antelope were likely to be found in the middle of the afternoon at a waterhole. As we drank together, they looked at me with astonishment. When I walked away, they continued drinking, as if they had established that I was not a hunter. Monkeys did not seem to be surprised by me at all. Some of them traveled alongside me, jumping from branch to branch and screaming to each other until they lost interest in me. Rabbits fled in silent disarray. As I walked closer and closer to my past, I was not feeling excitement, rather, countless grim questions lashed out at me. *What if everyone is dead? What if the house you seek never was? What do you think you're going to do, anyway?*

On the fourth day of my journey along this road, I came to a town where most of the houses were made of mud. Somewhere farther ahead I could see the tower of a church. *This is how far I was supposed to walk before asking someone for Dano,* I thought.

I was told that the name of this town was Diébougou. Dano was under its jurisdiction and located fifty-five kilometers to the north. The man I spoke to did not seem interested in knowing anything about me, nor was he in the mood to talk, but for the first time someone had actually given me a firm location of the town where I was born. Fifty kilometers felt like a day's walk. My heart pounded in my chest. Did I feel this excitement because I was going home at last? Or was it because I was close to an ending? There was no definitive answer.

The last part of my journey was almost twice the speed of the first part. I counted my steps ten at a time until I reached one hundred, then I started all over again until I lost the energy to do that. Farther east I encountered another crossroad. This one was marked. There was a sign that said that Dano was north from where I was.

I arrived at a marketplace where an immense crowd was bartering. I sat underneath a tree to catch my breath. The day was only two thirds over, so I did not think I was running out of time. After all, wasn't I home? Nobody had confirmed it yet, but I thought I remembered the marketplace and the huge kapok trees lining the dirt road that went through it. A man came over to me and said something that I did not understand. I tried to respond, but I had forgotten which language I was speaking in. What came out of my mouth was gibberish. I was exhausted, so I closed my eyes and slept, but not for long. When I woke up, there was a crowd around me.

Everybody was talking at the same time in a language I did not understand. A man addressed me in French. He asked if I was a stranger here. The sound of French in the middle of so much gibberish was invigorating. I heard myself say to him, "Oh—you speak French!"

"Of course I do. That's because I'm not from here. Where are you from?" His French was perfect. I told him my story in a nutshell.

"If the house of Bakhye is in Dano-Bagan, then it's across the river from here. That's what 'Dano-Bagan' means. It should not be difficult to find it unless everybody is dead. Here everybody knows everybody else. But just don't try to find someone by using his last name. Almost everybody has the same last name. Look, I'll walk you there if you want."

I got on my feet and looked at the man. He was slender, a little taller than me, but not older. He was dressed in an oversized shirt and in pants that ended in black leather shoes covered by a thin layer of yellow dust. He looked much cleaner than me in my dust-reddened uniform and filthy sneakers. His narrow eyes were almost hidden behind white glasses and his hair was bushy. Stretching out his hand, he said, "My name is Ouédraogo Lamoussa. You are?"

"Malidoma. I mean, Patrice—Patrice Somé. It's been so long since I last was here that I can barely remember where my parents live. But I'm sure I can tell my way from the river."

We cut through the crowd and took to the road, heading east again. The sight of the mud houses along the road brought back memories. I recognized the chief's headquarters, built like a fortress with its guarded entrances. I also noticed the minaret, crowned at its top with three ostrich eggs—the tallest mud building in town. Mr. Ouédraogo drew me out of my inspection by asking me how long I had been away.

"Oh, about fifteen years," I said almost without interest.

"Oh—so you're one of those who were chosen by God." He snorted. "Independence has put an end to all that crap. But your parents must have forgotten you by now. Fifteen years leaves plenty of time to die."

"Where did you go to school?" I did not like talking about death.

"In the city. There were fewer schools in colonial times than now. But the same is true for opportunities. Why are you coming home? You should have gone right to the city. With your education you would have found a job. That's what I would have done before coming home for a visit. There's nothing here. You can't expect to like something you never grew up with."

"I know. I don't know why I came home. It's complicated." I did not know how to respond. He had no idea that jobs and earning a livelihood were new realities for me. Before he had spoken to me, I had no ambition other than to get home. He had touched upon grave matters.

Interrupting my thoughts, he said, "Look, if you get tired of this, please look me up in the city. Ouagadougou is great. With your education you will find something you like."

We had crossed the river Guatazin and entered Dano-Bagan—"Dano-across-the-river." It was the same as I remembered it, less some minor changes such as trees being cut down here and there. One of the missing trees was the one under which my mother had given birth to me. The road through the village wound from creek to creek as it made its way to my parents' house. After hesitating at a couple of turns, we finally found it. Mr. Ouédraogo did not want to continue to the house. He said he did not like emotional scenes.

I sat on a pile of boards under a nim tree, the only shade tree near the house. The home I had left a decade and a half ago faced me silently. No one was in sight. Some chickens hunted for food in the nearby cornfield. Fifteen years of absence had changed my perception of earth homes. The compound did not have the same majesty. It did not look tall and imposing, and its simplicity was almost synonymous with desolation. Unconsciously I was looking at it with eyes that had been changed. Minor additions and modifications had been made. I noticed that the main entrance led directly into the inner yard, whereas fifteen years ago it had led first through the poultry room, then through the zangala, and then into the yard. I wanted to go inside to take a closer look, but something prevented me. The sun had nearly set, and I knew someone was going to come home sooner or later, so I decided to take a nap.

When I woke up the sun had disappeared. There were half a dozen naked people around me, all speaking Dagara, which I could no longer comprehend. They seemed excited by the fact that I had woken up. They were mostly kids and were extremely dirty. Most of them had sores all over their bodies that attracted countless flies. I was as interested in them as they were in me. We could only look at each other. It was not long before a young woman carrying wood appeared from behind the house. She dropped her load near the main entrance and spoke to the children. They responded by pointing at me. She greeted me in French.

I asked, "Is this the house of Bakhye?"

"No. This is Elie, my father's house. Bakhye is my grandfather." Her French was miserable, but it was better than the gibberish of the children. I said nothing. She walked inside the compound and came out with a calabash full of white liquid. She drank a small portion of it and handed the rest to me. I brought it to my mouth. It tasted sour, but it was drinkable. She took the rest and walked back into the compound. An old man arrived on a bicycle. He was thin, small, and fragile looking. He parked his bicycle against the wall and greeted me in Dagara. I responded in French. He spoke to the kids around me, looked at me for a while as if he were trying to identify who I was, then disappeared through the entrance of the compound.

Shortly afterward, an older woman arrived. Like the young woman, she had a load of dry wood on her head. She spoke to the kids as she came into sight of us. They in turn said something that made her look at me intensely. I wondered why she was staring at me so hard and I felt ill at ease. As if she were struggling with some decision, she walked forward and backward, continually turning her head toward the river and back to me. I lowered my eyes, picked up a piece of wood, and began moving dirt around.

Suddenly the woman screamed, "Malidoma, Patere, Malidoma!" She released her grip on her load of dry wood and tilted her head, sending the wood crashing to the ground. Then she rushed toward me. She knelt in front of me, grabbed my hands, and began wailing as if someone had just died. At first I was embarrassed and turned my face away. Her emotion was so sincere that the tears were rushing out of her eyes like water from a spring. I realized that emotion begets emotion, for I too could not restrain the tears that were welling from my eyes. They blurred the image of my mother as they rushed out, and we wept together, I silently, her making the sounds of someone in great pain.

The noise soon attracted more and more people. The old man reappeared from inside the compound, followed by the young woman who had brought the refreshment. My mother called my name again and cried more than ever. I noticed that the young woman was also in tears, but the old man was not. I read embarrassment in his face. He looked stunned, disoriented, and distressed.

My sister ran over to us, cut through the ever-increasing crowd, and joined my mother and me. She made loud cries, and her plump body swung to and fro as she ran her hands up and down my body. My mood turned to embarrassment. My tears dried up, and I wiped my eyes with the back of my hand.

The women cried much longer. They seemed unwilling to put an end to the electric impulse that had taken hold of them when they recognized me. I noticed that my father had disappeared into the inner yard again and returned with some ash in his left hand. He walked into the sacred room, where he remained for some time. When he reappeared, Mother almost forced me to my feet. She pointed a finger at Father. He stood still while she spoke to him in Dagara. When she was finished, Father said something and walked into the compound.

Mother motioned me toward the entrance of the compound. She was holding on to me as if I were a sick person who could not walk, and I gave in to her fancy. My sister held me from the opposite side. Thus, sandwiched between women, I entered the house the Jesuit priest had taken me away from some fifteen years ago. I was followed by a crowd eager to drink in every moment of my homecoming.

They seated me on a three-legged wooden stool placed against the wall next to an entrance. The sun had set. Darkness was rapidly enveloping the compound. I suddenly realized that where I was sitting used to be my grandfather's room, but it was no longer there.

Outside the door I could see some of the other buildings in the compound. To my right there was a large kitchen with a fire burning in a big fireplace. On top of the fire was a large clay pot. Farther right and facing south, I could see the door to the zangala, the same women's quarter I remembered from my childhood. This was the first thing I noticed that had not changed since I left. The other thing that had not changed was my father's quarter, situated south. Its entrance looked directly toward the zangala. It was the only entrance in the whole compound that had a wooden door.

It was pitch dark now and I was sleepy. My sister politely asked me to take a bath. I remembered it had been nearly eleven days since my last one in the seminary on the morning of my ill-fated eviction. In the washroom the bathwater was pre-warmed in a large clay pot. There was a local liquid soap made from a mixture of boiled shea butter and potassium. I remembered the process from when I was a child. My mother made soap for her family every fifth day of the week. My bath was refreshing and invigorating and it woke me up from my drowsiness. Afterward, Mother gave me a piece of cloth to cover my body with and took away my filthy clothes and sneakers. That night I tasted millet cake once again, the everyday food of the Dagara. As I lay down to sleep on the straw mat spread on a dirt platform, I noticed that this was the same place where, fifteen years ago, Grandfather had lain telling me things about my future. *And where is he now?* I wondered.

CHAPTER 11

HARD BEGINNINGS

 To truly appreciate sleep one must deserve it. To deserve sleep, one must work hard for it. It was wonderful to sleep, unmindful of threats, inside a room. Even though it felt odd to be home, just being inside a dwelling made me feel human again. I was as tired as if my body had postponed rest, real rest, during all those days of wandering in the bush. All my muscles demanded sleep with so much insistence that I sank into it irresistibly with an almost beatific surrender.

I was very sore when I woke up, and it took me a while to figure out where I was. First I thought I was still in the jungle because not far from me I could hear an animal making strange noises. My legs were stiff. I tried to get up in order to identify the source of this sound, which seemed to go on forever, but it was as if I were nailed to the ground. So I fell back into an agitated sleep, too agitated to keep me in it for long. When I woke again it was daylight and I was more aware of myself and what was going on. I realized that my mother was sitting next to me, crying discreetly so as not to wake me up, and I wondered if this had been the sound I had taken for an animal. When she noticed I was awake, she sniffed for a while like an engine that is running out of fuel. Then she became silent. I sat up and leaned against the mud wall. She left the room, I assumed to get me something to eat.

From inside my room I could tell that there were a lot of people outside. Voices of all ages and both sexes were conversing as if something exciting were going on. Normally, the owners of these voices would be sweating on the farm, waiting for their next meal to come to their rescue. But the rainy season was coming to an end. This is the time of the year when people say, "Even if you don't plow, you will eat." The millet had outgrown the grass and would yield grain no matter what. Judging by the coolness of the morning, which penetrated even into the small mud room I was in, it must have rained during the night.

My mother returned with some hot millet porridge in a calabash and some hard food. With it was a large Dagara spoon of a kind I had not seen in fifteen years. When she indicated that she wanted to feed me with it, I refused. I indicated that I could do it myself. But I also realized that she wanted to do something for me to make up for the nurturing that had been discontinued too early in my life. The millet porridge was warm and good, like the heart that served it to me. So I ate with an almost religious attitude. She watched my every movement with her tear-stained eyes and I wondered how long she had been sitting next to me while I slept. We did not talk because we could not, but a lot was exchanged anyway. I could sense her every feeling. She was all care, love, and sorrow, as if she understood that I had gone through immense suffering that her motherly care had been unavailable to alleviate.

Was she feeling sympathy for me or was she being apologetic, fearing her son's anger? I could not help but wonder about the family's seeming abandonment of me. Why had no one looked for me? Why had no one shown up to claim me? With those thoughts, I began to experience a different kind of feeling, one of anger. It surged like the fire in the kiln of the local metalworkers, voraciously fueled by my long exile. This anger was so intense that I thought for a moment it would kill me. But it didn't. It went away as it had come, though I knew it was never far.

My sister came in and greeted me in French once again. She sounded a lot more excited than she had the day before. I asked her where she had learned French.

"New Keretian Litter Porogaram," she said eagerly.* "The priest on the hill teach kids read-write. Want see write name me?" She picked up a stick and began scribbling on the dirt floor. I motioned for her to stop. She appeared disappointed, as if I had robbed her of something important. I inquired about the priest on the hill, whom I assumed was my nemesis, Father Maillot. "Gone home," she said. Kids started filling up the room. I recognized some of them as the ones who had been sitting next to

*The New Christian Literacy Program, initiated to functionally alphabetize indigenous people.

me the evening before, when I arrived home. I asked my sister who they were.

"Brothers of yours, sisters of yours." There were five of them, four brothers and a sister. I had been largely replaced. In the traditional world fecundity is the yardstick by which loss is compensated. Having children means being blessed by the gods and the ancestors. Four brothers and a sister testified to the fact that my parents had prayed a lot for replacement kids. That was how I felt in my heart, looking at all of them. It was impossible to tell how old anyone was. The oldest among them was called Laurent. He seemed unsure about how he fit into this whole thing, as if the general excitement caused by my arrival were beside the point. He always stood a little distance away.

The others had no problem enjoying the distraction my homecoming had caused. They all bore Christian names—Guillaume, Cyrille, Didié, Martine—and they looked Christian, too, with all the medals they wore around their necks. The church's brainwashing had been going on in this corner of the traditional world, only at a slower pace.

"How long did you go to school?" I asked my sister.

"Almost a whole year."

"Who else is going to school?"

"Cyrille and Didié will. Their age is ready."

The business of literacy was usually preceded by a heavy dose of catechism. In the minds of the villagers, there was no doubt that the God from across the sea was a learned person who bequeathed literacy on his believers. I could see that all my brothers and sisters had been alphabetized.

At that point my father came in, looking like an indicted man. His face was tense and overly serious, symptomatic of a person who was building arguments in his head. He ordered the room cleared except for my sister and my mother and sat down on a stool. But as soon as the kids were out, he knelt in front of me and grabbed my hands, speaking in Dagara, my forsaken mother tongue.

When he stopped, I replied in French, assuming that he had recited some profound welcoming formula, "Thank you. I'm well. I hope you too are fine." My sister's face was caught in a fit of hilarity. Then my mother began to speak with my father in Dagara. It became a rather odd dialogue and it was obvious that my mother was reproaching my father for something and that he was trying to justify himself. Her voice became harsh and her eyes angry. I did not know what was going on and asked my sister why she was trying not to laugh.

"Father said the spirit of Bakhye is great because you still alive. He said that he had been making sacrifices for you come home."

My body became hot. I felt cheated, as if someone had robbed me of the only heroic thing I had ever accomplished. I had battled my way home on foot almost three hundred kilometers through the jungle only to be told that someone else had made it possible. Which meant that all I had to do was walk.

I objected. "What! He made sacrifices all these years so that I could come back? Why didn't he just come get me? Why didn't he just ask that damn priest on the hill to bring me back? Ask him that! *Ask him!*"

My sister opened her mouth to speak, but nothing came out. "Tell him," I insisted.

Father spoke to her, indicating that he too wanted to know what was going on. "I hear you," she mumbled finally, looking at me. "But your words! I went to school nine months. I learned all. A few words I not learn and you pick these words. How can I say Father?"

"What! You mean you can't translate what I said?"

I was roaring at her. Father spoke to her in Dagara once again. She answered. It appeared that she had translated my remark. I watched Father carefully while he made some kind of a speech, his face set in annoyance. He was looking randomly around the room at everything except me. In the end, my sister turned toward me unhappily.

"Well!" I said, eager to hear the whole thing. She was trembling slightly, distressed at being in the middle of all this anger.

"Father says ancestors predict. Nobody can prevent."

And she was silent. I waited, certain she had more to say. My father had spoken for several minutes.

"That's it?" I asked, incredulous.

"Father say," she replied, nodding her head.

It became obvious that she did not want to translate everything for me. This angered me quite a bit.

"What do you take me for? What did he say?"

"I say what he say!" she replied in panic.

I knew I was not going to get anything out of her, or out of anyone in the room for that matter.

"I am among lunatics, idiots. God is a fool," I said out loud and in despair.

Between me and the people in front of me there was an unbridgeable chasm, so deep that it seemed it would take longer than I had been away, longer than anyone could afford, to bring us near one another again. It appeared that communication alone would not take care of it. Here was my own family, but emptied of the stuff that would make them a family to me. Everyone was absent as far as I was concerned. I sat there like a monumental question mark, feeling weak, alone, unheard.

"God, mmmnn . . . God," said my father, nodding his head. I wondered what he thought I had said. The warmth I had enjoyed in the silent company of my mother was long gone. There was no sense of home for me anymore. I began to feel like a fool who had bet on the wrong thing. This is what I had given up the priesthood for. I threw off my blanket and stood up. I needed to take a walk. After all those days en route, I still needed to keep moving on for a while longer.

"I'm going for a walk," I said. Everybody stood up with dismay written on their faces. The crowd in the compound outside also stood up as I appeared followed by my parents and my sister. Everybody was speaking. I decided to ignore them. My first day at home was a bad one.

If only I could remember how to speak Dagara! Noise without meaning is irritating, especially when you know that the noise is hiding from you something vitally important. There was a part of me that would have given anything to understand what Father was saying to me. . . .

The sun had already risen far above the horizon. The recently harvested millet field was quickly drying out from the predawn rainfall. *A useless rain,* I thought. I found myself walking under the huge baobab tree, recalling some of the things Grandfather used to tell me about these trees, especially the witches' meetings at night. His funeral had been performed under the shade of a baobab. *How long ago was that?* I had been so small, so young. My life felt like a game that had too many players. And now it was over and the baobab had seen it all. Being under the tree calmed me a little. Did it notice that I was bereft? I leaned against one of its gigantic protruding roots.

My mind went back to school and I began to sort out the good from the bad. What really made me quit the seminary? Didn't I want to be a priest? Sure I did, but I had wanted to find a home in a priestly vocation that concorded with my vision. I quit, not because someone told me I could not become a priest, but because I could no longer deal with the contradictions of Christianity. The Bible spoke of love and goodness, but all around me I had seen vanity, deception, and cruelty. I could no longer accept the sacrament from such unclean hands. So I did not come home because I was homesick, but because I could not become a priest. Was it worth all that I had forsaken? I could not decide.

The sun was heading toward the zenith and it was getting hotter and hotter, even in the shade. My parents' compound, the house of my ancestors, looked desolate. It had none of the majesty of the houses in the seminary. There was a sense of secretiveness in the layout of the compound that I did not understand. *What is the house hiding from?* I asked myself. The windows were tiny openings that looked like bullet holes in the battered walls. *That's what Western civilization wants to save,* I thought. I'd had my own ideas about salvation in the seminary. Now I was out of the picture. If this place needed salvation, it would have to figure it out for itself.

I had not noticed I was walking until I reached the river. At the end of the rainy season there was still a lot of water in its bed even though it looked shallow. Grass was growing out in the middle. I tried to remember what used to happen to me on these shores. Nothing, absolutely nothing appeared in my mind. Rather, I noticed that the grass was swiftly parting and that something was headed toward me. It stopped a few meters away and I saw that it was a crocodile. The two big eyes perched on the triangular ridges of its skull blinked a few times, then it resumed a statuelike immobility. We looked at each other. There, I thought, was a being who had never left home and would probably never want to. Why was he interested in me? Crocodiles did not stand and look at people as far as I could remember. I was not afraid of it, rather, I was puzzled. Looking into the eyes of the crocodile was soothing. It dawned on me that the Birifor clan had something in common with the crocodile. But what was it? I had no inkling. Once I had known of the friendship between the crocodile and my family. Now I had forgotten it, as I had forgotten so much else.

"Come get me," I yelled at the animal. "I am abandoned." The eyes of the crocodile blinked. I yelled again. It moved a few feet closer but did nothing. I grabbed a piece of dirt and threw it at him, urging him to hurry up. He floated there in his deadly immobility for a moment, then took a dive. By the movement of the grass, I realized that he was swimming away swiftly.

I heard a voice behind me and turned. There was a young boy, probably thirteen or fourteen, looking at me intently. He must have been watching me for a long time. He was half amused and half fascinated by my behavior. He was almost naked and about as tall as me, though he carried more muscle on his body. His face was covered with a vast smile that expressed his desire to communicate with me. He clapped his hands on his chest and bowed in greeting: *"Yaani."* This was a simple greeting that a person in my tribe could hear a hundred times a day. His gestures were emphatic, his voice soft. I nodded in response to show that I was friendly. He seemed familiar to me and I thought he might be one of the kids who had surrounded me when I first arrived in the village.

The boy came up to me and sat down quietly. After a while I turned and looked at him intently. Part of me did not like this proximity. He looked back at me and said, *"Nyangoli,"* hitting his chest with his hand. This was his name. I repeated it back to him. He nodded and smiled. Then I introduced myself. And he laughed out loud as if he knew me already. We sat there, him throwing stones into the river, me watching the stones glide on the surface of the water until they disappeared. He had nothing to say, but his presence took away part of my loneliness.

When I stood up, ready to go back to my parents' home, he stood up too. We walked together silently. He was throwing stones all the time, but kept pace with me. We arrived together and I invited him into my room.

My brothers followed and my room became crowded very quickly. Nyangoli spoke with my brothers, but this time I did not mind that I could not understand what they were talking about. I was experiencing a sense of renewal in my shattered psyche. A friendly social event was happening in my own room, and this made all the difference in the world. Somewhere in the gigantic dark tunnel of the absurdity of my situation was a thin filament of shining light, nameless but spelling unmistakable hope.

I learned later that Nyangoli was my male mother's son, that is, the son of my mother's brother, my uncle. Guisso, as this uncle was called, was a man of calm demeanor who, for weeks, would come to the house every morning and sit with me as quietly as if I were his own child. I wondered what these people were thinking, and why they were wasting their time on me, but I would have no answers until I relearned my native language. When that day came I understood that the taming of my anger was a task assigned to my male mother. After my ordeal, I had to be softened, quieted, sobered, and made to feel supported. A father cannot provide this for his son, especially when there is already a serious problem between them. There is a natural need for transfer of reference. I don't know how to explain it in Western terms. It is as though the father must at some point efface himself for the son to survive, and this is when the male mother becomes useful. The feminine in the male—the mother in the man—is an energy that can be triggered into wakefulness only by a male directly associated with the mother. The male mother is therefore thought of as someone who "carries water," the energy of peace, quiet, reconciliation, and healing.

Guisso was also a diviner and a healer whose priestly devotion to the village was unparalleled. And so, he and his son, Nyangoli, were performing their nurturing duties toward me now upon my return simply because my absence had delayed them. Whenever Nyangoli came to the house without his father, and this was almost always the case, he would try very hard to speak to me in Dagara. He was, in this manner, one of the persons who reintroduced me to my mother tongue. Guisso, on the other hand, was in charge of my soul. He was a boburo—a medicine man.

A little more than a month following my homecoming, my father woke me up very early in the morning and took me to Guisso and Nyangoli's house for my first divination. This was to be the beginning of my real transformation. A person who stays away from his home for a lengthy period of time leaves a great portion of his soul abroad when he returns. Nothing important can happen until the person is fully integrated again, that is, joined back together, body and soul. The boburo is in charge of determining how to do this. In my case, Guisso was going to find out what specific ritual would make me whole again.

We arrived at dawn. Guisso was already awake and meditating, perhaps about some former cases, but apparently waiting for us. He was seated on the *galiguo*, the part of the roof that overlooks the yard, with his legs hanging over the edge. When he saw us get off the old English bicycle and enter his compound, he stood up, coughed, and climbed down the ladder to meet us.

He pointed to an old piece of carved wood in a starlit corner. It looked like a chair. Although it had three legs, it was so rickety it could barely stand. My father sat on it while I sat against the earthen wall, using a bump built against the wall as a seat. We were in the zangala. Everything in it was darkened by the black smoke of the constantly burning fire. On the right side was a row of enormous clay jugs, some shining, some whitened by the remnants of yeast.

It was still too dark to see anything except the dancing fire. Off in the shadows I could hear the snores of Guisso's sleeping wives and children. This stopped, however, as soon as the divination began. The main entrance into this huge zangala looked like a large triangle, its bottom wider than the top by a half a meter or so. It reached from floor to ceiling and was never closed.

I looked at Guisso, who was absent from us, as if in a trance. In his body he seemed to carry all the years that have existed since God created anything, years that were quietly eating away at him. His total devotion to the welfare of his people guaranteed that he always looked tired. His thin bony legs, folded oddly around his waist, made him look like the materialization of something unearthly. His body smelled like death, yet the light in his eyes was intensely alive. He was a personified spirit, a man of nature and of planet Earth, with an undivided passion for his work.

"The *Kontomon*, the spirits, woke me up in the middle of the night and ordered me to stay awake," Guisso said after a long silence. "I insisted that they tell me why, but they are so stubborn. They refused."

That was the first time he had spoken since we had entered the room. All that time, he had been taking down shells and medicine tools, turning them over and over, putting some near him, some a little farther away. From time to time he would issue a growl of dissatisfaction. I watched with ever-increasing interest.

These medicine objects were for the most part a collection of the very things that an uninformed person would normally overlook because they were too natural, too trivial to attract attention. Who would be attracted to an old bone or the kind of stone that could be found anywhere? There were bones and stones and pieces of broken metal—remnants of tin cans, broken bicycle parts, and other unidentifiable metal objects. Some of these objects were tiny, others were a little larger, but all of them carried a sense of mystery. For the old man, power was in the trivial-looking thing, the thing that looked weak and valueless.

When his tools were finally in place, Guisso grabbed an old piece of wood shaped like a V. Its right side was half the length of its left side. He lifted it into the air, gazed fixedly in front of him as if in a dream, then placed the stick on a wooden circular platform no bigger than a dinner plate, its bottom buried in the floor. He and my father were facing each other. Guisso growled again, sneezed loudly, cleared his throat, turned his face toward the entrance door, and ejected something from his mouth that landed in the middle of the compound. Then he began to speak.

"The spirits are always like this. They do not care whether we need rest or not."

My father made a sympathetic noise and said, "They should take that into account in managing your work."

That seemed to encourage Guisso to complain more. "I do not belong to myself—and I wish I did! But it's been so long since I lost the taste of thinking about myself."

Father did not appear to have a lot to say. He emitted an *"Oon"* of acquiescence in response.

Guisso took hold of his spirit bell with his left hand. It was a rudimentary piece of metal, forged in the general form of a cup with a clapper in the middle. The bell emitted a noise that seemed to be coming from underwater. In his right hand Guisso held a gourd with an animal tail attached to its end. The gourd contained some beads and stones.

He began shaking everything with a power that surprised me. He spoke clearly and powerfully in a language I did not understand, but which struck every emotional cell of my body.

Guisso was sweating. His body was shaking with convulsions, and he looked as if he were suspended midway between his seat and the air. One could swear that an alien force had taken possession of him. Bent double, his eyes fixed upon the piece of wood in front of him, he spoke as if he were addressing an immense crowd. The shaker and the bell were making loud sounds that competed fiercely with the elder's voice.

When he finished, he was soaked in sweat. He put down the bell and the gourd and grabbed the V-stick, hitting it twice against the wooden platform. Father moved closer, raised his hands, and recited his own invocational prayer, then grabbed the stick below the place where Guisso held it. No sooner did he touch the stick than it rose with the hands of the two men into the air, drew a circle three times, and came back onto the wooden platform with a sharp impact. The dialogue with the other world had begun.

The stick rose once more and then began pounding the wooden platform wildly until Guisso said something that sounded like an order to stop. The hands of both men seemed unable to control the unpredictable motions of the stick, even though they hung on to it very tightly. Every word that came out of Guisso's throat was followed by a motion of the stick.

The wooden stick rose again and landed on Guisso's medicine tools. It searched for a while, then pointed to a dried chicken leg. Guisso picked it up and put it aside. He ordered, "Run."

The stick rose once more, then landed on something that looked like an empty cartridge. After this it pointed to a hen's feather, a metal box, a stone, and numerous other items. Each time, Guisso took them and put them aside. Presently, the stick just stood erect on the floor and would not move, even at Guisso's order.

"Is this all?" Guisso asked. The stick rose in the air and pounded twice on the wooden platform. By now I knew that this meant yes. This had not been hard to figure out. Each time the stick went to the ground instead of the wooden platform, there was an atmosphere of uncertainty. Each time it pounded twice on the wooden platform, there was joy and satisfaction. Guisso repeated his question five more times, and each time the stick responded in the same manner.

Convinced, he picked the first item and continued the interrogation. The divination went on for hours at an ever-increasing intensity, though it was difficult for me to always pay attention. It was hard to follow something I did not understand fully. Because of the language barrier, my curiosity could not always be satisfied. When the session was over, it was broad daylight. We moved into another room adjacent to the zangala. This room looked like a hidden medicine room and it was still as dark as a cloudy night. Guisso sprinkled me with some water contained in a clay jug. The water smelled bad. I was to find out later that in the village any good medicine smells as bad as the other world.

The rest of the day was spent sacrificing a huge number of chickens to a shrine. Some of the dead chickens were thrown into a ditch, others were cooked with various mixtures of roots and black medicine. Toward the middle of the afternoon we had a meal. The chicken meat was so heavy with medicine, I could not enjoy it—at the seminary I had become used to plain food. Guisso's family joined us and everybody had a great appetite except me.

Toward the evening we went into the medicine room once again and Guisso anointed me with a variety of potions, speaking all the while. At some point he cut my arm and rubbed something that burned unbearably into the wound. This was all part of a ritual done for my protection. I took it all in stoically. When we got back home, it was night.

In the days that followed, I felt as if some kind of transformation had begun. It was as if I had been given an emotional painkiller. I was not as irritable as I had been, and at night my dreams were no longer of the seminary, but of my ritual with Guisso. I shared my world with my mother and my sister on the one hand; and with Guisso—my male mother—and Nyangoli—my male sister—on the other hand. I could not have lived without these people. I also began the long process of forgiveness. The nurturing my mother gave me absolved her of most of my charges against her. My sister coached me in Dagara, a language that I was able to remember within a matter of months, and kept me informed of what was going on in the village when Nyangoli was not around. She told me that the village council had met several times to discuss my case and that people had been sent to perform a divination to ward off the bad things at work against me.

Despite the care and love around me, my life still felt unresolved. As the days passed, I noticed that elders came into our house very early every morning, did some ceremonies involving sacrifices and left. Guisso was there each time, even though his presence in my life was mostly silent. I grew attached to him, as if he were my own mother. Each time villagers met or did something on my behalf, my sister told me about it.

"And why didn't they tell me?" I always asked, annoyed.

"Because they don't have to," my sister inevitably responded neutrally.

My homecoming had produced a crisis in the village as a whole, but more particularly in my own family. With the sweeping changes under way in national politics and the economy, homecomings were becoming common throughout the thirty or so villages in the county of Dano. But most of the men coming home had not been transformed the way I had. These were the men who had been recruited to work on colonial projects, such as railroad building, gold mining, or plantation work. In the beginning they had been subjected to the rough discipline of conscripted labor, but independence changed all that. Now they had to be paid for their labor, and they no longer felt like slaves. A new culture was born, the culture of the working man who would live abroad because of his work but who could return to his village if he wanted. I, on the other hand, had acquired something different and infinitely more dangerous: literacy. As an educated man I had returned, not as a villager who had worked for the white man, but as a white man.

It all boiled down to the simple fact that I had been changed in a way unsuitable to village life, and that this transformation needed to be tamed if the village were to accept me as I was. People understood my kind of literacy as the business of whites and nontribal people. Even worse, they understood literacy as an eviction of a soul from its body—the taking over of the body by another spirit. Wasn't the white man notorious in the village for his brutality, his lack of morality and integrity? Didn't he take without asking and kill ruthlessly? To my people, to be literate meant to be possessed by this devil of brutality. It was not harmful to know a little, but to the elders, the ability to read, however magical it appeared, was dangerous. It made the literate person the bearer of a terrible epidemic. To read was to participate in an alien form of magic that was destructive to the tribe. I was useful, but my very usefulness was my undoing.

When people learned that I could write, they began coming to me to request my services as a scribe. They wanted to send letters to their relatives who had gone to Abidjan or Bouaké, on the Ivory Coast; to Kumasi; or to Accra or Sakoundé in Ghana. As I wrote, they watched, their eyes magnetized to the page as if I were performing a miracle. Soon the word spread and more people began to come. Very quickly I felt that I was becoming useful as a conduit, a translator, a kind of conveyor belt between people. They watched what they asked me to write take shape on the blank sheet of paper and were aghast as I spoke it back to them in bad Dagara.

Meanwhile, divination had revealed to the village council that I was able to read and write as well as the white man himself. It was even circulated that I knew more than the white man. This posed an additional problem to the elders, whom my father had told about my anger and inner turmoil. I never knew what else was being circulated in the village about me, but who I was and what I knew was seen as a serious threat.

Apprehensive, my sister kept telling me that I knew too much. She even asked if I could forget some of the things I knew in order to avoid trouble. I wondered why she did not understand that knowing certain things is terminal. Sometimes, when people came to ask me to write a letter, she would beg me to tell them I had forgotten writing, or a great deal of it at least. When I refused to do this, she would say that I should write more slowly and stop frequently to think. That way I would convey the sense that I was not as knowledgeable as everyone thought I was.

Learning Dagara did not diminish this impression. In six months I was able to speak reasonably well, that is, a little better than my sister spoke French. Meanwhile, Father and I had decided that we would postpone our conflict until such time as it was possible to communicate to each other directly. What choice did I have? Actually, this postponement helped, softening my anger and helping me to forget a lot of what I had initially felt. As I concentrated more on learning my native language, the distance I felt between me and my family diminished.

I remember the day I first greeted my father in Dagara. He had just arrived home from an errand on his bicycle. Profoundly moved, Father rushed to hug me. His face radiated joy—his own son had spoken to him in the language of the ancestors! This was twelve days after my arrival. I had been in a good mood that day, but my mood disappeared fast as tears of sadness overwhelmed me. A father was happy because his twenty-year-old son was able to speak his mother tongue. What fatal irony had postponed everything till now? My father thought I was crying out of joy, so he tried to reciprocate. But he found out quickly enough that I was crying for something else and he cut his gladness short. Though it is dangerous in my culture for men to cry outside of the funeral context, this did not apply to me. I was not initiated, so I was not really a man.

That evening he asked me to follow him into a dark medicine room. He knelt and I imitated him. Then he began a long speech in front of the shrine of the ancestors. I could not understand much, but it seemed to me he was giving thanks. This was the first time I had appeared in front of the sacred since I had left the seminary. I came out of the medicine room wondering if Father had made a pledge to the ancestors about me and, perhaps, that our interaction that afternoon had given him a clue as to the outcome of that pledge. At that point I could only guess what was going on around me, and such speculation often filled me with sadness.

No matter what my father did to bridge the gap between us, I never felt close to him. My involvement with him was cold on my side, a little warmer on his side, and always uncertain. I needed answers. He wanted to prove something to me by being active with me at the level of the spirit. Whenever the situation would seem appropriate to him, he would drag me to the ancestral shrine with water and ash for a quick ceremony. When he had asked me to follow him into the medicine room that evening, I knew that our relationship was moving one step up. What the step was, I did not know. Something had changed between us, but only the future would reveal its exact nature.

CHAPTER 12

TRYING TO FIT
BACK INTO VILLAGE LIFE

 The cold season of November through January had passed, followed by the days of heat. In April it became humid with the sudden coming of the rain. Fields were being prepared for planting and the air smelled damp, like an egg about to hatch. Every morning I followed my brothers to the farm and watched them work, thinking that their literacy in farming was a perfect match for mine in another area. Initially, I had tried to work with them, but I was so clumsy I was more of a hindrance than a help. My father suggested that I watch and learn instead.

Before the fields can be sown, there had to be a planting ceremony. It began with a community ritual at the house of the chief of the earth shrine. Every head of a household brought sample seeds to the priest. We brought red millet, white millet, corn, groundnuts, beans, and grains my father wouldn't name because naming them would kill them. Among the Dagara, some things are known not for what they are, but for what they do. The Dagara avoid identifying them in order to ensure that their magical properties stay alive. In the village, anything referred to as *Yélé* or *Bomo* falls into this category.

The seeds that my father would not name were magical seeds. They were not supposed to grow into plants, but were related to the seeds to be planted the way a shepherd is related to his flock. Father said that Grand-father had used them in his medicine room when he was alive, and through them was able to see everything that was happening on the farm. Grand-father also used a clay pot full of water as one of his surveillance tools. To-day, my father does not know how to use that pot. He blames this on his poor relationship with his father, which was the result of his not having the privilege of a relationship with his grandfather. My father had also lost the secret of the unnamed seeds, which knew when something was wrong with other plant life on the farm. Father did not have a medicine room, as Grandfather had. Much knowledge had been lost with my grandfather's death, but the tradition continued even in its incompleteness. Colonialism and Christianity were responsible for the discontinuity of much tribal knowledge. Perhaps if Father hadn't rejected the religion of his ancestors all those years, Grandfather would have been able to pass down much more to him.

At the beginning of the planting ceremony, the priest of the earth shrine would take a single seed from each basket and deposit it in the lap of the spirit of the earth shrine. The following day, villagers, generally men, would perform a similar ceremony at their respective farms in the presence of the members of their families. This ceremony would be followed by the actual planting of the crops.

To plant crops, the planter, generally a woman, bends down and digs a tiny hole with a hoe she holds in her right hand. Into it she deposits several grains held between the thumb and the first finger of the left hand. Then the hole is closed. The entire activity takes a few seconds. The right hand digs, the left hand pours seeds, the right hand closes up. If it rains that night, the grains will rise. If not, the birds will come digging as soon as the farm is deserted. Birds can smell seeds, even when buried, and besides, they watch all day while people plant, waiting for their chance.

From early May to mid-August, we went to the farm every morning and worked hard till the middle of the afternoon. My mother would bring us lunch sometime before the sun reached the zenith and we would eat in silence, as is the Dagara custom. We did not rest after the meal and it was very difficult for me to work in the afternoon with my belly full. In the seminary, we used to take long naps after lunch, and habits, good or bad, are hard to break. By evening I was so exhausted, all I could do was wash, eat, and go to sleep.

My brothers, who felt stronger after dinner, sat in the compound, and told stories and competed in riddles till they all fell asleep. The rainy season is tough, but it is even tougher for the one whose body is not used to indig-enous life. My life in the seminary had been smoother, quieter, far less de-manding in terms of physical energy even when we had athletic training.

Indigenous life is a constant physical exercise. From plowing the earth with your bare hands to running after an antelope during the hunt to carrying huge stacks of wood for the fireplace, the body is constantly involved in expending energy. It is not surprising that my people don't have weight problems. The energy each person burns during the day is incalculable. No wonder the amount of food available always seems insufficient. My younger brothers always behaved as if they were starving. They would gulp down an enormous dish and yet keep sniffing around as if they had not eaten anything at all. Guillaume told me one day that he never knew what satiation felt like. He said he stopped eating when there was no more to eat.

When my mother prepared meals, she always made two servings, one for the males and the other for the females. Father presided over male meals and she presided over female meals. We always sat in a circle around the dish. The grown-ups sat on stools, and the young sat with their left legs folded under their butts as a seat. The evening meal, about ten o'clock, was the most important of the day. It gathered together the whole family, including visitors, since in the Dagara tradition no visitor can be denied food.

Dinner began with the hand-washing ceremony. The male leader was first, followed by the next-oldest person and so on till the youngest had washed. The first bit of food was always offered to the spirit of the earth shrine. This is called a clearance bite. My father always performed this ceremony. He would take a bit of cake and dip it into the sauce, say something rapidly between his teeth, and then throw the thing away as if he did not want it. The dog loved it—even though it was not destined for him but for the Spirit of the earth shrine. Sometime the dog would catch it in midair and swallow it at once as if he did not want to know what it tasted like.

Then my father, who pretended not to pay attention to the fate of the first bite, would prepare another for himself. I noticed that his portion was larger. He would stick the whole portion into his mouth, hold it in there for a few seconds, and then nod his head before swallowing it. This was the signal that the dinner was safe to eat. Seven hands assaulted the dishes, determined to empty them, and the meal was enjoyed in silence. For the Dagara, there is no such thing as a plate for each person, because in the context of a real community, separate plates cultivate separateness. The older people were supposed to stop eating first, allowing the youngest to finish it all up. Anyone who burps is expected to stop eating immediately, as that indicates that he or she is full.

Eating with one's hands is a fascinating art. You are supposed to lick your fingers one by one after each swallow, starting with the front of each of the four fingers, then their backs, and finally the thumb. Then the entire finger must be taken into the mouth and carefully sucked. The person presiding over the meal is in charge of making sure that these rules are followed carefully. Consequently, any voice you hear rising during a meal is the leader's voice correcting bad eating habits mostly related to finger-licking. Children who are very hungry don't take the time to lick their fingers properly, so someone must be there to instruct them in good table manners.

In the seminary, even though spoons, forks, and knives were always provided, we were never prohibited from eating with our hands except tacitly when a priest was among us. Thus, the only thing from my childhood that I never forgot was eating with my hands. I did so in the seminary as a way to stay in touch with something that seemed ancestral.

My brothers were masterful at eating with their hands. Watching them at work around the huge bowl of food was like watching a performance. The agility with which they carried food, solid or liquid, to their mouths had something of the religious about it, as if the food were a living entity performing a lifework on behalf of someone who needed it. The fact that eating is done communally, and is gender specific, adds to its feeling of being a ritual.

It took me a while to get used to eating out of a common dish again. Accustomed as I was in the seminary to having my own plate and cutlery, it was rather unpleasant to participate in a meal that seemed, underneath the delicate, artistic, and focused gestures of the diners, like a fierce competition. The speed with which my brothers ate amazed me and discouraged any attempt on my part to rival them.

In the beginning I took my time, unmindful of running out of food, and so I was always on the verge of not eating enough. At first I was silent about my hunger. But my mother noticed it and discreetly intervened. She always put an extra plate in my room for me before she went to bed. One night I asked her why.

She hesitated, then said, "I do not think I can recover from fifteen seasons of life without you."

"But I am not hungry. I eat well with everybody."

"You need not tell me this. I am your mother."

"Since when are you my mother?"

She burst into tears. I felt sorry for her. My outburst made me realize, however, that I had not fully forgiven her. I felt cruel and ungrateful, but something prevented me from apologizing. Was my wounded ego all too eager to feed on the feelings of others?

Mother defended herself. "After we found out you were gone, I cried for months on end. I had a big fight with your father and asked him to find you and bring you home. He went out to get you several times, sometimes spending days away before returning empty-handed."

"Where did he go? I was just up the hill. How could he not find me?"

"I knew, and he also knew very well, where you were. The priest, the priest . . . *those priests.* Your father was going against the will of the foreign god, but we fought anyway. It was no use. The priest kept saying that only God could release you if he changed his mind. In the meantime he would not let anyone interfere with you. So your father prayed for your release, and I cried for it. I could not pray. I was too angry at God. Believe me, it was a nightmare for all of us."

So according to Mother I was a victim of the divine will. The thought rolled through my mind, clothed in irony. "If it was God's will that I be snatched from my home, whose god was that? You believed the priest on the hill was equipped with the power to detect the slightest will of God, what makes God happy, or angry, or indifferent. That's an odd power."

A lot of what I had said was in French. Even though I had been home for nearly nine months, I still did not have enough vocabulary to articulate everything in plain Dagara. Because I lost my language at such an early age, and learned another under such terrible duress, I was never again able to communicate in Dagara with anywhere near my fluency in French or English. I can't even think in my native language, and to the best of my memory, I never did.

In spite of my linguistic difficulties, my mother understood. "Did you suffer a lot?" she asked, her voice strangled by sobs.

"The ways of God are always painful for humans to follow. I was not alone and that made things easier."

"What was it like there?"

"Where? On the mission hill? You know what the mission hill is like. The seminary is the same, but many times bigger, with houses on top of houses. It is a whole village. We lived like a tribe. Our elders were all white. The ancestors were far away in Europe. We spent all our time getting acquainted with them."

"Did you like the white man there?"

"I liked the god I discovered. I didn't like the god I was asked to abide by. I respected some of the ancestors I found in the white man's history, but I didn't like them being called my ancestors and I didn't like the fact that my own ancestors were never mentioned."

"It is not possible to like the ancestors of people who take without asking, who harm in the name of their own god. I hate to talk like this, but you are my son."

"Grandfather was with me in my life there. He really helped me make it through."

"Your grandfather Bakhye?"

"Yes! He was always there at the major intersections of my life. I do not know if this is what made the difference, but he kept me in touch with my ancestors."

"How did he do that?"

"Sometimes he would appear to me in my dreams. Sometimes I wouldn't even need to go to sleep. While my mind burned with a desire to rest because it could not find an answer to some absurdity imposed on me, the thought of Grandfather would always come into my consciousness."

Mother looked a little surprised, but I knew she understood. After all, it was my grandfather who first saw what I would have to endure later, and understood it as part of the burden of being Malidoma—the one who befriends his enemies.

"Someday you should tell your father about this. I am sure he would like to hear about it. And please let me feed you. I know you are grown up. You should be married now. Please let me catch up with fifteen seasons of not having you with me. I am a mother. May I include you in who I am?"

"I will eat. I am sleepy too."

"Do both, then."

I felt as if a bridge now linked my mother to me. It had just been erected—or perhaps it was already there.

▲　　▼　　▲

August is a wet month in the tropics, but the abundance of rain is never taken as an evil thing. It is also the month when the millet grows faster and the hardships of farming are substantially reduced. Talk about the harvest begins to circulate, as well as talk about *Baor,* which means "knowledge" but is really a reference to initiation.

One evening after dinner I went to my room while the rest of the family gathered around for storytelling. My mother used to leave a shea-oil lamp burning in my room for me. It emitted such a feeble light that one had to be a half meter from it to see anything. There was no way of making more light at night, and no one wanted any. I had light because I was not yet a real village person.

Among the Dagara, darkness is sacred. It is forbidden to illuminate it, for light scares the Spirit away. Our night is the day of the Spirit and of the ancestors, who come to us to tell us what lies on our life paths. To have light around you is like saying that you would rather ignore this wonderful opportunity to be shown the way. To the Dagara, such an attitude is inconceivable. The one exception to this rule is a bonfire. Though they emit a powerful glow, they are not prohibited because there is always drumming around them, and the beat of the drum cancels out the light.

Villagers are expected to learn how to function in the dark. I was given light because I had lost the ability to deal with darkness, and each time people saw the timid light of the shea-oil lamp in my room, they would walk away from it as if it signaled the presence of someone playing with the elements of the cosmos. No young man ever came to sit by me at night.

That evening, after Mother lighted the lamp and left, my father came in. He had entered so discreetly that I did not notice him until he cleared his throat to announce both his presence and his intention to speak. I cleared mine too in response. I had nothing to say. There was always a sense of uneasiness and emptiness when I found myself alone with Father, as if a chasm lay between him and me that both of us would have to jump into to find out how our destinies were linked. But neither of us dared initiate this exploration. Neither of us knew how to do it.

He addressed me with the formal Dagara greeting that presages something deep to come. Then he said he had met with the village council and wanted to speak to me about it.

"Was the meeting about me?" I asked.

"Yes, and several others in the past have also been about you."

"You have been having meetings about me ever since I returned?"

"Yes—of course. This is not because you are the first one to return to the village, but because you are the first to carry into the village the kind of knowledge you have. Knowing what you know is not common. It means that you have received the white man's Baor. His spirit lives in you. In a way you are not here yet. It's as if the real you is somewhere else, still trying to find the route home. The you sitting here in front of me is like the priest who came here fifteen years ago and took you away from us. Your soul is in his hands. This is what the counsel is worried about."

"Am I responsible for allowing my soul to be stolen?"

"You know you're not. No one is looking for someone to blame. No one is responsible for this. What lies in the mind of fate is always undecipherable."

"I should not have come home, then!"

"You can't say that, because you are a tool to the fate of your name. No one knows if coming back is right or wrong, but you can't escape your destiny."

"So why am I of such great concern?"

"I have already explained that. You carry something in you, something very subtle, something that comes from your contact with the whites— and now you want to be here where you once belonged. You cannot live here as you are now without turning this place into what you are. This is what the white man did throughout the land of the Black man. He could not be here without subverting our home to fit his needs. The people of this village all know that the white man's ways mean death. All these white people that came here to make trouble for us are possessed by the troubled ghosts of their ancestors. This is because where the white men come from, people don't grieve. Because their dead are not at peace, the living cannot be either. This is terrible. These people are empty inside. Someone who does not have an inside cannot teach anyone anything.

"You are not white, and because you were born here, you must be made to fit into this place. You must be able to come home completely before your white nature changes your village by forcing it to come to you. When a person has been changed the way you have, one of two things always happens: either you die into the old part of yourself—and that is painful—or you make everything else die into you. The first one is human. The second one is not. In the first case, wisdom is at work. In the second case, fear is at work. The elders want to give you the chance to adjust to your village before you make it adjust to you."

"So what is going on in the elders' minds?"

"I don't know what they feel in their bellies, but I think they have many concerns. What you know has sealed you into a place that is unfamiliar to us—and yet you are here. One of our concerns is whether it is possible for you to be here and there at the same time."

I did not know what to make of anything Father was saying or how to respond. The seriousness in his voice convinced me that the elders considered this matter of prime importance. But why should their worries bother me?

"You said that what I know is keeping me somewhere else, and now you ask if I can be in two places at the same time. Isn't that what I have been doing since the day I left this compound? While I was away, I was always dreaming about being back here. Now, every day I see the things I experience here in terms of the seminary. I can't forget knowing how to read and write. And I don't want anyone to accuse me of anything behind my back."

"I know how your belly feels. I am not trying to punish you for what you know, nor is the council trying to blame you for what happened to you. Some of the elders look at your experience among the whites as a good omen. They have seen you read and write, but they want to ensure that you get something else in addition to the white man's knowledge so that you can be more present among us.

"The problem we are facing with you is not about an individual. It is about a community trying to learn from the past. Everyone has suffered at the hands of the white man, whether it be at school, in his church, or on the roads, working for him. The spirit that animates the whites is extremely restless—and powerful when it comes to keeping that restlessness alive. Wherever he goes he brings a new order, the order of unrest. It keeps him always tense and uneasy, but that is the only way he can exist. It took our community a long time to come to understand this. The white man is not strong—he's scared. His whiteness is made of terror, or otherwise he would not be white. He is consumed by his terror and wrestles with it to stay alive. Until he is at peace with himself, no one around him ever will be. The elders want to quiet the white man in your soul. They do not know how, but they would like to try something."

"And what is it that they have in mind?"

"Baor—initiation. They requested that I ask you this: would you agree to submit to this season's Baor ritual? It will teach you the way of your ancestors and probably make you more a part of us than you are now."

"Do I have a choice?"

"I don't know. . . . You can say no, but no one knows what may happen. What I do know is that experiencing Baor will bring your soul back home and you will stop being a stranger to yourself and to us."

In other words, according to the council I had not yet arrived home. I did not know myself yet, nor did I understand the extent of the fragmentation within my psyche. The elders were aware of the forces at play within me, and their concern translated into a desire to provide a cure for the forces that did not want me to come home. There was no doubt in my mind that within this whole village, even within my family, I was the only person who did not fit in. I had believed that time was going to change all this. As I became more and more accustomed to traditional life, I assumed I would be able to throw off the cloak of literacy that separated me from my people and become adequately integrated into the realm of nature, within which the village found its meaning. Indigenous people find their rhythms in nature. Westerners, on the other hand, seem to seek meaning in the realm of the machine, where one finds neither peace nor wholeness, but ceaseless movement. In the West, people are always frenetically rushing somewhere in the countless lanes of the multiple highways of progress.

Now the elders were suggesting that a sure way to cure me would be to go to the school of the ancestors and to be trained according to custom. This had never been tried before. As if he had been following my thoughts, Father continued from where my reflections left off.

"This situation has never occurred before—a man going into Baor after having been initiated into something else. I don't know how deeply your experience among the whites has affected you. No one else seems to be able to tell either. What we are all sure about is that Baor will be a serious challenge to you because you know things that Baor would rather you didn't. This knowledge will be like a wall in front of you that will want to keep you from digging into yourself the way people are expected to during this kind of experience."

I thought about this business of knowing things that initiation would rather I didn't, and it dawned on me that literacy, from the traditional point of view, occupies a space within the psyche that is reserved for something else. So my knowing how to read and write meant that I would never be able to access certain traditional knowledge as long I lived.

My father continued. "Two diviners were assigned the task of designing a medicine that might help you. You remember what we did with Guisso? The others did not have to work with you directly. Last night they reported to the council that they don't think their medicine is going to transform you all the way through. This means that there are certain things that don't want to be broken in you. The difficult part is that for your Baor to succeed, these things must be broken. It would be better for you if these things within you could be broken before Baor; otherwise this may all be an experiment that might not work. I am worried about you. I can't advise you whether to do this or not. I just carry the words of the elders. I want you to live."

"Why do the diviners think the medicine they have prepared for me will not work all the way?"

"There is a ghost in you; something dead that does not like to confront anything having to do with life. This thing will be on the defensive each time you try to come alive. For you to live as one of us, that one is going to have to die. Right now it is prepared to fight. Fire is cooking violence and resistance inside of you. If you allow the violence to have its way, it will kill you. I don't know what is fueling that violence, no one seems to know, but it is a ghost that comes from the white world. Though it is not alive as a human being is alive, it still smells its death."

I could understand Father's concern at my level of preparation for the initiatory experience, but I could not understand why he was so afraid for me. I knew nothing about Baor. When I was a small child, I had been too busy with Grandfather to realize that people were being initiated. I did remember his explaining to me that everything he told me would not have to be understood right away. Would Baor help me to understand some of what he had shared with me?

I was not afraid of dying. Wasn't I already dead in some sense, trapped between worlds as I was? If Baor was a way out of this trap, what choice did I have? If it would make my homecoming real, could I say no? And why was everyone so concerned about me, anyway, when they could offer nothing better to rescue my divided soul?

Part of me was curious about what made my father hesitate. What did Baor really entail? What dangers did it hold? When I asked him to tell me about it, he replied, "Accidents occur in these things. People die in Baor every year. It is part of the experience. If people who have never been outside the ancestral circle fall victim, what about a person who has lived most of his life outside? That's why I am afraid for you."

Father was not in the mood to discuss the details of the experience even though I was eager to know all about it. He kept saying that he could not tell me much because knowing about it would hinder me from the experience. I, on the other hand, was convinced that the more I knew, the more I could increase me chances of survival.

At last he said in a firm and convincing tone, "Knowing what Baor is will not protect you. It will only save you from being initiated. This is not what you need. You cannot want Baor and protection at the same time—it's like wanting day and night at the same time. The very reason you need Baor is because you grew up protected. Protection is toxic to the person being safeguarded. This is because no one can effectively protect anyone. When you protect something, the thing you are keeping safe decays.

"People come into this life with a purpose that enables them to protect themselves. You are your own and best guardian. You go into Baor to save yourself from the lethal protection of other people. If I told you what my Baor was like, I would have to be your protector for the rest of your life, and that is deadly."

All this seemed utterly strange to me. How had our conversation led to this? I began to feel suspicious and confused, as if the whole idea of Baor were some sort of trap to get rid of me. In the seminary, hadn't I read novels in which such things happened?

When I tried to discuss my fears with my father, he declined any further conversation. "The night is late and there is work to do at sunrise. The elders will want to meet with us in the evening. That's also what I came to tell you."

He left without wishing me goodnight.

The timid red light bleeding out of my lamp flickered and went out. There was no more shea oil to feed it. My head was heavy with thought, though I felt too exhausted to deal with it. I wanted to think, but I also wanted to rest. I lay down defenseless and let sleep take over.

CHAPTER 13

THE MEETING
AT THE EARTH SHRINE

The next day Father came back from the farm a little earlier than usual. I could almost hear him thinking, caught up in a net of perplexities that no one could help him solve. He looked pitiful. I knew that he was trying his best to win my sympathy and forgiveness about my abduction, the pain of my homecoming, and the pending initiation.

He paced back and forth like a man searching for something but unable to name what it was. He did not notice me. I was sitting outside the compound in the same place I had sat in when I arrived. After a while I began to wonder whether his failure to notice me was because of the nature of the place I was sitting. Perhaps it was a place that swallowed whoever came near it into invisibility. Or perhaps it was just that a worried, crowded mind blurs the eyes.

Father disappeared into the compound and I decided to go after him, just in case he wanted to talk to me about the meeting ahead. I did not see him, but there was a line of ash in front of his door and in front of mine. I began to understand that the meeting with the elders had great significance for him. Otherwise he would not have performed this ritual. One spreads ash when something is threatening to go wrong and must be stopped before it gets out of hand. What was he afraid of? Father walked out of the medicine room, where he had just finished doing something.

He was still carrying some ash. He headed toward the shrine of the ancestors, inside the goats' room. I followed him.

He knelt and I imitated his gesture. The place smelled of goat and sheep dung. In front of us were two statues holding hands, the Dagara symbols of the ancestral masculine and feminine so important to the maintenance of a home. Partially concealed behind a mud wall and resting on a mud platform, the statues could not be clearly seen.

Father stretched out the hand in which he held the ash and spoke breathlessly. "It is not bad news that I bring to your attention. A man of faith never leaves home without a word to you, the true keepers of this compound. I come to announce that we are going to meet the council of the elders and to ask that you be with us to inspire us to speak the truth. All I want is peace for this family and for everyone in it. May we arrive there in peace and come back home in peace. I bring this ash to you so you may use it to stop anything that might hinder this meeting from going well."

Saying this, Father poured the ash all around the statues. Then we both stood and walked out of the room silently.

We were the first to arrive at the meeting place, a little clearing outside the house of the priest of the earth shrine. In the center of the clearing was a circle made by six stones, and in the middle of that was the statue of Dawera, the community lawmaker. Seen from a little distance, the statue looked like the same cross on which Jesus died, made of wood from an unknown tree. But, as you get closer, its appearance is terrible. The top side of it has the face of an elder in trance with his hands outstretched as if to placate something. On either side of the body pours water, while from his feet burst flames. It was not calming to look at this statue. When I saw it, I suddenly felt tense.

The god Dawera can see without being seen and is a representative of supreme justice. He polices the tribe, always on the lookout for lawbreakers, and warns those who think they can get away with minor violations such as theft or lies. When someone is suspected of lying, this is the symbol they are asked to swear on. Nobody wants to have to say anything in the presence of Dawera because he sees everyone down to the bottom of his or her soul. This, coupled with his striking resemblance to the Christian cross, made me dread the meeting.

The elders began to arrive one by one. First came the priest of the earth shrine, Kyéré. The meeting place was just behind his compound, yet he was late. Kyéré was so old that he walked with the support of two canes. He would put one cane in front of him, lean on it, and move his leg forward, then repeat the process for the other leg. He resembled a skeleton set in motion by a remote control. I felt the urge to help the old man, but I did not know how. I hesitated because I did not know what my father would think of me if I did, or whether this was customary or not. Anyway, did he want help? He seemed to be in no hurry to get to the meeting place. Every five or ten feet he would stop for a period of time longer than the one it took him to walk that distance. Then he would resume his painful progress.

As he came into speaking range, he noticed us. "It's been a long time since I became a four-legged. I have forgotten how fast the two-legged move. You must have jumped over here. My older son saw you as you walked out of the bush and into the surface of my property. I thought I should let you come closer. Then you vanished and here you are. Did you jump over?

"Yes," my father replied. People never say no to questions like this. It is not polite. No implies denial. No one wants to deny, but to make it possible for all things to be affirmative. What they do or say in the next sentence, however, gives the real answer to the question, so Father added, "We just walked at the same speed. There was nobody at the outskirts of the compound when we got here."

He spoke these words in a soft tone, different from the one he normally used at home. There was no doubt that he felt the authority of the old man.

The priest spoke again. "Then I do not wish you to live to be a four-legged. See, every morning when I wake up, it takes me a while before I can tell where I am. I always think I am in the country of the ghosts. My legs won't let me live here in this life, and I can't go to my ancestors, where I won't need them anymore."

My father looked embarrassed, as if he did not know how to talk to the chief. He growled, sputtered, and tried to laugh; then, realizing that he should not laugh, he turned the unfinished laughter into a clearing of throat and ventured, "There should be someone to help you. Why do you have to do this alone? I will ask my daughter to come over if you need some help."

The chief laughed, or rather, he emitted an elephantlike sound that I interpreted as laughter. I too was on the verge of exploding with laughter because of the comical way in which the old man was talking, but I could not laugh—out of respect. He could not talk and walk at the same time and he could not listen and walk at the same time.

"Your daughter will cost me three cows, two barrels of cowrie shells, seven sheep, and as many chickens as I have fingers left on my hands."

I looked at his hands. He had six fingers on each one. The sixth finger was a useless protrusion the size of the small toe, with an incomplete nail on it.

"Wasn't that what you gave as a dowry for his mother?" he asked, pointing one of his sticks at me. "Now, I don't think I can do that. So I'll just use my own daughters until someone dares to want them. By that time I should be ready to get rid of this damn body of mine. I can't use my wives because all four of them have lost their sight. Sounds like a conspiracy, if you ask me. Why would four women decide to go blind, all in the same year? Can you answer that? I know that Napo, my oldest, was having some problems seeing this side of reality. I did not worry about her because she was old enough to not care anymore. A woman who stops bearing children should turn her sight to other things anyway. But the three others—what business did they have to think that the affliction of their superior co-wife was an order that they too should get rid of their sight? You figure out this riddle for me. Isn't this a perfect example of blackmail? Now I can't ask them for anything."

The chief was obviously in a good mood. Father, out of respect for old age, was too nervous to participate in the chief's bantering. He said, "I was just trying to help. It looks as if you would get here quicker if you stopped speaking."

This much was true. The chief looked as if he planned to never stop talking, but he took my father's advice seriously and began to move again. Eventually he made it to one of the large granite stones, let his hands glide down the sticks, and sat down. His appearance was unearthly. His spirit was so unlike his body that it felt as if two living entities were competing with each other. The level of detachment he had with his body was an unmistakable sign of the work of the spirit in a person who knows what ultimately lasts and what does not. Kyéré had abandoned any notion of external aesthetics, but one could see beneath the surface of his wasted body a spirit far more beautiful than any representation of the divine. The experience of such a spirit made me disregard the ugliness of his body as something superfluous to the expression of beauty, integrity, honesty, and genuine life that glowed all around him.

The priest of the earth shrine reminded me of Grandfather, and made me understand why the wise pay little attention to their bodies. In their world dirt has no negative effect on life because they have no concept of its being evil. These earth people live like Mother Earth—their cleanliness is in their spirits. I wondered if those who spend their lives obsessed with looking beautiful are not fighting to cover up something ugly deep within. Our shallow appreciation of outward beauty might be more a confused reaction to the memory of true beauty than an actual encounter with it. In that case the beauty that exists on the outside of a person would serve only as a reminder to us of the real beauty of the spirit behind it. These elders had long ago understood this and chose to focus their energies where they really count—on matters of the soul.

All of this went through my mind as I watched the priest of the earth shrine sit. He put his sticks away, breathed contentedly, and saluted my father as if he had just met him. The other elders arived, quickly and silently. The sun was about to set and they were all late.

Presently each of the six stones had a man on it. Each elder was assigned a stone to use until he died. Each time a stone was left empty by death, the chief of the earth shrine selected another man among the grandfathers and great-grandfathers of the community. The priest of the earth shrine is always succeeded at his death by the eldest of his sons from his first wife. So this circle had existed since time immemorial. The once-gray stones had been used for so long that they were polished and blackened with age.

The chief declared the beginning of the meeting by clearing his throat loudly. "We are here tonight to water our garden. But this is not like our regular watering, for that which grows in our garden needs far more water than we had believed. A few months ago, this grandson of ours found his way back to his roots, coming out of the wilderness where the white man lives—the one who hunts men. When the spirits have a plan for someone, he survives even the unsurvivable.

"We know this boy is here for a reason. I have summoned you together so that we can find out if there is something we can do to help him get home. The last time we met, Bofing, our diviner and ash-thrower,* said he could not tell us if this boy can pass through Baor and learn what he must learn. We want to see if there is a chance that he can."

A short, stout elder seated directly opposite the chief began speaking, almost interrupting the chief. "What are we doing here? Are we letting a wanderer who has become a stranger because he stayed away too long trouble the peace of our council? This is not the first time someone has come back from the wild. Why should we act as if his arrival were so special that we had to invite him to sit here? Why should we let this uninitiated kid come to this sacred place with a father who obviously has no knowledge of what makes an elder an elder? We are violating our principles today, compromising the sacredness of this circle. Our ancestors will judge us for doing this."

"Fiensu," the chief replied, "we are talking about a drizzle, not about a tempest. When I sent Dogo—whom we all agreed should design the medicine to help this boy get through Baor—to divine on this matter, the ancestors told us something that convinced me of the appropriateness of inviting this boy and his father to come here. You cannot ignore the fact that the dawn hides the coming day; otherwise you may be unprepared

---

*An ash-thrower negotiates with the spirits for the resolution of a conflict that involves a person and a spirit.

when the day comes. The destiny of this grandchild has been known since his birth. We want to make an offer to him, a risky offer, and we want to hear him say yes so the rest of our plans can proceed."

"Well, why didn't you tell us that in the first place? When we last met it was clear to all of us that we were facing a delicate and dangerous situation. We have agreed that all must be done in the interest of the village, not that of any individual. Even if you had it all checked out, our responsibility requires exercise of the highest caution."

I felt sorry for Fiensu. Obviously he hated anything out of the ordinary and had little sympathy for anyone who did not fit into established categories.

Dogo, who was seated next to him, spoke. "When the chief asked me to consult with the spirits, I did not know what to expect. All I knew was that when Bofing performed his divination, he could not guarantee that his medicine was going to work during Baor because he could not locate the boy's *Siè* [double]."

I was alarmed when I heard him say this. The Siè is a person's spirit, the part of him or her that is connected to the ancestral world. A person who is suffering from serious psychological problems is said to have left his spirit somewhere. Living away from your double is like living with chaos, terror, and insecurity.

Dogo continued. "I don't know how someone can live without a Siè. I suppose that this is what happens when someone is swallowed by a foreign way of life. Now, Bofing is not a member of the council of Baor this season, so he will not be able to oversee the working of the medicine for this boy. But Guisso, who has worked with the boy ever since he arrived, knows him better than any one of us, and he thinks he can succeed. I consulted with the spirits for a yes-or-no answer, which I communicated to the chief. That is why he convened this meeting."

"Thank you, Dogo, for your useful clarification," Fiensu said. "But the cloud in my head left me even before you explained matters to me. All I'm saying is that someone should have told us this before. But somehow I still don't like the idea that we are making such a fuss about this boy. Last rainy season one just like him came back from Ghana. The lad was fine. He brought back a lot of nice things with him too. Then he left."

"I hear you fine, Fiensu," Kyéré said, "but we all know that this return is different. This boy seems to have left himself behind. And he wants to stay. He wants to be one of us."

For reasons I couldn't understand, Fiensu would not stop arguing. His sarcastic character was made worse perhaps because he was the youngest and the proudest of the council. "I don't think someone who paints language on a paper should be trusted," he continued. "This boy speaks too fast. He has no respect for anyone. He yells at his family—his father can testify to that. If we do not do something, and soon, he may turn out to be some sand in our food. Something has to be done."

Bofing came to my defense. He spoke as if he were trying to appeal to Fiensu's sense of compassion. "I thought that this is what we came here this evening to do. We are talking about one of our sons. I remember Malidoma as a little boy, bright-eyed, cheerful, obedient. We all looked to him as one with a promising future. Bakhye, his grandfather, who sat where you now sit in this council, told us everything about him that we needed to know—that he was a good boy with a good spirit who would help us preserve our ways. How can we throw him out when he has crawled across the world to return to our hearts?"

I didn't remember any elder looking at me as a child with a promising future, nor did I believe that my future held anything promising. From the direction that this meeting was taking, it seemed more likely that the opposite was true. Hadn't I made trouble that propelled me into this place? Didn't this man have to defend me?

"You're a sentimental fart," Fiensu said scornfully, prepared to stand his ground. I lost my sympathy for him. "When that white priest left with Malidoma on his back, do you think that he did not know that he was creating a time bomb to come back and destroy our village, the juice of our lives? Water that has been spilled cannot be collected again."

"But what about the destiny assigned to the boy at birth?" Kyéré argued. "He is the first male child of his parents and must be the one to become the priest of his family after his father dies. We all know that if he is not initiated, this will be the first time we have ever disobeyed the ancestors. This is a risk we have to take. We have to get Malidoma back with us or he is gone."

The passionate intervention of the priest of the earth shrine seemed to slow Fiensu down a bit. He fell silent, a silence loud enough to indicate that he was hatching something. Then he said, "Our knowledge is not the best. The white man's is better—and this boy knows it. Personally, I can't compete with the white man, and I don't like the idea of trying to fight against something when I know I can't win. I have an idea—let Malidoma go back where he came from."

"He is one of us, Fiensu," the chief replied.

Father, who had kept silent longer than he could bear, pleaded with the elders. "He came back from the wilderness because he really cares about us. He doesn't want to leave his village like all these other children today, daydreaming their lives away about being modern, going to the cities. If we let them all go, if we let my son go, we'll die without a trace. Our civilization will end. And we will be responsible."

"I still say send him away!" Fiensu insisted. "There are things you can never make someone forget, and we can't make him forget what he experienced."

Bofing didn't like this. He continued on from where his argument had ended earlier. "Send him away and you'll add to what he can never forget. What he experienced can be good for us."

"I can't see how," Fiensu said. "If we want to know what he knows, we will have to ask him to teach us. If we do this, we give him too much power. Do you think it is good for a boy to teach his elders? I don't think so."

Bofing disagreed. "What alternatives do we have? If we don't want to know what he knows, that means we don't want him among us. This is terrible."

"What is terrible," said Fiensu, "is when we allow him to infect everybody with this sickness."

"Fiensu, let me finish before you infect everyone with discord," said Kyéré, who by now was unable to contain his irritation. "When I consulted the ancestors about Malidoma this morning, I was advised that we have to open ourselves to this boy and welcome him back because throughout his exile he's never forgotten us. The ancestors told me that when he lived in the village, he was always close to his grandfather, our Bakhye, his real teacher. I also learned that he came back because his grandfather told him to. The ancestors said that he will be our mouth, and through him the white man will become friends with us. Let us bring forward our wisdom and recognize what our duties are to him. We will offer him Baor. Now, I want to ask the father of this boy what he wants for his son."

I liked the chief for saying what he had said and I felt he knew me better than I knew myself. But the question he asked my father seemed to take Father by surprise. He jerked around and looked at me appealingly, as if for guidance. Then he looked at the six elders. When he saw that we were waiting for him to speak, he cleared his throat and ventured, "Thank you for offering me the honor of speaking. I feel like a child here. As a father I know I should be clear about what I want for my son, but you know I have not been with him very much since his grandfather left us. I want him to do whatever he can in order to be a part of the family and the community, but I do not know if this is what he wants. I don't know what to say in this situation."

Fiensu took over. "What are you trying to say, young man?" he asked my father.

"I mean that what my son wants is what I want."

"I'll still wait to hear the man in you speak," Fiensu said, "for you have not spoken yet."

"I have to be honest about what I think when it comes to my son. I don't know how to speak for him. Only he does. My answer came from my heart and my belly."

"Do you all hear that? Here is a man who doesn't know his role toward his own son. Are you the real father of this boy or are you his son?" I began to hate the man because I saw his strategy. He had been humiliated by the chief and now he was trying to take it out on my father.

I could not remain quiet. "What my father wants is what I want." True, I held some grudges against Father, but I could not stand by when he was attacked and not defend him. "He wants me to be initiated. The chief wants me to be initiated. Everybody wants me to be initiated. And I will be initiated. Whether it works for me or not, I have nothing to lose. If something happens to me and I can't make it, that's my business. I will do anything to belong to my community and to my family."

Fiensu leaped off his stone seat as if something had bitten him. He grabbed his machete and raised it high. "Who asked you to speak?" he shouted. "Since when do babies speak to their elders without being asked?"

Everybody began to talk at once. I sensed that they wanted to calm Fiensu down without making him look as if he were in the wrong. I knew I had done something improper, but I did not care. I did not feel sorry for what I said, even though I was uneasy that I had disturbed the sanctity of a council meeting. My anger at Fiensu had nothing to do with the council. To me he was a person before being a councilman.

Finally, the chief managed to make himself heard. "Stop! Let's not give this boy the impression that this is the way our meetings go. I asked a question and the response came to me. This is what we wanted to hear. You can't walk naked into the rain and expect to keep your body dry. This is the first time the council has met with individual persons. A change in tradition requires a change in the way things happen. I am not sorry for this boy's behavior. For a long time this council has been ignoring the fact that a new day is forcing itself upon us. We are becoming outdated without knowing it. If the council is going to continue to exist in this community, we have to pay more attention to those who return from the wild. We cannot change the things that have happened to us. Our recent past is flooded with strangers coming from far away into our land and staying with us against our will."

"That's true." The man who spoke had not said a thing since he arrived.

Another man ventured, "I think the old days are giving birth to new suns. What I don't know is what will make them shine."

"Thank you Daziè, thank you Signè," said Kyéré. He indicated me. "There, sitting among us, is an expression of this new sun. He said he wants to get the chance to shine. I say we must let him, and give him our blessing. He knows things that we don't know. Let him learn what we know. Who knows what will come out of him, fired as he will be in the kiln of two knowing paths? What do you say—all of you?"

"I agree," said Daziè. "I can think of at least one good thing that we will gain if the bad does not prevent it from happening. The people who taught him all he knows do not know a thing about us. We don't know about them either. Who is the white man? What is his medicine like? Who can actually answer these questions for us? I think that if we open the belly of this little boy, we will see a lot of things we needed to know about from the beginning. I don't like to live with something I don't know, nor do I want to throw it away because I don't understand it. We all believe that there is a reason why things come together. I say, let this boy be initiated."

Everyone else agreed, but Fiensu said nothing. He was brooding over something. For a while it felt as if the whole council were waiting on him, waiting for his word, as if everything depended upon it. Finally, sensing this, he said, "If that's what the council wants, who am I to say no?"

The chief thanked him and everybody nodded. We could barely see each other by then. The night had quietly swallowed us. The meeting came to a close and we began to disperse.

Before leaving, Fiensu went to the chief and said, "Next time, Kyéré, would you avoid making a fool of me?"

"I promise it will not happen again."

"Thank you."

My father and I came to say goodbye to the chief. As we approached him, I heard him murmur, "Avoid making a fool of you, Fiensu? Not yet." Then he greeted my father and smiled at me. He had no teeth.

That night I tried in vain to sleep. Something major had happened to me. I had seen a council meeting and I had seen how hard decisions were to make. I finally understood my father's hesitation when he had first mentioned Baor to me. A page of my life was being turned. I was going to be initiated as soon as harvest was over.

CHAPTER 14

ΜY FIRST NIGHT
AT THE INITIATION CAMP

 Time flew. The millet fields were generous and the harvest was good. The hard work of collecting and transporting grain from the farm to the roof of houses where it waited to be put into the granaries was over. Now, in the fallow season, the villagers turned their attention to spiritual matters, to initiation. The dry season would be painfully idle if there was nothing else to do. One afternoon I was sitting outside with my sister when a town crier came running to my father's house. In a Dagara village, the town crier is considered an envoy of the spirit. He does not greet people or otherwise behave normally, for he is possessed by the message he has been commissioned to convey. He appears very agitated while doing so because he is responding to what the spirits have told him to do.

Out of breath, he stopped in front of us, mumbled something, and drew a cross on the mud wall of the women's quarter. He said nothing, but instead sang a bizarre song. As he was about to go away, I stopped him.

"Wait a minute. What's all this about?"

"What? You don't know? Well, a child who lives in this house will become a man—if he lives that long. . . ."

This answer transfixed me. I sat down. I had imagined that Baor was scheduled for the middle of the dry season.

Seeing my perplexity, my sister tried to clarify things for me. "You cannot be told about it until the day before. If you know ahead of time, something is wrong."

"So my initiation begins tomorrow—and I am not the least prepared for it."

"Your not knowing is your being prepared."

"Did anybody in this house know?"

"How would anyone know? The council of initiation is very secretive."

I had become accustomed to being relaxed about initiation since that evening at the council's quarter. Now, the sudden proximity of the experience brought my blood to boiling heat. That night I could not sleep. Each time I closed my eyes, I saw ghosts all over the place. I lived the whole night in the country of ghosts, and the only time I was able to sleep Grandfather appeared to me. He was dressed in the same ragged clothes he wore fifteen years ago.

He greeted me in French. Shocked, I replied, "Grandfather—you speak French?"

"Of course I do. I'm dead. Look, I want you to know that this is another journey of pain."

I was half awake. I sat up in bed to make sure that I was fully understanding what Grandfather was saying to me.

Noticing this, he continued. "I said that this initiation is another journey of pain, but you're going to the real school now. I hope you're feeling strong. If you see a Kontomblé, just remember you've seen them before."

When I woke up I could not even remember how Grandfather had left or how the dream had ended. I awakened because Father was calling me to inform me that we had something to do together before I was taken out of the village. Then he disappeared.

My brain was crowded. I sat on my bed, trying to sort things out.

No one bothered me until the middle of the afternoon, when Father called me again. The house seemed to be deserted. I walked out of my room into the inner yard, where Father was waiting for me. He held ash in one hand and a bowl of water in the other. He handed me the water and I followed him into the medicine room.

We knelt down and he began. "Walai!" he said, saluting the spirits. "To the rising of the sun, to the powers of life. To you who established the directives and the meaning of crossing the bridge from nonperson to person through the hard road of knowledge. Here is another one who leaves his warm home and comes to you seeking the path of memory. The road is dangerous, the process uncertain, but with your protection, upon which we rely, he will return to us a man. Let him come back alive."

Father motioned to me to hand him the water, which he sprinkled onto the spirits, the statues of the male and female ancestors. He had already done the same with the ash in his hands. Then he continued, "Take this ash and give him the power of his ancestors. Take this water to seal the contract between us that he will return from his journey with a heart turned toward his tribe and a soul toward his ancestors."

He then turned to me and said, "The time has come. I will not have much to say to you again until . . . I may never say anything to you again unless you come back. I have done what a father should do, the rest is in your hands. Please come back to us."

The whole family was outside watching. When I followed Father out into the compound, everybody looked at me with sympathy. My younger brothers were staring at me as if I were going on a long journey with no specific time of return. I had no idea how long I was going to be absent. We all walked away from the house toward the outskirts of the village. As we neared the bush, more and more people joined us. There was a large group of young adolescents, maybe thirteen, maybe fourteen years old packed together at the edge of the bush. They looked so young that I felt out of place. They were all naked.

Nakedness is very common in the tribe. It is not a shameful thing; it is an expression of one's relationship with the spirit of nature. To be naked is to be open-hearted. Normally, kids stay naked until puberty and even beyond. It was only with the introduction of cheap cloth from the West, through Goodwill and other Christian organizations, that nakedness began to be associated with shame.

The naked kids were singing. As I came closer I could hear their words.

My little family I leave today.
My great Family I meet tomorrow.
Father, don't worry, I shall come back,
Mother, don't cry, I am a man.

As the sun rises and the sun sets
My body into them shall melt,
And one with you and them
Forever and ever I shall be . . .

As the candidates for initiation passed through the crowd, they took off their shirts and shorts. Their families embraced them. Some family members grabbed their hands and sobbed with them; perhaps they were saying goodbye for the last time. There were so many young men that I could not count them all. Many of them were strangers to me. My father asked me to take my clothes off. I obeyed him, but I felt ashamed. No one paid any attention to my nakedness, however. In the village, clothing attracts more attention than nakedness. My sister was weeping when she grabbed my hand. A little annoyed by this display of emotion, I pulled myself loose and joined the group of candidates who were singing—

> . . . *To become a man I must go,*
> *Into Nature's womb I must return,*
> *But when I come back,*
> *The joy of rebirth for you I will sing.*
>
> *My little family I leave today.*
> *My great Family I meet tomorrow.*
> *Father, don't worry, I shall come back,*
> *Mother, don't cry, I am a man.*

We sang as we walked into the belly of the bush, swallowed by the trees. We were not walking in any order. I felt driven forward by the crowd of kids and my feet moved automatically. *How many of us are going into the bush to be initiated? How many villages are represented here?* I wanted to ask someone, but I felt what I can only describe as a palpable pressure against asking questions. The air around me was charged with the sensation that something serious was happening, something so big that to start trying to put it into words would desecrate it or go counter to the whole purpose of the gathering. So I kept quiet and did as everyone else was doing. Besides, people were singing and walking too fast for conversation. I decided that later I would seize the first opportunity to find out who my fellow initiates were.

The initiation camp was a rudimentary clearing in the center of the bush, hidden in the midst of a grassy savanna by the protective walls of the surrounding mountains and foothills. Envisioning a place where the marvelous and the supernatural could happen naturally, I had imagined a decor of talismanic medicine tools—hyenas' tails sewn onto elephant skin to enhance vision, courage and determination; dried lions' hearts for special intrepid missions; hunting relics for mystical rites; catskin bags containing nonmaterial attack instruments, and the like. But the clearing turned out to be a just a circle like the one in the middle of a farm that farmers reserve for the harvested crop before they carry it home. Maybe that's what Baor was supposed to mean—a return to or a harvest of simplicity. In this case we were the crop.

The area was divided into two circular sections. The larger was used as a place of instruction and a sleeping area for the neophytes. Thirty meters away was another circle reserved for the five elders in charge of the rites of Baor. Each of the five elders had a straw mat for a bed. Each mat was brand new. At the center of the elders' circle there was a fireplace and a little hut. I assumed the hut contained the teaching tools for the six weeks to come.

All the evidence suggested that the elders seemed to know exactly what they were about to get us into.

Our circle, on the other hand, was virtually empty when we got there. We began by collecting leaves from trees to make beds for the coming night and dry wood for the fire. As soon as we arrived, the elders disappeared and we were given directions by a coach—a graduate from a previous training—who was in charge of practical organizational matters. We knew that the elders were there somewhere, but we didn't see them until nightfall, when they appeared suddenly out of nowhere to begin our training.

Meanwhile, as we prepared for the night, I wondered what we were supposed to do for dinner. No one talked or asked any questions, and the general silence was beginning to annoy me. I asked my friend Nyangoli if women from the village were going to bring us dinner since we had not eaten since morning. Nyangoli was busy dexterously tearing the leaves off a branch he had stripped from a tree. Without turning his head, he matter-of-factly said that if a woman showed up here, she would be cut to pieces and roasted.

"How are we going to eat, then?" I asked, surprised.

"We did not come out here to eat. If you're hungry, have dinner anywhere you can as long as you do not disturb the schedule."

"Do you know how many of us are here?" I asked as a way to change the subject.

"Three times twenty plus three. Five villages altogether," he replied. That's a Dagara count for sixty-three.

When darkness fell that first night, our coach roared at us to prepare for the circle of fire. He communicated with his hunter's *Wélé,* whistling the words rather than singing them. The Wélé looks like a five-inch flute, with two holes on the right side and one hole on the left side. The Dagara language is a tone language, that is to say, it is spoken like a chant. It is customary on important ritual occasions to blow words through this flute. Each sound has a code meaning, and people take this kind of message more seriously.

The coach's summons came while a group of us was outside the initiation circle, still collecting dry wood or fresh leaves. I had little knowledge of musical language, and all I understood was something about gathering around the "sun of the night." The rest of the message seemed like perfect gibberish to me. The communication was very complex, and it almost seemed like the coach took a personal interest in polishing his musical language into something too advanced for illiterate musical interpreters like me.

Sensing my difficulty, Nyangoli translated for me. "He says that the sun is going to lie down for the night. As the blanket of darkness spreads over the land of the gods, the ancestors have requested the elders to ask him to summon us to gather for the instructional ceremony. That's what he said word for word."

"What's this supposed to mean?"

"Nothing," replied Nyangoli, uninterested. "Very soon the elders will show up to tell us what we're going to be doing out here. That's all there is to it."

I was becoming conscious of entering an unknown space. The message of the flute was the first mystery. How many more were to come?

When we returned to the initiation circle, nearly everybody was gathered there. The sun had set and the twilight was at its height, about to yield the last bit of its daylight to the overwhelming impress of the night. In the middle of the circle, a little hole had been dug. Around it pieces of dry wood were being planted. Smaller pieces of wood went on top. More wood was added until a fireplace was built. The coach supervised this, aided by those nearest him. Candidates who could not help, because there were so many of us, either stood and watched or continued preparing their beds. It was pitch dark by the time the fire was ready to be lit.

The coach plunged his hand into his medicine bag, bringing out two firestones. He placed dry grass next to the fireplace, and scratched the firestones one against the other. A spark flew out onto the grass, but was ineffective. He repeated his gesture a number of times until smoke finally began to rise from the pile of dry grass. One of the boys knelt down and blew onto the fire. He did not seem to be in any hurry. He began slowly, with his eyes closed, as if trying to incorporate the spark that was slowly consuming the dry grass into his inner self. In the meantime the coach was mumbling some words—a prayer to the divinities of the South, to the god of metal, and to *Daziè* the lightbearer.

His prayer ended when the grass ignited. Then he lit a bundle of dry millet stems from the burning grass. He lifted the stems into the air, prayed again to the gods, and touched the fire to the wood. Soon the fire drove back the blackness of the night. Our shadows moved rhythmically with the flames that danced to the roar of their own music. As if compelled by an invisible force, the group intoned the song of light:

> *O light of burning fire,*
> *Clean the mud of the night*
> *That sticks to the lids of my sight.*

> *O instrument of my sight,*
> *Do not close the lids of my eyes*
> *Even when you eat the wood to ash.*

Can I see without your light?
Can I live without your heat?
Can I survive your plight?

O light of burning fire . . .

I did not remember having heard the song before, but the music was inviting, calming to the mind (mine was still restless thinking about food), and
soothing to the heart. I mumbled along, wishing I knew how to sing it like
everybody else. But I had been away too long. In the middle of the circle
that we had instinctively formed, the coach was directing the singing. The
song got inside of you, burning your heart like fire. I was quickly caught
up with its rhythms, words, melody. We held each other's hands and swayed
in cadence. It was intoxicating to sing in the middle of the bush at night—
even on an empty stomach . . .

The elders chose this time to make a dramatic entrance. They looked
like living skeletons, half naked and covered with white lines painted on
their faces, necks, bellies, and backs. Each elder wore ritual cotton shorts.
They were voluminous and looked from afar like bags. Their thin black
bodies were not visible in the dark, just the white, almost phosphorescent
lines painted on them. In addition each elder was carrying his medicine
bag, made of feline skin. They walked in a line, slowly, quietly, and imper-
turbably. When shrouded in the darkness, far away from the fire, their
bodies were luminescent, but as they came closer, into the light, the luminescence disappeared.

Their presence intensified the song. We sang more furiously as if the
force of the elders, suddenly available, were a gift that flowed from the
power of being old. Our teachers walked around the fireplace in the center
of the circle—three times clockwise and three times counterclockwise.
They did not sing with us. When they stopped their procession the song
stopped as if by enchantment. Nobody asked us to stop singing—we simply lost the song. It departed from us as if a force had removed it from our
lips as a calabash of water is removed from the thirsty lips of its drinker.
The silence that followed was as thick as the darkness behind us in the bush.

One of the elders pulled something out of his bag, a pouch with an
end like a tail. One could see long, mysterious, stiff hairs sprouting from
the pouch as if they grew there. He brought the thing to his mouth and
said something silently. Only his lips moved. Then he directed the tail end
of the pouch toward the fire and uttered something in primal language.
The color of the fire changed to violet and increased its roar. We still held
each other's hands. The elder moved close to the fire, speaking again in primal tongue. With each of his movements, the fire grew taller and taller

until the violet flame stood almost six meters in the air. From then on I heard nothing and thought nothing.

The violet fire looked like a ghost with flaming arms, one of which held a flaming stick. The legs seemed to be covered by a robe, all of flame, roaring horribly. The elders had disappeared as if they had removed themselves unseen from the center of the circle. Only this ghost remained, roaring with a deep voice. I suddenly knew what we were going to be doing in the next six sets of five days, which make up the Dagara week, but nobody seemed to have told me this. Rather, this knowledge seemed to have been poured directly into my consciousness. I could not tell if it had been there before, or had come after the fire was turned into a ghost. Can a thirsty throat feel quenched without the cool sensation of drinking? Can a starving belly feel full without the pleasure of eating? The schedule of Baor was somehow poured into us. Later I found out that everybody knew what I now knew.

I doubt that the whole thing took more than thirty minutes, but when I came back to myself, the ghost was becoming a regular fire again. It receded slowly—reluctantly, as if fearing a trap—into the fire. The elder responsible for this magical event was standing in front of the fire. He was thin, tall, and rigid-looking. His body and mind were entirely fixed upon his creation. His eyes were wide open and dilated. The other elders were still standing where they had been before. They had been there all the time, and I suspected that my impression that they had vanished had something to do with the mysterious presence in the fire.

The coach ordered us to sit. Four elders posted themselves around us in four different corners—the four directions—facing each other. The fifth elder, the one responsible for the initial experience, still stood in the middle of the circle next to the fireplace. Walking slowly around the circle, he spoke incessantly and breathlessly as if he were in a hurry to get a job done. Somehow what he said did not sound strange to me or—I found out later—to anyone. It was as if he were putting into words something we all knew, something we had never questioned and could never verbalize.

What he said was this: The place where he was standing was the center. Each one of us possessed a center that he had grown away from after birth. To be born was to lose contact with our center, and to grow from childhood to adulthood was to walk away from it.

"The center is both within and without. It is everywhere. But we must realize it exists, find it, and be with it, for without the center we cannot tell who we are, where we come from, and where we are going."

He explained that the purpose of Baor was to find our center. This school specialized in repairing the wear and tear incurred in the course of thirteen rainy seasons of life. I was twenty. Had I been home all that time, I would have gone through this process seven years ago. I wondered if I was catching up too late but then thought, better late than never.

"No one's center is like someone else's. Find your own center, not the center of your neighbor; not the center of your father or mother or family or ancestor but that center which is yours and yours alone."

While he spoke, he held his medicine pouch with the stiff tail pointing upward. He walked slowly as if moved by an imperceptible force and animated by a vibrant youth that knew no fatigue. He said that each one of us is a circle like the circle we had formed around the fire. We are both the circle and its center. Without a circle there is no center and vice versa. We listened carefully, acquiescing from within us.

"When there is a center there are four live parts to the circle: the rising part in the east and its right side, the north, and the setting part in the west and its right side, the south. All human beings are circles. Our setting part represents the coolness of water. It provides the peace of the body and the soul, and bridges the gap between how we look on the outside and how we are on the inside. It brings us to our family, the village, the community. It makes us many. The god of the setting side is the god of the water, the water we drink, the water that quenches our thirst.

"Its opponent is the rising part, the fire, the god that makes us do, feel, see, love, and hate. The fire has power, a great power of motion both within us and without. Outside of us, it drives us toward one another, toward the execution of our respective duties, toward the planning of our lives. We act and react because this rising power is in us and with us. Inside of us, the fire pulls the spiritual forces beyond us toward us. The fire within us is what causes our real family—those we are always drawn to when we see them—to identify us. From the realm where the ancestors dwell this fire can be seen in each and every one of us, shining like the stars that you see above your heads. Imagine what would happen if you did not have this fire. You would be a dead star, invisible, wild, and dangerous.

"Yes! The fire within us is never dead, therefore it never needs to be reborn. When we know, without being told, that we must perform a certain sacrifice or ritual, we know because the fire tells us this. Through the fire within we dialogue constantly with those we left behind us by being born. The fire is the rope that links us with our real home that we abandoned when we died into being human. We leave our real homes to come into this life, but there is nothing wrong with this. You will understand why long before the end of your learning here. But I am not in charge of telling you this. Why should I be? I can't tell anyone what his personal truth is—and who would I be to even try?"

The elder stopped walking, but his eyes never quit the fire in front of him. He stared at it with such intensity that he seemed to be seeing another ghost emerge from it. From the four corners of the circle the other elders watched him. I could clearly see the dancing fire in their unblinking eyes.

The Dagara view fire much differently from Westerners, both literally and figuratively. The two ideas are almost exact opposites. In the West, fire is thought of as something wild, dangerous, and unmanageable. It drives the individual into uncontrolled fits of passion and a restless pursuit of material things. It always seemed humorous to me that there are fire departments in America and Europe. To a Dagara, the craziness that fire inspires in the West comes from the fact that fire is upset that Western people have forgotten their purpose in life.

My eyes moved from the elder to the neophytes sitting around the fire. Each had a different posture, as if they had become stones, or human dolls stuffed with straw. They had lost control of their bodies. For a short time I felt I was the only conscious person there. The others had shifted into a closer relationship with what the elder in the center of the circle was teaching us. But how did they perform the shift? Why was I an outsider, incapable of entering into the same state of intensity I could see in every face?

As my gaze wandered around the circle, it only confirmed my aloneness. Nobody noticed me looking. They were all preoccupied with what they were doing. Why was it so hard for me to participate fully like everybody else? What or who was distracting me?

I tried to concentrate, but the more I tried to focus my attention, the more I realized how alone I was in this circle of inert men. I could not even sense those next to me. My body had stopped registering anyone's presence because there was no one around for it to respond to. I could not even fully experience my fear: someone else was being afraid for me. . . . I felt as if the elder were still speaking, but I was the only person in the circle unable to hear him.

Suddenly my perceptions changed, turning inside out in an instant. No—the elder had been speaking all the time! He had never stopped talking and gazing into the fire. This new perception, however, did not help stabilize me in reality. Instead, I felt as if I were jumping from one contradiction to another, from one strange realization to another, registering reality in an abnormal way. I was too busy trying to make sense out of something that was probably supposed to challenge my habitual perceptions.

I became conscious of an overwhelming urge to analyze and intellectualize everything I was seeing and experiencing. This impulse to question was cold and purposeless. I was tired of getting nowhere in my thoughts, tired of being constantly defeated in my understanding. I felt trapped, caught inside a stone wall, trying uselessly to break out. But I didn't know where I would be if I escaped.

Something inside of me began screaming for me to break out of this spell of isolation. I asked myself, *Where am I if I am the only one alive in this circle?* Where are these people—the elders, the neophytes, my friend Nyangoli, who is sitting next to me as stiff as a dead piece of wood? The fire was still emitting its roaring sound, but it too had stopped moving. Everybody and everything around me was like a museum piece, and I had become a visitor to that museum.

It was then that the bush around us narrowed. I was quite certain that the trees had moved closer, but how much closer I could not tell. I felt as if everything around me, other than the strangely immobile fire and my companions, had come to life—a strange life. I could not assess this state by any yardstick other than that of my own absolute certitude.

All around me and underneath me I could feel life pulsating, down to the smallest piece of dirt on the ground. The way this life expressed itself was otherworldly: sounds were blue or green, colors were loud. I saw incandescent visions and apparitions, breathing color amid persistent immobility. Everything seemed alive with meaning. Even the stonelike circle of people partook of the same cacophony of meaning. Each person was like the sum total of all the emanations taking place. The people, however, were not in charge of the operation of the universe around them—they were dependent on it and they were useful to it as well.

The elder in the center of the circle was the most intriguing to watch. He looked like an impalpable being in fusion, an amalgamation of colors, sounds of varying pitch, and innumerable forms. All of his smallest constituent parts—his cells and the bacteria in his body, even the tiniest atomic particles of his being—had come alive. He was not moving, but the colors, the sounds, and the life forms were. Without being able to put it into words, I understood what was happening, for at that stage of consciousness there is no difference between meaning and being. Things had become their meaning and I knew that was the lesson for the evening. I also understood that this was the kind of knowledge I was going to become gradually acquainted with—not by going outside of myself, but by looking within myself and a few others. For now, all I could do was to feel and honor the effects of the subtle invisible world breaking through my own blindness and preempting my perceptions. How acquiescent one becomes when face to face with the pure universal energy!

CHAPTER 15

TRYING TO SEE

 I am not sure how this session ended. What I do recall is a huge rock, weighing tons, being hurled at me. I saw it coming, but it was traveling so fast I had little time to avoid it. All I could do was stretch out my hands like a shield to protect my face. This gesture was a joke masquerading as a defense, but it was all I had. The rock hit me with an explosive sound. At that point I could see myself—flat like a cartoon cut out of a cardboard—lying on the ground . . . but there was no rock.

Suddenly I heard a familiar voice. "Malidoma—you are late."

I looked around and realized I was still sitting up, as I had been before the vision at the fire. Nyangoli was speaking to me. It had not been a boulder that had hit me, but Nyangoli striking me gently to get my attention.

"I had to hit you to get you back here," he explained. "You don't want to be left behind."

The fire was nearly dead. The flame had died after consuming every splinter of wood. There were no elders in the center of the circle or anywhere else. Only the coach remained. He asked if everyone was back, but when nobody replied, he did not seem to mind. He already knew the answer to his question. "The night of your education has begun," he said. "It will be a sleepless night until the dawn of your awakening. You will live more wonders, see and feel different things, and be changed from then on. It is my job to tell you that this is not a game. I have noticed that some of you are already having a hard time staying with the group. You must learn to not fight back. This is not a wrestling field. You came here to accept death because you want to live. You may never find new life if you begin by falling behind."

I had no idea what he was talking about. I looked at Nyangoli, hoping for an answer, but he turned away. I looked at Toori, who was sitting on my left side. He smiled bitterly, as if he were sorry for me and wished he could help.

"Tomorrow we will begin working with your sight," the coach continued. "You must learn to see. Without good sight you can't continue with the other sessions. When you have learned to see well, you will journey one by one to your respective places in this world and find every piece of your self. For now, I want you to sleep. Put your weary bodies to rest for the night and put your spirits in a state of awareness. There will be no further pause in this instruction until it is all over."

Part of me understood him and part of me did not. The part that understood knew that my days and nights were going to be lived as if I were in a dream in which worlds collided and different realities confronted one another. I knew that my survival was dependent upon a supreme effort not to resist the initiation process or to set up rules and measurements to control the flow of information presented to me. I knew too that somehow I was unlearning something. Whatever previous ideas I had cherished about the world were going to change. Reality was going to shift, with my cooperation. And if that was not given, would reality try to come and take me away with her anyway? From the first day, my traditional education was like an ending; something was being terminated with no appeal.

There was, however, a part that did not know what to do with all these changes. Myriads of questions were slowing down my journey toward traditional knowledge. I longed for debates, for theories, for criticism: clearly a legacy of the white world. But, I kept telling myself, one cannot continuously ask questions. One cannot always sculpt theories to frame experience, or top experience with the roof of theory. The techniques of indigenous learning were revealing themselves before my eyes, sweeping away my preconceived notions of how learning was accomplished. The contrast between this state of mind and what I had been accustomed to at the seminary was the same as the difference between liquid and solid. It seemed to me that Dagara knowledge was liquid in the sense that what I was learning was living, breathing, flexible, and spontaneous. What I was learning made sense only in terms of relationship. It was not fixed, even when it appeared to be so. For example trees are not immobile, they travel like us from place to place. By contrast, I could see that the Western knowledge I had been given had the nature of a solid because it is wrapped in logical rhetoric to such a degree that it it stiff and inflexible. The learning one gets from a book, from the canons of the written tradition, is very different from the living, breathing knowledge that an elder has to offer—and different from the knowledge that comes from within, from the soul.

Still, I kept asking myself questions. Could one reality contradict another? What kind of new reality was I being introduced to? What is reality predicated upon? I had in a matter of only a few hours accumulated so much new information that I was feeling intolerably burdened by it, yet I could not analyze how this had happened. An old man had started speaking and suddenly I began knowing, or remembering something. I told myself firmly that I must do something about my mental restlessness—shut it down or control it. If I could not, I knew it would be my undoing. How did I know this? I simply felt it, a certainty that was powerful and unmistakable.

That night I forgot what food meant. The hunger I had felt at dusk vanished as if panicked by what had transpired. My body was in a state of such intensity that I could not focus on something as mundane as hunger. I pulsated rhythmically with the vibration of the Earth: green, yellow, blue, and white—I could see these colors everywhere around me. Anything that lived carried them or a combination of them. The initiates were lying on their rudimentary straw-and-leaf beds. The night was cold, so cold I felt an overpowering need to cover my naked body. But all I and the other students had to curl beneath was cold leaves: we were naked and were going to remain naked for the rest of the initiation. I shivered timidly in response to the chill from the dust-laden wind. It had been quite some time since the coach dismissed us, yet I was not asleep and sensed that nobody else was either. I wondered what spell we were under. Perhaps the coach was right and I was resisting, questioning, fighting back too hard. I tried to blank out my mind by turning my attention to my own restlessness. For a while I felt as if I were out of my body, standing in front of myself watching. This could not be, I thought, but I could not afford to contest anything anymore. I decided this was a trick of the mind I would come to understand later. For now, I wanted to sleep, to escape thought by making my mind the subject of its own activity.

As I held tight to the perspective of watching my own body, my attention was caught by something behind it. I began to glimpse the intermittent apparition of a pair of eyes that seemed to hang in the darkness as if they were unconnected to anyone. I realized they must have been there for quite some time, but that I had noticed them only when they blinked. They were obviously looking at me, and I stared back. Enveloped in the frightening darkness of the night, the body—whatever it was—was hidden by the shapeless darkness. All I could see were two luminous oval lenses that rolled from left to right, from right to left. As soon as I focused on the eyes, the questions, objections, and fears I had been fretting over vanished. The eyes had a magnetic effect: they were seductive, cajoling, and—I knew—capable of generating the most abject panic if they desired. But as the eyes watched me watch them, I was incapable of feeling any fear. I do not know how long this staring contest lasted. I had no notion of time passing. Suddenly the eyes rose into the air, as if they were attached to a huge bird. Tilting my head back, I watched them leave. I was still able to see with a strange double perspective—I still saw myself in front of the eyes, and saw the eyes behind my sleeping body. . . .

I felt very cold and realized that day was breaking. The coach was pouring cold water on each sleeper. This undignified wake-up ritual would be customary throughout our time of probation in the bush.

"You can't stay here. Up—up everybody up!" he shouted. I sat up and watched the coach splash water onto the last sleepers. Some of them leaped up from their beds aggressively. One guy jumped up, mumbled something, then flipped into the air like an acrobat and landed on his feet, crouched as if ready for a fight. When he realized he was still in the last episode of a nightmare, he looked around shamefaced, lowered his head, and sat down.

"Hurry," the coach commanded. "You must eat right now, for as soon as the sun rises, we must begin teaching you the tree knowledge. You don't have to eat if you don't want to. Actually, the emptier your stomach is, the easier it will be for you to learn. Other things within us are better nurtured when the body is not fed."

I didn't see any food being prepared. I wondered how he expected us to have breakfast. In the village? But we weren't supposed to be seen by any villager until the last day. Too exhausted to try to figure things out, I decided to behave as if I knew where to get food. I watched Nyangoli walk into the bush and I followed. He moved as if he did not notice me, but I knew that he sensed I was behind him. I followed him in silence until he stopped at a *gaa* tree. Then he climbed the tree and began eating the fruits. I hesitated for a while, then did the same. We ate silently. I was beginning to understand that Nyangoli needed his silence. It must have helped him, for he did not look as devastated or lost as I did. Somehow his attitude communicated to me that there was a subtle method to the way we were being taught in this rough school. I found this attitude profound in someone seven years younger than I was.

Breakfast was quick—I did not feel particularly hungry after a night on the edge of sanity. I decided to stop eating *gaa* as soon as my friend stopped. Nyangoli finished. As we walked together back to the camp, I ventured to start a chat. "I had a horrible dream last night . . ." I said, moving closer to him.

"Everybody had one," he responded without any show of curiosity as to the content of my nightmare.

"How do you know?"

Nyangoli stopped and looked into my eyes as if trying to pluck out some knowledge he knew was hidden there. His face was cold and impassive, yet there was an air of concern in his look. He seemed about to say something, but refrained at the last minute. I had hoped he was going to answer me, but he didn't. Finally he commented that he hoped I was going to give myself a break and allow what was happening to me to sink in.

When we arrived back at the initiation camp, it was almost deserted. Those present were being given the assignment of the day: tree knowledge. I had expected a general meeting of the type we had the night before, but nothing like that happened. Instead, we were placed in groups of five to fifteen and asked to walk a little distance away. Each initiate should select a sizable tree. We were to sit, stand, or kneel about twenty meters from the tree and look hard at it. We were supposed to see something, but were not told what. Each elder was assigned a certain number of students. Apparently his task was to supervise this boring training and to make sure that we saw what we were expected to see.

The tree I chose was about ten meters high, with a trunk less than a meter in diameter: a *yila* tree. I chose a comfortable place to sit and began staring. The sun had risen higher and the freezing temperature of the morning was quickly turning warm. I gazed at the tree faithfully, as I had been told to. For the next five hours nothing happened. The exercise merely became more and more exasperating, since I had nothing but a tree to look at. The same sun that had warmed me up, freeing me from the chill of the night, was now slowly baking me.

To distract myself from this torment, I started thinking about something else. Hadn't I suffered worse than this in the seminary? And was this really a test of seeing or was it just an endurance test? The heat of the sun was more palpable than anything else. It was irresistibly taking possession of my senses. I fought this distraction by thinking about how satisfying it would be to survive this ordeal, to prove that I could do what the others could. The heat, however, was impossible to ignore. Sweat fell into my eyes, which were soon burning painfully. The only way to alleviate this distress was to rub my eyes with the back of my hand, but my hands were too sweaty to be helpful. So I kept my eyes closed. In my struggle against the crippling effect of the heat, I forgot the tree: I was dragged away from my task.

Sitting there with my eyes shut, I felt the impatience and frustration of someone who has something to do but can't get to it. My helplessness in the grip of a simple natural phenomenon was extremely irritating to me. I had to act. My eyes still closed, I got up and scratched around for the leaves of a plant or anything that I could use as a towel. Suddenly a voice behind me commanded, "Back to work—now!"

I explained that I could not see because there was sweat in my eyes. The elder laughed, as if what I had said was rubbish.

"What do you think you are doing?" he said. "You think cleaning your eyes will help you see better? Anyway, do as you wish. There is a plant right in front of you that will help."

I wiped my eyes with the plant and returned to my position. The elder who had spoken to me wore a ragged *balbir* that barely covered his emaciated body. Kola meal that he had been chewing dripped from his red-stained mouth. He was still rhythmically pounding the rest of the nut between his toothless jaws. Sitting at his ease in the shade of a tree, he watched me with interest, as if I were a specimen destined for a secret experiment.

I resumed my gazing assignment. The momentary change of posture seemed to have done something good to my body, and for a while it was willing to cooperate with me. The sweating had cooled me by this point, and the distraction caused by the heat of the day diminished. On the way back to my tree, I had noticed that some of the other students were casually strolling around. Why didn't the elder pick on them instead of me? I was almost certain I had seen at least three boys walk back toward the camp.

"You will not get anywhere if your thoughts are watching one thing and your eyes another. The boys you just saw are through with their assignment so they are free to go do something else."

It was the elder who had spoken before. I did not respond. How did he know that I was thinking about something else, let alone about these other students? I figured he must have noticed me looking at them in astonishment as I was returning to my place by the tree after taking care of my eyes. *You cannot see another person's thoughts,* I told myself. Reassured by that conclusion, I continued to let my thoughts wander while my eyes were locked onto the yila tree. A little later, when I heard the elder begin to sing, I wondered if he too were trying to divert himself from the boredom of this task: watching somebody watch something must have been just as monotonous as staring at nothing.

That thought made me feel better, but not for long. The song the elder was singing was not a commonplace one. It was an old healing melody to which any words could be sung that fitted the situation at hand.

> The blind man had two eyes
> That saw things that moved
> And things that did not move.

He thought he was not blind
And was proud to see,
But when asked to see the moving
In the thing that does not move
He decided he was blind.
His eyes would not believe
That the still was not still
And that the moving could cease
Because the only thing the moving knew
Was move move and move.
Seeing has become blindness
And that which does not move
Knows you lie to yourself
When you lend trust to what you see now.

I listened to the elder sing his mournful song over and over, and it made my body react in strange ways. Instead of hearing the song in a normal way with my ears, I felt instead as if I were hearing it in my body, my bones, my blood, and my cells. With each repetition, the meaning of the song seemed different and more helpful to me in some way. Though my eyes were fixed on the tree, my attention was on the singer. Soon I had no doubt that the elder was singing about me.

"See anything yet?"

He had stopped singing. I realized he expected me to see something now. What I wanted to tell him was that my tree would never stop being what it was, and that looking at it would not make it any more or less of a yila. Instead, I decided I was going to be polite. So I responded with a mere "No."

"Keep looking," he said and resumed his song.

I stole a quick glance at him. He wasn't even looking in my direction and he didn't seem to care one bit about what I was doing.

As evening approached, it became cooler. All around me I heard the voices of my fellow students. Some of them were familiar, others less so. I guessed that I was again falling behind the group in my assignment, since they seemed to have completed theirs. But I figured that soon I was going to be released anyway since the day was almost over.

Another elder joined my supervisor and they began to discuss me. I listened carefully.

"How is he doing?" the newcomer asked.

"In his belly he is a full-bred white. He can't see," my supervisor replied. "The white man's medicine must have damaged *vuur* [spirit]. But his soul is still in him. That's why I said a year ago—that for his own sake he should not be involved in initiation. But Kyéré silenced me as if I were speaking nonsense. Now, if this boy can't even wipe his eyes, how do you think he is going to clean his body? We are barely a day into Baor and he is already trailing behind."

There was a moment of silence punctuated by coughing and spitting. Even though I could not see well, I felt their presence very powerfully. The newcomer asked if I could see anything. I replied that I could see nothing but the same damn tree. He laughed compassionately and then ignored me.

They returned to their chat, and my supervisor said, "You would assume that a person like him would have an easy time, since he has some white man's blood in his medicine bag. He can think like them. And isn't the white man's medicine supposed to be really powerful? They have traveled beyond the seas to parts of the world really wondrous. This boy here is a riddle to me—I can't figure him out."

The voice of my supervisor sounded grave, as if he were announcing an unknowable doom. I wondered why he felt sorry for me. I was just doing what I was told, or at least trying to. It was not my fault if I couldn't see anything in the tree.

"Whatever he learned in the school of the white man must be hurting his ability to push through the veil. Something they did to him is telling him not to see this tree. But why would they do that? You cannot teach a child to conspire against himself. What kind of teacher would teach something like that? Surely the white man didn't do that to him. Can it be that the white man's power can be experienced only if he first buries the truth? How can a person have knowledge if he can't see?"

The second elder was clearly exasperated. He did not seem to be speaking to my supervisor anymore, but wrestling with a theoretical challenge. For him too I was obviously a riddle. There was something about me, something about the way I was not assimilating my lessons and the way my body was not reacting properly to the most important instructions, that attracted the curiosity of these old scholars. They watched me like a dog that has seen a worm for the first time.

CHAPTER 16

THE WORLD OF THE FIRE, THE SONG OF THE STARS

As I continued to watch the tree, I knew I was also being watched. Even after overhearing the conversation of my teachers, I could not help wonder what they really thought of me. I vacillated between two ways of thinking about myself. In the first I saw myself as a living example of the white man's medicine successfully competing against the medicine of the indigenous world—a force to be reckoned with. In the second I was convinced that everyone saw me as incompetent and foolish. The first idea inflated me with pride. Perhaps, I thought, the elders would let me go on, realizing that there was nothing to be done. The second thought took this pride away. As more time passed and my tree stayed the same, I told myself that I should have thought the last thought first. Was there something I was supposed to do that I was not doing? What veil was I supposed to push through? My assignment had been to sit at a respectable distance from the tree and never lose sight of it. Other than getting up for a moment to wipe the sweat out of my eyes, I could not see how I had done anything so far that would have ruined my status as a student in good standing. I had successfully demonstrated my ability to be patient, obedient, and present all day long.

Darkness came. The elders left and the coach appeared. "That's it for today," he said. "If you were not able to see while you had light, how do you expect to do so now that the moonless night is coming on? Do you plan to use some starlight?"

Seizing this opportunity to converse with the coach, I asked him what I was expected to see. I had a good look at him since he was now standing right in front of me. He was dirty, his belly was callused, and stinking, as if he had shared his last meal with the vultures. He was very tall. Though he was pitch black, his blackness seemed to be artificial, acquired through years and years of studied neglect.

I knew that most villagers took a bath with soap only once a year. But even those who bathed that rarely looked cleaner than the coach did. At least you could still see some of their pores. The coach's body, however, was covered with a massive layer of stinking black crust. His face was illuminated by two transcendent colors: red and white. The whites of his eyes moved constantly in a frightening manner, rolling in circles in their sockets. Even though it is the Dagara custom to avoid looking directly into someone's eyes—to do so is to intrude into the other's secret world—the coach seemed to take this to a greater extreme than anyone I had ever met. As he stood facing me, he never rested his eyes on me. Instead, they darted back and forth, left to right, as if they were trying to follow the trajectory of something moving about behind me. The red color on his face was near his mouth, which looked like a volcano. He licked his chapped lips with the dexterity of someone who just concluded a delicious meal. His mouth was the only clean area on his body.

He broke the spell by walking away. I stood up, stretched my legs, and followed him from a distance.

Suddenly I knew I had failed that day, not because of the coach's remarks, but because I felt failure from the depths of my being. I still did not know what I was supposed to see, or what was preventing me from seeing what I was supposed to see. The day was over, the night had come, and other things were going to pile themselves upon me in addition to this failure. I had already missed a traditional deadline. This was a little frustrating, but, worse, fear was creeping into my consciousness as I remembered Father telling me about the dangers of initiation. Was there something in this tree-gazing exercise that could kill me?

Back at the camp I saw Nyangoli remaking his bed along with the other initiates. He noticed my arrival, as did everyone else, but merely continued what he was doing. The heat of the day had dried the soft leaves we had slept on the night before, and they had to be replaced with fresh ones. Nobody told me what I was supposed to do next, so I set to work remaking my bed. It was getting darker and darker. Some of the boys had already finished their beds and gone off to build the campfire for the nightly vigil. Nyangoli, however, waited for me. He even tried to help me lay out the leaves of my bed. Momentarily comforted, I looked at him, hoping for sympathy. He looked away, probably embarrassed for me because of my failure.

I understood his dilemma. This poor kid was probably being berated by the other students because of his friendship with a whitened Black. I remembered something that had happened a year ago, when I had not been back in the village for long. Nyangoli was teaching me how to use a bow and an arrow, and some of the kids were laughing at him for playing the father toward an older guy like me. "You can't make a woman into a man," one of them said, laughing. *"Mwin* [the supreme god] himself made that mistake once when he created a human being with both male and female organs. He corrected this mistake a long time ago—so don't go repeating it."

Nyangoli was making a sacrifice by being my friend. Though he didn't say a word to me as he helped me make my bed, I knew that beneath his action was something profound, carefully hidden. I was very moved.

Through Nyangoli I had learned of the villagers' inability to discuss esoteric knowledge and of their love and respect for the hidden. This had taught me to be less vocal about certain subjects that I perceived were not supposed to be talked about. This silence on taboo topics, however, had never kept me from learning from Nyangoli. His very existence and actions spoke clearly about these unspoken things, and his body language was more eloquent than speech. At no time did I notice this better than when he was helping me, as he was now.

When we had finished with the bed, we walked over to the campfire circle. Nobody had noticed our absence or seemed to care that we were arriving late. The elder was already lighting the kindling, and the sparks he made quickly turned into a large fire that illuminated the faces that were busy feeding it. We took our positions in the circle and waited in silence.

The sound of the *kuor,* a ceremonial drum, rose, speaking the words of the ritual that was to take place. It was usually high-pitched, but was punctuated now and then by a single bass note. The specific meaning of its rhythms was not immediately graspable, but its tones extended and intensified the sacredness of the moment. As if it were listening, the fire responded almost immediately by flashing its flames upward, changing its color from orange to violet. Though the voice of the drum came from behind me, I could not tell if it was near or far. Its location was not important as long as its voice could be heard and its effect felt. Soon the circle opened from the south side. Five students entered, followed by the elders. The students were holding pots of paint which they set down beside the fire.

The elders positioned themselves at the corners of the four directions, and the coach examined the pots and their contents, pouring medicine into each of them. I had no clues as to what was going to happen tonight, and I was uneasy, realizing how powerfully last night's events had affected me. As I thought about my failure, I was afraid. If there was a continuity between experiences, if the success of one guaranteed the success of the other, then I was the least prepared initiate at the fire circle tonight.

The elder in the center of the circle took one of the pots and began to paint on the coach's body with a brush. First he took some paint that shone red and made a series of lines on the coach's face, running from one ear to another. Then he added some lines that ran from one cheek to the other, above and below the nose. He added a circle around the mouth.

The symbolism of the patterns of the face paint was indecipherable to me, though I sensed that the lines had meaning. As the elder painted the coach, he spoke all the while in primal language, the language elders learn as a tool to fulfill their responsibilities. Primal language is the language of the spirit, and of creation. When uttered under certain circumstances it has the power to manifest what is uttered. Primal language is also dangerous because of the potential it has to be lethal. I still remember the first time I heard Grandfather speak it during my childhood. He used it as a retaliatory weapon against a vulture who had defecated on his bald head. He faced the tree where the bird was sitting, uttered a few sentences, and the poor thing came crashing to the ground. When I rushed over to grab it, it was ash. Because of the potency of primal language, only certain elders are given custody of it.

As I watched the elder paint, I also intuited that there was a connection between what he said and the almost mechanical precision of his drawing. The way the brush ran looked almost magical. It was a dance that responded to the way the drum spoke. The dancing of the brush also responded to the dancing of the flames. I became aware that there was a connection between the rhythm of the drum, the dance of the fire, and the manner in which meaning was inscribed on the coach's face. Upon completion, the pattern on his face was a combination of colors: white, red, green, blue, and yellow.

The elder then moved on to the coach's chest, drawing a long vertical white line that ran from below the neck to the navel. Then he drew a series of yellow horizontal lines that crossed the vertical line from east to west. These lines on the chest made the coach look like he was carrying his bones outside his body. The painted patterns became even more complicated when the elder started painting on the legs.

I stopped paying attention to the painting as my attention was drawn to what the coach and the elder were saying to each other. It began as a murmur, as if they were merely communicating practical information to each other. Soon they seemed to be reciting prayers as part of the ritual. Their language was not primal language, nor was it the common tongue. As they spoke, the drum intensified. The fire grew bigger and roared louder as the old man busied himself on the coach, transforming him into a fantasm.

When the elder was finished, he threw his brush into the fire, which bucked and roared. The other elders then entered the circle and in a flash had painted the five students who had helped them carry the paint pots. Then each student came and painted one of us with whatever he had at hand. One of them approached me with a potful of green paint. I shut my eyes. He ran the brush upward and downward, right to left, all over my body. The paint was warm. I wondered if it would ever come off. . . .

When I opened my eyes the circle looked like a wonderland. The fire was alive in a magnificent way. It had ceased to be fire and become a luminescent circle of dynamism, the window into a marvelous world populated by Lilliputians. They were suspended in the middle of it, singing a curious melody. I watched these beings, magnetized by their unceasing motion. They were suspended in midair. I realized that they appeared small only because they were far away, yet I also knew that this was happening in the fire right there in front of me. The song that rose from the fire did not necessarily come from the floating people, but seemed to emanate from everywhere and everything. Soon the luminescent circle of the fire grew bigger and bigger. I could not tell what exactly was happening, but I did not care. It felt great.

Everybody began singing one of those songs you suddenly know the words to, as if you had learned it in a previous life. I lost the analytical part of my mind and was drawn irresistibly into participation. I sang full-throated, clapped my hands, and danced. I could not see the other people, but I knew everybody was there. I could perceive their presence by a different sensory apparatus than the usual five senses. Soon I experienced myself in the same way, as if I were invisible, yet all the more concrete, cogent, powerful, and inalienable. This feeling was wonderful. Never before had I experienced something so real, so true, and so befitting a human being.

When invited into the dynamic circle of fire, we did not hesitate. I do not recall who made the invitation, but I don't think it was an elder. Rather, the invitation came from the Angels who floated in it. The land in the middle of the fire was a vast natural place with trees that burned but were not consumed. The fire they burned with was as bright and pure as the purest gold in the world—and I was in the middle of it.

The grass was also in flames, golden and non-burning. I came to a river—flowing golden liquid like fresh lava running down a hill. The river made me experience an indescribable relief a thousand times more powerful than any earthly sensation. When I jumped into it in a moment of excess and foolishness, the effect produced by my contact with the water was so powerful that I blacked out.

When I awoke, the night was far gone. I could tell this by the position of the shepherd star, which had already risen high in the sky. Dawn was close. I was lying, wet and cold, on the bank of a familiar village river some three kilometers from where we had the painting ceremony at dusk. I was more exhausted and surprised than frightened. I stood up and started the trek back to the initiation camp while images crowded my mind.

One thing I noticed: although it was still pitch-black night, I did not hesitate about where I was going for one single moment. Somehow I felt as if I were being mechanically drawn toward the camp by an irresistible force that I did not mind having around me.

When I finally arrived, dawn was only a few moments away. The few students I saw were sound asleep. Nyangoli and Touri were not on their foliage couches, and I thought they must have been left behind in the wondrous experience of the night. When I lay down on the cold leaves, I could not sleep and I did not try to. Instead, I watched the sky above me. As I gazed at it, I felt an immense nostalgia, as if voices from afar were calling to me. . . .

The voices seemed to emanate from each of the tiny stars that lit the sky. A feeling of sadness and pain I cannot put into words overtook me, and I surrendered to it gently as if it were natural to feel what I felt. As to what had really happened to me during the course of the night, my mind never once tried to analyze it. The proximity of the silent darkness spoke comforting words to my heart, and I felt the friendliness of the trees and the grass surrounding the camp. This invisible presence of the stillness resurrected an intense sense of home and comfort within me.

As more students entered the camp, they proceeded straight to their beds. They looked like moving shadows. Finally, I saw Nyangoli arrive. He looked at me with surprise, and then he stretched himself out on his couch and immediately seemed to fall into a deep sleep. I had no desire to disturb him. Soon the bird of dawn sang, announcing to the spirits and to all nocturnal species that it was time to find refuge. I had never seen the shy secretive bird of dawn, but my brother once told me that it looks like an owl with flaming eyes.

I listened to its melody while my eyes remained locked onto the dark scintillating sky. I was so aware of the life of everything around me that it felt as if the entire bush were filled with heavy traffic. The trees were gallantly oscillating as if in response to the cold breeze of the dawn, and this breeze seemed a carrier of countless life forms, including spirits who were returning to their point of origin.

Nyangoli began to snore. As if that snore were a signal that I should rest while I had the chance, I suddenly felt the need to sleep. The quiet of the night, the communion with the stars, the song of the bird of dawn, and the dance of the bush produced in me a feeling of immense peace and nostalgia. I wanted to join with the stars way up there in the infinite spaces of the cosmic realm. There was the night and there was the bush and there was me. Nothing else mattered. I did not even notice that I had been crying quietly until the stars became blurred.

My tears were the language of the longing that I felt to merge with the stars. They sent a message to them, sharing something I could never express in human terms, and I felt the sky accept my tears as a response to their attention. The bright scintillating lights came closer and closer until I could see only a few of them. The closer they got, the bigger and brighter they became. The stars brought the day to me, their day, pulsating, breathing the stuff that keeps the cosmos in order.

The closer the stars came to me, the louder this breathing became. The light they emitted became so blinding that I was forced to close my eyes. I knew, however, that I was not hallucinating. How long I remained in that state I do not know. I only know that Nyangoli woke me up to announce that the day had come.

CHAPTER 17

IN THE ARMS
OF THE GREEN LADY

 The next day I was ordered to resume my gazing exercise. The others were gone, probably getting on with their initiation. I had not had time to speak to Nyangoli, either after waking up at daybreak or during the more opportune time of breakfast, but just being with him had made me feel better. My friend embodied all that I was trying to become. To be near him was to have a frame of reference for all my confused feelings, and that somehow comforted me.

As I took up my position in front of the tree, I noticed that I was not as restless as I had been the day before. I was able to get to work with a relatively quiet mind that took the task at hand seriously. Today I was more eager to explore the new avenue made available to me by this opportunity. There was, however, a greater number of curious elders watching me than the day before. Four of the five elders had gathered to see me gaze at the yila tree, as if someone had told them there was an unusual event occurring on the sidelines of the initiation ceremonies. I felt the anxiety of someone who is being monitored—stupid, as I had at school when I sinned and was asked to wear the hated goat symbol.

I had to show these old men that I could do something. I concentrated my sight on the tree. *This,* I thought to myself, *is a gaze that has substance and meaning—the look in my eyes embodies challenge.* I was determined to overcome the opacity of the physical by my commitment to *see.* By now I had figured out that I was expected to see something other than the tree itself—something that still was the tree, but uninvented, unmediated, pure. I stared intensely. I was more confident than I had been yesterday, and my level of distraction was minimal. For the first time I had stopped asking myself questions. There was a goal to reach, and I did not want to continue lagging behind everybody else. So I attacked the tree with the drill of my sight.

The sun rose, and with it came the heat. I penetrated the depths of my body, cooking every cell along the way. As I locked on to the tree, the heat locked on to me. The contest was hard, for I did not want to waste another day fighting against the sun and other distractions. I was determined to do better this time. I began by deciding the sun did not exist. Only me and my tree existed in this whole universe. But my denial of the heat became more and more impossible to sustain as the sun got closer and closer to the zenith. To make things worse, some insect decided to bite me on my bare back. Instinctively, I reached back and hit myself very hard. I heard the elders laugh at me, exchange some words, then laugh again. Meanwhile, a large area on my back was getting swollen. I guessed that I had been stung by a bee.

Presently, the area needed to be scratched but I could not afford to do so for fear of being laughed at again. It was apparent that they were enjoying watching me wrestle with my ordeal. I decided I was not going to think about my back either. In the meantime the sweat that the heat of the sun had forced out of me was dripping slowly down my body, tickling me in sensitive areas. I thought about designing a strategy to diminish thinking about sweat running down my body, but I couldn't do it. It was beyond me. Trying to ignore the sweat only made me think about it more. It also served to irritate the part of my body that had been stung. As if envious of my wandering attention, the pain rose sharply from the area of the bite and drew my hand around to scratch it. The elders noticed this and, as before, murmured to one another. I saw them shake their heads in agreement, then look away from me.

I resolved that I would not continue to torture myself for the sake of a tree. Since I could not openly defy the elders (that would have meant the end of me), I would trick them. They expected me to see something, so I would make something up. How would they know I was lying? The understanding of traditional education I had gained from my year in the village had taught me that one was always introduced to the very thing that is part of one's own world. I had also learned that the world of the self in the universe of these elders was autonomous. Knowing meant knowing one's own world as it truly was, not as someone else told you it should be.

Wasn't this gazing assignment just one of the many contexts designed by the elders to allow each of us to come to grips with that esoteric universe of the self?

I called out to the elders and told them that I was seeing an antelope staring at me. It was gigantic and brownish, with a white line on its side and another between its eyes. I said that it was looking at me as if it intended to hunt me, and I asked them, "Can a tree become an antelope and vice versa?" While speaking, I made sure I never looked their way because I knew they would then detect that something was wrong. I wanted to convey the impression that I was fascinated with this apparition. In so doing, I hoped to increase the credibility of my invention.

Their reaction, however, was the opposite of what I had expected. Though I was not looking at them, I could sense the impact of their surprise in the air around me. They all stood up as if shocked. Then the elder who had been my supervisor the day before asked me what else the antelope was doing. I said it was sitting on its hind legs. This time they all burst out laughing and kept laughing for what seemed like a very long time.

"An antelope sitting on its hind legs?" my supervisor said in between laughs. "Keep looking."

They cackled and gleefully patted one another on the back. When they finally calmed down, one of them said, "What did I tell you? This boy is fighting against himself. I can't believe it. This falsehood is not his own invention. He would never have thought of this kind of thing himself. The white men have initiated him into acting this way. He has lived around them too long, and now he has become a liar too. If his *Vuur* were not stained with white, he would know that this life has no room for lies."

I felt as if I had been stabbed. I was ashamed of myself, so much so that I felt the urge to bury myself, right on the spot, to escape the presence of the elders. How did they know that I had lied? How could I win their trust, now that I had so stupidly lost it? All I could do was to pretend I did not hear them. After they had their fill of laughter, they ignored me. Tears insidiously crawled out of my eyes and ran down my face, mixed with sweat.

I was crying because of my sense of failure. What was wrong with me that I could not do what I was being asked to? Sitting in front of this tree and failing at my first initiation task made my being different from everyone else even more painful and intolerable. For here I was—being laughed at! Here I was—caught in a lie. My feelings were a mixture of everything: aloneness, broken pride, anger, alienation, ostracism, segregation.

Through my tears, I managed to continue keeping an eye on the tree.

Then I suddenly began speaking to it, as if I had finally discovered that it had a life of its own. I told it all about my discontent and my sadness and how I felt that it had abandoned me to the shame of lying and of being laughed at. I complained that my failure must have its roots in the fact that the spirit of my grandfather had defaulted from his duties toward me a long time ago. He had brought me here to be humiliated and thrown away like trash. I addressed Grandfather, accusing him of standing between me and this tree and delaying my traditional education. I told him I did not deserve this and begged him to take me away if he could not allow me to have a normal education like everybody else in the camp.

I then spoke to the tree again, not angrily, but respectfully. I told her that, after all, it was not her fault that I could not see, but mine. I simply lacked the ability. What I really needed to do was to come to terms with my own emptiness and lack of sight, because I knew *she* would always be there when I needed to use her to take a close look at my own shortcomings and inadequacies.

My words were sincere: I felt them while I said them. My pain had receded somewhat, and I found I could now focus better on the tree. It was around midafternoon, but I was not really interested in the time. I had something more important to deal with, for suddenly there was a flash in my spirit like mild lightning, and a cool breeze ran down my spine and into the ground where I had been sitting for the past one and a half days. My entire body felt cool. The sun, the forest, and the elders and I understood that I was in another reality, witnessing a miracle. All the trees around my yila were glowing like fires or breathing lights. I felt weightless, as if I were at the center of a universe where everything was looking at me as if I were naked, weak, and innocent. For a moment I experienced a deep fear that I imagined was similar to what one feels when one is told that death is inevitably on its way. Indeed, I thought I was dead. I thought that something must have happened while I was trying to reconcile myself to the shame of being caught in a lie.

To substantiate my impression, I thought about the hardships of the day—the baking heat of the sun and my sweat falling into my eyes and burning them like pepper. I had lost all sense of chronology. I told myself that this is what the world looked like when one had first expired. I felt as if I were being quite reasonable. I could still think and respond to sensations around me, but I was no longer experiencing the biting heat of the sun or my restless mind trying to keep busy or ignoring my assignment. Where I was now was just plain real.

When I looked once more at the yila, I became aware that it was not a tree at all. How had I ever seen it as such? I do not know how this transformation occurred. Things were not happening logically, but as if this were a dream. Out of nowhere, in the place where the tree had stood, appeared a tall woman dressed in black from head to foot. She resembled a nun, although her outfit did not seem religious. Her tunic was silky and black as the night. She wore a veil over her face, but I could tell that behind this veil was an extremely beautiful and powerful entity. I could sense the intensity emanating from her, and that intensity exercised an irresistible magnetic pull. To give in to that pull was like drinking water after a day of wandering in the desert.

My body felt like it was floating, as if I were a small child being lulled by a nurturing presence that was trying to calm me by singing soothing lullabies and rocking me rhythmically. I felt as if I were floating weightless in a small body of water. My eyes locked on to the lady in the veil, and the feeling of being drawn toward her increased. For a moment I was overcome with shyness, uneasiness, and a feeling of inappropriateness, and I had to lower my eyes. When I looked again, she had lifted her veil, revealing an unearthly face. She was green, light green. Even her eyes were green, though very small and luminescent. She was smiling and her teeth were the color of violet and had light emanating from them. The greenness in her had nothing to do with the color of her skin. She was green from the inside out, as if her body were filled with green fluid. I do not know how I knew this, but this green was the expression of immeasurable love.

Never before had I felt so much love. I felt as if I had missed her all my life and was grateful to heaven for having finally released her back to me. We knew each other, but at the time I could not tell why, when, or how. I also could not tell the nature of our love. It was not romantic or filial; it was a love that surpassed any known classifications. Like two loved ones who had been apart for an unduly long period of time, we dashed toward each other and flung ourself into each other's arms.

The sensation of embracing her body blew my body into countless pieces, which became millions of conscious cells, all longing to reunite with the whole that was her. If they could not unite with her, it felt as if they could not live. Each one was adrift and in need of her to anchor itself back in place. There are no words to paint what it felt like to be in the hands of the green lady in the black veil. We exploded into each other in a cosmic contact that send us floating adrift in the ether in countless intertwined forms. In the course of this baffling experience, I felt as if I were moving backward in time and forward in space.

While she held me in her embrace, the green lady spoke to me for a long time in the softest voice that ever was. She was so much taller than I was that I felt like a small boy in her powerful arms. She placed her lips close to my left ear and she spoke so softly and tenderly to me that nothing escaped my attention. I cried abundantly the whole time, not because what she told me was sad, but because every word produced an indescribable sensation of nostalgia and longing in me.

Human beings are often unable to receive because we do not know what to ask for. We are sometimes unable to get what we need because we do not know what we want. If this was happiness that I felt, then no human could sustain this amount of well-being for even a day. You would have to be dead or changed into a something capable of handling these unearthly feelings in order to live with them. The part in us that yearns for these kinds of feelings and experiences is not human. It does not know that it lives in a body that can withstand only a certain amount of this kind of experience at a time. If humans were to feel this way all the time, they would probably not be able to do anything other than shed tears of happiness for the rest of their lives—which, in that case, would be very short.

Human beings never feel that they have enough of anything. Ofttimes what we say we want is real in words only. If we ever understood the genuine desires of our hearts at any given moment, we might reconsider the things we waste our energy pining for. If we could always get what we thought we wanted, we would quickly exhaust our weak arsenal of petty desires and discover with shame that all along we had been cheating ourselves.

Love consumes its object voraciously. Consequently, we can only experience its shadow. Happiness does not last forever because we do not have the power to contain it. It has the appetite of a ferocious carnivore that has been starved for a long time—this is how much love and bliss and happiness there is in nature, in the place that was there before we existed in it.

I cannot repeat the speech of the green lady. It lives in me because it enjoys the privilege of secrecy. For me to disclose it would be to dishonor and diminish it. The power of nature exists in its silence. Human words cannot encode meaning because human language has access only to the shadow of meaning. The speech of the green lady was intended to stay alive in silence, so let it be.

I loosened my grip, lifted my wet face up to hers, and read departure in her eyes. I did not know where she was returning to, but wherever it was I did not want her to go without me. My feelings for her were so strong I felt that I would be able to brave anything to stay with her, nor did I think there was any reason we should part after having been separated for so long. Her face, however, said I could not go where she was going and that this was one of those imperatives that one had to respond to without negotiation. Things had to stay as they were. In despair I clung harder to her soft body, unable to do anything else. My eyes closed as my grip tightened, and the soft body under my hands became rough.

When I opened my eyes I realized I was desperately hugging the yila tree. It was the same as it had been before. Meanwhile, the elders had moved closer to me, obviously watching everything I had been doing. I heard one of them say, "They are always like this. First they resist and play dumb when there are a lot of things waiting to be done, and then when it happens, they won't let go either. Children are so full of contradictions. The very experience you rejected before with lies, you are now accepting without apology."

This seemed to have been directed at me. I looked up at the elder who spoke. He met my eyes, and I felt no further need to be holding on to the tree.

"Go find something to eat, and make your bed for the night," he said gently.

It was then I noticed that the sun had set. My experience had lasted several hours, but the time had felt so short!

When I arrived back at the camping circle, the students were almost done making up their sleeping places. Nyangoli in his faithfulness was discreetly waiting for me. He looked relieved when I appeared, so relieved that, for the first time since we had arrived at the camp, he spoke to me first. "You're still alive! *Walai.*"

"Yes—of course," I replied, feeling in the mood to chat. "The day was challenging but not too bad."

"I feel you are gradually becoming a bush person. That will help a lot in the days to come. I don't know how to tell you this, but I've been afraid for you since the first day. Now I do not think I should worry anymore. I can see in your eyes that you are getting over to the other side. You were not there when you arrived."

"What is the other side?" I inquired, feeling that I had learned nothing so far and that this might be my chance to satisfy my curiosity.

"When you arrived here, your Siè was out of you. That is dangerous for what we are doing here. You have to keep your Siè inside to make sure you can be pulled back to this side of reality after you've done your learning. Otherwise your soul will forget that it is connected with your body and abandon you. Somebody must have done something to heal you today."

"You mean a medicine person performed a ceremony to fix me from a distance?" I asked. "But who?"

I knew what it meant when the Siè is out of a person. That person is prone to unnecessary pride and passion, loses his humility, and can't tolerate feeling vulnerable. I knew too that the only way this situation could be rectified was by performing a ceremony with a black chicken. When I returned from the seminary, my father had done this once without explaining to me what he was doing. After the ritual he had told me that a foreknowledge of its function would have voided its effectiveness. I had never heard of this ceremony being done from a distance before, but obviously something in me had been strengthened and helped.

It was getting dark, and my sleeping place had not been replenished. Nyangoli helped me change the leaves, and together we joined the rest of the group for the customary fire ceremony.

CHAPTER 18

RETURNING TO THE SOURCE

 My experience of "seeing" the lady in the tree had worked a major change in the way I perceived things as well as in my ability to respond to the diverse experiences that constituted my education in the open-air classroom of the bush. This change in perspective did not affect the logical, common-sense part of my mind. Rather, it operated as an alternative way of being in the world that competed with my previous mind-set—mostly acquired in the Jesuit seminary.

My visual horizon had grown disproportionately. I was discovering that the eye is a machine that, even at its best, can still be improved, and that there is more to sight than just physical seeing. I began to understand that human sight creates its own obstacles, stops seeing where the general consensus says it should. But since my experience with the tree, I began to perceive that we are often watched at close distance by beings that we ourselves cannot see, and that when we do see these otherworldly beings, it is often only after they have given us permission to see further—and only after they have made some adjustment in themselves to preserve their integrity. And isn't it also true that there is something secret about everything and everybody?

What we see in everyday life is not nature lying to us, but nature encoding reality in ways we can come to terms with under ordinary circumstances. Nature looks the way it looks because of the way we are. We could not live our whole lives on the ecstatic level of the sacred. Our senses would soon become exhausted and the daily business of living would never get done. There does, however, come a time when one must learn to move between the two ways of "seeing" reality in order to become a whole person.

Traditional education consists of three parts: enlargement of one's ability to see, destabilization of the body's habit of being bound to one plane of being, and the ability to voyage transdimensionally and return. Enlarging one's vision and abilities has nothing supernatural about it, rather it is "natural" to be a part of nature and to participate in a wider understanding of reality.

Overcoming the fixity of the body is the hardest part of initiation. As with the seeing exercise, there is a lot of unconscious resistance taking place. There is also a great deal of fear to be overcome. One must travel to the other side of fear, crossing the great plains of terror and panic to arrive at the quiet one feels in the absence of fear. Only then does true transformation really begin to happen. It feels strange to not be afraid when one thinks one should be; but this is the condition for the voyage to other worlds. This metamorphosis cannot happen as long as the body is weighed down by heaviness. One must go through a process of relearning, enforcement of these lessons, and the consolidation of new knowledge. This kind of education is nothing less than a return to one's true self, that is, to the divine within us.

After my intense experience with the green lady, I began to understand when it was useful to analyze what I was learning and when it was better to discontinue analysis. That night when Nyangoli and I joined the group for the fire ceremony, I knew the experience was going to be less traumatic than before. I had successfully reunited with the energy of the vegetable world. Its imprints were going to serve as the preparation for my next series of experiences. As the fire rose, chasing away the darkness within the circle, there was something especially magical in it tonight. As the darkness receded, I heard the fire speak to it, and I felt that tonight there was nothing violent or threatening about its gigantic, flaming proportions.

One of the elders intoned a fire-dance rhythm in a slow voice, while the elder in the center spoke. "Fire is seeing . . . fire is dreaming . . . fire is living." He spat at it and a flame jolted up violet with a loud voice as if it had been fed with gasoline. Satisfied with the result, the elder continued. "Fire lives, and tonight is the night of fire—our own fire within that burns like this one here. We must merge with this fire, be one with it, to let our dreams come alive. For in the belly of the fire rests our ancestral lives, in it is who we have always been, who we truly are, and who we must be now."

While speaking, the old man walked slowly around the fire. Sometimes his voice rose in a crescendo, sending a chill into all of us. The drum followed every intonation of the elder's voice as if he and the fire were one in delivering the message that the power of the fire was in all of us. Meanwhile, the flames appeared to have changed, moving through all the colors of the rainbow, gradually, as if in response to what the elder was saying. We stood in circle, hand in hand, somber. The silence was absolute.

For a while only three voices were heard: the voice of the fire responding to the voice of the elder, the sound of the elder speaking to the fire, and the voice of the drum. The last two voices were familiar—part of the ordinary world—but the voice of the fire was getting stranger and stranger. As the elder spoke, the fire grew bigger and bigger, hotter and hotter; yet suddenly a wave of cold enveloped all of us. First, I began shivering and noticed that everyone around me was too. I wanted to try to figure out how something that was so hot could be so cold, but I had no time for analysis. The elder was now inside the fire, walking in circles and speaking. In his hand he held a hyena skull, all alight and burning with an unearthly fire.

Each time the elder's voice rose higher in the air, the drum also rose in volume, the fire grew taller, and the skull became more luminescent, light breezing out of it. All of us had our concentration glued to the center of the circle, and it felt to me as if our combined attention were producing this phenomenon we were witnessing. Soon my hearing became confused and began to register strange noises. What I heard was almost like gibberish. Voices seemed to emanate from all over the place, but a lot of the ones behind me were coming closer and closer at an alarming rate. The elder's voice was getting more and more distant, the drum more timid, and the fire had no more center. It felt as if I were in the center of it except that, instead of feeling hot, I felt very cold.

The voices behind me were now in front of me. They belonged to people, red people just as real as I was. Some were tall and some were small . . . but there was no real fixity in their appearance. This crowd was gathered in an unusual place, a place that had no equivalent to anything I had seen before. The place where they stood seemed groundless. It appeared as a dark carpet surrounded with a multiplicity of stars, creating the illusion of a crowd standing in the middle of outer space. It felt like we were all floating together in the cosmos. None of the people present had any resemblance to any person I had ever encountered before on Earth, yet the place was familiar and I knew these people were the ones I belonged to. I was observing myself being the center of the unfolding drama. They all listened avidly as I, clothed in the most extravagant fashion, addressed them. Part of myself was an observer and the other part was a busy actor in this drama, doing all the things he knew how to do well.

On an altar in front of me were three baby girls. I did not know where their parents were, but I knew what my task was. I stretched my hands toward the altar and said something I could not hear. Suddenly, a light beam dropped onto the babies from an invisible ceiling and began rotating counterclockwise. It rotated slowly at first, then moved faster. All the while the crowd prayed in a language I could understand then, but cannot remember now. After what seemed a long time, the babies and the altar rose up, encased in a planetary sphere.

The planet with the babies standing up in the middle of it rolled away and then shot southward. I lowered my hands and brought them together clasped over my chest, as if to give thanks to some divinity for a job well done. The crowd also bowed and gave thanks in their own language.

The illumination of this scene, which seemed to have no source, disappeared, but I found I had expected that. As if pushed by an instinct that wanted to respond to these people's need, whatever it was, I tried to walk toward the crowd. But I could not get near them. A force field prevented this from happening. Each time I came close to it, I would be thrown back gently to where I had been before.

Each time I touched the force field, an immense lightning bolt shot out, as if two high-voltage wires had touched each other. Although this had no effect upon me, it had a tremendously powerful effect upon the crowd. Three times I struck the force field, and each time the crowd went into a delirium of bliss. I began to wish I could share their bliss, but I had no more power over what I was doing to them than they had power to make me stop doing it. As I hit the force field for the third time, I moved backward with my hands outstretched toward the crowd. I could see myself becoming smaller and smaller, as if an irresistible force were carrying me away from this throng of people whom I loved and who loved me. I could still see their countless hands outstretched toward me as if in an ultimate appeal to bring me back or to express their appreciation for the bliss that I had brought them. I watched myself fade away and back into the northern part of the circle around the fire, north, the place of water.

My dream had lasted for a long time. A few of the others were already back from the dream world, but a whole lot more were still there. The latter included the elder in the center of the circle and the drummer, whose hand was now suspended in the midst of an uncompleted rhythm. He was most intriguing to look at. He appeared like a perfect sculpture carved out of the best ceremonial tree. Those that were still in the dream world were no less stiff in their appearance. Some had their eyes wide open, others had them closed. The latter were not frightening. The former were—their eyes were projected out into the infinite. The abject depths into which they had plunged their sight could be shared with no one, nor could anyone disturb the intensity of their dream. Those who had their eyes closed were more earthly-looking. One could imagine that they were either in prayer or simply sleeping.

For a while the whole circle of neophytes and elders stood at the edge between worlds. Some had crossed back to the narrow reality of this world, others were refusing to return, at least for the moment. Suddenly, the elder in the center who had initiated the dream journey came back to himself. I saw him move his left hand and then blink his eyes. He took a deep breath and cleared his throat.

Some of the other students immediately followed him. One of them uttered a slight yell of surprise, as if he did not believe in what he was being brought back to. A good third of the initiates were still dreaming fast, including the elder drummer. The old man in the center went over to his colleague and produced some ash. He sprinkled the drummer with the ash and uttered some words and the drummer resumed his drumming.

The drummer's return was strange. First, he completed his suspended rhythm, then he started all over with a different, very syncopated rhythm to which he added some humming. He had a bad voice and I thought to myself that it would have been better not to spoil the power of the drum's speech with such a profane addition.

In the Dagara culture the drum is a transportation device that carries the listener into other worlds. Only the sound of a drum has the power to help one travel in this specific way. This magic works only when the drummer coaxes special rhythms, not just banging noises, out of it. The journeys that can be taken with the drum concern not only the listener, but the drummer too. Where the soundship goes, everybody goes. To refuse to drum is to refuse to travel. To forget how to drum is to forget how to feel.

Presently, with the drummer's return to Earth, there was a different dynamism within the circle. Those of us who were half here and half there completed our return. Some of the young men who had looked as if they were awake suddenly jolted into complete consciousness, fully realizing where they were.

The elder in the center took care of those who had not yet come back. He said a few words to each one of them, spat on them, and as if by enchantment they returned to life. Some came back rather reluctantly, as if they were being awakened from a great sleep that was still incomplete. These students mumbled some disapproving words and then obediently remained awake. Others, who obviously had not expected anyone to disturb them, screamed and jumped in surprise. They looked around, made a quick visual assessment of where they were, then sat quietly.

For the most part this waking-up process was comical, but though everybody watched, no one laughed. By the time the last person was brought back to Earth the drummer had stopped and we were prepared to listen.

The elder spoke again. "Our ancestors used to say that unless you return to the other world, you will not know the difference between there and here. You now know where you were before becoming part of this family of people. You know what you were doing, so you know what you came here to do. You know how good you were at doing things, so know how thorough you must be in trying to help others here. No one must tell the anyone else where he went, what he saw, or what happened until the initiation is all over.

"This information is for you alone. It belongs to you. What you were taught in the other world should not leave the pit of consciousness in your belly or you will lose it once again and have to search for it in the storms of everyday living. Do not let your tongue betray you. You will wish you had cut it off. What you've learned is like a fish who lives in the water. To speak it is to pull the fish out of the water. It will cease to breathe and you will be both murderer and murdered.

"Our ancestors survived because they knew how to keep things unspoken. If you want to survive, then learn from their wisdom. This matter is now in your hands. Tonight, when you go to sleep, those of you who have not finished your task will have to leave your body to complete it. You are now able to tell where you are, who you are, and what you are doing. Now you understand that your body is a shell and that when you are encased in that shell, there are only a limited number of things that can be done under these circumstances.

"You must get used to changing modes of awareness depending on what task you are being asked to perform. You must be alert to the way in which you are looking at things, and know at any time the place from which you are looking at them. Your survival depends on this. In the days to come, you will confront situations similar to the ones you have already been through. Be able to recognize where you are, for if you fail, there is little that anyone can do for you."

Here the old man paused. He walked over to the drummer and muttered something in his ear. Then he walked west and did the same thing to the elder who was posted there, and to the elders in the south and the north. When he was finished, he came back to the center, walked around the fire clockwise a few times, and resumed speaking. He no longer held the hyena's skull, but a walking stick.

"The dream world is real," he said. "It's more real than what you are observing now. Why? I'm not going to give you the answer to this. I'll let you find out yourself. You are your own best evidence, your own best witness; but you must be aware that we have no knowledge or maps of the frontier between these worlds. So when one of you gets lost in one of them, neither I nor any one of my colleagues can do anything to retrieve you. This boy will be denied death. You can't die in the dream world, and that's a terrible thing.

"But because you will be there with a body, you will suffer. It is horrible. We have a few of the tribe in there right now. They come to us while we are in trance to see if anyone has finally discovered the road back home. Please be vigilant. As much as we want you to know the secret of your nature, we do not want you to be damaged in the process. We want this to be an opportunity to repair the damage of forgetting already worked on you by your own growth. But we will be greatly grieved if any of you come to misfortune."

The elder paused again. He seemed so human in the way he taught us caution. He radiated dignity, pride, and wisdom; but above all it was his humility that stood out. I believed his words even though I did not understand most of what he was saying. I could not help asking myself, however, what would be so terrible about remaining in one of those strange worlds. I knew from personal experience that each time I had gone somewhere unearthly, I had experienced sadness at the end of the journey, as if to return were to disconnect myself from something fundamental, something much more meaningful than the meaninglessness of the world here. The old man seemed to see this very pleasantness as one more reason not to linger too long, because we might then lose the option to return. Why was he insisting so strongly that we return? And why were these students who had lost the way back unhappy?

Although up to this point we had left our bodies behind each time we had traveled interdimensionally, I knew that the experience we had just completed was meant to be a preparation for taking our bodies with us. I had traveled far in a body that was but a shadow of my real body, and I had returned. In the course of these journeys I did not feel any different than I felt in the body I inhabited now.

I slept badly that night. My consciousness was populated by a crowd of images. The green lady came back and spoke briefly to me again. She had news from some friends. She held a bundle of herbs in her green hand. "This will be your first medicine," she said.

The eyes also appeared again. This time I was able to understand the message behind their blinking. They were no threat to me. They just wanted to talk. I winked my own eyes in response. When morning came, I still felt the same way I had when I went to bed. My body did not feel rested at all, but I could not tell whether I was merely tired or suffering from stress. The other students seemed in no better shape. Some were speaking aloud, and others were weeping violently. Perhaps they were completing the dreams they had started earlier. I listened to them for a while, trying to understand those who were talking, but they were speaking in tongues. I could not understand them, so I ignored them.

CHAPTER 19

OPENING THE PORTAL

 The next day was a busy one. There were many things to do and no one had time to chat. First, the elders had all of us running around the camp like wild animals while some kind of preparations were in progress in their quarters. The sky was hazy, dirtied by yellow dust thrown up by the wind, thinly blanketing the sun. This haziness, however, did not make today any cooler than yesterday. As the sun climbed higher and higher, so did the heat. The running did not help. Never before had we been asked to run, and I wondered what kind of physical fitness we needed for the task ahead.

We kept going till the sun had almost reached the zenith. We ran almost mechanically, absent from our bodies, only praying that we didn't run ourselves to death. With grim humor I wondered whether the elders meant to put to the test the extent to which we had absorbed the lessons taught us the night before.

Flashes of images of my dream experience crowded my mind as I ran, as if to save me from the boredom and the pain of jogging in the baking heat. These images took away the sensations of my body, helping me to focus my attention elsewhere. I kept seeing another me mediating on behalf of a crowd of believers. What religion was that ceremony informed by? Where could it have been taking place? I had heard that we usually come to Earth from other planets that are more evolved and less in need of mediation. Our errand on this planet is informed by a decision to partake in the building of the Earth's cosmic origin, and to promote awareness of our celestial identity to others who are less evolved. Our elders taught that some of the universe's inhabitants were as much in need of help as others had the need to help them. This Earth was one of the many places where those who craved to help could find this desire easily satisfied, and where those who needed help could easily become recipients of it. But what help could I possibly give when I needed it so badly myself?

We were requested to rejoin the five elders. The coach, who had been leading the jogging exercise, stopped and turned to us. He stretched out his hand. "Close your eyes. Stay in line, hold each other by the elbow and walk slowly into the circle of the elders. You will open your eyes only when I tell you to."

I closed my eyes and walked behind Nyangoli. When we got to the elders' quarters, I saw four elders holding a buffalo skin less than a meter above a circle of the same diameter. The circle was delineated with ash and some sort of black medicine. Around the circle, partly hidden by the shadow thrown by the buffalo skin, I could see chicken feathers: indication of a sacrifice. The elders were very agitated. They held the skin tightly. The only one not holding the skin was dressed as a warrior, with the pink phosphorescent paint of invisibility on his body. On his back he carried a bulging, feline-skin bag filled with a magical arsenal. In his left hand he held a wand. He was finishing up a chant that he must have begun a long time before our arrival, for he was sweating just like us.

Shortly after we arrived, he stopped singing and circled around the four elders who were holding the skin. The coach asked us to form two lines and to stay put while the elder prepared to tell us what the day's task was going to be. The coach then took the drum, sat down next to the ceremonial place, and began striking it slowly and distinctly. His wet hands produced a hoarse sound as if the drum did not want to be addressed by hands dripping with sweat.

From afar the buffalo skin held by the elders looked like the recently completed roof of a hut, ready to be put in place. Beneath it I noticed dripping green gelatinlike material that reminded me of the fermentation produced by algae in the middle of the rainy season. Whether it was seeing this strange phenomenon in the middle of the dry season or some other reason, the sight of the little space beneath the skin gave me a sensation of extreme coolness.

The officiating elder came over to us and prepared to speak. I took a long look at his magic staff. It was carved in an otherwordly shape representing two rows of faces that were half human and half animal. Both rows of faces rested on a shape that reminded me of what my father used to call "the soul's state prior to entering the human body"—an oval shape carved in a way that suggested it was ready to become something else, or to create something else in concert with the two faces above it. The whole array was so intense that the carved faces seemed constricted as if in terrible pain. The top of the wand took the shape of a dome from which carved rays of light radiated vividly. There seemed to be a connection between what we were going to do and what that wand symbolized.

"Today you will have to spend time with all of yourselves—earthly body and soul—in the world below us," the elder began. "There is nothing to fear. What you will pass through is a light hole. It won't hurt your body. It will just lighten it a little so that you can stay in the other world long enough to remember where you have come from. Those who want to live a serious life go there and come back. Those who don't want to live a serious life go there—but don't come back.

"I want to assume that you all want to fulfill your duties on this Earth. You saw what those duties were last night, and you all know that you are here because you are dead there. Today there is yet another world for you to go to. If you think trivial thoughts once you are there, you might try to convince yourself that you can stay, but you can't. If you stay in that world without going through your life and death here, the people there will only acknowledge you as a ghost, just the way we deal with ghosts here in this world."

The old man stopped. I understood little of what he had said, but there was no doubt that another serious event was about to take place. The gelatinous coolness of the swamplike material pouring out of the skin began to make some sense. This was the light hole. Through the agency of the skin, it communicated with another world. But what exactly was the function of the skin?

The elder began speaking again. "You will enter the light hole one by one. Each one of you will run until he gets close to the skin. Then you must jump." Saying this, he jumped, humorously, and laughed.

"Keep your feet tightly together like a woman who knows decency. Hold your arms firmly against your body, otherwise you will cut them off as you enter the light hole. Your body cannot be turned into light until it is entirely in the light. If your hands overlap the circle when your body enters the hole, your body will be disconnected from your hands—and you will not be able to come back. These are important precautions to take: *do not forget.*" He spat out the kola nut that he had been pounding in his mouth while speaking and coughed loudly.

Suddenly things began to make sense to me. The light hole was a gateway to an alternate world. Access to it required conversion of the body cells into a form of energy that is light. We would feel like spirits for as long as the experience lasted, unless there were ways of making the whole thing last forever. I could not think of any reason that would make me decide to stay in a world of light as a ghost in order to be with the normal citizens who were there.

The elder asked if we had all understood what we were supposed to do. No one said a word, and he took our silence as acquiescence. He continued. "Once in the hole, do not let yourself fall indefinitely. You will go too far and we will lose you. Instead, as soon as you are in, notice the countless lines of light. They have many colors. You can see them if you keep your eyes open, but it takes an effort to open your eyes. No one can do that for you. The lines are there for you to use. Grab them and hold on to them. When you have grasped a wire of light, you will float. There is nothing to fear after that. Just float. Everything else will be taken care of. Do you understand me?"

Again there followed the heavy silence of acquiescence. I could already imagine myself plunging into a wild world that was not a dream this time and trying to figure things out once I got there. I knew it was midafternoon because the heat of the sun was biting into our skin very hard as if it were trying to boil away the unevaporated sweat on our bodies. The elder had rejoined his colleagues and they were convening one last time before we were to go.

Never had I felt so alone with myself, so responsible for myself, so careful about myself. All the previous experiences had been intense in their own way. We had been given the chance to acquaint ourselves with and become accustomed to the dream world, the supernatural realm, and to magic. So far we had survived the tricks of these old men.

This time, however, we were being sent somewhere wholesale: body and soul together, with the possibility of never returning. That was no joke. I could not even imagine what would happen if I were unable to get back. I wondered what it would be like never to die, but also never to live—to be a ghost trapped in a crack between the worlds, severed from both with no hope of any help. *No!* I thought. There cannot be such a thing. . . .

Then I remembered the horror stories my father had told me of children who went to initiation and never came back and the abject terror of shamans who saw them in their divination water or shells, crying for help. At the time those stories had sounded like legends to me. Now I was convinced of their reality.

So these old men were exposing us to an initiation rite that was highly dangerous. What should I do? There were not many choices, nor were we in a situation where we could simply say no.

Meanwhile the elders had begun chanting and swinging the skin back and forth. It appeared to me that the amount of green gelatin oozing out of it was increasing. The elders intensified their formula in primal language while the drum intoned a breathless rhythm. Around us an energy field of immense magnitude was developing. My first sensation was that of a coolness that soon developed into an icy cold all around us. Our bodies reacted to the change of temperature by shivering violently. My teeth were chattering, and I soon felt like I was losing control of the function of my organs.

The green gelatin became violet and danced like burning methane. The light hole was circular, with a diameter no bigger than a meter. When the chanting and drumming ended, the elders were holding a window into the world the chief had spoken about earlier. I could glimpse only a small part of it. I thought I saw a sky, but it could have been the reflection of the sky above made violet by the substance in the light hole.

The elder came to us and said, "The gate is open. I will test it up by throwing a stone into it. If the stone makes a flaming noise in its descent, the gate is real. If not, the stone will just fall to the ground. That will mean we did a poor job." He turned his face toward the magic circle. I heard him add, mostly to himself, "Which is impossible. . . ."

He picked up a stone, walked closer to the circle, and hurled it at the center of the skin, right through the gate. The rock disappeared and we heard a noise like that of sustained thunder. The sound receded into the distance. Satisfied, the elder ordered the first dive to begin.

The boy at the front of the line ran the ten meters that separated him from the infernal circle and jumped high above the skin. We saw him descend, legs first, arms straight, right through the skin—and disappear into the world below. I thought I saw his body turn violet as he was descending, just before he vanished, but it all went too fast. His disappearance was followed by a thunderous rumbling and an unearthly human scream. I felt a chill run down my spine even though it would not be my turn for quite some time.

The elders looked down, as if searching for the boy. One of them said, "He must be there." The officiating elder was very excited. He held his magic wand erect, high in the air, as if to ward off any negative spirits that might take an interest in a ritual involving live beings filled with blood—the oil of the dead. The elder walked around the circle a few times and then ordered the four holding the skin to pull. They lifted the skin and made a tossing motion with it, as if it were a container with something in it they wanted to pour out.

The violet light stretched higher and higher, sticking stubbornly to the skin right until they made the tossing motion. At that moment the light stretched itself out past the other side of the skin, detached itself, and flew through the air about ten meters. The blob of light landed on the ground noisily and lo! there was our boy, still recovering from something that his face registered as a nightmare.

Parts of his body still carried tongues of violet fire that he fought to remove. His body was violet colored at first, then it became green, and then dark as usual. He grew still, then stood up and walked toward the elders. They dismissed him to go hunt for food. I looked at him with envy and curiosity. *What had happened to him?* He did not even look back at those of us who were waiting for our turn. He walked away as if happy to have the ordeal over with.

Meanwhile another gate was ready. The officiating elder ordered the second in line to run for it. The boy ran and jumped, disappearing into the circle like a rock tossed into a dark pond. Again the same rumbling noise followed. The violet of the circle darkened, as if the force field that had produced this gate needed to manifest more energy to support itself. Again the elders looked down in search of the boy. Each glance was as anxious and interested as the previous one.

This time, however, I noticed that the drumming was frenetic. The drummer looked like an animated statue in conspiracy with the diabolic ritual in progress. Humans in tune with magical power cease to act with normal coordination, and the drummer appeared to be in the midst of a severe epileptic crisis. His muscles were tensed, his face was aghast, and his eyes stared into the infinite as if he were being electrocuted by an alien magnetic force. His hands spoke on the drum as if they moved independently of his will. He no longer seemed human.

The officiating elder suddenly shouted "Pull!" The four elders lifted the skin, and the circular gateway followed as if resisting. This time it appeared as if the elders needed more strength to do the same job they had done before. Finally the gate surrendered and the violet light was ejected from the skin with immense speed. The light ball shot into the air, soared, and crashed nearby. Unlike the previous ball, which had regurgitated a person immediately after its descent, this ball rolled onto itself with a roaring noise before the boy appeared. The initiate remained on the ground, motionless.

The officiating elder ran over to him and struck him with his wand. The poor lad screamed as if mortally wounded. He was lying in a pool of greenish slippery fluid, and part of his body looked lacerated while another part appeared to be burned. He kept screaming while the drum tried to cover up the awful sound. The screams turned into a howling and weeping that cast a pall over the entire assembly.

I wanted to go help him get up on his feet and take care of his wounds, but there was nothing I or anybody else could do. I could not explain what had happened to him or what had caused his agony. He was lying on his side, his face toward us, his arms covered by a thin layer of the green gelatin, trying to free himself from the part of his body that was still burning, for not all the flaming tongues of violet had disappeared. The council abandoned him to his fate and continued. A new gate was opened, and another boy was ordered to dive. . . .

The next five who jumped made it. Each entry ended with a re-entry similar to that of the first initiate. In objective time each passage took from one to three minutes, but this short time appeared infinite. In the meantime the boy who was hurt had finally fallen asleep in the sun, in a pool of greenish fluid that had coagulated and turned hard. Even the thin film on his arm had formed a crust. As I looked, magnetized by the phenomenon, I realized that something strange was happening to him: he too had coagulated, becoming hard as a rock. He looked more like an artifact or a reclining statue than a real person. He was immobile, and his body had lost the suppleness of a living body.

For a moment it crossed my mind that he was dead.

My turn was approaching. Three other boys had successfully completed their task, and I was now fifth in line. Divided as my attention was between the abject image of the unfortunate boy turned into stone and the speed with which the ceremony was going, I did not know what to concentrate on. I decided that the plight of our fellow student was the most serious question. *Why is he turning into something else?* I panicked; I had to have an answer before my turn came or I would not survive my journey. My eyes moved jerkily from the boy to the gateway and back again when something even more terrible occurred: the elders pulled on the skin and nothing happened.

Everything stopped. The officiating elder said something in primal language. Then he pulled out a gray-colored medicine, mixed it rapidly with water, and poured it onto the exact place in the circle where the disappearance had occurred. He filled his mouth with water that he took from a magic bag and ejected it in a long stream that shot into the circle like a liquid spike being drilled through a steel surface. The circle gradually turned to smoke, like a cloud in formation. After the elder emptied his mouth, he stretched his wand toward the cloud and said, *"Mouké, Souja, vapla, namati."*

Each word produced a loud noise inside the ever-thickening cloud, but nothing else happened. The four elders covered the cloud with the skin and waited. Then they pulled hard. Nothing happened. The officiating elder and the others repeated the procedure a second time, then a third. As they exchanged anguished glances, I realized I had just witnessed an unsuccessful retrieval. They resumed their work.

My heart froze and I shivered. I had seen death—a bizarre death, since there was nothing left behind to remind the living of any painful separation. My eyes had been glued to the mutating body of the suffering boy, and I had not seen the last candidate jump through the magic gate, so I had no idea who he was. But I could imagine his cries for help while drifting away into the bottomless depths of an unfathomable place.

A terminal event had taken place right before it was my turn to jump. I was less bothered by the boy's fate than by the dire possibilities it presented in terms of my own. The elder was obviously correct when he had announced that we must be aware of the dangers and take precautions. Had this accident occurred because of the boy's disobedience? How would I ever know? Was it possible that he had not held on to the colored wire of light? Was there something that this boy now knew that the elders did not that had caused his fall into the cracks between the worlds? Whatever had happened, nothing seemed fair to me—neither his disappearance nor the fact that I would have to take my turn at passing through the gateway. . . .

Part of me felt angry and wanted to revolt. Why was initiation so hard, so dangerous? Why did growth have to be so violent? Why did it require all these painstaking rituals? Until today things had been difficult, but at least nothing had happened that appeared to constitute a threat to anybody's life. Now here was a real catastrophe, very likely a death. There was nothing anyone could do for this boy who disappeared. He was trapped forever. And then there was the sleeping thing over there that nobody paid any attention to. Was he dead yet? If not, then he needed immediate help.

But help was the last thing he was going to get, since everybody was busy doing his job. Like the boy who fell irretrievably into the cracks between the worlds, this one was also trapped in a crack. The difference was that he existed in the fresh air of this world. *Why*, I asked myself again, *couldn't knowledge be acquired more safely?*

CHAPTER 20

THROUGH THE LIGHT HOLE

I was now one boy away from passing through the volcanic gate, and its unfriendly roar was scraping my nerves to an unbearable tension. I wanted to blot out of my mind the dreadful thought that something was going to go wrong and that I was going to become one of those green fiendish human gelatins, a leftover of a psychic catastrophe. It was important for me to remain focused, to continually recite the prayer of the ancestors, and to approach the gateway to the other world as quietly as someone who was coming home. But I did not know how to be calm in the face of this. Here was the window to the underworld made plain in front of me, the legendary made real. There was no avoiding this ordeal. I needed every faculty the universe had given me at birth and every bit of awareness I could harness, for the easy part of my initiation was over.

For the first time in my life I feared death. Things that I had once thought important were now becoming insignificant in the face of the real issue: death. A merciless avenger was demolishing things inside me as if they had become irrelevant.

To the village elders, who were openly inimical to the idea of introducing me to the secrets of the ancestors, my death would confirm their suspicions of the foolishness of trying to initiate me—as well as prevent any future initiations of this sort. I decided that for the sake of argument, for my own sake, and for the sake of the people who would come after me, I had to survive. Images of the seminary rushed into my mind with stormy intensity. I saw myself in the classrooms, the playground, the chapel, and the refectory, struggling to make sense out of the chaos of a world vision I had come to understand as belonging to someone else. The dream of my grandfather calling me home, the fight with the priest, the walk through the jungle, the terror of an uncertain future—all reminded me that it was imperative for me to complete *this* journey. *Where,* I asked myself, *is my fear coming from? Have I waited this long to receive my real education only to doubt my ability to survive it?*

The boy in front of me was ordered to run for the gate. It was my dear friend, Nyangoli. He ran fiercely. He had patiently waited for his turn, as calm as a ewe at the gate of the slaughterhouse. Many times in the last half hour I had tried unsuccessfully to involve him in my worries, but he remained aloof. Now I realized that his cool, silent presence had emanated a certain comfort that I had been unaware of until just now. Nyangoli jumped into the burning circle and disappeared in a flash. As I waited for him, I held my breath in support, thinking that his survival would increase my chances of making it. It was not long before he was pulled out safe and sound. Unlike the boys before him, no screams issued from his mouth, no groans from his throat.

He brushed the miniature violet tongues of fire from his body the way one brushes dirt from a suit and walked away. This adolescent was a master of adjustment whom nothing could faze. As he walked away, our eyes met and in a flash we communicated. This brief contact was all that I needed at the moment—it was power enough to lift a mountain.

The gate was quickly reconstructed. It was my turn. I heard the officiating elder order me to run. I inhaled deeply and dashed forward. My body was weightless. I could barely feel it. I could see the circle of light rushing closer and closer, as if it were not me going toward it but the gate coming toward me. Soon it filled my entire field of vision. About a meter away, I jumped high above the gateway and dived in.

▲   ▼   ▲

At first my body felt extremely cold, as if I had fallen into a freezer. Then, almost immediately, I felt myself descending rapidly. My rate of speed was vertiginous, throwing my sense completely out of kilter and making it impossible for me to control my descent. I wanted to scream, but lacked the elements that permit a scream to occur.

I could not open my eyes though I felt that with every passing second

I descended another dozen kilometers. Where was I going? What strange gravity was pulling me downward? But I had no time to ask such questions, let alone answer them. What I wanted, what I had to do most urgently now, was to open my eyes and grab at a wire of light. That thought came to me in a flash, but my furious fall was making every conscious action impossible to take, as if I were a slave to the speed with which I was being pulled downward.

I gathered every bit of willpower that was left in me and focused it onto my eyes. I had to open them. I needed to accomplish this saving gesture. Redirecting my attention from my headlong fall to my eyes, I pushed hard. Every effort I made seemed to produce some result, slight but sufficient to be noticeable. I knew that I could achieve something if I continued to press on my eyelids with the power of my desire.

Slowly, like the dawn breaking, I began to see light. At first it was like an aurora borealis, shot with areas of dark and ones of extreme luminescence—rays of such intensity they made me think of the cosmos in expansion or a cosmogony in progress. The light was so powerful that it would have fried my sight into blindness under ordinary circumstances, but somehow I was able to gaze at the skies of the underworld and survive. Everywhere around me it looked as if there were continuous explosions taking place, and each one released an immense force field that took hold of the universe.

Very quickly this luminescence changed, transforming itself into countless colors, a symphony of luminescent wires, all in motion and breathing life. My instincts for survival took over and I grabbed the one closest to me. My stop was sudden and noiseless, brutal yet painless. I knew my descent had come to an end. It took a moment for me to collect myself and remember what it was I was supposed to do before starting to worry about returning home.

I wondered how long my descent had been. Was it enough or too much? I decided I could not think about that now. Meanwhile, something interesting caught my attention: the wire of light I held in my hands: a bundle of countless fibers clustered together to form an environment of light waves that reminded me of the Milky Way. The Milky Way, however, looks commonplace by comparison. It is one color, hazy and boring. The light strands I held in my hand were a live bundle in which tiny cells of changing colors moved slowly upward within what looked like a thin tube of translucent glass.

Each cell twinkled. They were alive—and so was the whole bundle. Each cell lived as a whole within a whole. I sensed this, but I could not figure out the relationship between the individual cells and the light bundle. Where was I holding the bundle? I had no idea. I could not see my hands where they held tightly to it, and I was puzzled about this. When I looked down, hoping to see my naked body, it too was invisible. I was not there, yet I was—an invisible presence bathing in the light of my invisibility.

Was it possible for someone to be blind to his own presence? Perhaps my inability to see myself was directly connected to my perception of the environment; but why, if I could see everything around me, could I not see myself? My inability to see my body, however, did not challenge the conviction I had that my body was there. Maybe, I ruminated, my body was truly absent but compensated for by an overwhelming presence of consciousness. Perhaps I had fallen into a visibility too high to contain the crudity of my body. At the same time I realized that I did not feel terrified, nor did I feel strained, that is, it did not take much energy to hold on to this bundle of light. I concluded that I must also be weightless.

I decided I would test myself to see whether I still had a body or not. I brought my left hand toward my chest. I searched in vain. There was no chest; yet I knew it was there, just the same way that I knew that my hand was there. Nothing can't search for something. Though the elder had assured me I would come here in my body, I had lost the sense of my own physicality as I experienced it on the Earth plane. I was now visible only to my consciousness.

Where, then, was my physical body? I had little time to explore this subject, as I needed to fix my full attention on the immediate environment. The most powerful presence was the light, which everywhere breathed life. The spaces in between myself and the light source were blurred, imprecise like a city at night, but I felt presences in these spaces, too, to a lesser degree. I was aware of motion, as if a consciousness or an intelligence were moving about undisturbed by my presence. I thought I glimpsed a huge face with countless eyes that moved past me and continued upward, but I dismissed thoughts of this apparition for fear of awakening panic in myself.

When I concentrated on my surroundings, something seemed to awaken in me. I began hearing—a sensation I had not been aware of before. I could not tell what I was hearing, but it sounded as if it were coming from underwater. It was the same thunderous rumbling sound I had heard earlier (it felt like days ago now), prior to my leap through the gateway.

I also heard something that sounded like a mixture of laughter and a humming complaint. This sound floated up and down, as if transported by waves toward the infinite. The noise came from nowhere precise, instead, it seemed to come from all around me. I tried to hold my breath in order to listen for more meaningful sounds and discovered that there was no breath to be held—yet I knew I breathed just as surely as I knew I still had a body. I could hear the sounds of breathing all around me, the sound of my own breath and the breath of something else, and I became convinced that somebody was breathing for both me and himself.

Meanwhile the unearthly underwater sounds continued floating around me, sourceless. Soon they were followed by other noises coming from below. When I looked down to see if I could see where the new sounds were coming from, I almost lost control. The space beneath me was terrifying. It was violent, as if it were a volcano in action, and there was no end to it. I was not surprised by the endlessness—I had expected something like this from the beginning when I had seemed to fall very far and fast, but the volcanic action was not very reassuring. The bundles of light wires ended in the volcano, as if they were fed by the power coming out of it. Like a living entity, the volcano opened and closed periodically.

Each closing sent dark spaces moving upward along the wires and produced a great dimming of the light everywhere. Each opening of the volcano pumped myriads of light cells into the wires, creating a powerful light beam that ignited the cosmos infinitely. These cycles of darkness and light lasted for irregular intervals of time. The dimensions of the burning opening of the volcano appeared to be infinite. I became convinced that the sounds I was hearing all emanated from there.

I had the feeling that I was caught in the middle of a vast intelligence, something that knew I was there and wanted to do something to me. I was still holding on to the bundle of light, as well as to my own sense of being fully conscious and physically present in this strange world.

From the beginning, since I jumped into this place, I had been experiencing a sense of hysteria that made me constantly want to scream. It was not the kind of hysteria generated by fear, but the kind that comes from a vertiginous fall. Even though I had stopped my descent by grabbing this bundle, I was still in a state of tremendous excitement. At times I experienced this excitement as the sensation of being jolted. The next moment I had the impression that countless ants were crawling upward over my body, producing an imperative need to scratch that could never be satisfied because I could not find a body to scratch.

There are moments when no mind is capable of putting certain kinds of feelings into words, when speech is a meager instrument for communicating the reality of a situation. Words, by their very nature, are limited, mere representations of the real, human-made pieces of utterances. Reality exists independently from language.

Because I felt weightless, my finite consciousness concluded that the world below was a weightless one where everything articulated itself in light and dark. The real workings of this world, however, were too complex to figure out, though I strongly sensed that there was an incontestable meaning and irreplaceable function to every element within it.

I do not know how long I stayed there, trying to read these cosmic hieroglyphics spread in front of me. I was severely limited in what I could do, hanging as I was on to a bundle of light wires that felt like rubber.

There were moments when I fervently wished I could go someplace and explore, but I remembered what the elders had said. I remembered also that I had taken a rather long time to open my eyes, and therefore might have gone too far down to be pulled out.

The temptation to let go and explore was there anyway, caressing my mind in an increasingly inviting manner. If I could only go exploring, I could gain greater knowledge and expand my consciousness tremendously. I was especially curious about a mountain a few miles in front of me that reminded me of the pyramids of Egypt, which I had seen in the geography books at the seminary. Nothing had ever looked more beautiful than this living mountain crowned with gold and luminescent sapphires and all kinds of precious metals. Every bit of it pulsed with motion and life.

The mountain drew me toward it invitingly. Its force of attraction was so compelling that the only way I could avoid succumbing was to take my eyes away from it. But no sooner was that done than I began to wonder why, if I couldn't go there, I could not at least take a look. This thought being completed, I would look back at the mountain and it would appear more beautiful, more inviting, and more insistent than before. My only escape would be, again, to look away from it.

The music was also music coming from it, producing a sound so enticing and so sweet that it made me want to cry. The third time I looked at the mountain, I thought I saw someone within it. High up on its slope something that looked like a mirror or a door had just appeared, and someone seemed to be standing on the other side of it, looking at me or at something beyond me. I could see only the upper part of this person, who appeared to have an odd coloration—pinkish, greenish, and reddish. I thought he must be rather big since the mountain was a great distance away, and he still looked huge. His chest filled two thirds of the large opening.

His eyes were especially disconcerting: like fiery globes that protruded unaesthetically out of their sockets. Each globe contained a red circle and a green circle that kept rolling one inside the other counterclockwise indefinitely. The eyes moved from left to right and back again from time to time, as if to confirm that they were alive. As I looked at them, I felt an immense magnetic force overwhelm me and pull me toward the mountain. I followed, incapable of resisting, but somehow I managed not to let go of the bundle I was holding.

As I moved nearer, I felt myself moving faster and faster. My speed seemed to double with every second that passed, as if the faster I moved, the faster I had to go. Soon I realized I was going to crash into the mountain. Fearing the pain of the impact, I closed my eyes. Suddenly I heard a great noise and felt an extremely painful burning sensation all over my body. I opened my eyes and released my hold on the bundle.

I had been pulled out of the gate. I was covered with small flames. Though I fought hard to put them out with my bare hands, I was not doing a good job. I needed to work faster to fight the fire that was consuming me. I had no time to think about what had taken place. The pain was very bad. I rolled on the ground. When the flames were finally extinguished and I was somewhat recovered from my crashing return, I realized that the boy behind me had already been sent through the gate, and that I was being regarded enviously by those who were still waiting.

The elders either did not care or else were too busy to notice me. Even though it felt like I had spent the whole afternoon in the light hole, the sun had not moved an inch from where it had been when it was my turn to jump. I lay on the ground, exhausted. I got up and took a look at the body that had been invisible to me for so long. There were scattered burns all over it—I still carry the scars—and the burns were stinging from the sweat that began to pour from my skin.

As I walked away, I had to think about each leg before I could lift it or put it down again. I had to remember how to walk, and actually practice it. If I did not think of them individually, my legs seemed to vanish.

I must have looked like I was traversing a minefield. For some reason I could hold one foot up high in the air for an indefinite amount of time without feeling any imbalance, as if the other foot were perfectly capable of holding me up forever.

My eyesight too had changed, becoming super-receptive to everything around me. Details that I would have overlooked before were suddenly very prominent. A termite that I was about to crush under my bare foot suddenly grew enormous, as if to make me notice it. As soon as I changed the direction of my foot, it became small again. I saw a spider's web, and the spider grew huge just in time for me to avoid running into it. It too returned to normal size as soon as I passed by it.

None of this surprised me. What could have astonished me by then? The horizon of reality had increased exponentially. I took this for granted, not because I was exhausted but because by now I had seen too much. I understood what was happening to me from deep within myself, using a logic that did not come from my brain.

▲　　　▼　　　▲

Back at the camp, I met Nyangoli just returning from the deep bush. He had a dead monkey in one hand and some dry wood in the other.

"You want to help me?" he asked. "The sun isn't down, and we should have our first real meal before dark since we don't know what kind of ordeals are left ahead of us."

"Where did you get the monkey?" I asked, just for the sake of saying something.

Nyangoli was a skilled hunter who could practically kill with his bare hands. He could smell game half a kilometer away and spot it with the precision of a hunting dog.

"There was a bunch of them on a big tree in the middle of the river. You know monkeys don't swim. I knocked one of them off balance with a stick and let him drown. Nothing to it." He began making a fire.

I could not bear to stand near the fire because of my painful burns. Nyangoli looked at them but said nothing. I did not ask him anything about his experience either. We spoke about simple things. Nyangoli told me how to hunt porcupines—where to locate them at night and how to petrify them before making a kill. He also told me how he had learned the technique of "high" hunting—hunting large animals—from his father a few years ago, and how his father had shown him how to use the medicine of invisibility. This medicine was the only way to hunt large animals such as buffalo, lions, or elephants without becoming the hunted.

Nyangoli said he never knew if he was invisible or not because he could not ask the animal to tell him. His father had always told him never to strike an animal while still invisible. I said I didn't understand that.

"Me neither," continued Nyangoli, "at least in the beginning, for I thought if I missed it and the animal got mad, at least I could remain hidden. But, you see, the animal is not a fool. If it guesses you are hunting it while invisible, it will go into dimensional seeing and petrify you there, preventing you from coming back to this world. See, when you are hidden, you are not from here. The animal, however, does not need to hide itself from the hunter because . . ." Here he hesitated, and I thought, *He must be getting ready to tell me a family secret.* Finally he continued. "Because it does not need to. Well! This is a hunter's secret. But you must know that when I heard that being hidden like this meant being vulnerable to the animal, I was scared to even try it."

"Then how would you hunt large animals?"

"I wouldn't hunt them. I don't have to."

There was another long silence while Nyangoli fixed his attention on barbecuing the monkey. While he cooked, my mind kept returning to my experiences in the underworld. I could not stop remembering the eyes of that thing that pulled me out; nor could I establish the connection between the mountain, the portal in it, and the horizontal journey that had ended with my being ejected out of the gate. I could not figure out how I had gone in vertically and fallen so far, then exited horizontally.

We ate in silence. The monkey meat tasted great. It was a little tough, but it was the first decent meal I'd eaten since I couldn't remember when.

As we ate, the sun went down. I noticed that the other students had returned and regrouped in small teams. They were either doing what we were, cooking dinner, or just sitting and chatting quietly.

Did the weight of experience always reduce one to silence, or was it that we simply did not feel like speaking? It was strange to feel so uncommunicative about the ordeal we had all been through. Here I was, with a unique opportunity to discuss my strange experience with my most trusted friend, and instead we were speaking as if nothing had occurred. As if to acquiesce, the coming of darkness informed us it was time to join the circle. We heard it together, and left our dinner space silently.

CHAPTER 21

THE WORLD AT THE BOTTOM OF THE POOL

That night I dreamed that a bull spat on my face. When the dream began, my father and I were visiting a nearby village to consult a diviner on the delicate subject of my future. As I watched the diviner interact with us, I seemed to be entering a new life, a new realm of meaning, discovering a new way of reading the world and my role in it. All the things the two men were doing looked and sounded familiar to me. The diviner picked up his medicine bag and began pouring strange things on the dirt floor. His working tools were unsophisticated: dried birds' legs with claws attached, contorted animal bones, pieces of metal, copper wire probably taken from an abandoned bicycle's brake system, a talismanic object hidden within the carefully sewn skin of a mysterious animal. There were pieces of corn *thud,* the body around which the grains stick, various types of stones, and other things I could not even tell the origin of. These things were so old-looking that they had become almost unidentifiable.

I did not know the diviner's name, but it did not seem to matter, for my father knew him well and had often consulted with him. The diviner knew me for my father's son and that was enough for him. He could not say my Christian name because he could not pronounce the "r"—he had lost too many teeth.

I do not recall what was said in the reading. What I was aware of, however, was that every one of these unimpressive objects was a whole book that traditional literacy could open and read. The diviner had picked several of these objects and built a story in which I was the central symbol. I was fascinated by the ease with which he was operating in his domain, reading at great length out of the book of an old animal bone some story about me having been chewed up and spit into the sun, where I became dry and stiff and unable to respond to the commands of my destiny.

I thought, *The book of a bone.*

The diviner picked out another item, a metallic object. Holding it, he spoke of faraway countries and cultures of wires and metals. He described men riding in strange boxes that moved by themselves; restless, moving parts hidden inside these boxes; and many other mysterious metal things not of his world. He spoke on and on, monotonously, about these medicine items. To him, they constituted an immense supply of information hidden behind the seeming triviality of their appearance.

When we left it was dark. My father's bicycle did not have a headlight and we rode very slowly, hitting bump after bump on the narrow trail going home. Father was guessing the way, for the night was so dark that only the trees were still visible because they were darker than the night itself. We had barely entered the village when the drive chain came off the gears and we had to stop to put it back on. I stood there in the dark, unable to see a foot in front of me, while my father fixed the invisible bicycle's chain. Suddenly a huge bull appeared out of nowhere.

I could see the bull because he was all white with only one dark spot between his eyes. His fierce gaze was even more frightening than a normal bull's because he was standing on his hind legs, making him almost twice as tall as usual. One of his front legs was pointing at me while the other was waving frantically, as if he were having a problem staying in balance in this awkward position. After a while he began speaking the words, "You, you, you," over and over again. Each "you" sent a spray of slimy saliva onto my face. I was panic-stricken and unable to yell.

Focused on the chain, my father did not notice anything for a while. When he stood up and saw the terrible creature, he groaned and reached for the machete that was hanging on his bicycle frame.

At the same moment the bull turned around, brought his front legs down, and charged toward a small bush. My father ran after him, but when the bull vanished into the bush, Father gave up and came back to me. I was more frightened than ever. We mounted the bicycle and rode home without further problems, even though I was still terror-stricken by the event. As we reached home, my father said, "It was the diviner testing us."

When I woke up the next morning, I was still frightened by the image of that horrible creature. I looked around reflexively. When I realized it was just a dream, I felt relieved. I was certain that the dream was a message from my father. What did it mean? Nyangoli noticed the distressed expression on my face and patted me on the shoulder in support. We got up and joined the others, who were gathering around the coach.

The coach led us westward, single file, toward the mountains. As we passed the spot where the ceremony of the light hole had taken place the day before, I noticed that there was no trace of the injured boy. Instead, the place where he had landed was covered with the kind of worms that crawl on piles of dung. No one paid much attention, but somehow I knew that the other boys had not forgotten. I found myself wondering if it was worse to be caught inside the gate or to be pulled out burned and cut to pieces.

I remembered the icy cold of the gateway and felt a cold chill run down my spine. How terrible it would be to live forever, naked in an icy climate, with no loved ones to provide the tiniest comfort. Why should anyone be allowed to risk his life just for the sake of becoming oversensitive? For I was becoming more and more aware of my extreme sensitivity to everything surrounding me. There were so many details flooding my senses that I could not possibly handle them all.

Silently, we walked out of the camp and into the wilderness, heading toward the mountains. The elders were not visible today. I wondered what had happened to them. As we came close to the mountains, the coach ordered us to find something to eat before continuing. This was the first time a general food break was ordered. He didn't have to speak twice. The line shattered like a rat migration disturbed by a mighty hunter. Nyangoli and I rallied from the heat of our march. He made a large staff from a branch he had broken off a tree and began to clear the bush in front of us as we walked.

There were many kinds of fruit trees here, but I was not familiar with any of them. Nyangoli did not seem interested in fruit, however. As he beat the bush, he kept his eyes riveted on to the ground. I was empty-handed. He suggested I grab a stone or two. We did not speak much. Suddenly a rabbit leaped out of a bush Nyangoli had struck and headed straight for me. Instinctively, I lifted my hand to throw the stone at it, but I suddenly remembered that rabbits are the children of the Kontomblé. I recalled the little elder sitting on a cloud and reminding me that the rabbit too had a mother.

I just couldn't do it. Helplessly, I watched the animal run past me. Nyangoli watched me with surprise, but he did not say anything. We continued our hunting.

It was not long before I heard him pound hard on the ground. By the time I was beside him, he was picking up the huge blacksnake whose head he had severed from its body.

"This should be enough for the two of us," he said.

I was a little apprehensive. Ever since my return to the village, I had not eaten a snake. I did not even know if my family ate snakes. Every clan has a food taboo, but I did not know mine because no one had ever told me. I could not afford to dwell on these kinds of thoughts, however, because I was too hungry.

We rejoined the group and got back in line. The sun had almost reached the zenith when we arrived at the first mountain range. Our progress had been slowed because of the steep incline and the intense heat. We had all eaten our fill and our bellies were so stuffed that we felt sluggish and uncomfortable. We all sweated.

We reached the top of the first mountain in our accustomed silence. All around us was a flat grassy land scattered with low trees. Cows and bulls grazed nearby. I noticed that one of the bulls looked like the one that had attacked me in the dream. It met my eyes briefly, then walked away. Farther west was a series of taller mountains. We had stopped at the first range. The other was about a day's walk away.

The coach sat down and, exhausted, we all did the same. No one wanted to know if this was the place where we were to meet the elders. Just then, however, they appeared, walking toward us. All five marched in a line, each carrying his medicine bag and walking stick. Walking past us as if we didn't exist, they headed farther south, toward where the cattle had grazed. As soon as they disappeared, the coach ordered us to get up and follow them. We walked in their direction for a while until we found out that they were now behind us. How did that happen? None of us knew. We turned around and stopped, waiting. The sun was biting our naked skins.

The elders sat down a dozen feet away and beckoned us to sit on the stony ground in front of them, as if they had not noticed that we were already sitting. One of them pulled out a tobacco pack made from a hollow gourd covered with an iguana skin. The powdered tobacco must have become clogged in the neck of the gourd, for the old man grabbed a small pointed stick and began digging into it, rolling the stick around inside it. He hit the gourd several times against his knee and peered into it with one eye. Nodding with satisfaction, he offered the pack to a colleague, who opened his hand to receive the tobacco and deposited it inside his lower lip.

Thus was tobacco shared among the council of the elders while we sat facing them, some of us watching them, others busy taking care of their digestion.

The lead elder began to speak. "I see that you are all ready to return to the realm of shadow and mist where you had your beginning. He who does not know where he comes from cannot know why he came here and what he came to this place to do. There is no reason to live if you forget what you're here for. Yesterday you all saw that there is life in other dimensions, right?"

He asked this question skeptically, as if we did not believe him. Some of us nodded, others emitted sounds of affirmation.

"I want you to be prepared to return to where you were before you came here. Before you were born, your family learned who you were and what your purpose is. You chose to be born within a particular family because that made your purpose easier to fulfill. While still in your mother's womb, you told the living certain things to remember. But even if they were to tell you these things, would you believe them? Would you trust them enough? You would not, because when we come here and take on human form, we change our opinions like the wind. When you do not know who you are, you follow the knowledge of the wind.

"There are details about your identity that you alone will have to discover, and that's what you have come to initiation to go and find out. To come to this planet you first had to plunge into the depths of a chasm. In order to return to where you came from, you will do the same thing."

I knew the elder was speaking figuratively. There were no real chasms in the mountain for us to leap into, and even if there had been, the exercise would have been so similar to yesterday's experience with the light hole that it would seem like a useless repetition of something we had already learned.

Something odd was going on inside of me. For the first time since the initiation had begun, the words of the elders did not make me feel strange. I discovered that I could remain calm, finally quieting my relentless questioning. My heart could continue beating at the same pace, even in the face of an intense experience. The sense that I might die was not as strong as it had been in the beginning. This time I felt certain I would survive.

It was clear that we had come to the mountains to plunge once again into the infernal and hermetic order of another world, a world different from the ones we had seen before. How many of them were there? This world and endless layers of reality? The elders seemed to have no doubt about the existence of all these worlds. They knew a great many of them.

I recalled the words of one of the medicine men to whom I had been explaining how I came to abandon the school of the white man. He said, "Our minds know better than we are able and willing to admit the existence of many more things than we are willing to accept. The spirit and the mind are one. Their vision is greater, much greater than the vision we experience in the ordinary world. Nothing can be imagined that is not already there in the outer and inner worlds. Your mind is a responder; it receives. It does not make things up. It can't imagine what does not exist. The blessing in this is that you are your mind. That is also a curse. When you refuse to accept the reality of your mind, you refuse yourself, and that is bad."

Is it possible, then, that everything my mind could imagine exists somewhere in some other world? Where, then, is the place for that which is not real? In the world of my people there is nothing but reality, alone without its opposite. When something comes into our lives that we label as impossible, like a buffalo running into a hole one foot in diameter, or a brand-new landscape opening up right before us, an elder would interpret this way of thinking as a manifestation of our own rigidity in the face of a new idea. When we resist expansion, we foster the unreal, serving that part of our ego that wants to limit growth and experience. In the context of the traditional world, the geography of consciousness is very expansive. Consequently, in the mind of a villager, the unreal is just a new and yet unconfirmed reality in the vocabulary of consciousness. It is brought to us by the ancestors. A little hospitality toward it will quickly make it part of us.

It was now late afternoon. No one seemed to be in a hurry. The elders were chatting quietly. Meanwhile, the coach was dividing us into five uneven groups, the earth people, the fire people, the nature people, the water people, and the iron people. When he was finished, each group was assigned an elder who took them away. The fire people went down the mountain slope, the nature people walked a little distance and stopped there, the iron people went into the bush nearby, and the earth people were asked to stay where they were.

I was one of the water people. Our elder took us to a canyon on the other side of the mountain. Along its bottom a stream of water two or three feet wide flowed toward the valley. We followed the water upstream until we reached a large, cavelike opening in the mountain and entered. Inside was a pool, its cold water boiling noisily, sending jets of spray upward. Farther back in the chamber was a narrow, impenetrable opening out of which came more water. It was surrounded by plants. We sat around the edges of the pool. It was cool there, at the edge of the water and away from the sun. Nobody spoke a word. We simply felt.

The silence was good. I did not want to try to guess what was going to happen here. I only wanted to let my body experience the coolness of the water and the peace it brought into my heart and mind.

We sat like that for a long time before the leader spoke. "This water has been here since time immemorial. It protects the doorway to the ancestors. Only the sick are brought here, for healing. This water is the roof of the world you are going to visit for a while. You will jump into the pool one after the other. There is no bottom as there is in the village river, instead there is a world. When you jump in, do not waste your time in the watery area or you will drown. You will have to let yourself sink down as fast as you can until you stop. If you still have fear, let it go or you will drown."

He produced some medicine out of his pocket and gave each one of us some to eat. It tasted bitter at first, but then it made you feel drunk or dazed. The elder asked us to stand up and follow him as he began walking around the pool. I looked down into the water. I could see the bottom of the pool, visible under the crystal clarity of the water. It did not appear deep, though I could not be sure. There were nine of us, walking one behind the other, waiting for further orders. Suddenly the old man picked up a skinny little kid and hurled him into the water. The boy yelled as he crashed into the pool and disappeared as if sucked down by some invisible force. The jets of spray stopped for a while and a few bubbles appeared on the surface.

Everyone's eyes were locked on to the water. As if by enchantment, we saw the boy, hands stretched out in front of him, diving down like a bird in a bright sky. Soon he was too far away to be seen. The water began boiling again. I instinctively looked behind me, and there was the elder staring at me with a malicious smile that seemed to say, "Now it's your turn, buddy."

I did not wait to be thrown into the water. Holding my breath, I plunged. I immediately found myself caught by a powerful current. I kept my eyes closed. I did not have the feeling of moving downward, but rather as if I were being flown horizontally underneath the mountain. Keeping my eyes tightly shut, I passed screaming noises and rushed forward, pulled by an irresistible gravity toward the north. When I opened my eyes, there was no water around me.

For a while I thought I had drowned, but I dismissed the thought as a mental reaction to an alien environment. Everywhere around me it seemed to be dusk. I could not see very far and I could not tell if I was standing up or sitting or even still flying. I felt as if I were just a shapeless consciousness in the middle of a misty presence that was everywhere around me. Only shadows were visible, some foggy, some smoky, some light, some dark. They moved like clouds or smoke. Some of these shadows had the distinctive shapes of human beings, while others were just two-dimensional cutouts or unspecifiable shapes.

In this world, I could see myself clearly, but I felt as if I weighed nothing, for it was very hard for me to stay put on the ground. I was constantly being pulled upward. I had to resist this attraction any way I could. The concentration required to keep my feet on the ground was painful. The world under the water was not a world in any way comparable to ours, nor would one particularly want to live in it. The voices I had been hearing all along became more distinct and I realized they were musical—a conversation between drums, xylophone, and singing voices. I could feel rather than see a presence close to me, but I was not frightened or curious or surprised. I just was.

This presence had been pouring information into my heart since I arrived. I had no power to resist or to act on what was going on. When I could finally make out the shape of the creature that was working on me, I saw that it was a dolphin. It had come to nurse me like a mother.

▲   ▼   ▲

The power of quiet is great. It generates the same feelings in everything one encounters. It vibrates with the cosmic rhythm of oneness. It is everywhere, available to anyone at any time. It is us, the force within that makes us stable, trusting, and loving. It is contemplation contemplating us. Peace is letting go—returning to the silence that cannot enter the realm of words because it is too pure to be contained in words. This is why the tree, the stone, the river, and the mountain are quiet.

There was no water in that world beneath the pool. My journey was perhaps all an illusion. When I came to my senses back in the cave, standing in the shallow water of the pool, I could not help but weep at having returned to a strange world. As in the experience with the green lady, my underwater journey had brought a powerful feeling of nostalgia surging out of my heart. I felt a tremendous longing for what I had seen and experienced under the water. I knew this wholeness and peace was what I deserved, what everyone deserved at every moment of his or her life. Coming back to the cave was like being exiled from my home. My face was as wet with tears as my body was with water.

There was no one else in the cave. When I looked outside, I saw, grazing a few hundred feet away, the same bull I had seen in my dream the night before. It was not standing on its hind legs, but staring at me intensely, as if it too had recognized me from a previous dream. The sun was about to set. My experience under the water had obviously taken all afternoon. I stopped weeping and responded with intensity to the bull, whose eyes blinked several times ferociously. It turned around, walked away down the hill, and disappeared.

As the bull disappeared, the elder appeared in its identical place and walked toward the pool. He glanced at me furtively, as if he did not want me to know he was looking at me. It occurred to me that I might have been the first one to come back.

The elder beckoned to me to come out of the cave. As I approached him, he held his hands stretched toward me. Instinctively, I stretched out my hands toward him. They met and I felt like I had a grandfather. We walked hand-in-hand, he leading, I behind, toward the top of the mountain where we had met the elders earlier that day.

"You spent a long time in there," he said. "Almost the whole day. I almost thought you were never going to be reborn. Just keep being strong."

As we neared the meeting place, everybody was there. The elder released my hand before we appeared in front of the others. The crowd was silent. We approached them without speaking and took our places, I with the young men, the old man with the council of the elders.

CHAPTER 22

BURIALS, LESSONS, AND
JOURNEYS

 That night at the camp we had no nightly ritual with fire and drum. Everybody was unusually quiet, as if in deep meditation. No one wanted to disturb anyone. I did not even notice Nyangoli's presence next to me. He had been with the mineral people while I had gone into the water. We were nearing the end of our training. I did not yet know how far we still had to go, but somehow I knew that we had covered a huge amount of ground. I could not fully understand the meaning of most of the trials we had been put through, nor could I contain them in words. Every initiation has its esoteric and exoteric parts. As the years have passed, I have realized that some things can be told and others not. Telling diminishes what is told. Only what has been integrated by the human aspect of ourselves can be shared with others. I have also come to believe that things stay alive proportionally to how much silence there is around them. Meaning does not need words to exist.

There are times, however, when words do come to us. My experiences could not pass from me to you without the agency of words. But remember: the word is not the meaning and the meaning is not the word. At best words are merely a vehicle, a very shaky and second-rate means of human communication. This is because meaning does not have a body. Shamans tell us that, were meaning to come to us fully unveiled, it would turn us

258

into it; that is, it would kill us. This is why we must content ourselves with whispers and glimmerings of meaning. The closer we get to it, the wiser we become.

For two nights in a row we did something terrible to each other. The first night, half of us had to commit the other half to the ground. It was a hard and painstaking job. We spent the days digging our own graves and the nights burying each other. The coach had given each pair of initiates a machete and a hoe. We had the choice of digging a deep vertical grave or a horizontal shallow one. Those who chose the vertical grave were given an extra tool because it was hard to dig in the dry earth. Some who had chosen to dig vertically changed their minds after a while because after two or three feet of laborious digging they kept hitting rocks. Everybody looked for a smooth, porous place to experience what it would feel to be confined to their final resting place.

The day was animated by the drum of the coach and consistently macabre because of the smell of death. We had gone through so much pain already. Why were we required to commit our bodies to a grave while we were still alive? The elders had given us no explanation. In fact, they had not even appeared. It was the coach who took charge of the burial operation. The work was completed by midafternoon. Those who were to be buried standing had dug a hole able to contain their bodies up to the chin. Those who were to be buried lying on their backs dug a horizontal hole capable of doing the same thing.

As soon as it became dark, we were asked to get started. The coach presided over the ceremony, going from grave to grave to assist with the burial. With ash he made a white ring around the hole and covered the body of the boy to be buried with some strange oil. Then he and the guardian lifted the boy and put him into the grave. While the coach went to work with the next pair, the boy's partner would fill up the grave with dirt. When the coach came to Nyangoli and me, we had not decided who was going to go first. My heart was beating violently. I decided I was going to wait till tomorrow night.

Nyangoli, who did not mind either way, let his body be covered with oil, and with the help of the coach was put to rest in the ground. Our grave was horizontal. I began putting the dirt back into the hole. Some heavy chunks fell on Nyangoli and he protested, joking that he was not dead yet. I proceeded at a slower pace until only his head was above ground. Then I walked outside of the circle of ash to look at my friend. Nyangoli was a living head. Only his eyes moved swiftly in the dim light as if to compensate for the sudden stillness his body had entered into.

He seemed amazingly fragile and vulnerable. I asked if he felt anything. He merely said that we should have dug a vertical grave for that way we would not have to bear the weight of all that dirt all night. Then he said he would rather not talk anymore because he sensed a great challenge ahead, so I shut up and moved closer to him. I sat down, put my hand on his head, and waited. Nyangoli had his eyes closed.

The silence of the night was troubled by screams. They came out of nowhere, simultaneously. My body shivered. A cold sweat ran down my spine and my skin tightened with goose bumps. I looked at Nyangoli. His eyes were still closed and his breath came very slowly. His head was hot. I felt the urge to speak to him, but I remembered he would rather not talk.

The screams came back; this time synchronized and accompanied by voices. I heard someone scream, *"Leave me alone, I don't want to go! Please— someone tell him to leave me alone."*

Another voice complained of fire being everywhere. That voice said the bush had become a huge flame and that we had to flee immediately. The voice kept repeating that he would go if no one else wanted to because he wasn't going to wait around to be burned to death. That constant refrain gave me chills. I could tell that the voice was operating on a different plane. The boy who owned it seemed to be out of his grave and moving around freely. His cries seemed to come from everywhere.

Other voices joined in, making a concert in the night: cries and miserable, pitiful weeping that went on for hours, then mutated into hallucinations. The night was long, too long, I felt, for me to survive it. I was amazed by Nyangoli. He said nothing, did nothing. His breath remained slow and regular. There was a long silence between his inhalations and exhalations, and a much longer one between each cycle. I went to sleep seated next to him, my hand resting on his head. . . .

When I opened my eyes it was dawn. I did not open them because of the light but because the coach hit the drum. Voices were still crying. The time had come for the "resurrection," and I waited for the coach to tell me what to do next. He walked from grave to grave, carrying some very cold water that he poured onto the head of each buried boy while speaking strange words. Then he would order the removal of the dirt from the grave.

The morning moved slowly. The resurrected initiates were all sick and weak. They lay down while we took care of them, bringing them food and water. Nyangoli, who had remained in the grave for another hour or so after the dirt was completely removed from his body, did not stay still for a very long time after that. I had gone hunting for some sweet fruits while he lay there. When I returned, he was exercising his legs. Our eyes met but we said nothing. I did not want to know what he had been through. Or maybe I already knew. When the night approached, my heart pounded inside my chest as if this were going to be the harshest test of all.

It was. The ordeal of being buried alive had nothing to do with fear, but it was filled with pain. Pain is a sister to fear. They have a strange relationship with each other. Fear is the resistance against death. Pain confirms that resistance. There was also another side to being buried alive—a sense of complete submission. When my body was buried, for the first few moments I did not feel anything but weight, tremendous weight upon me. I understood why Nyangoli had remarked that we should have dug a vertical grave.

The next thing I experienced was intense heat that made my body sweat. That was the sensation that triggered the pain. I closed my eyes and tried to think about something else. But you cannot outwit pain. Any contraction of your muscles will diminish it just enough for you to want to hold that position for a while, but you cannot remain contracted forever because a good contraction makes it impossible to breathe. The intake of air creates sensations again. Breathing is to pain what fuel is to fire.

I was the first to scream. Screaming outwits pain because pain is one of the body's languages. To speak back at pain is to scream. While you scream the pain listens or waits till you're done in order to speak back. That way there is an endless dialogue of stubborn entities talking to each other.

There are no words to describe how it feels to be buried alive. The first several hours, while I was still conscious, I was only trying not to make a fool out of myself after the superb handling of the situation by Nyangoli the night before. But Nyangoli was superhuman. No normally constituted human being could spend the night packed with so much dirt and so much heat without uttering a sound. The heat from a naked body, unable to dissipate, gets trapped in the dirt and so comes back to you. When you begin to sweat and itch, there is no remedy because you can't move. Slowly your sweat turns the dirt immediately surrounding your body into a layer of scalding, sticky mud. As the heat increases with the weight of the dirt, the mind cannot tolerate being in the body any longer, so it leaves. When I began hallucinating, that was better because it did not include the pain anymore. There came a moment when all the screaming and yelling were no longer having any effect on the excruciating pain. At that point something else took over.

The whole area around me suddenly became light, as if the sun had risen. *Am I dreaming?* I wondered. *Or have I passed out?* All around me was a mob of smoky people, or rather, smoke shaped into human form. I was still conscious of being buried and was looking forward to be taken out of the grave since the day had suddenly broken, but these smoky people would not dig me up. They just moved round and round me as if waiting for me to do something. I decided I was going to have to take care of myself. I found out that I could move my hand perfectly easily and that there was no more weight on my body. I got up out of the grave myself and felt good about it. I was not sweating, nor was I feeling any pain at all. I wondered where these feelings had gone.

The misty crowd rallied around me as soon as I exited from the grave. Their faces at last were solid and real. Most of them were white faces, faces like those of my professors back in the seminary. Other faces were black, but there were fewer of these. Yet other faces were neither white nor black—I could not classify them. All of them were familiar, but I did not know their names. They did not look angry, or surprised, or curious. They were just looking at me. I walked farther into the bush and they followed me, gently at first, and then very eagerly. I walked for a long time until I reached a clearing. Then I stopped and sat. They sat too.

From then on whatever happened was not under my control. A force greater than me, greater than them, greater than all of our forces combined, was instructing us on things we could not resist. The circle began to swing clockwise, slowly at first, then very quickly, so quickly we all became only one consciousness, one entity in motion in the open space of the cosmos. My body got colder and colder as we swung though the vast open cosmos in a perpetual circular motion. The cold began to increase to the point where I could not stand it anymore and I tried to shake my body in order to warm it up. It was then that I opened my eyes.

The coach had poured cold water on my head, and the cold liquid was dripped all around me.

Impassively, Nyangoli began to dig around me. I was too weak to realize I was at the end of the ordeal. He dug me out, but I could not move. He left me there, the wind caressing my body while he went in search of food. I fell asleep. When I awoke, the sun was high in the sky and it was already hot. The morning dew was quickly evaporating from the grass even though there were still some remnants of coolness in the air.

That day was also a very quiet one. Nothing happened communally because the elders wanted to see us one by one. They started with the fire people. There were about fifteen of them. One by one they went and came back, their faces unchanged. I was not really curious about what went on at these encounters, although this was the first time we would be meeting privately with the elders since we left the village.

At that point I did not know exactly how many days we had spent in the camp. I did know we were not far from returning home. I could tell by the way I felt. Part of myself did not care one way or another about returning. I felt as if I could have lived in the bush for the rest of my life without complaining. I had an unshakable sense of well-being and unity with nature. The plants around me were all glowing violet, and the trees kept moving their branches as if they were noticing my presence. I was happy to be noticed that way. I knew nature loved me and I was happy to love nature back.

I could even hear nature, its relentless vibration of love and its slow movements. Its nurturing power fed me through my nose and my pores, sustaining my vital senses. I was aware that nature also fed itself in a way that I was not able to understand, but I knew it was not the kind of meal I could consume. I had friends in the trees and in the grass.

While the others were being interviewed, I took a walk in the bush, enjoying my rediscovery of the array of nature's wonders. My perceptions had become hyperbolic, spanning both the small and the large. I was able to notice the most minute crawling insect concealed beneath the tiniest blade of grass. I could see the different personalities of the trees and larger plants. Even their roots were visible to me. Some appeared as a vast network growing out in all directions, others were simply a single tubercle on top of which stood the plant erect and content. I saw the medicine and the healing power in all of them.

I remembered the blind healer in the village who worked at night and slept during the day. The man was so skilled at conversing with trees that he baffled even his fellow medicine men with his spectacular talent for obtaining medicine from nature. His consultations always ended in the middle of the night. Then the patient was ordered to follow him into the bush. There he would speak to Mother Nature in a strange language, giving her a list of illnesses. She would respond in a buzzing language, telling him which plants he needed to gather.

Then the vegetal world would awake in the middle of darkness, every tree and every plant—all speaking to the man at once. For the witness it was gibberish, but for the blind healer it made sense. He would translate, telling each patient that such and such a tree said his fruit, dried and pounded and then mixed with salted water and drunk, would take care of the disease in question. Another plant would say that it couldn't do anything by itself, but that if the patient could talk to another plant (whose name the healer knew) and mix their substances together, their combined energies could kill such and such an illness.

Some trees said they did not want to be touched or disturbed because they were going through *Amanda,* a metamorphosis process that requires total seclusion. In such a state their vegetal substances could be very harmful. Yet other plants were busy helping their neighbors and could not help humans because of that. Their medicine, which did much good to the other trees, would be harmful to humans.

The healer was totally dependent on this dialogue with the vegetal in his work. He often said that the vegetal world was better than the human one because it knew more than we did, and because it is of a finer species than we are. The vegetal can get along without us, but we cannot progress without the help of the vegetal.

When I returned to the quarter, the water people were being interviewed. I had no idea how far into the interview with the water people the elders had been while I was away in the bush, but when I saw the last one

OF WATER AND THE SPIRIT

coming back, I decided I must be next. No one opposed my decision. The elders were seated in a circle. The one who had walked with me on the mountain ordered me to sit in the middle of the circle. Then they all stretched their hands toward me and recited a prayer that seemed very long to me. It was very calming.

I lowered my head and concentrated on the prayer. I could not understand the words because they were at the same time Dagara and not Dagara. When they were done, the head of the initiation council took some ash and made a circle around me. Another one produced a black sticky substance and anointed me on the forehead, the spine, the elbow, and the chest, making a cross sign each time. Then the whole group began to speak again in that strange language, one after the other. They were apparently reciting a prayer that had to be said word by word, one person at a time.

Recited this way, the prayer took a long time to complete. I knew it was over when they all said the same sentence three times together.

The head of the council spoke. "The next two days are important for you. Do you know this area of the wild?"

"I do not," was my reply.

"It won't matter," continued the elder. "The mountains we went to the day before today are a place you can find again. You must return there and look for a cave shaped like an egg. It won't take you long to find it because there is no other cave that shape anywhere else. When darkness comes, you will go looking for that cave. Enter it and allow yourself to be guided to the Kontomblé world. There is nothing to fear. It is like here, but it is not here. You must return with what these beings will give you. That will be your first medicine. You must come back, and you must be back here before sunrise. Nobody will be with you on this journey, so you are on your own. Have you understood?"

I said yes because I did not think I was authorized to ask questions. The presence of these elders all around me was very strange. I felt as if they were responsible for a kind of numbing vibration that made me unable to be inquisitive. I did not have a clue about what they meant by entering a cave and letting myself be taken into another world that was like here but not here. There was, nonetheless, a certain level of trust that I had for them that forbade me to ask questions. I knew that whatever was going to happen would happen. I was being asked to go somewhere and to bring something back.

I had learned that it is not customary for a grown Dagara to be nosy and suspicious. Those traits are a sign that one has not reached the level of maturity required for true experience. The Dagara refrains from asking questions when faced with a riddle because questioning and being answered destroys one's chance to learn for oneself. Questions are the mind's way of trying to destroy a mystery. The mind of the village elder has become accustomed to living with questions while his heart dances with the "answer." Besides, I had no more fear left to fuel my desire for information. Before, my heart would have leaped violently inside me, beating frenetically; but now I just felt privileged to deserve the attention of so much wisdom and power.

When I returned to the camp, Nyangoli asked if I wanted to journey with him tonight. He was going in the same direction, to the same mountain, but his cave was more distant than mine. Several other boys wanted to join us. The day was monotonous. Preparing for this journey made us all the more silent. No one questioned the specifics of his mission. The assignment weighed on us as we waited for the sun to set. Finally, before it had quite disappeared below the horizon, the drum sounded to announce that it was time to go.

We walked slowly out of the camp and into the thick of the forest toward the mountains. The journey was much slower as night fell than it had been the day before. It was made even worse because of the sudden sensation that forces were walking alongside of us, constantly distracting us from the road. In truth, there was no road. We were the road—a patrol of five boys heading for the mountains.

We reached a clearing, a place where we could see the sky. Ebele suggested we rest a while. We figured we were about halfway to our destinations. Nyangoli began pointing out constellations—the Triad, the Dog Star, the Monkey Star, and the Rabbit Star—and said that even though it was almost the middle of the night, we had to continue. All of a sudden the starry sky disappeared and a huge bird that looked like a turtle, its wings outstretched and its eyes red, appeared. None of us had seen such a bird before. We had only heard of this sort of thing in stories.

The first boy to see it screamed and rushed into the thick of the forest. We followed him instinctively. The wingbeat of the turtle-bird moved the treetops and bent the tall grass. It was obviously pursuing us. We ran as fast as we could, following each other closely. We could feel the wind from the turtle-bird's wings.

We had almost reached the foot of the mountain when the bird swooped up high and in a flash vanished, leaving us panting with exhaustion and wondering why we had bothered to run.

We began to speak about the location of our specific assignments. Each one involved entering a cave. Since I knew he was a mineral person, I asked Nyangoli where the mountain was that was shaped like an egg. He told me it was in the second range. I still had a lot of walking to do, and so did he, since his cave was situated at the far end of the mountain. As we reached the first range, one of the boys left the group.

We were walking faster than we had the other day because we wanted to get there. Soon we came to a river. The water was quiet, dark, and mighty. Without hesitation, Nyangoli entered it and we followed. The river was usually shallow, though at one point the water was up to our shoulders. As we neared the shore, the boy at the end of the line yelled and said that he was being bitten by something big. I stopped in dismay. Just as he screamed that he could not breathe, Nyangoli grabbed my hand and pulled me toward the bank.

It was so dark that no one could even guess the nature of the thing that had attacked the boy. I began to imagine that it could be anywhere in the water, swimming swiftly toward one of us as its next victim. This thought frightened me and the water suddenly seemed cold. What kind of creature could devour a human so quickly in the middle of the night? The other boys were also rushing toward the shore. The unfortunate boy had stopped screaming by the time we had all reached safety. He was not visible on the surface of the dark water that was made even darker by the night. Tears crawled down my cheeks as I stood there, unable to save him. The other initiates had not even stopped to offer a moment of silence.

We walked at a much slower pace now, as we were almost at the flank of the second mountain range. Troubled by the recent tragedy, I could not focus on the task ahead. *Who is next?* I wondered. Nyangoli left me as we reached the flank of the elevation. As he walked away, he pointed toward my egg-shaped cave. Something within us was prohibiting us from using words to communicate. As if by telepathy, I could feel Nyangoli say he would see me at sunrise at the initiation headquarters, and in a flash he had disappeared, swallowed by the night.

The other boys had also vanished. I knew they were not far away, but the night was good at burying us. I was alone.

CHAPTER 23

JOURNEY INTO THE UNDERWORLD

The egg-shaped cave was not far, but the journey was going to be steep—uphill all the way. In the thick darkness of the night, I figured it would take me about a half hour to get there, but my progress became slower and slower. The terrain was unpredictable: rocks everywhere, some hidden and painful when stepped upon, others so large they formed a natural barrier that I had to work my way around.

Even when there were no large rocks, the loose gravelly ground was no help. My feet slid in search of a grip while the mountain kept getting steeper and steeper. Soon I had to use my arms to drag myself forward safely. My thoughts went out to Nyangoli and the others, who at that very moment were also progressing toward their respective caves. I wondered how hard it was for them, or if they thought about me.

I heard erratic breathing, as if an animal were sniffing at something. I hid behind a rock and listened more carefully. Soon I heard noises everywhere, the sounds of hoofs and paws, panting, throats being cleared, yelping. Out of the blackness above me appeared a thin snow-white man holding a stick and walking downhill. He was probably two feet tall. His long hair was thick and stood straight up all over his tiny head as if petrified by some kind of grease. I realized that I was able to see him only because all around him there was a halo of light, bright as day. Behind him came a herd of animals of all kinds. Leading them all was a pack of porcupines, some large, some small, all walking in a loosely ordered manner. They had fierce glowing eyes and thorny bodies.

Following behind the porcupines came the tiny squirrels. They ran all the time, hopping in and out of the line. Most of the other animals in the pack were unknown to me, but I recognized some of the bigger ones by their horns and the shapes of their bodies: antelope, gazelles, buffalo, ostriches, elephants, rhinos, lions, and giraffes. The line was endless. I remembered the stories that circulated in the village about where the animals in the bush had disappeared to since the introduction by the white colonials of guns and wholesale killing and hunting. I thought, *So this is where they have run to—they hide inside the cave as long as humans are awake and come into the open air at night to feed undisturbed.*

I held my breath and waited for the endless parade to end. I figured they were going to the river below. At the end of the line there was another tiny man. This one carried a cane on his shoulders and was dressed in a beige uniform. For half a foot around him it was day. He never noticed my presence or, if he did, it did not bother him. He walked behind an animal that looked like a horse with a wing in the middle of the back. There was no doubt that these animals had come out of the cave I was going into. I imagined it had to be extremely big to accommodate so many different species.

The sniffing sound I had heard in the beginning came from an animal the size of a raccoon. Attracted by the unusual smell I was emitting, it had quit the line like a recalcitrant schoolboy and sniffed its way over to me. Now it stood on one side of the rock while I hid on the other. It inhaled deeply and, like a skilled hunter, crawled slowly toward me. My mind was moving fast. I had to design a protocol for dealing with my new companion, and I wondered whether a rock pounded heavily on its dumb head would do the job. Then I would not have to worry about food for the next day. After completing my mission, I could pick the animal up on my way back to the camp and roast it while my friends and I shared stories about our respective adventures.

The stupid beast moved closer. I held both my breath and the stone, ready to exhale at the same moment the deadly rock made a hole in the creature's head. I never got to do any of this. Instead my hand froze in the act of bringing down the rock. Petrified, I realized that the creature I had taken for a raccoon was actually a rabbit. To my amazement he began to speak, telling me the secret of my journey to the underworld: "You still do not get it, man. After all these years here you are again, eager to hurt me."

The voice was not really coming out of the rabbit's mouth, but from some unspecifiable source. It came to me as if by an infusion from an unseen needle into the most receptive part of my being. I could neither resist the communication nor respond to it. I wondered what he meant by "after all these years." I had no clue. Our eyes were locked onto one another, his luminous, mine illumined.

The rabbit had something like a hiccup that interrupted his speech every few words. "You are going to visit *my* home now (hiccup), yet you continue to try to kill me in yours (hiccup). My father sent me to tell you (hiccup) that he is waiting for you (hiccup). He has been chosen to be your guide (hiccup). I hope that when you come back from your visit (hiccup) we will be friends at last (hiccup). See (hiccup), when you were a kid chasing me in the bush, I tricked you into following me to my father (hiccup). I knew that wherever I ran, you would run (hiccup). You thought you found me, but it's me that found you (several hiccups). Do you still remember what my father told you? I see you don't (hiccup). It does not matter (hiccup). Ask your mother when you go home (hiccup). She still remembers that day. Your absence the whole afternoon almost scared her soul out of her body (several hiccups). She thought you had been eaten by one of us (hiccup). Ask her when you go home—and now, welcome to my father's home (hiccup). I must go join my fellows."

In a flash the rabbit was gone. I stood there immobilized by a force field, still holding the stone. After all I'd been through in the last few weeks, there was no surprise left in me. I was disappointed, though. Someone had showed up to talk to me about my journey into the cave, but just as quickly he had disappeared.

When I could move again, I realized I was freezing. I had to continue walking in order to keep myself warm. The egg-shaped cave was still several hundred feet away at the top of the mountain. The way was getting so steep that I sometimes had to use my arms as much as my legs in order to stay balanced. I wondered how the mineral people had made it when they came here a few days ago; but of course then it was day and now it was night. The rocks offered just enough of a grip to prevent me from falling off. So I went that way, jumping from rock to rock till I reached the entrance to the magical cave.

It looked like any other cave, a dwelling for bats and crawling things; and it smelled of rotting dung. Countless animals, domestic as well as savage, had defecated in it while taking a nap during the unforgiving heat of the day. The entrance was sealed by darkness and looked blacker than the night. Around it, the ground was as soft as that of a beach, as if the cave were an ocean whose shore was a resting place for dwellers of both worlds: the underworld and the one above.

I remembered someone telling me—I believe it was Grandfather—that the underworld people call our world the underworld too. It all depended on your point of view. Regardless of which world you are in, reaching the other always requires a downward motion.

I could not endure the thought of entering the thick blackness of the cave, so I decided to light my way in. There was some straw nearby, which I gathered into a bundle, and plenty of firestones. I collected a few and struck a spark to ignite the straw. I blew on it to get it going and, carrying my torch, I entered the cave.

It felt like a womb. The floor was sandy and dusty and I noticed with surprise that the walls were perfectly carved out of red granite. There were animal footprints everywhere. On the roof of the cave, there was a colony of bats. They screamed when I directed the light of the torch at them. Some took disorderly flight and exited the cave.

The bats that remained looked at me, as if trying to figure out what could possibly have made me come here at this time of night. I could not help thinking what a great meal I could make with only a couple of bats.

Like the walls of the cave, the roof, far above me, was smoothly carved. This could not be a natural geological site, I told myself: some higher intelligence must have carefully carved it, to serve the purpose for which I was sent here. The smooth, soft ground at first seemed like a playground or a resting place, but as I moved farther into the bowels of the cave, its walls became narrower and the floor less even. I was unable to continue walking, even crouched over, so I crawled. Pieces of pointed stones bit into my soft flesh like nails into butter. I continued to hold on to the burning torch.

The cave was getting dangerously narrow, so cramped I could not have defended myself against crawling things, nor could I have turned around and escaped. But I could not worry about it. The space seemed custom-made to fit me. My fire went out, but it was getting to be a nuisance anyway. I lay there resting and watched the sparks die. The blackness closed in.

I closed my eyes in an effort to blot out images of what would happen if I had to back out.

When I opened them again, I could see something that looked like a light a little distance ahead of me. At first I imagined it was a one-eyed prehistoric animal that had taken an interest in me. Then I remembered what the rabbit had told me. The light magnetized me. It did not move or blink or twinkle. I decided to move closer. It grew bigger and bigger, and soon I realized that it was not an eye but the sky I was seeing. I had reached the other side of the mountain! The cave must be, I thought, a tunnel that pierced straight through the mountain.

I was encouraged to move forward more confidently. *So this is the elders' idea of the underworld,* I thought. *Just another unpleasant ordeal to test my courage one last time.* By now I felt that I was beyond fear. I still had a few minor concerns, especially about my knees, which were bleeding heavily from the cuts caused by the stones. But I was confidently prepared to get the ordeal over with and to go back to the camp to report that there was no underworld anywhere in my assigned cave. On my hands and knees, I scrambled toward the exit.

▲   ▼   ▲

Writing about what came next is an extremely difficult task. What I have been able to convey so far of my experience in the underworld seems very limited, sometimes insignificant compared to what really happened. The basic problem is that whole sequences of events occurred without words, and that is what blocks the telling. When I try to describe them, I feel like I am walking barefoot on a thorny path. Not only do I have to mind where I put my feet, but the walking is so tedious that covering a short distance seems to take a long time. I know I am not doing justice to the experience, but how else can I tell you about it if I don't use words? While I am trying to negotiate these events into language, however, I have no illusion about the weakness of words in the face of certain overwhelming realities. I also know that the reader may have great difficulty fitting some of the things I am writing about into his or her own reality. I am doing the best I can. Bear with me.

It was dawn when I finally crawled out of the narrow tunnel back into a world that at first looked familiar, but soon turned into something else as my body caught up with its vibration. At first I felt an indescribable shock as I was barraged by numberless sensations. This place was so noisy I could not resist the urge to shout, "Stop!" Everything was screaming, and each shriek seemed directed at me. Soon, however, I discovered that it was I who was screaming.

The sun was about to rise. The sky was so clear I knew it was going to be a sunny day. But where was I? When I asked this question in my mind, I heard it so loud in and around me that the tears rushed out of my eyes. I thought again, *Why am I hurting myself so badly?* and instantly felt sorry for ever having thought anything in the first place. Thinking was excruciatingly painful, but I could not stop my thoughts, no matter what I did. In the meantime I felt an immense cold envelop me, a cold so bad that I could not even shiver, yet I could not even question this because thinking was such torture. I kept making monumental efforts to postpone mental activities, but my mind refused to cooperate.

We were in the cold season of the year, but it never got like this. The tropical winter is a combination of the Western fall and early summer. Temperatures become cooler during the middle of the night, but never to the point I was feeling. It was then that I realized I was in the underworld.

The realization came again like a scream into my ears. It made my body shiver again, not out of cold but out of fear—the same terror I thought I had definitively fought and overcome over the last weeks. Meanwhile, I had to do something about thinking, because thinking was torturing me beyond anything I could imagine. I felt something warm on my cheeks. When I brought my hand up to touch it, I discovered that blood was dripping out of my ears.

I have to stop thinking, I said to myself, and every thought was like a sting inside my ears. I was living inside a huge loudspeaker blasting to full capacity. My survival depended upon my ability to find the wires that transmitted these sounds and cut them. But if I myself were the wires, how could I do that? I sat down, closed my eyes, took a deep breath, and held it. I do not know how long I remained without breathing. I was conscious only of the fact that the volume of the noises in and around me was beginning to dim.

Slowly the screaming receded and with it the pain and the cold. From scream it changed into bearable sound, then into a whisper, and finally into silence.

The speech of silence is achieved when words, and their potential ability to hurt meaning, are done away with. Words entrap meaning, torture it, slice it into pieces the way a butcher cuts the meat of a slaughtered animal and serves it to us. The speech of silence has profound respect for the integrity of meaning as an entity separate from language. In silence, meaning is no longer heard, but felt; and feeling is the best hearing, the best instrument for recording meaning. Meaning is made welcome as it is and treated with respect.

Humans become meaning when they get as close to it as this. The way I felt when I had finally reached this stage cannot be described. The unresolvable conflicts that had tortured my being when I entered the realm of the underworld had been deleted, uncovering another layer of myself that collaborated better with my ability to receive meaning. That layer saved me from killing myself with the murderous knife of inner noisiness.

As my mind cleared and I came out from the interior of the inner loudspeaker, I experienced a peace similar to that which I had experienced with the green lady and during my water journey. Peace came as a surrender, as a successful discovery of a resting place, a home. It helped me at every level of my being, and was therefore more than welcome. It saved my life. I had forgotten if I was still breathing or not, but it no longer mattered. I was conscious, aware, knowing and remembering that this is the way things are and the way they should be. I was finally able to begin to explore.

The underworld is not under our world and probably not above it either. It is a world all by itself. Where I was, nature was beautiful, much finer than in the world I had left behind. The abundant green and violet colors that surrounded me gave the sky a special touch. It was not blue like our sky, but of a different color. The trees were of different species too, tall and large beyond anything I had seen before, and their majesty and serenity suggested great knowledge of the world they lived in. I felt both at home and not at home. I could not sort out the part of me that was not at home, but fortunately my critical-thinking mechanism was turned off.

Even though the trees hid a lot, I could see for a great distance, for I stood on a high elevation. Far in front of me were chains of strangely shaped mountains. Some looked like humans, others like animals. Though I somehow knew that each one carried great meaning, I could not decipher that meaning at this time. There was no need to. What was strange was that I remembered seeing those very shapes configured in Guisso's medicine room. They were modeled out of clay and stood as a backdrop to the animals and humans carved in wood that occupied the forefront of the medicine room. I had seen them there when we met for our first divination session.

The valley below me was crowded with all types of animals grazing along the shores of a river that ran northward. I could not tell them apart from this distance. They looked like tropical animals, yet they had certain characteristics that did not correspond with the beasts in the world above. As I sat there watching them, I felt the urge to stand up and move toward them. None of them paid attention to my presence. They were all busy grazing or chasing one another or making love. It was as if I weren't there.

Before walking down toward the river, I turned around to take a good look at where I had come in so that I might remember it when I needed to leave. It didn't surprise me to see neither doorway nor cave. The scene in front of me was similar to the one behind: trees, animals, mountains and valley without end. But somehow I was not shocked, nor critical, nor frightened.

All I did was look back and forth several times to make sure that the images and landscape concorded. When I felt the urge to move downward deep within my unconscious, I obeyed it without hesitation.

CHAPTER 24

A MISSION IN THE
UNDERWORLD

The inner compulsion I was feeling took the form of an order to proceed to the river. This urge tolerated no resistance. It did not have to, because by now I had forgotten how to resist. As I began to walk, I become aware of a feeling of weightlessness. My movements were unusually agile and my progress seemed effortless.

The clear waters of the river seemed to originate from the mountains farther south. I could not tell how deep these waters were, even though at points the river bottom was clearly visible. As I neared the shore, I stopped and gazed into the water. It occurred to me that I should be seeing my reflection, but for some reason I didn't.

Because my mind was no longer busily producing thoughts, I was unable to stop questioning. Though several things were happening all around me at once, I could not give anything my attention. I knew, for example, that there was someone near me, though I could not see him. I was unable to wonder who he was or what his business was with me; nor did he bother to try to tell me. I could not remember anything linear that had happened on my way into this place, including the rabbit's message. I was fully present to what I was doing.

A bird flew over to me and circled around my neck several times, so close I could have grabbed it. Then it landed on the surface of the water and floated for a while before flying off downstream. Almost immediately, I felt a pull to enter the water, and I knew something was about to happen. As I stepped into the river, I could feel that its bottom was uneven and slippery. Soon, to my surprise, I discovered that I was walking almost on top of the water, which felt warm and agreeable to the touch. The river generated a sensation of delight, and my chilled body soon warmed up to match its temperature.

As I reached the middle of the river I realized that I was walking on something that was like a slightly immersed bridge. As I neared the opposite bank, I looked down and saw my right foot land between two large, staring crocodile eyes. I looked away at once and experienced a strange sinking sensation in my spine. As if it knew I was now aware of it, the crocodile moved downward, bringing the water level close to my knees.

I knew beyond doubt that the strange sensation in my spine was responsible for what had occurred; yet I was not afraid. It was normal that crocodiles would team up to form a bridge for me. I had seen them come to my grandfather's funeral. The crocodile has always had a special relationship with my clan, based upon a long-ago story of mutual cooperation; and after my return from the seminary, a crocodile had come to me at the river outside my village. In the real world crocodiles are neither intelligent nor very attractive. A totem animal, however, takes its association with humans very seriously. There had to be three or four crocodiles of sizable length to cover the entire width of the river.

When I finished crossing the river, I never looked back. I felt a pull to walk downstream following the riverbank and I followed these instructions without hesitation.

Everywhere birds and animals were enjoying the peaceful and serene vibration that nature gave off close to the river. None of them seemed disturbed by my presence, nor was I by theirs, though some would have been quite terrifying to me under other circumstances. There was, for example, a huge python with a hairy head that held itself up from the ground with two short, powerful clawed legs. As I walked close to it, it stood on guard and rolled its red eyes in their sockets.

Some of the creatures I saw that day looked like animals from my world, and some were very strange. After I passed the python, I noticed a woman-fish in the water, swimming downstream parallel to me and going at the same speed. I could tell she was part woman because of her braided hair and the huge pair of breasts that hung heavily below her chin. Farther ahead was a family of large monkeys that sat quietly on the beach, watching me approach. One was holding a child in her lap the same way a human mother would. I walked past them in the same quiet manner as I had walked past the others.

I do not recall how long I walked, nor how much distance I covered, but suddenly I felt as if I were being asked to leave the river and walk into the bush. As usual, I obeyed.

There were scattered trees in the area I was heading toward. The grass was so tall that I could barely see any distance ahead of me as I walked. The most visible thing was the sky, which still retained the same appearance of imminent dawn that it had displayed when I first entered this realm.

I did not wonder where the light came from or why the sun wasn't rising. It seemed normal to me that the underworld could do without direct sunlight and that nature would prosper anyway. I became aware that I was sweating, though I did not feel hot. I decided I must have been walking for a long time. The grass and the trees began to get shorter and shorter, as if I were entering the savanna region of the underworld. All around me were shea trees, just as they appeared in the outside world. I continued my progress unconcerned.

Finally, I saw a tree that distinguished itself from the others by its unusual size. Tall and heavily branched, with large shining leaves, it held night inside its foliage. Under its vast canopy smaller trees of diverse nature were grouped according to species, as if by special design. As I came closer, I noticed that they formed a circle around the big tree as if parading underneath it. I walked straight to the trunk of the large tree, making my way through the smaller ones.

The big tree was elevated on huge branching roots. They reminded any who approached that the tree had the same silhouette below the ground as it had above. I counted six large roots reaching into the ground, and the same number of large branches some fifteen meters above. The trunk of the tree was covered with a gelatinous substance that reminded me of the fluid that covered the boy who had died after returning through the door of light. It never occurred to me to touch it.

Under the roots of the tree was a bluish-violet stone that glowed as I looked at it. It had a very bright center whose light increased and decreased, making the stone seem as if it were breathing. I had never seen its like before. Were it not for its glow and its strange color, I would have taken it as a white firestone. It was small enough to be easily grasped in my hand and I suddenly felt the compulsion to do so.

The roots of the tree seemed to form a shield around the stone. To reach the stone, I had to kneel and lean my body at an almost perpendicular angle to the opening between a pair of roots. As I grasped the stone and brought it out through the opening in the roots, it began to glow fiercely. I felt my body growing colder and colder. The stone felt like an ice cube. It stuck to my hand as if some force were holding it there from inside of me. When I stood up and opened my hand, it would not fall off, but clung there, stinging me.

Against my will I closed my fingers around it. My hand was shaking, and so was my whole body. Just as I could not stop holding the stone, I could not stop looking at it. My eyes began to tear in reaction to the luminosity that was getting far too high for the naked eye. It was like a battle. I wanted to get rid of the stone, and the stone would not let go of me. I tried prying it off my palm with the help of my other hand. It too became stuck.

It was then that I realized that I was on my own to solve this problem, just as I had been when I had first entered this realm and encountered the unbearable noise level. My hand had taken on a violet color as if the irradiation of the stone were infectious. The violet glow spread slowly from my palm to my fingers. It was so powerful that I could clearly see it shining through the back of the hand stuck on top of it. The cold I was experiencing was similar to the cold I had felt earlier, only now it was more ferocious.

The warm tears pouring out of my eyes quickly froze, blurring my vision. First it felt as if I were looking through a glass window that grew fatter and fatter from the inside until I seemed to be looking at the world from the inside of a huge crystal house. In the meantime, the violet infection that had begun in my hand was spreading irremediably. Like a statue, I watched the gradual icing of myself occur from my hands to my arms and outward to the rest of my body. My thoughts and motor abilities; my ability to discriminate, notice, and register; everything that makes a human feel distinct from things and from other humans was gone.

Soon I felt as if I were in the middle of a huge violet egg that had no shell. Inside the egg there was a whole world, and I was in it. Time had ceased to exist, and there was no sense of motion in anything.

In that moment of awareness, I had an epiphany, that the light we encounter on the road of death is our being in the act of coming home to itself. I understood that light is our natural state, but that we human beings must help each other as we move toward the shores of light. We must be born and die many times to reach the light, and ten thousand years can pass in a flash. Being in the light is knowing we must get others into it. The soul that has already attained perfect enlightenment returns to life in compassion to help other souls along their journey.

The light is where we belong. Everyone who is not in the light is looking forward to being there. So we leave the light to go and experience the need for light, and thus come back to it anew.

Then it was as if I were seeing a series of my own past lives, beginning very far back in time. I was in a village, but it was not quite the kind of village I was used to, because there were no mud houses to be seen anywhere. Instead there were invisible dwellings carved inside of nature, or dwellings that nature itself had carved for the living. Many homes were built using living, growing trees. The branches of the trees were still fresh even though the houses had been there for a long time. Other homes sat like birds' nests on branches with fresh leaves growing out of them.

In that village I was a young boy who grew very fast into a man. Everything about our lives was magical. We were a family of dwarfs who played at being giants, and we rode in a chariot through the clouds. It rained abundantly and it felt good to be naked in the rain.

Next, I saw myself as a man in migration with many other men, women, and children. Our magical realm had collapsed. The reason for this collapse was the anger of the gods. Someone had cut down a sacred tree, but we discovered this only after it was too late. At that point, there was nothing we could do but leave. As we walked south, we left behind a civilization in smoke. The pyramids we had built rose defiantly above the smoke of our burnt past. The future we walked toward had no contours. The journey was rough. The wide river we walked along was the only living thing in a lifeless emptiness.

The days came and went and we walked. Images from our magnificent past still flashed painfully in our minds. Our sense of loss was immense. Nothing was magical anymore because everything had become ordinary and without power. To be deprived of one's nature is a terrible loss.

Some of the people I traveled with stopped at the first sign of vegetation and promised to rebuild. Others continued farther south and stopped in the thick of the jungle thinking, "No one will find us here, and our gods will never be harmed." I was one of the latter. We began by raising an altar to a female divinity, and a shrine to our supreme guardian. The green life came back. It was slow and long and sweet. But we could regain nothing of the powers we had before. We prayed to our gods and to the spirits of our priests that had given their lives so that we might live to rebuild, asking them for their intervention in our great desire to remember. We wanted to believe that they could restore these powers to us. The following generation participated in our rituals with little attachment. Although the great numbers of our offspring signaled a divine blessing, the support of the gods was now limited. The heritage of our magical past was no longer available to us.

We could not pierce the primal realm of nature to become part of it as we used to be. We could no longer raise mighty pyramids for our gods. As the original pioneers grew old and joined the light, there was no need for the tribe to linger in nostalgic rituals anymore. And thus it was that, having risen to the highest level of spiritual and cultural achievement, we had to come down once more.

When I returned from the light the next time, I tended domestic beasts and lived most of the time in the forest, where my best friends lived, a group of supernatural beings. They were of a world nearby and could travel into my world even though I could not go into theirs. Because the human world at that time was infested with great unrest and hostility, I soon gave up going back to civilization. I began to live exclusively in the realm of nature, where my magical companions had made a cozy place for me inside a hollow tree.

The supernatural beings who had befriended me showed me many secrets. One of these was a potion that could make you invisible. Another could transform the body into anything you wished. You had only to drink and utter the name of the thing you wanted to be. My friends also instructed me in magical speech.

We communicated together in a language that I did not speak but understood perfectly. And so I lived out my life with the beings in the wild, as a friend to them and a caretaker of my fellow humans who came to see me there when they needed some kind of cure. None of their ailments were serious, and I healed some with decoctions and others with words and/or willpower. After a long existence of dedication to the ills of others, I decided to leave this life, and so I joined the light.

It felt strange and yet very familiar to see myself reborn as a household head, a man who possessed knowledge of caretaking and the mysteries of nature. Our household was large and filled with life. Two important shrines, one dedicated to nature and one dedicated to the ancestors, occupied a central role in my everyday life and responsibilities. There were duties to fulfill in the wild too. I was a hunter, both of medicine and of animals.

I was Sabare, the ancestor that my grandfather had told me about. Roles were well distributed in my household, and the tasks of keeping the family running smoothly were executed in ways that kept us together appreciably well. I had brothers who helped share the responsibilities of the compound, and their competence gradually enabled me to live a great part of my life in the wild, hunting. Then I would go back to my village, give the animal to my strongest brother, and order him to skin it and give the food to the family.

Nature, however, sometimes plays tricks on both humans and animals. Sometimes a spirit will take the shape of an animal to explore the wild at greater leisure. The hunter who mistakes a supernatural animal for a simple one invites serious trouble.

One day I tracked a deer and shot a poisoned arrow at it. To my great astonishment it turned into a bull and charged me. Remembering from my last life how to change my shape, I quickly turned into a bird and flew to the top of a tree that I judged high enough to protect me from the bull. At that moment, however, the bull disappeared and a menacing vulture rushed toward me.

I had just enough time to remember that a porcupine will counter the temper of a vulture, so I flew down and turned into a porcupine. The vulture disappeared and I was immediately enveloped by clouds of smoke that made me cough and sneeze to the point where I had to shift form again. I decided to become a bush in the middle of a wide clearing I had reached. No sooner had I turned into a bush than there was another bush next to me that threatened to invade me. When I moved, it moved closer until finally I gave up.

"Do with me as you wish. I know I should have recognized what you truly were. Whoever you are, I am at your mercy."

Saying this, I resumed my human form and the bush beside me became a very beautiful white lady. She looked like a human, except that her breasts hung from her back instead of her front, and she had three eyes. She was taller than I was and wore a loincloth that entrapped her legs so that she could walk only by tiptoeing.

She took me to her world, which was reached through a hole in a rock on a hill. Even though this home was inside a rock, it was larger than my house and a large family lived in it.

The men were naked and almost half the size of the women, who were dressed in colorful, undifferentiated outfits. The white lady took me to her room, slept with me, and announced that until further notice I was going to be her husband. She taught me strange things. They were all about humans, especially how to get into their dreams. I went home in spirit and entered into my younger brother's dream and confirmed what he had divined about me, that I was not dead but detained by a magical woman whose world was in a rock.

As the years passed, however, my brother grew more and more concerned about what the divination had told him. He began to seriously consider organizing my funeral ritual.

I expressed my concerns to my wife, who said that we must go tell them not to perform the funeral ritual because then I would die for real. I asked her how we could do that. She said, "Don't worry. We will arrive there one evening, me in the form of a white horse, you as yourself. I will stay nearby while you talk to your brothers. Do not drink or eat anything from them. I know this last goes against your customs of hospitality, but you are not to do anything other than tell them not to perform your funeral ritual." And so we went and did as we were supposed to do.

My life was neither sad nor happy. I had three children with my new wife. I could not tell if they were boys or girls. They were simply children. In the world of these beings, women had great powers that men took for granted. The women ran almost everything. I was a special case because I was a man from another world, and I had power too because my wife shared her knowledge with me.

Over the years I returned to my brother several times in his dreams. After his death, when his eldest son took charge of the medicine, it was harder to communicate with the family. The mind of this eldest son was so powerful that he could blot me out of his dreams. Because of this I became more and more focused on my life in the rock.

The men of the world within the rock were so amorphous that I never connected with any of them as friends. I wanted so much to be a part of the dynamics of the women's life that I felt rejected when I was not invited to any of their great events.

One night there was a meeting of the medicine women going on at the same time as the women warriors' vigil. I knew my wife was at the healer's ceremony that night, so I sneaked in to try and see what role she was playing. By mistake I stumbled into the meeting of the female warriors and got caught by one of their guards. Because I was a man, I was sentenced to death. I was going to be hurled into what they called the chasm of oblivion.

My wife was distressed by the situation but did not have enough power to repeal the decision. I lived alone in confinement awaiting my execution. The day came, and I was taken to the edge of a cliff. The crowd was big, most of it composed of women warriors. My wife came to me and whispered in my ear that I was going to be returned to my human family as a child of my own grandson.

My children were also present at the execution. There was some kind of coldness between us. They did not cry, and I did not cry. It did not matter. Nor did the prophecy uttered by my wife impress me very much since I was waiting for my death.

As a last message she told me that because of what I had learned, and because of my hunting habits, I was not going to have a quiet life at home. "Once you have belonged here, you can never belong anywhere else," she added sternly.

Someone pushed me violently from behind and down I went. The downward motion was very familiar. It reminded me of my fall through the light hole into another world. The difference was that in this case I fell into a big pool of liquid and was held floating inside it like a fish. I did not stay there long, however. I remember an event right before my birth that frightened me. There was a loud noise and the voice of someone asking me who I was. I kept telling the person, but he kept asking the same question over and over again. Then the voice demanded that I state my purpose, and

I told him the story of my life in the world in a rock, including my execution day when I was hurled down a cliff.

All of a sudden I was drawn toward a very large black hole. I rolled and rolled, trying to resist its horrifying magnetic pull, but I was like a leaf detached from its branch and hurled around by the wind of a storm. As I entered the darkness, I felt an immense asphyxia that was going to kill me if I did not scream. So I screamed.

CHAPTER 25

RETURNING FROM THE UNDERWORLD

The sensation inside the black hole seemed overwhelming. I was sucked inward by a magnetism that seemed particularly designed for my body. Feeling compressed, I screamed in order to survive. The scream produced a chain of echoes around that made me feel as if I were being welcomed somewhere. Suddenly, everything came to a standstill. All around me was a deep silence.

It was then that I realized I was standing back under the enormous tree, still holding the stone in my hands. It was still glowing, but it was not sticking to my hands anymore. I no longer felt cold either. I could remember the entire experience I had just lived through, but it bore the aftertaste of a fantastic dream. Actually, I felt more like myself than I had ever felt before. My ability to think and wonder about things had been restored to me. I could question what was going on around me again without feeling pain.

For the first time I could wonder if all this had really happened. It was wonderful to have my mind restored to me—an inquisitive mind that wanted to know everything ahead of time, a turbulent mind quick at getting confused the minute something looked suspicious, a restless mind that chose to set itself into a useless hyperactive mode at the slightest unusual thing. Presently, this mind informed me that I needed to get organized very fast. First I needed to know my whereabouts. I wanted to leave very urgently. Something in me willed it. Now that my experience was ended, I was eager to get out of this realm. One thing I understood immediately after my mind was restored to me was the death sentence and my fall into the black hole. There is a saying in the village that with death, one world grieves a loss while another celebrates a birth. Could this be what reincarnation is about?

I walked away from the tree to a place where I could see the horizon and looked around. In the direction I thought I had come from, everything was hidden behind a thick jungle. Farther north, I saw some mountains that appeared familiar, but were nowhere near a day's walk. The need to return to the initiation camp grew stronger and stronger in me until finally all I could do was to circle around and around in search of a solution. The thought of retracing my steps was not appealing, especially when it included the part about crossing the river on the backs of crocodiles. Besides, I had lost track of the hole where I had exited from the mountain. I continued circling around the tree, making wider and wider orbits.

Suddenly, out of nowhere, I saw a girl, a real village daughter, as my people would call her. She was carrying a clay pot containing water. Most of her naked body was wet with the water that had splashed out of the pot as she walked. She was heavily beaded up around her waist; strand after strand of colorful beads typical of what young village girls wear. This signaled that she was nearing puberty. For a while I felt an immense relief at finding her. There was no doubt that she knew where she was going and must have some reasonable knowledge of this region. I did not have to call out to her since we practically walked into each other.

She stopped, looked me over swiftly in the typical village way, then kept her face lowered and her eyes on the ground. I was so happy to see another human being in this realm, especially after what had happened to me, that I almost hugged her. Though I had wanted to inquire about this region and her business in it, I instead found myself asking her for directions. She looked around at the four directions, one after the other, and said pointing west, "You see these mountains over there?" There was a line of three mountains. One looked like an elderly woman, the other like a dog, and the last one like a formless mass.

"Yes."

"Go to the dog mountain, the one in the middle, and cross to the other side of it. There is a cave there. That is your way home." Saying this, she walked away. I watched her, stunned, till she disappeared behind a grove. The trees hid her.

I began to sort things out in my mind, trying to make the new experiences in my brain agree with one another, when I felt a profound sense of urgency. It felt like a sudden, unspecified sense of danger. I began to rush toward the dog mountain. Everything else around me—landscape, trees, rivers, hills—faded out. The dog mountain appeared on my visual horizon like a picture. By the time I reached it, I did not even know how much distance I had covered.

From then on everything was done in a rush. I found the cave the girl had told me about and ran in. It became dark as soon as I reached its interior. I reproached myself for not having taken the time to make a torch, but I wasn't very hard on myself. As I walked farther into the cave, I noticed that it did not get any darker. Then I realized it must be nighttime in the world I was going back to because I could see some stars twinkling ahead of me. Their light was unmistakable. I walked toward them, but suddenly stopped and realized that I couldn't be seeing stars. I was still inside the cave. Looking up, I found out that I was indeed inside the cave, but near the exit. I could see the stony ceiling there two or three feet above me. I had crossed back through the mountain almost instantaneously, without even having to crawl this time. How had all this happened? Looking behind me, I realized that this cave was like any other cave, as black as the black hole of my dream, with no suggestion of a light existing on the other side of it. There was no suggestion of the place on the other side of it where I had come in.

Meanwhile, the night in our world was nearing its end. I could see the shepherd star high up in the sky, brightest among the bright stars, and I thought, *The animals from the underworld must have come back from their nightly errand. I wish I had met that rabbit for one last time.*

Something bit me inside my hand. I looked. It was the blue stone, my only proof that what had happened had been real. As I looked at it this time, it remained undifferentiated. Only its otherworldly color defied the obscurity of the night. It never glowed again. I closed my hand around it. I had nothing to put it in, but the direct contact with it was extremely valuable to me. I needed it. I prepared myself for the long trip back down the mountain, jumping from stone to stone. Then I realized there were no stones anywhere near the size I had walked on before. I looked again very hard. Where was I?

When I turned around to check the cave behind me, I realized it was not the egg-shaped cave I had first entered. I looked at the shepherd star again. No doubt about it, I was east of the camp, but how could that have happened? I had exited the mountain over fifteen kilometers from the place where I had entered.

I began walking west toward the camp. The ground was covered with tiny gravel and sparse grass, ideal for walking with bare feet. I rushed down to the valley and began trekking at a regular pace while I reviewed the events that had just happened.

My entry into the underworld was too painful to dwell upon. I had no way of comprehending what caused these inner noises that had tortured me so. The cold itself was also incomprehensible. The girl who had told me how to get out of the cave intrigued me the most. It was not her presence there that fascinated me, but her timely appearance just when I needed some direction. Her manners and her look were so ordinary after all the exotic things that I had experienced that she made me feel at home instantly. Why a girl rather than a boy? Without her, I would have still been in the underworld, looking for the exit. I felt as if I owed it to her to try to complete my journey before sunrise. If I could do that, I would probably be the only one to finish before the deadline. I took pleasure at the thought of being the first to arrive at the camp, feeling exceptional and proud of having gone through it all.

Nonetheless, I could not stop thinking that I should have stayed with the girl a little while longer to get to know her. A village girl would never ask questions of a man—it went against our customs. Instead, it had been my responsibility to inquire about things. I should have asked what she was doing in the region and where she was heading rather than ask for simple directions. I could have obtained valuable information about the underworld from her, especially about where people lived there. What was I going to tell the elders, that all I had brought them was a stone? What if they told me it had been my last opportunity for knowledge and that I had let it go?

It had all happened so suddenly, and I had been confused about finding a way out of the place . . . and where had the immense sense of urgency come from? I began making excuses for myself.

I continued trying to make sense of my experiences. When I thought about the crocodiles who had made a living bridge for me across the river, the recollection was neither frightening nor painful. I even wondered if the rabbit's father had arranged for the crocodiles to give me a lift across the river. I also could not help thinking that if the crocodiles had made a bridge across the river when we were first heading for the mountains as a group, it might have saved a life. The unfortunate boy who had died so horribly, attacked by the underwater creatures, might have survived.

Initiation is an extremely individualistic, self-centered activity. The camaraderie you feel with the elders and the other boys may try to hide that, but ultimately no one will save you if you fail to remember what you need to survive. No friend will do for you what you are supposed to do for yourself in order to further your own process. We, as a group, do not constitute a "village" where people support one another spontaneously. Our purpose is not to save one another if the need arises, but to learn.

The real society is the one we left behind. Those who survive the ordeal of initiation will have the privilege of being reintegrated into it as real people. The community is a body in which every individual is a cell. No harmful or inappropriate cell is allowed to remain in the body. One way or the other, it will be ejected. One must learn how to function as a healthy cell in order to earn the privilege of staying in the body and keeping it alive.

Just as we came in this world alone, so we remember alone. The elders who facilitate our act of remembering do not mind what we remember as long as we do exactly what we are supposed to do, according to our true nature. So it seems that, after all, at the deepest level the Dagara are an incurably private people. The sharing of our knowledge stops at the doors of the esoteric. During the rituals of initiation or daily life, the presence of the other is symbolic. What I know may be dangerous for you to know and vice versa.

Furthermore, to try to learn what the other knows is to distract oneself from really acting upon one's own memory. Our memory is not something static that we petrify and store in the inner museum of our being. We already have everything we need for life inside of us. If we do not act upon these memories, we fail to live in this transient world. Some live in order to remember and others live because they do remember. I began to realize that everything I had experienced in my month of initiation was about learning how to recall what I already knew.

The careful reader may be asking him- or herself right now why I say I have been in the bush for a month when I have only described six or seven days and nights. I have had to trick the reader in this way in order to provide a sense of continuity to my narrative. This trick was necessary because without areas of silence, I would not have been able to tell you about my initiation experience at all. What I have shared with you here is very potent and special information. Before I sat down to write this book, I first had to get permission from my council of elders. The episodes I have been able to present in this book are the ones Guisso thought I could speak about. There are others that I am not at liberty to ever write about. They constitute the bulk of the initiatory experience and its most secret parts.

As I walked toward the camp, my mind came back to me fully. I was now able to fit things into their right perspective, one that made all the violence I had seen, all the hallucinations and interactions with the magic of the natural world make sense. All of a sudden the conflicts that had roared in me had ceased to exist thanks to the powerful intervention of initiation. The emptiness that had filled me when I had joined the group over thirty days ago, and the suffering I had undergone to achieve true arrival, now seemed justified.

I was full. I felt content, oriented, and unconcerned. I was home. Yet I did not know what exactly permitted me to feel the way I felt. The hardships of initiation did not flow along an even gradient of learning like the education I had been accustomed to at the seminary. At the outset, initiation had appeared like a set of weird, unconnected events; but their result was a state of surrender, and, much later, contentment. At the seminary I had grown away from myself into a mold that tried to make me into someone I wasn't, while all the while I craved for myself. As long as we are not ourselves, we will try to be what other people are. If these people are also not themselves, the result is terrible. During the Dagara initiation process, I grew into myself. The problems I had became resolved as I entered into my own true nature.

When I finally reached the initiation quarter, the night was nearly over and the eastern sky was brightening. Without a word, I handed the stone to the first elder I saw and waited for instructions. The old man looked at it very carefully and nodded with satisfaction as he passed it on to another elder who examined it in the same manner before passing it along. I waited till they had all looked at the magic stone. Then the elder to whom I had first given the stone got up, walked a little apart from the circle, and beckoned to me.

I remembered the girl in the underworld whom I had failed to speak with longer. Apprehensive and anxious, I realized that I needed to confess my "failure" to the elder then and there to escape from this strange feeling. I joined the elder and we walked in silence for a while till he sat down on the grass. I imitated him. We remained that way for a while in silence until he spoke.

"Look at me," he said.

I looked at him. He was emaciated and his painted face did not seem to have any individual characteristics about it. For me, the elders were archetypal. They were symbols or conduits, not necessarily humans. Why should I try to change that? I was a little embarrassed to be looking so boldly into the face of an elder. This is not something one does unless directly ordered to. I had learned that quickly after my return from the seminary.

"What do you see?" the old man inquired.

I wondered what he meant. I did not know him personally, so I could not see anything other than a man in him.

"Look hard," he insisted. He moved his face closer to mine. I was a bit frightened by the dark holes of his eyes, which contrasted so greatly with the extreme whiteness of his painted face. I saw nothing in those eyes, even though I could sense that he was tense with excitement. As if unable to hold back any longer, he said, "I am Guisso—the same Guisso who first worked on you when you returned from the white man's initiation place, the one you and your father have been consulting ever since. Don't you remember? It was only last rainy season. Don't you recognize me?"

I remembered the man whose house my father and I had visited early one morning, to find him sitting at the edge of his zangala. Then he had said that my case was the fulfillment of his career—that he had been waiting for me for two years. I remembered that a few weeks later he had prepared medicine for us and then tested it out later when we were on the way home by showing himself to us as a white bull standing on its hind legs in the middle of the night. Then it had been a dream, but now I understood it. The white bull is the symbol of prosperity and life. It is what suitors give as dowries when they come seeking their brides. The image of the white bull came to memory, and the white cow on the hill, and the man who had held me by the hand as we walked toward the rest of the people after my experience under the water. It all made sense.

"It's me," he said again with satisfaction. "I knew you did not recognize me. You could not, and it was good that you didn't. I am very pleased with your success in this last mission. You are now one of us. I am happy for you. Are you glad to know the way of your ancestors?"

"Yes," I replied mechanically. I did not know whether I knew the way of my ancestors yet, but it felt wonderful to be sitting next to a delighted elder. Guisso's heart was fatherly, loving, and satisfied. He had revealed his identity to me because now there was no more danger. The intensity of his joy showed me how much he had been looking forward to the day when he could see me come home. He had watched out for me secretly all along without my having an inkling of his support.

I was so touched by his poise and wisdom that all I wanted to do was sit beside him in silence. Guisso, however, wanted to talk.

"It's all over now. We will be going home soon. There will be no further missions or exercises. You are now a man, that is, you are your own mission. Do not be worried anymore. The last mission was the most dangerous and you made it. I am happy."

"We lost someone on the way to the mountains," I ventured.

"We know. Someone always gets lost. There are four who will never go home. You are not one of them, yet if there was someone best fitted to being overcome by this experience it was you. But you do have real hunter's blood underneath your skin, after all."

"Who is that girl I met in the underworld?" I asked.

Guisso's eyes narrowed and he frowned. "You met a girl in the underworld? Oh! That could have something to do with what happened to you when you found the stone. See, that's your experience. I don't know why it had to be a girl. A long time ago, when I was going through this, I also went to the underworld. A snake showed me the way out. No one knows what is going to happen before you get there. I am glad you saw a real person, even though it must have been a transformation. It does not matter now, as long as you are here. You do not need to understand everything right away. You can't. You have the rest of your life to figure out the meaning of what really went on during the six weeks you spent here. So don't be in any hurry. Be happy you did not stay behind."

Our conversation was not running in the direction I had wished. My mind was boiling with images that needed to be fitted into one another, but Guisso seemed only to want to get reacquainted before we returned to the village. So I resumed the posture of the listener who does not ask questions.

When he saw this, he said, "I see you need to rest. You will need to be ready when packing time comes. And since you have nothing to do between now and then, why don't you take it easy? I'll get going with my business too, and we will meet again many times before I die."

Saying this, he got up and walked away before I could utter another word.

At the sleeping quarter I found Nyangoli snoring. I lay down quietly to avoid waking him. The sun had not quite risen and there were no more stars to be seen in the brightly lit sky. I slept. When I woke up, Nyangoli was sitting next to me. The heat of the sun must have wakened me, for I was sweating profusely. Nyangoli asked if I was hungry and we went into the bush in search of something to eat.

That afternoon was quiet. For the first time since we had arrived at the camp, we had some real free time. No commands came from anyone, not even the order to have free time. We used it in silence. Overwhelmed by our last mission, we communicated with one another silently, as if sound were prohibited. People walked at random around the camp, alone or in groups, hands crossed behind their backs as if they were meditating on what had just happened.

The elders, on the other hand, seemed busy. By the end of the afternoon they had sacrificed some fowl and a black goat to the nature shrine, a dog to the spirits of the underworld, and a black goat to the ancestors. No one knew where these domestic animals came from or who delivered them to the council.

We were going home the following day, but we were leaving without some of our number. Those who had been absorbed had to be honored, and this is what the elders were doing. We could not participate in these ceremonies because we were still too "open." A newly initiated person is as vulnerable as a sick person who has passed the most critical stage of his or her illness and is now convalescing. No one had to tell us not to participate in the funeral ritual of the departed ones. We knew.

That night we did nothing. As if humbled by all the intense days, we went to sleep very early. As I lay there watching the crescent moon, I thought to myself, *What if I had gone to the moon last night?* The Earth has so many vortex points through which one can reach almost anywhere. Far beyond the moon, the stars twinkled rhythmically, dancing to unheard cosmic music. I neither admired this perfect harmony, nor felt detached from it. Somehow I could just be and let be. The sound of a snoring sleeper knocked at the doors of my ears and my thoughts followed it backward to its source.

A man asleep is like a child in nature's lap. It does not take trust to reach this level of abandonment, only the craving. Yesterday a boy, today a man, but still the same person. It is too hard to be a man, yet I wanted to live my life. So I went to sleep.

CHAPTER 26

HOMECOMING AND
CELEBRATION

 As the initiates walked in single file toward the village, it was easy to envision the kind of homecoming waiting for us there. The trees, the grass, the stones, and the village itself all seemed a part of it. I felt both a sense of closure and the turmoil of a new beginning. The feeling of completion was real because I had not died. The other initiates also radiated a sense of peace and completion. We were at the ending of boyhood, coming home to begin new lives as men.

The elders arrived first at the boundary between village and forest. From a few hundred meters away we would hear fragments of the ritual of return passing between them and the authorities of the village. That was the elders' final official action. When the ritual words had been spoken, they surrendered us to an exhilarated community, overwhelmed, just as we were, by our return.

We all felt as if we had been to the end of the world and back. None of us could respond adequately to such an exhibition of joy. We knew we were the cause of it, but somehow we had lost the stamina to celebrate our victory.

Someone fired a gun as a welcoming salute. The noise shocked my ears in the same way they had been shocked by the screaming sounds in the underworld. They jerked and became quiet. Meanwhile the crowd, as if stirred to greater jubilation by the gunshot, became hysterical, rushing at us as if we were manna dropped by God into the middle of the village. Mothers collided with their sons—now become men—in a concert of emotional jabbering, while sisters wept quietly nearby. My mother came to me and held my arms in hers for a while, her moist gaze locked on to mine. The moment was infinite in every respect. I no longer felt any anger toward her. In her eyes I saw a great depth of love from a heart that knew nothing else, yet I did not have the energy to reciprocate. I could only acknowledge her love.

Sometimes silence speaks better than words. My sister Zanta stood by, devoutly observing what went on between my mother and me. Farther away, Father stood surrounded by the rest of the family, who waited in calm communion. As Mother released me, Zanta stepped forward and shook hands with me, wishing me good homecoming in French. That drew a smile from me. Then we went over to join my father, my four brothers, and the rest of the family. My father did not speak to me yet, but we exchanged a silent glance as we headed home.

Even the house looked different. An annex had been erected next to Father's quarter. Painted white with a mixture of cow dung and ash, it was elegant and inviting. I was overjoyed to see it because I understood what it symbolized. Every house to which a boy was returning from initiation had an extension or a special quarter painted white, the color of hospitality. Nothing else in the compound had changed, but the structure of the inner yard with the doors opening into individual rooms seemed especially inviting now because the design included me.

The door to my room was also white. My father opened it and beckoned for me to enter. The room was cool and dark. Its single tiny window, facing east, let in little light. The cow dung that served as a finish for the walls exhaled a strong smell, but I got used to it quickly. I walked to the mud bed that was built almost against the wall. It was covered with a straw mat and a blanket. I felt as if I wanted to lie down, but my sister pointed to the stool near the bed. I remembered that I was not supposed to touch anything modern until after the customary bath, so I sat and rested on the mud stool, which felt cool against my naked body. It too was built against the wall.

Mother brought the customary welcoming refreshment, millet cake and tamarind juice mixed into water. I drank it straight down while the family looked on. It tasted good. It was then that my father spoke for the first time. He recited some welcoming words in an unemotional voice and wished me well. I did not know how to respond, so I remained silent. My sister then announced that a bucket of bathwater had been put in the washroom for me and that more would be available as the need arose.

I walked out into the sunlight, which hit me as if I had been in the dark for days. The washroom, open to the sky, felt like a beach except that the water was in a clay pot. Fetched by women from the nearby river, the water had been warmed up in the kitchen. There was a cake of local soap nearby, made from mixing potassium or ash juice with indigenous oil. It was round and gray and smelled like ammonia.

My washcloth was made from the pounded root of a tree. It smelled aromatic. The contact with the warm water revitalized me. As I filled up the calabash that floated in the clay jug and poured its content over my body, I could not help thinking of how difficult it was to become a man in a traditional setting. It had taken six weeks of perilous adventures to bring me to the point where I could ritually wash away the impurities of my previous state. After that I would be able to touch the soft cloth of my mud bed.

I thought about those who had never made it back home. Knowing that their sons were lost between the worlds, what were their families doing at this moment? I had not had time to notice if anyone looked sorrowful at the welcoming place, but now I wondered about the bereaved families. What were they feeling at this moment of general celebration? True, the villagers had seen more men coming home than it had lost, but the universal joy was overshadowed by a mystery more profound than the honoring of our newfound manhood. I shook my head partly to get the water out of my hair, since there was no towel, but also to shake these heavy thoughts out of my mind.

Still wet, I returned to my room where my father was waiting for me, holding my first traditional suit. We began a dressing ritual. The suit had three components. The first was a pair of bulky pants called a short. They looked like an oval barrel with two brief extensions at the bottom for the legs to exit from. The top of the short was wide enough to fit three additional people. To make it fit just one, there was a rope sewn inside the cotton fabric of the waistband. When pulled, the rope gathered the pants into a good fit. The fabric of the legs was decorated with family medicine designs.

The main part of the suit was an oversized boubou. Its sleeves were long enough to cover my arms. On the front and back of this suit were images from the underworld, the family earth shrine, the nature shrine, and the ancestral shrine. A bird, the symbolic messenger of nature, sat on top of the nature shrine and looked out over the panorama of the underworld. A chameleon, symbol of adaptability and compatibility, stood beside the ancestral shrine, and several hieroglyphics symbolized the family medicine gathered over centuries.

The final component of this ensemble was a hat, much simpler in design. It resembled a crown. The seven cones at the top represented the seven secrets of the medicine of our clan. The image of the chameleon was embroidered on either side. A star, symbol of leadership, was embroidered on the front.

My father took the pants, held them stretched out in his hands, and murmured prayers. First he faced north: "This suit will be worn in conformity with the way of our elders whose bodies have returned to nature and whole spirits watch over us day and night. This suit will be a living shrine for the medicine of our clan, the Birifor, and a tribute to the medicine of Bakhye that I inherited and that also belongs to his grandson.

"This suit will be a tribute to the continuity of our ways and will shine forth truth wherever it goes and whenever it is on this man's body."

Then he faced the sun, lifted the suit upward three times, and gave it to me to put on. I introduced my leg into the immense pants, searching for the tiny exits intended for my feet. It took some struggling to get the thing to hang around my waist, and the contact of the cotton against my skin felt soft and strange. In six weeks I had learned to live without clothes. I would need time to get used to them again. The boubou was easy to put on: my body disappeared into it like a vessel caught in the clouds.

With the hat on, I felt like an elder. Over fifteen years ago I had seen them in this very kind of outfit for the first time. Now it was my turn. My father backed away, took a long look at me, and exhaled an "*oon*" of satisfaction. With that, he invited me to come out into the compound yard. My movements were as noisy as if I were a huge bird taking flight. In the yard, I felt as if I were on stage. Everyone in the house came out to take a look.

My mother could not seem to get enough of me. She kept walking around and around me until I felt dizzy. We were supposed to go to the village circle for a dance ceremony, the last one before the feast. Everyone got dressed and, surrounded by my loved ones, I left the house.

A crowd was already there. The xylophone played tunes that were strange to me but not to the others, who were singing along. As soon as we arrived, Father led me to a house where the other initiates were waiting for our official appearance in our gala outfits. Our clothing had changed us so much it was hard to tell who was who. We said nothing. Only the music of the xylophone outside reached our ears, and even its voice did not last very long.

Suddenly the silence was broken by another gunshot. The sound of the xylophone began again, accompanied by a drum that roared out rhythms as if it were angry at something. The music as the xylophone was familiar. It was the song of return:

> *I had a date in the bush*
> *With all the gods,*
> *So I went.*

I had a date in the bush
With all the trees,
So I went.
I had a date in the mountain
with the Kontomblé.
I went because I had to go.

I had to go away to learn
How to know.
I had to go away to learn
How to grow.
I had to go away to learn
How to stay here.

So I went and knocked at doors
Locked in front of me.
I craved to enter.
Oh, little did I know
The doors did not lead outside.

It was all in me.
I was the room and the door.
It was all in me.
I just had to remember.

And I learned that I lived
Always and everywhere.
I learned that I knew everything,
Only I had forgotten.
I learned that I grew
Only I had overlooked things.
Now I am back, remembering.

I want to be what I know I am,
And take the road we always
Forget to take.
Because I heard the smell
Of the things forgotten
*And my belly was touched.**

*In Dagara you "hear" smell, you don't smell something. That which is picked up by the olfactory sense is sound being heard in that way. The same thing applies to the tactile. But you can both hear and see taste.

That's why I had a date with the bush.
That's why I had a date with the hill.
That's why I had a date with the world
Under.
Now, Father, I'll take you home.
I am back.

The villagers sang along with the xylophone while the drum pounded the rhythm with frenetic joy. The coach came into the room where we were waiting. He was carrying a beat marker and a pair of small cymbals, one attached to his thumb and the other to his middle finger. He marked the beat by hitting the cymbals against each other. He also had a whistle that he blew continually as if to alert us to something. We lined behind him by the exit.

He blew the whistle even harder, then leaped out, dancing. He danced around in a circle, then faced the doorway, where we waited. We moved out rhythmically, in single file, and followed him toward the dancing circle. The crowd cheered as two gunshots blasted the atmosphere. We arrived at the xylophone and circled it. I did not know the dance steps very well, but I kept an eye on the coach, who with the help of his whistle told us when to turn, when to stop, and when to move.

As we circled the xylophone and the drum, walking in tune with them, a power surged up from the depth of my belly, climbed the steps of my spine, and invaded my heart, making it throb frantically. When this power reached my eyes, they filled with tears of joy. I thought: *What a commencement exercise this is!* How was it possible that I was here while others, who had seemed better prepared, were not? How had I survived the ordeal? I could hardly believe I was a participant in a traditional festivity in which no one saw me as an outsider.

The memory of fifteen years of brainwashing in the seminary, an institution that claimed the supremacy of knowledge, stood timidly in a corner of my mind, as if afraid of competing with what I now knew. I thought to myself that a person who lives in denial of who he really is must have a hard time living, because he would have to invent meaning and purpose from the ground up. No one can tell us who we are or how we must live. That knowledge can be found only within. To deny our true nature can only cause us tremendous pain.

The sun was about to set. Its fading light gently illuminated the cloud of dust surrounding our celebration. The crowd had become ecstatic. Hands were clapping all around us, as if we were performing something magical. I did not know if I was dancing or just walking along, lost in the dream world. I felt the touch of the cotton fabric of my clothes each time I took a step forward or backward. The rest of the time the cloth merely hid me. It felt good to be concealed—I was happily invisible.

The dance was entering its third cycle. The circle of over sixty dancing initiates looked like a huge precious ring presented as a gift to the villagers. I could clearly see what happiness means. It poured out of every face like a flow of pearls given to a bride. The people were not just singing along and watching us dance. They were also participating. The coach, the leader of the ceremony, could barely be seen in the middle of the thick clouds of red dust stirred up by hundreds of bare feet pounding on the dry soil. His whistle was getting fainter, but he still used it as his voice, signaling to us what steps to execute next.

He blew his whistle and we jumped and spun in a circle, transforming our clothing into immense outstretched umbrellas under which one could see our tiny bodies flashing in rhythmical ambulation. In perfect synchronization, everyone went right, then left, then center. Then, in an ultimate move, the entire circle sat. Xylophone players, singers, clappers, whistlers—everybody stopped simultaneously. There was a profound silence. Then everyone woke from the trance, and our circle broke into a single line that went back into the house it had exited from. The initiation dance was over.

But for the villagers, the feast had barely begun. The music now played only for them and they danced to it tirelessly. We initiates were no longer obligated to do anything. Packed next to each other like migratory birds in the small medicine room, we held hands and held our breath for a moment in acknowledgment of the ancestral shrine. Then we lifted our hands gradually and emitted a sound of release that broke into a roar as our hands reached skyward.

This time we did not exit the room in formation. Some of us joined the dancing; others, like me, headed home with their families. The day was over, and it had been a full one. I had come back home as a member of my village. I felt immensely pleased, but I could not find an effective way of expressing this to my loved ones. Perhaps I was too tired or my feelings were too great for words, or perhaps they just needed silence. Whatever the reason, I honored it. Walking home from the village circle, I felt as if the vault of the sky were watching over my every step while my family, elated by my return, served as a shield that surrounded me as if I were a precious and endangered species to be saved at all cost.

At home, a crowd that had not made it to the dancing ground was waiting, drinking millet beer. I noticed Guisso seated at my father's door, along with the other councilmen of the village: Fiensu, Kyéré, Dapla, Daziè, and Gourzin. They too had skipped the dance ceremony.

My father was among them. I remembered seeing him at the beginning of the initiation dance but not afterward. As I walked in, Guisso motioned for me to come and join them. I picked a stool and sat. He was smiling, his face luminescent with joy, but the others looked grave. They wore the kind of face that councilmen put on when they are busy cooking up deep things to say.

Fiensu finally spoke. "They say that wisdom comes with age and re-membering. They say it comes with a sharp eye. But I did not see what was hidden in you, Malidoma."

I was not sure what he meant, so I did not respond. Guisso urged Fiensu to be more explicit. He and the other elders knew what he was going to tell me, but it was obvious that Fiensu was not very enthusiastic about having to say it.

They argued among themselves for a while. Then, as if convinced that he owed me an apology, Fiensu continued. "When you first came from the white man's country, you caused the council a lot of talking. Because you knew what the white man knows, I thought you were a danger to our way of life. We all know that wherever the white man goes, he is the predator and everybody else his potential victim. So when the others thought you should be initiated, I opposed the idea. I had a good reason: you can bring words from out of your mind and put them on paper for all to see. How can a dog-thought and a cat-thought—two contradictory ideas—live to-gether in the same person?

"But today as I look at you, you are part of us and also part of them. That's what baffles me. For how can you be part of them and part of us at the same time? When I opposed your initiation, it was because I wanted you to live. I never thought you would make it. But here you are, all flesh and blood. I owe a chicken and a goat to the nature shrine."

Kyéré laughed with contentment, spat out some kola nut, then cleared his throat and spoke. "Thank you, Fiensu, for saying this in front of this young man and all of us. Today I can say that he is a little better than us because he knows more than all of us here. Who else in this whole village is the kind of person he is now?"

He grabbed an empty calabash and offered it to Fiensu, who sat in front of a large calabash full of millet beer. "Cut me a drink," he said. "This thing will always be remembered as the impossible denied impos-sibility. We don't want to burden this child with our talk now. This day is his day to celebrate as he wishes. Let him go. We can talk to him later."

He drained his beer in a gulp and poured the dregs away. They made an explosive sound upon contact with the ground. Satisfied, he emitted a loud burp, grabbed his walking stick, and slowly stood up.

Fiensu, however, had more to say. "You can't believe that I was *all* wrong. You wanted the boy initiated because you thought that our educa-tion was going to clean him up from the white man's education. I wanted him out of initiation to save him from death. Today you're making me into the bad guy because he survived. Have you checked to see how he feels about being in the middle of two worlds? You can't because you're not in his skin. Even the Kontomblé can't because their reasoning is not capable of doing justice to this issue. I can only imagine how strange it must feel to not really belong because of what you know. Guisso, when you looked into his initiation at the white man's school, what did you find? Tell him. I told him what I knew about him before he went to the initiation camp. You too must tell him what you know."

Fiensu was getting excited now. Guisso seemed annoyed. "We're not here to make confessions to this young man, but to tell him how pleased we are with him. Let's not turn our original intent into a disquieting babble. If I did not know what I know about his learning at the white man's school, I myself would have objected to his initiation because the whole process is about remembering. You can remember things you know, but you can't unknow things you remember. The Kontomblé told me the boy was an apprentice feeding on the white man's knowledge. That's why he could be initiated. Are you happy now that you got me to say these things in front of him?" The information that Guisso had was not troubling, but it was Guisso's habit as a mentor not to be talkative about me. A mentor does not talk about his student with other people. Guisso knew that the context here was exceptional, but still he felt uncomfortable.

"You bet I am. Do you think that I'll let myself be turned into an evil now that the boy can sit with us and talk to us directly? He is as much my son as he is yours. Now let's celebrate because today is his day."

Part of me felt amused as I listened to these elders while another part struggled to stay calm. The part that wanted to stay calm was fighting the urge to say something nasty to Fiensu. I wanted to tell him that I could never be his son, but I did not succumb to this urge. Instead, I tried to show discipline by avoiding open conflict, and I did not really have to go out of my way to do that. I was a different person now than I had been, and it was easy to stay silent.

My silence seemed to have spoken louder than words, for Fiensu looked at me, baffled. Kyéré nodded, the kind of nodding that acknowledges the proximity of wisdom. I overheard Daziè say something to Gourzin to the effect that it takes the special knowledge I possessed to maintain this quiet on a day like this.

It was already getting dark outside. Guisso seemed to want to carry on his discussion with Fiensu about remembering and learning how to know. Kyéré, who had suspended his leavetaking when Fiensu began to speak, now decided to complete it. "I must go home. Everybody is out celebrating and the whole house is a ghost house now. Someone must always stay at home to make it a place for the living."

No one tried to stop him. He did not have to explain why he had to go. Wasn't he the chief of the earth shrine? This was the first time he had come to my father's house since the funeral of my grandfather. The chief seldom goes anywhere; everybody comes to him. So coming to my father's home was a high honor. It was also an honor that almost all the members of the village council were here at the same time.

The only one missing was Bofing, whose rheumatism had knocked the function out of his legs. My father was beatific. He could not hide his joy at seeing what was happening in his own house. He tried to stop the chief from going home so soon, saying that the thanksgiving meal was yet to come, but the chief replied that he had come to see me, and having done so, he had no interest in anything else.

Feeling a little awkward in the midst of so many personalities, I decided I would go to my room, get comfortable, and enjoy a little privacy. I had never had a room before. I changed and put on my old seminary clothing, which resembles Boy Scout attire but is white. It felt very tight, but it was bearable. After a month and a half of living naked, I could no longer tell what was fashionable or appropriate. My brothers came in and we poured some drinks. The quiet of our sharing contrasted with the sounds of revelry reaching us from outside. The drinking had opened up people's throats and they began to sing. It was the sound of homecoming, the kind that tells you that you are linked to people who care. I liked what I heard, a melody never experienced before, so peaceful it produced within me a joy beyond definition. I understood that what makes a village a village is the underlying presence of the unfathomable joy of being connected to everyone and everything.

EPILOGUE:
THE FEARFUL RETURN

"I am coming to get your son's help to speak to my son who lives in the wilderness."

I recognized Fiensu from his voice. When he was brought into my quarter by my father, I was not in the least ready to talk with him. I had not forgotten. But Fiensu was a tough, persistent man who plainly shared the tribal belief in natural inequality based on each man and woman's connection with secret medicine. As the saying goes, *Sata sa gnata*—Difference is better than resemblance. The wisdom of village life celebrates difference—not material inequality but variations of depth in people's relationship with the otherworld. They see this difference as an opportunity for people in the tribe to benefit from each other's knowledge and to demonstrate their ability to share. Known in the village as one of those who had through intensive research tapped into the secrets of lobie, Fiensu had won respect and status as an elder, accorded him not just because he knew the workings of these lobie, but because he never used their power against anyone.

Fiensu's aggressiveness stemmed from the fact that he was probably the youngest councilman in village history. He was only in his early fifties, and he felt that he had to constantly prove himself. He was, I came to understand, an outstanding example of a man who had made it to the top. In a culture where what you become is often the result of who and what your family is, Councilman Fiensu was the traditional version of the man from the slum become famous. When he was growing up, his family was in ruins, partly because of bad leadership and partly because not one young male returned alive from initiation. How Fiensu had made it back, no one knew, for it is impossible for someone to hope for a successful initiation if he comes from an untidy, disorganized family.

Fiensu had proven them wrong. He was a miracle. His return was the beginning of a new era in his compound, and he rebuilt his family from scratch. His seven wives gave birth to thirty-nine children. He was grandfather to nearly twice that number and great-grandfather to a dozen more. Thus, in traditional terms, Fiensu was successful. Not only did no deaths occur under his leadership—because crises were dealt with before they happened—but Fiensu was constantly testing new secret medicines.

For me, however, he was still the man who had opposed my initiation and said I should be kicked out of the village. And I would never be able to forget what he had told my father and myself the day I returned from initiation.

Several months had gone by since the ordeal of my passage into adulthood. Ever since my true return I had been feeling an immense silence within me. It was a silence that I could not, even with great effort, penetrate. The memory of my years of absence from the village had suspended itself, and I felt as if my mind had stopped functioning. Once crowded with millions of incessant thoughts, my head now felt as hollow as an empty stomach. Once in a while I would dream of being back in the seminary, but everyone in the dream—all the students and priests—would be naked and act as if we were at an initiation camp.

Nyangoli and I had become even closer. He was always with me. We went fishing and hunting together, and he showed me how to tap beehives and get their honey. And he taught me the many useful things that any Dagara knows—how to dig out wild rats, how to use a bow and arrow, how to whistle a message so as not to scare an animal one was hunting, how to weave a straw hat. He was my teacher and friend. In return I told him about Europe, the Europe I had found in books. I told him about wars, guns, and machines—and about the white man. I even taught him a bit of French: the alphabet and how to write his name. He was fascinated by the process that made language visible.

One day Nyangoli told me of his intention to go to the Ivory Coast. This shocked me profoundly. Of all the people who had gone to initiation, I had thought Nyangoli was the least attracted to modernity. But I knew too that he craved for adventure, not just the kind I had had, but one that would provide him with opportunities for material gratification. He believed that his spiritual strength would translate into luck in the wilderness of modernity so that he would be able to bring things home to make his life a little more comfortable. And besides, it was becoming fashionable that someone in every family be called a "been to," a person who had successfully gone into the wilderness and come back from it without becoming a threat to the village. In fact, it felt to me as if the whole village was flirting with the city.

Nyangoli said he wanted to buy a bicycle and some clothing. He said he wished he knew how to write as well as I did because it seemed to be an initiation into something that was irresistibly creeping into our village. For him, it was good to have survived initiation, but the real survival was yet to be won. Initiation was only a beginning. Nyangoli dreamed of seeing the city and getting a chance to seek some of the things there. He said he had been craving these things since he was very young and that even initiation had not effaced his desire to have them.

When he spoke this way, I felt weak, as if a huge world had fallen on my shoulders and defeat had followed me into my very roots. I wanted to argue, to explain that he shouldn't feel this way or want these things, but my debilitation was real. It was the result of a feeling of pessimism that had crept into my comfortable soul. Was I waking up from a good dream into a nightmare? As modernity crept into my village, everything I held dear in my heart was disappearing. But my friend had his mind made up, for he needed the very stuff I had run away from.

After Nyangoli left for the white wilderness, I began to comprehend that there were quite a few villagers who had already left for the city in search of goods for their families. The worst of it was that one of Fiensu's first sons had gone to the city. It angered me. For a man as conservative as Fiensu to allow his own son to taste the modern world while he argued that, as a man who had dwelt in it, I was a danger to the village was not fair. There was something contradictory in the way he acted around me. I thought that perhaps at bottom he was either uncomfortable with my literacy or jealous of my father, a noncouncilman, for having such a son.

One morning Fiensu came to seek my help in writing a letter to his son in the city; he had heard that someone in the village was going there and could deliver it. A good villager, he entered my room without knocking. He sat down, pulled out a box of tobacco, and poured some into his mouth.

"I want to send talk to my son in the wilderness. You should know him since you lived there too," he said after a brief greeting.

"The wilderness is big. Is your son going to school there?" I ventured. I had said the word "school" in French.

"What is 'school'?"

"School is where you get initiated into the white man's way of knowing," I explained. Fiensu thought about this, then ordered, "Get your things and draw what I am going to tell you to send to him." He growled, spat some dark juice out of his mouth, and began. "Tell him it's been too long since I last saw him and that I would like him to come home for a cleansing ceremony. Tell him he should be prepared, when he comes home, to buy a sheep and several hens. Tell him too, and make sure you say this right, tell him . . . but I'm not sure I should say this. Well, tell him anyway that his wife has been found and that he should come home to get her before somebody else wants her."

"Wait."

"Why? What is the problem?"

"Speaking with your hand is not like speaking with your mouth," I explained. "The hand speaks slower because it must make sure it guides the stick to say things right. If you speak too fast, my memory will not be able to retain everything you say."

Without listening, he continued. "Say all this first and then tell him I will expect him at home two and a half market days from today. Kids in the wilderness are impossible to understand. You have to repeat things over and over before they hear you. They look like somebody has hit them in the belly, so that their bellies do not work anymore except when food comes into them.* And this wilderness must be a hell of oblivion. Why do they take so long to send words to their parents?"

"Do you want me to say all this too?" I knew he did not, but I wanted to make him discreetly aware of the fact that it was impossible for me to write and listen at the same time.

"Have you said everything already? No—don't say anything until I ask you to."

When we finished, I folded the letter and put it into the envelope. "Your son must have an address or something," I said.

"What's an address?"

"It's what helps you find somebody in the wilderness."

"My son does not need an address. He is a person. Anybody can find him."

"All right. So what's his name?"

"Just say, 'Fiensu's son.' That's what they call him here and that's what they should call him there—because that's who he is."

I wrote *Fiensu's Son* on the envelope and gave it to him. He went out and thanked my father.

▲　　▼　　▲

Nyangoli's departure depressed me. My sense of loss equaled the eagerness I had felt to be with him. For a while I did not know where to go or

---

*The Dagara believes that truth emanates from the belly. When someone is out of touch with truth, his belly serves only as a place to digest food (truth) into stinking excrement.

what to do, so I stayed home and tried to keep busy. Wasting no time, Mother had already made plans for me involving the daughter of a distant relative. I had never met her, but her existence was not less real because of that. Although I had mixed feelings about arranged marriages, I was not totally opposed to the idea. After all, I wanted to be like everyone else.

One night my father woke me up. I was used to being pulled out of sleep before dawn since my return from initiation, for it was customary to get up at a wee hour to perform ceremonies or to discuss serious matters. He said he had come to speak with me about something that had come up at a council meeting concerning me. My first reaction was embarrassment. What had I done wrong now?

Father explained. "I don't quite know how to tell you this, because I don't want to make a mistake in the way I say it, but do you remember what the chief said about you and your sudden return?"

"I don't remember much of that meeting except that Fiensu made me very ill-at-ease."

"The chief said that he had found out through divination that you are supposed to be our mouth. Do you remember this?"

"Not really. But it sounds like something the chief would say."

"Well, he said it again the other day."

"He did?"

"Yes."

"So what does that mean?"

"It means they want you to return to the white man's realm."

I thought I had misunderstood. The memory of my experience in the seminary burst onto the screen of my mind as if it were a movie. Then my brain fell into my stomach, leaving my mind empty of thoughts. At that moment I felt fatigue overcome me. I could neither object nor agree. In a flash I experienced the futility of all that had preceded this night, of all my efforts to escape from the influences of the white world. For a moment I felt the old rage rising within me, but I controlled myself, drawing from resources I did not know I had. I simply asked, "What do they mean? Am I not one of the members of this village?"

"Of course. Everyone knows that. But things are happening fast. . . ."

"What things are happening fast? What have they to do with me?"

"As an initiate, the council thinks you could be more useful to us being away from here."

"This sounds like the words of Fiensu. He is still trying to figure out a way to get rid of me, even after everything that has happened."

"No—it's not him. The chief said that you are the way that the hyena and the goat can learn to walk together because you know both the ways of the Dagara and the ways of the whites."

"All I know is reading and writing and the terror of the white man's world. I just want to be left alone."

"I understand. But let me tell you this. When the white man first came into this village, he cost me a wife and four children. They are all buried out there—next to the big baobab tree. So I understand what you mean. Your staying here would mean my not losing you, and believe me, I am tired of losing my children to the white man. But you see, the council does not view things the same way. The elders see in you a person capable of taming the white man because you know something that he does not know—the medicine of an initiated man—and because you know what he knows as well. The white man needs to know who we really are, and he needs to be told by someone who speaks his language and ours. Go. Tell him."

"I can't," I said instinctively. How could I? No one in good alignment with his higher self would contemplate such a venture. And where was I supposed to go? Back to the Jesuit school? To the city?

The image of myself as an eternal wanderer came into my mind in all of its monstrous absurdity. I was deeply frightened because of all the uncertainties that accompanied this vision. It made me feel weak. Here I was, just becoming a person, learning to be sure about certain things in my life, and now I was plunged back into confusion! I did not know how to effectively object to a recommendation by the council, and I knew better than to even try. So the part of myself that knew I had to obey overcame the part of me that revolted.

I could not even think of my future in any detail. My life had suddenly become bleak, like a dark bottomless hole into which I had inadvertently wandered.

Seeing my distress, my father said, "I know how you feel. And I would not want to be in your place. But your own grandfather told you when you were very young that you would have to go and live in the white world, and I think your fate is pursuing you. Since you came back from the initiation camp, I have consulted diviner after diviner. This has been at the center of every finding about you. You survived initiation in order to help us survive. We can't survive if you stay here."

"But how am I going to survive so that you can survive?"

"Just go away. The ancestors will tell you what to do. They will provide."

We sat quietly, facing each other in the dark. For a long time we said nothing, needing time to let everything soak in. I was tired—tired in my soul, tired with the kind of exhaustion that cannot be named. But I knew what my father meant. I knew what the council meant. I will never have a home.

▲　　　▼　　　▲

A few days later my father and I went to Guisso's home for a divination session and a ritual. It was clear to us that what was happening to me was something beyond what anyone could handle on his own. My frustration was not directed at anybody in particular, only toward the formless fate that had singled me out to be different when all I wanted was to stay here and be part of my tribe.

Guisso had been my mentor since my return from the seminary. With him I had learned to trust what I remembered by working closely with him. I used to spend whole days sitting next to him while he divined for others, explaining what had gone wrong in their lives and warning them of what would happen if certain matters were not paid attention to. He refused to answer questions from me on the ground that I already knew the answers. He would simply urge me to look at the instruments of divination more carefully. After a year, I could see the basic patterns of the divination book. Though I still had difficulties, I knew what it signified to have a mentor. The mentor shares the same world as the mentored, and therefore neither really knows more than the other.

Even though he was older and knew more from experience, Guisso did not want to allow me to fall into the illusion that I was his student. At first it was annoying since I wanted a teacher and he wanted a colleague. But when I overcame this need, he became more vocal and we talked more to each other as he worked on people. He attached value to my suggestions, and even began to ask for them. I volunteered information instinctively. Sometimes he would even let me talk to the person involved. Without a mentor a young man is a disempowered knower.

So it was natural that my father should bring me to Guisso to help me cope with the distressing news we had received from the council of elders.

After a brief consultation with his medicine objects, Guisso said to me, "Go and let yourself to be swallowed. Your ancestors will do the rest."

Though I knew he, as my male mother, meant to bring me comfort with these words, I also knew that he had no personal experience of what the world outside of tribal boundaries was like. These well-meaning words brought me no comfort. Instead, my thoughts kept going around and around. I had just arrived in the village. I had fought to belong here. My painful and difficult initiation had helped me immensely. Now, just as I was on the point of being accepted, I was being gently but inexorably expelled. . . .

Not heeding my silent protest, Guisso continued. "The challenge of a man is to act in accordance with what he remembers. You are not as young as you think you are. In you I see an elder, weighed down by the energy of his ancestors, and, knowing that, Fate is asking him to live as a man who remembers. You cannot be who you truly are until you can put what you remember into action in your life."

My heart was pounding hard against the walls of my chest as he pronounced these words. Each of them felt like a heavy stone falling into my ears and traversing down into my belly, where truth resides. Perhaps I expected some sort of last-minute reprieve.

Guisso looked into his medicine for a long time, then continued. "You don't search for something you already have. It's like the story of the man who spent the whole day looking for his machete while it hung on his shoulder. Had he not felt thirsty and gone to a creek where the machete fell off as he bent down to drink, how much longer would he have spent looking for the damn thing? I tell you, this man had a sick memory. You can't wait until the knowledge you already have about your destiny falls off your back. That takes too long. You must remember. Remembering means submitting to your fate.

"Once you have obeyed, the ancestors will be able to intervene in all the good ways they can. That includes helping you with all the things you cannot know about until you have allowed yourself to be swallowed into the wilderness.

"The spirit of the land of this tribe has always been with you. Remember, you're an orphan who was recovered to his nest. Several seasons ago, when you escaped from the white man and came back to us, our ancestors had already predicted your return to the healers. The ancestors arranged the things that happened to you when you were a child and they helped you survive these experiences. They helped you come back from your initiation ordeal. They will ensure that you survive in the white man's wilderness as well.

"You are not going there for the adventure—you are under orders as an initiated man. Why be anxious? After all they have done for you, do you still not have enough trust in your own ancestors? Your fear comes from the fact that you are still conditioned by your experiences as a child in the white man's world. This time you are going there as a prepared adult, an initiated man, journeying with the ancestors. Your worries are human worries, not spirit-induced ones."

Having made his point, he asked me to pour my medicine into his. He wanted to show me yet more evidence that I should shake off the yoke of my unfounded concerns. I removed my medicine bag from around my neck and poured its contents into Guisso's medicine circle.

Guisso looked intently. I followed him closely. He asked, "Do you see what I see?"

"Yes." I saw that what he said was true.

▲   ▼   ▲

When I finally left for Ouagadougou, the capital city, it was with the conviction that the support coming from the elders and the ancestors was genuine. How did I let myself be convinced? I will never be able to explain.
There are certain things that just carry you away. I think I went because I
had finally stopped arguing. And maybe I was a little afraid of the consequences of ignoring the elders' recommendation. Because of the Jesuits
I was already in conflict with the white world. Could I also afford to op-
pose the indigenous one?

Elders and mentors have an irreplaceable function in the life of any
community. Without them the young are lost—their overflowing energies
wasted in useless pursuits. The old must live in the young like a grounding
force that tames the tendency toward bold but senseless actions and shows
them the path of wisdom. In the absence of elders, the impetuosity of
youth becomes the slow death of the community—which is exactly what
Guisso had shown me by the way in which he worked with me.

I decided that the best thing for me to do in the city was to attend a
four-year college. I was lucky because school was only about twelve hours
away from the village by motorbike. I loved the commute, and rode home
whenever I could. My father and Guisso continued to be my principal
teachers in the ancestral ways, silently competing with the modern education I was receiving.

It was a great irony that I, a college student, continued to be more interested in what was going on in the minds of my elders than in the ideas
propagated in the university classrooms. Was it because the more I grasped
of the modern world, the more the traditional cried out to be known? On
the other hand, there was a reciprocity: I felt at times that understanding of
one contributed to the comprehension of the other.

I still often suffered from being a man of two worlds: conflicting
worlds that, when combined, could elevate me to a plane of perception
from which I often saw situations through two different points of view—
neither of which ever seemed to quite match up with the other. At times
that double perspective landed me in bizarre and uncomfortable situations.
It sealed me off from my fellow students, who were all trying desperately
to become nontraditional people. How often I grieved to hear unjust and
ignorant comments aimed at village life! The students hated the ways of
the village and displayed scorn and revulsion toward anything that did not
come out of books. The logic of the school totally contradicted village
knowledge, and they carefully nurtured their feelings. There, in the city, at
the college, the book had replaced the elder.

Because the two worlds could not be brought into harmony—and indeed I had the feeling that it never occurred to any of the students but my-self to even *try* to live in both of them—most of the young men and women were confused: they were neither Westernized nor traditionalized. My enduring passion for magic, rituals, and ceremonies reassured me that the traditional world had swallowed me and that I was resisting the white world—or maybe I had grown to be a man trapped between the white and the traditional worlds. Because I was alone in my efforts, I had no basis by which to explain to anyone the kind of world I was living in.

After four years of hard work, I was rewarded with three bachelor de-grees, a free airline ticket, and a scholarship at the Sorbonne. For me, going to France was to allow myself to be swallowed deeper. While get-ting ready to leave, I kept hearing Guisso's voice repeating the old admoni-tion: "Go and allow yourself to be swallowed." By now I could have faith in his word. The elders do not see the details, they see the overall picture. If the overall pattern is good, the hardship of the details does not matter. Somehow I felt I was not traveling alone. Guisso was with me, as was the spirit of my grandfather, Bakhye, and behind them was the weight of Grandfather's vision. I was finally living out the destiny foretold by my name—Malidoma—he who makes friends with the stranger/enemy. An entire culture was going abroad to be swallowed.